GATEWAYS TO ACADEMIC WRITING

GATEWAYS TO ACADEMIC WRITING

Effective Sentences, Paragraphs, and Essays

Alan Meyers
Harry S Truman College

Longman

Gateways to Academic Writing:
Effective Sentences, Paragraphs, and Essays

Pearson Education, 10 Bank Street, White Plains, NY 10606

The present work is an authorized adaptation of *Writing with Confidence: Writing Effective Sentences and Paragraphs*, 7th edition, by Alan Meyers, Copyright © 2003 by Addison Wesley Longman, Inc.

Executive editor: Laura Le Dréan
Development editors: Ann Grogg, Joan Poole
Senior production editor: Kathleen Silloway
Art director: Ann France
Marketing manager: Joe Chapple
Manufacturing manager: Nancy Flaggman
Cover and text design: Ann France
Cover and text image: © Ben Wood/CORBIS
Text composition: ElectraGraphics, Inc.
Text font: 10/12 Palatino
Text art: ElectraGraphics, Inc.
Text credits: See page vi
Photo credits: **p. 66,** © Copyright The British Museum; **p. 137,** ©Corbis/Francis G. Mayer;
  p. 296, ©Corbis/Historical Picture Archive; **p. 320,** ©Corbis/Bettmann;
  p. 324, ©Corbis/Bettmann; **p. 327,** ©Corbis/Bettmann; **p. 346,** Peter G. Veit/Copyright, National Geographic Society.

Library of Congress Cataloging-in-Publication Data

Meyers, Alan
  Gateways to academic writing : effective sentences, paragraphs, and essays
/ by Alan Meyers.
    p. cm.
  Includes index.
  ISBN 0-13-140888-7
  1. English language—Paragraphs—Problems, exercises, etc. 2. English
language—Sentences—Problems, exercises, etc. 3. English
language—Rhetoric—Problems, exercises, etc. 4. Academic
writing—Problems, exercises, etc. I. Title.
PE1439.M47 2004
808'.0428—dc22   2004011278

Printed in the United States of America
  6 7 8 9 10-BAH-09 08

To my two Anns

Text Credits

Chapter 2: **p. 18,** Danny Labin. From *"G" is for Growing: Thirty Years of Research on Children and Sesame Street.* Edited by: Shalom M. Fisch and Rosemarie T. Truglio, 2001. Lawrence Erlbaum Associates, Publishers. Mahwah, New Jersey.

Chapter 5: **p. 53,** From *The Color of Water* by James McBride. Copyright © 1996 by James McBride. Used by permission of G. P. Putnam's Sons, a division of Penguin Putnam Inc.

Chapter 6: **p. 62,** "Rules of the Game," from THE JOY LUCK CLUB by Amy Tan, copyright © 1989 by Amy Tan. Used by permission of G. P. Putnam's Sons, a division of Putnam Group (USA) Inc.

Chapter 8: **p. 75,** "The Beekeeper" by Sue Hubbell. © 1984. Reprinted with permission of Darhansoff, Verrill, & Feldman Literary Agents; **p. 78,** Krups User's Manual.

Chapter 12: **p. 103,** "The Allergy Epidemic" by Jerry Adler, *Newsweek,* September 22, 2003. ©2003 Newsweek, Inc. All rights reserved. Reprinted by permission.

Chapter 20: **p. 243, 244,** "Old Civilizations of the 'New World' " from *That's Not in My American History Book: A Compilation of Little-Known Events and Forgotten Heroes* by Thomas Ayres. Copyright 2000.

Chapter 29: **p. 369,** Ella Clark, INDIAN LEGENDS OF THE PACIFIC NORTHWEST. Copyright © 1953 The Regents of the University of California; © renewed 1981 Ella E. Clark.

Additional Readings

p. 399, "Needing and Wanting Are Different" by Jimmy Carrasquillo, *Newsweek,* November 16, 1992. Reprinted by permission of the author.

p. 405, "The Natchez Indians," adapted from *The People's Almanac #3* by David Wallechinsky and Irving Wallace. Adapted by permission of the author.

p. 406, "The Legacy of Generation Ñ" by Christy Haubegger from *Newsweek,* July 12, 1999, copyright © 1999 Newsweek, Inc. All Rights Reserved. Reprinted with permission.

p. 408, "Out of the Sweatshop And Into the World" by David Masello from *Newsweek,* June 24, 2002. All Rights Reserved. Reprinted by permission.

p. 410, "The Struggle to Be an All-American Girl" by Elizabeth Wong, © 1980. Reprinted by permission of the author.

p. 412, "Melting Pot" from *Living Out Loud* by Anna Quindlen. Copyright © 1987 by Anna Quindlen. Reprinted by permission of Random House, Inc.

Brief Contents

Detailed Contents

Rhetorical Contents

About the Author

Alan Meyers has been teaching in the City Colleges of Chicago since 1968 and at Harry S Truman College since 1976, where he has been Chair of the Communications Department since 1990. His honors include being named Distinguished Professor, Illinois Community College Trustees Association Teacher of the Year, and American Association of Higher Education Exemplary Teacher in 1991. He is author or coauthor of nine other textbooks.

Preface

Gateways to Academic Writing presents a fully integrated program of instruction for students who are writing in English as a first, second, third, or fourth language. The four units of the book address (1) the global issues of the writing process, which includes exploring ideas, organizing, drafting, revising, editing, and proofreading for sentences, paragraphs, and essays; (2) ten modes of writing, including narration, all forms of exposition, persuasion, and summary and response; (3) an introduction to grammatical terminology, sentence structures, and verb tenses and forms; and (4) extended practice with the grammar and mechanics of English.

Students will find the explanations and exercises practical and clear and supplemented with visual aids: in-chapter outlines and diagrams, as well as unit-ending Guidelines for Success that summarize essential points of the chapter content. Moreover, students will find the content engaging and often humorous. The majority of the exercises and examples are thematically focused on fascinating and unusual information about a variety of topics, including odd facts about the past, animals, and famous (and not so famous) individuals in U.S. history.

Content Overview

- **Unit I: Developing Your Writing Skills.** These four chapters introduce students to the writing process, to composing paragraphs and essays, and to revising and editing their work. Separate chapters focus on a four-step sequence of planning, drafting, revision, and editing; the shape and form of the paragraph; the shape and form of the essay; and a full exploration of the revision process.
- **Unit II: Different Modes of Writing.** Each of the ten chapters in this unit includes a professional model followed by discussion questions; an explanation and diagram of paragraph order; a step-by-step guide through a single writing assignment; revision guidelines that encourage collaborative revision; a student model and discussion questions; and additional writing assignments.
- **Unit III: Gateways to Grammar and Structure.** The three chapters in this unit lay the grammatical foundation for instruction in grammar and sentence structure. The chapters introduce key terminology, the basic sentence patterns, verb tenses in the active and passive voice, modal constructions, and the conditionals.
- **Unit IV: Editing with Care.** Chapters in this unit cover the most important issues to address in the editing stages of the writing process: subject-verb agreement, past-tense and past-participle verb forms, pronoun forms, use of modifiers, comparative and superlative forms of adjectives and adverbs, phrasal verbs, articles, and prepositions. Additionally, five chapters focus on all aspects of joining sentences correctly, beginning with identifying and eliminating fragments, followed by instruction in the use of coordination, subordination, and relative pronouns, and concluding with comma splices and run-ons. Two more chapters offer instruction in spelling and punctuation.
- **Additional Readings.** These nine high-interest essays (three of which are written by students) provide models of the rhetorical modes, practice in close reading, questions for analysis, and prompts for additional writing.

- **Appendices.** Appendices list the most common irregular verbs; the most commonly misspelled words; verbs that take infinitive objects, gerund objects, or both; common phrasal verbs; and common expressions that use prepositions.
- **Glossary.** The glossary defines the key terms used throughout the book.

Features

The following features make the text a valuable and flexible tool for both instructor and student.

- **Emphasis on the Writing Process.** Writing Well in Six Steps in Chapter 1 engages students in an easily mastered sequence that constitutes the writing process. Each of the ten chapters in Unit II guides students through these steps as they apply to different modes of writing. The chapters also emphasize outlining, writing topic sentences and thesis statements, developing and supporting claims, establishing clear transitions, and writing effective conclusions.
- **Simple and Direct Explanations.** Discussions focus on what students must know to generate effective paragraphs, essays, and sentences while increasing their facility with language and eliminating errors. Key terms are highlighted and explained in the text, and repeated in a glossary at the back of the book.
- **Multifaceted Presentation of Each Paragraph (and Essay) Mode.** Each chapter in Unit II includes both professional and student models, along with discussion questions on their structure and suggestions for writing. The chapters also demonstrate how the model paragraph or essay takes shape through the stages of the writing process, all of which are illustrated or diagrammed.
- **Chapter on the Essay.** This chapter describes the structure and purpose of the essay, relating it to a well-wrought paragraph and demonstrating the roles of individual paragraphs within the essay.
- **Chapter on Report Writing.** This chapter explains and illustrates how to write clear and accurate reports in both academic and occupational contexts.
- **Chapter on Persuasion.** Extending the scope of writing beyond exposition, this chapter instructs students on how to present their viewpoints convincingly to others.
- **Chapter on Summarizing and Responding.** This chapter provides skills that aid students in the writing of term papers, essay examinations, and other types of academic work. Students learn to locate and explain key ideas objectively and then interpret and analyze these ideas.
- **Gateways to Grammar and Structure in Unit III.** This important three-chapter unit provides an overview of grammatical terminology, the parts of speech, independent and dependent clauses, the major sentence patterns, verb forms, the verb tenses, active and passive voice, the modals (and their perfect and progressive forms), and four conditional sentence patterns. These "gateway" chapters teach or remind students of the terms and concepts they'll need for understanding and practicing the sentence-level corrections that are the focus of Unit IV.
- **Mechanics in Unit IV.** This book's final chapters are a handbooklike section on punctuation, quoting, spelling, apostrophe use, hyphenation, and capitalization.
- **Chapter Goals.** Behavioral outcomes are listed at the beginning of each chapter, focusing students on the skills they will learn and practice.
- **High-Interest Exercises and Models.** Working with engaging materials in connected discourse, the chapters introduce writing skills within a meaningful and highly enjoyable content. Selections include biographies of Abraham Lincoln, George Washington, Benjamin Franklin, Harriet Tubman, Diamond Jim Brady, Thomas

Edison, Cornelius Vanderbilt, Sequoyah, Jesse Owens, Jim Thorpe, Babe Didrikson Zaharias, Dian Fossey, and others; narrations of events in American history (for example, the signing of the Declaration of Independence, Custer's Last Stand) and of the origins of superstitions, of April Fool's Day, Thanksgiving, New Year's Day, as well as interesting facts on various animals such as zebras, leopards, lions, cats, some unusual dogs, and a talking gorilla; and some interesting Native American legends. This entertaining subject matter serves a more serious purpose as well: It exemplifies that people write to communicate ideas, and if ideas are worth saying, they are worth saying well. As students read and then rewrite or revise an exercise, they discover that interesting ideas become clearer and even more interesting.

- **Optional Collaborative Activities.** Suggestions for out-of-class and in-class partnered or group work expand learning opportunities. Paragraph writing assignments include Revision Guidelines that encourage (but do not require) peer response and editing. Predicting activities provide additional opportunities for collaboration while stressing the interrelationship between writer and reader.
- **Mastery Learning Capabilities.** Each chapter in Unit IV concludes with two Editing for Mastery exercises in which students apply and assess the skills they have learned, restudy those applications if necessary, and then engage in further assessment.
- **Comprehensive Treatment of Verbs.** Focusing on one of the most troublesome hurdles for English language learners—verbs—the book devotes four chapters to verb tenses, verb forms, verb phrases, and phrasal verbs.
- **Chapter-Ending Summary Boxes.** These highlighted summaries help students identify and review the important points to practice, and they serve as additional reference aids in revising and editing.
- **Student Models.** Student models appear not only in each chapter in Unit II but also as three of the additional readings.
- **Unit-Ending Guidelines for Success.** Each unit concludes with spreads called Guidelines for Success that summarize the key points.
- **Writing Assignments Based on Readings.** Suggestions for writing follow each of the readings, both within chapters and in the Additional Readings section at the end of the book. These suggestions include writing in response to a reading.
- **Tips Boxes.** Within the margins of every chapter are helpful advice and mnemonic aids.
- **Glossary.** Key terms are highlighted in the text and defined in a glossary at the back of the book.

Acknowledgments

I could not have achieved this result without the assistance, advice, and support of colleagues and students. I thank my colleagues at Truman College and the City Colleges of Chicago, who constantly offer me advice, comfort, and encouragement. I thank my students, who continually teach me how the writing process works and should be addressed. I especially thank the group of students—some of them from my classes, others from other colleges—who have contributed paragraphs and essays to the text: Linder Anim, Bozena Budżyńska, Giuliano Correia, Veronica Fleeton, Tuyet-Ahn Van, Mirham Mahmutagic, Monica Radu, Max Rodriguez-Reyes, Sara Sebring, Amra Skocic, Jane Smith, and Erica Teal. Professor Patricia W. Kato of Chattanooga State Community College, Chattanooga, Tennessee, deserves my special thanks for providing several of the reading selections and student paragraphs for the book. And so does Professor Sherry F. Gott of Danville Community College, Danville, Virginia, who provided Jane Smith's student essay.

I thank the reviewers of the manuscript, whose invaluable criticisms and suggestions have helped steer me in the right direction: **Marsha Abramovich,** Tidewater Community College, Virginia Beach, VA; **Deanna Cecil,** University of California–San Diego, La Jolla, CA; **Jayne Leshinsky,** Spring International Language Center, Denver, CO; **Miriam Moore,** Raritan Valley Community College, Somerville, NJ; **Mary Jane Onnen,** Glendale Community College, Glendale, AZ; **Nancy Price,** University of Missouri, Columbia, MO; **Luis Quesada,** Miami Dade Community College, Hialeah, FL; **Esther Robbins,** Prince George's Community College, Largo, MD.

I also thank the people at Pearson Longman for their work in the copyediting and production of the text. I thank my Acquisitions Editor, Laura Le Dréan, whose vision, insight, imagination, and flexibility made this whole project work. I thank Kathleen Silloway and Joan Poole for their keen eyes and minds in editing this manuscript, and their good cheer throughout the process. And I could never thank enough my Development Editor, Ann Hofstra Grogg, who has guided me so brilliantly through the many stages of creating this text.

Finally, I thank my wife, Ann, who has been my loving companion for almost four decades, and my daughter, Sarah, and son, Bradley, who continue to make me proud of their achievements.

Alan Meyers

Developing Your Writing Skills

The word *writing* comes from a verb. That means it's an activity—a process. Writing is a way to produce language, which you do naturally when you speak. You say something, think of more to say, perhaps correct something you've said, and then move on to the next statement. Writing isn't much different, except that you take more time to think about your subject, the person or people you'll be discussing it with, and the goal you hope to achieve in that discussion. And, if you're writing in a second language, you also take more time to revise your work. You consider your choice of words, their form, and their grammar to make sure that they clearly express what you intend to say.

The four chapters in this unit will show you how to work through the writing process. They'll describe how to discover and organize your thoughts, how to write them down, and how to rewrite and revise them so that they achieve your goals. These chapters suggest ways to make your writing interesting, direct, and clear.

Don't worry if you're unsure about the writing process or about expressing your ideas in English. The chapters in this unit will take you through it step by step. Follow the steps, and you will learn to write well. ■

1 The Writing Process

Writing well comes from working through a *process* of writing. The page you're reading right now is the finished product of many hours of composing and revising. You don't see the pages that went into the trash along the way: the notes, the early drafts, and the later ones. You don't see the changes made in response to student reactions, the advice from other professors, and the comments of editors. But the process does work, and it will work for you, too. In this chapter, you'll examine the steps in that process. You'll see

- ways to gather and shape ideas
- ways to get your first draft on paper or entered in the computer
- ways to revise and edit your work

Speaking and Writing

Writing is speaking to others on paper—or on a computer screen. Writing is partly a talent, but it's mostly a skill, and like any skill, it improves with practice. Writing is also an *action*—a process of discovering and organizing your ideas, putting them on paper, and reshaping and revising them.

Consider what speaking is all about: sharing an idea, giving information, expressing a greeting, stating an opinion, or sending a warning. That is, you speak because you have

1. something to say
2. a reason for saying it
3. someone to say it to

Of course, when you speak, you also see and hear your listeners. You answer their questions and restate ideas. And when you speak, you are also exploring your thoughts. You correct yourself, give examples, or even change your mind. In short, you are both stating and examining your thoughts as you say them aloud.

Writing is much like speaking—a way to discover and communicate your ideas. Unlike speaking, however, it doesn't happen all at once. You cannot see and hear your readers, so you must think about their reactions. You must choose a subject that will interest them and try to present it in an interesting way. You must present your ideas in a logical order. You must read what you write and then rewrite it until you express your meaning strongly and clearly.

You cannot do all of these things at once. Any good paragraph or essay goes through many stages before it's finished. First, you may simply explore ideas as you put them into words, lists, or charts. And at this point, you shouldn't worry about grammar or exact word choice. Afterward, you can write a first draft. Then you can examine your ideas, rearrange them, add to them, and probably rewrite the draft. Perhaps you'll revise your ideas and wording in several drafts until you're confident that your audience will understand and care about what you have to say.

Writing Well in Six Steps

No two writers approach writing in exactly the same way. But they generally follow a series of actions that looks something like this:

1. **Explore ideas**
   a. Consider the subject
   b. Consider the purpose
   c. Consider the audience
2. **Prewrite—using one or more of these methods**
   a. Brainstorming
   b. Clustering
   c. Freewriting
3. **Organize**
   a. Select
   b. Outline
4. **Write a first draft**
   a. Write quickly to record your thoughts
   b. Put notes and new ideas in the margins
5. **Revise the draft**
   a. Read it aloud
   b. Add or omit material, and move material around
6. **Produce the final copy**
   a. Edit
   b. Copy over, or print a clean copy
   c. Read carefully for errors, and then make another clean copy

The rest of the chapter will examine each step in detail. As you read, you'll also have a chance to practice each of these steps in exercises. Together, these exercises will help you produce a final draft of a paragraph.

Step 1: Explore Ideas

Writing first involves discovering your ideas. So before you sit down to write, let your mind explore freely. Thoughts will occur to you while traveling to work, eating dinner, or lying on the couch. Record those thoughts by writing on whatever you can—napkins, scraps of paper, or even the back of your hand.

Eventually, though, you should focus your exploration more systematically. As in speaking, you must have something to say, a reason for saying it, and someone to say it to.

Ask yourself three questions:

- What is my subject?
- What is my purpose?
- Who is my audience?

These are always the first questions writers ask themselves when they're genuinely interested in communication—and not in just completing assignments.

Your Subject

Ask yourself, *what is my* **subject**—the material I want to write about—*and what do I know about it?* The subjects that are most interesting to your audience are usually those that you find most interesting. Choose a subject that you care about and know about (or can find out about). Then you'll have something interesting to say, and you'll say it more clearly and confidently.

Academic assignments sometimes give you freedom to choose your subject. Often, though, you must select and then narrow your subject from a general assignment. You'll practice doing that in the exercise that follows.

EXERCISE 1	Exploring a Subject

Here's an example of a general assignment. Write a paragraph about a job you know well. (If you've never had a job, choose a "job" you've been responsible for at home.)

To write about this subject, begin by exploring your ideas. Ask yourself the following:

- What jobs have I done or am I doing now?
- What do I know about these jobs?
- Which jobs (or parts of one job) do I feel strongly about? What do I love or hate? What parts make me angry or happy?

  Now choose the job, and search for more detail.

- What tools or materials do I use in my job?
- How do I perform each task?
- Which tasks are most interesting or boring?
- What examples or little stories best illustrate these points?

  Make notes of your answers. Which answers seem the most interesting? Think about how you can narrow your subject. What job will you choose—and what specific idea about the job should you discuss?

Your Purpose

Now ask yourself, *what is my* **purpose?** Communicating always has a purpose: to inform, to persuade, or to entertain—or maybe to do all three. You could, for example, *inform* your classmates about some procedures at your job. You could also *persuade* your classmates that they should find (or avoid) a job like yours. Or you could simply *entertain* your classmates with examples of odd incidents you've experienced at your job.

EXERCISE 2 | Defining Purpose

Exploring Purpose

Share your answers to Exercise 2. Suggest ways to revise one sentence so that it begins three different paragraphs: one that informs, one that entertains, and one that persuades. For example:

a. (inform) Glassmaking began almost 5,000 years ago in Egypt.

b. (entertain) Perhaps the Egyptians were nosy, so they invented glass windows to look inside their buildings.

c. (persuade) Glass making may seem unimportant, but it is probably one of the most important inventions in the last 5,000 years.

List a few details that will follow each sentence.

Each of the following sentences could begin a paragraph. Read each sentence and then predict the purpose of the paragraph. Will it probably *inform, entertain,* or *persuade?* There may be more than one possibility. Be prepared to explain your answers.

1. Glassmaking began almost 5,000 years ago in Egypt. _____*inform*_____

2. The United States must offer low-cost health care to all. _____

3. The United States began minting coins in 1792. _____

4. Few sights are as magnificent as the setting of the orange-red sun as it disappears beneath the deep waves of Florida's Gulf Coast. _____

5. Smoking may be pleasurable, but can you continue to risk your life for the sake of that pleasure? _____

6. With the score tied and just seconds left on the clock, Jordan stepped to the free-throw line. _____

Your Audience

Ask yourself, *who is my audience?* The answer to that question will determine what you say about your subject and what purpose you hope to achieve. For example, you might need to explain a lot to a reader who's never heard of your subject, but explain much less to a reader who knows the subject well. Or you might need to provide a lot of evidence to persuade a reader who doesn't agree with your opinion, but provide far less for someone who tends to agree with you.

EXERCISE 3 | Adjusting for Audience

Read the following subjects. List two or three points you would include if you were writing to the different audiences specified.

1. *Subject:* the value of popular music

   a. *Audience:* people between the ages of eighteen and thirty
   enjoyment from listening and dancing

   b. *Audience:* professional musicians
   profits, enjoyment, fame

2. *Subject:* the benefits of diets

   a. *Audience:* overweight adults

   b. *Audience:* athletes

3. *Subject:* the benefits of attending your college

    a. *Audience:* high school seniors

    _____

    b. *Audience:* people whose first language is not English

    _____

    c. *Audience:* older, returning students

    _____

Step 2: Prewrite

The second step of the writing process involves writing your thoughts on paper or on the computer. Don't worry about grammar, exact word choice, spelling, or punctuation, because you'll probably change your mind and your wording later anyway. This step is called **prewriting.** It's a time to relax, to write quickly, and to begin organizing your thoughts. This process can even be fun!

Brainstorming

One way to capture your thoughts is by **brainstorming**, or listing thoughts as they come to you. Here's an example from a student who has been asked to describe a job:

> *Deliver pizza for Guido's Grand Pizza*
> *Pay: minimum wage plus tips*
> *work nights, 6 to 10*
> *boss is impatient*
> *must use cell phone*
> *hate some customers*
> *lady who always complains*
> *sleepy guy who answers bell after six rings*
> *four young guys who always forget to tip*

You might also brainstorm a second or third time to generate more ideas.

Clustering

In **clustering,** you write your subject in the middle of the page and then circle it. You write related ideas around the circle as they occur to you. Then you circle the ideas and connect them to your subject circle. These related ideas are like *branches.*

You can then add more branches to the subject circle or to the related ideas as they occur to you. A completed clustering chart might look like this:

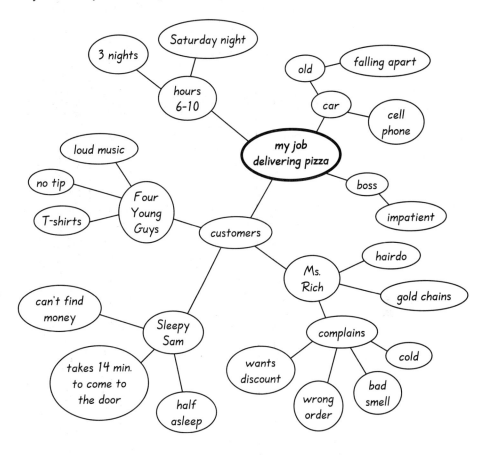

Freewriting

Another way to get started is by **freewriting.** You simply write about the subject without worrying about sentence structure, spelling, logic, and grammar. Write as you would speak so that you can get your ideas down fast. Following is an example of how a freewriting might begin:

> I work part-time delivering pizza for Guido's Grand Pizza. My hours are 6 to 10 three nights during the week and on Saturday evening. I drive an old car held together with wire and chewing gum. I have to use a cell phone because new orders come in all night, I need directions, and some customers won't open the door unless I call. Customers can be difficult. One woman, I'll call her Ms. Rich, thinks she is very important. Every time I deliver a pizza, she complains. It's cold, it's not what she ordered, it smells funny. (Of course, she keeps on ordering.) All her gold bracelets and jewelry . . .

Your freewriting may be disorganized, but that's all right. It's just a way to put ideas into words that you can look at, expand on, change, or omit. And you can use freewriting (or brainstorming or clustering) *any time* you aren't sure what to say or how to say it, even in the middle of composing a first or second draft. Getting words on the page will help you generate ideas, even if you know you will change them later.

EXERCISE 4	Prewriting a Paragraph

Return to the subject you chose in Exercise 1. Consider how the subject might interest your classmates. Limit the subject to a specific job and consider your purpose and audience: Will you inform, persuade, or entertain your readers? Limiting the subject will help you determine what to say. Ask yourself, *what information would be most useful, interesting, or convincing?*

Then do a brainstorming list, a clustering diagram, and a freewriting page so that you can sample each of these techniques. Which one do you like best?

Step 3: Organize

After you've put your ideas into words, you can begin to organize them. This process involves selecting, subtracting, and adding ideas, and then outlining them.

Selecting, Subtracting, and Adding

Think again about your purpose and audience. What goal do you want to accomplish—to inform, persuade, or entertain? What point do you want to make? And what should you tell your readers so that you can accomplish those goals? Return to your prewriting and do the following:

- Underline or highlight the best ideas in your brainstorming list. Then rewrite the list, putting related ideas together. Add to the list as more ideas occur to you, and remove or ignore the parts that aren't related to your choices.
- Choose the part of the clustering diagram that has the best ideas. Do a second clustering diagram that explores those ideas in greater detail. Ignore the parts of the original diagram that aren't related to your choice.
- Circle or highlight the best parts of your freewriting. Do a second or even a third freewriting on them. Ignore the parts of each freewriting that aren't related to your choice. And focus more specifically on your subject and add more details.

For example, the pizza delivery writer might decide to entertain his classmates—and to make the point that his job is actually fun. So he'd select only humorous information about the customers he typically serves: Ms. Rich, Sleepy Sam, and the Young Guys. He wouldn't use the unimportant details or the ones that don't develop his point—perhaps the ones about his cell phone and maybe even his working hours. And he would add more details to develop the humor.

Outlining

After deciding to focus on customers, the pizza delivery writer can make an informal outline. The three customers are the main categories, which he lists and numbers. Then he includes some supporting details under each category. The outline would look something like this:

1. *Ms. Rich*

   Answers door wearing gold bracelets and other jewelry

   Complains about the pizza

      One time: too cold

      Another time: it smells funny

      Another time: wants a discount

2. *Sleepy Sam*

   Arrives after 14 minutes

   Half asleep

   Can't find money, finally gives me $20 and doesn't count the change

3. *The Young Guys*

   Loud music

   Wearing T-shirts

   Never tip me

EXERCISE 5	Selecting and Outlining

Return to the materials you prepared in Exercise 4, and consider your purpose and audience. What point do you want to make, and to whom? Select your ideas by underlining, circling, or highlighting them. Arrange the ideas in an informal outline. Remove the ideas and details that don't fit the outline. If some parts of the outline don't contain as much material as other parts do, add some more details for those parts.

Step 4: Write a First Draft

You've done some prewriting, selected your best ideas, expanded on them, and arranged them in some reasonable order. Now you can begin the first draft of your paragraph. At this point don't, worry about being "perfect." New ideas will come to you later, and you may discover a better arrangement of ideas. So write fast, as if you were speaking to your readers. If an idea occurs to you that belongs earlier in the draft, make a note about it in the margin, write it on a second sheet of paper, or click your mouse at the spot where you want to insert it. Here is an example of the part of the first draft that developed from the freewriting:

TIPS

For Drafting

1. Say something aloud before you write it.
2. Write fast by hand or by computer.
3. Use only one side of the paper.
4. Leave wide margins and double-space to make room for changes.
5. Save your work every five or ten minutes on the computer.

> *I have a part-time job delivering pizzas for Guido's Grand Pizza three nights a week and on Saturday nights. I don't mind driving an old car held together with wire and chewing gum, but the customers can be difficult. One woman, I'll call her Ms. Rich, answers the door wearing all sorts of jewelry. Every time I deliver a pizza, she complains about something. Once she opened the box and told me she wanted triple extra cheese, not double. She even demanded a discount. I had to give her the discount or eat the pizza myself. . . .*

EXERCISE 6	Drafting a Paragraph

Write a first draft based on the selecting and outlining you did in Exercise 5.

Step 5: Revise the Draft

TIPS

For Revising

1. Make notes in the margins—or write new material on separate sheets of paper.
2. Circle words you think you misspelled or will want to change later.
3. Tape or staple additions where you want them to go.
4. On the computer, use cut-and-paste or insert commands to move things around.
5. Print out a double-spaced copy for revisions: Slow down and revise in pencil.

Revising is among the most important steps of writing, especially for people who write in a second language. It's the part of the writing process that may take the most time. For that reason, Chapter 3 explains the revising process fully. Work hard on revising, and take advantage of the resources available to you: your instructor, tutors, writing workshops, and the writing center if your school has them.

Here's a procedure for revising. After completing your first draft, put it away for awhile. It's hard to think about changing and correcting your work immediately after you finish a draft. Better ideas may come to you the day after you've done the first draft. You also will probably notice more things to change. If you've composed it on the computer, print out a hard copy to work on later. When you come back to your writing, read it carefully. Study its organization, word choice, and details. You'll probably find things to omit and think of some things to add. Don't be satisfied with changing just a few words. Add ideas, remove ideas that don't fit, rearrange sections, say sentences differently, and substitute words. Write new sections and draw arrows to where they will go, or compose them on the computer and insert them. If your work is too messy afterward, then make a clean copy before going any further.

Here's part of the first draft on delivering pizza that the writer decided to revise. He added some specific details to make it more interesting:

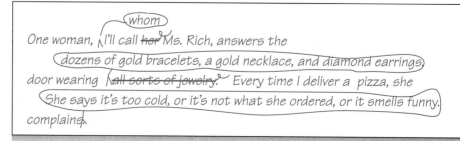

Concentrate. Read what's actually on the page; resist the tendency to read what you *think* you said. Now read your work again very carefully. Make notes for changes in the margins and above the lines. Challenge what you've written. Don't ask yourself and others, "Can this be understood?" but instead, "Can this be misunderstood?" Make a clean copy of your work and challenge it again. Don't stop revising until you're satisfied with (or even proud of) what you've produced.

EXERCISE 7 | **Revising Your Paragraph**

Review the draft you composed in Exercise 6 one or more times. Make changes on the original version. Read your paper aloud so that you can hear the words and rhythms of the sentences. Read the paper to someone else, too, and ask that person for comments and suggestions. But don't have him or her do the revising for you; that's your job.

Step 6: Produce the Final Copy

TIPS

For Being Smarter than Your Computer

1. Use the spell checker, but be careful. The computer highlights only incorrectly spelled words—not correctly spelled (but wrong) word choices (for example, *low* when you mean *law*, or *wants* when you mean *once*).

2. Be careful when using a grammar checker. It catches many errors, but sometimes it finds errors where no errors exist.

3. Use the thesaurus—a dictionary of **synonyms** —to broaden your word choice, but choose the words you know and know how to use correctly.

After you've finished revising your paragraph, you can begin the final copy. Prepare it according to your instructor's guidelines, or follow the tips on page 12. Before you're finished, however, you need to pay attention to details you've ignored while getting your ideas on paper and shaping them to fit your purpose and audience. You want people to judge your ideas, not your mistakes.

Editing

Now that you have revised your work, you can **edit** it. Check it carefully. Focus on grammar, word choice, verb forms, punctuation, and spelling—the real challenges for people writing in a second language. Use your dictionary and any other reference materials you need. Again, take full advantage of the resources available to you, including this book. Each of the chapters in Units III and IV deals with a specific aspect of grammar, word order, word forms, or punctuation. The chapters also include useful checklists to help in editing your work.

Read the paper more than once. Copy it over or print it out again with all your corrections. This draft should be neat and should represent your best effort.

Proofreading

Proofreading means carefully examining the final copy again. Check the corrections you made. Are they accurate? Are they complete? Did you make any new errors? Read through the paper slowly. Place a ruler under each line to focus your eyes. If necessary, make a new, clean copy—and then proofread that copy. This is the stage during which you will produce the final and best draft.

Here's the edited and proofread final draft of the paper on delivering pizza:

I work part-time three weeknights and on Saturday night delivering for Guido's Grand Pizza. I don't mind driving an old car held together with wire and chewing gum, but the customers can be difficult. One regular customer, Ms. Rich, answers the door wearing dozens of gold bracelets, a gold necklace, *and diamond earrings. She always complains the pizza is too cold, or it's not what she ordered, or it smells funny. Once she looked in the box and screamed that she wanted triple extra cheese, not double. She even demanded a discount. I charged her $2 less rather than lose the sale and eat the pizza myself. Another customer, Sleepy Sam, takes fourteen minutes to answer the door after I ring the bell six times. He arrives half asleep and sways back and forth like a man on a ship in a storm. Sometimes I think I could give him cheese on cardboard and he wouldn't know the difference. He can't find money in the pockets of his torn pants, but eventually he gives me a $20 bill and doesn't count the change. Then there are the Young Guys. When one of them opens the door, the loud music from the apartment hurts my ears. He grabs the pizza, pays me, and gives me a thank-you but never a tip. The customers are not always friendly, but they make the job interesting. Besides, it pays for my school tuition and books— and it's better than no job at all.*

Notice that this final draft is more entertaining than the original. All of its content develops the main point. Its sentences are clear. And it has plenty of details.

You can get similar results by following the steps in the writing process described in this chapter. In fact, you may wish to return to this chapter every time you write, until the process becomes a habit.

EXERCISE 8 | Editing and Proofreading Your Work

Look over your revised paragraph from Exercise 7 carefully. Correct mistakes in spelling, grammar, and punctuation. Proofread it more than once. Keep looking for and correcting errors. Make a final clean copy, and proofread it, too.

IN SUMMARY   The Writing Process

- Consider your subject, your purpose, and your audience.
- Discover your ideas by putting them into words through brainstorming, clustering, or freewriting.
- Select your best ideas and expand on them.
- Arrange your ideas in a logical order.
- Write a first draft (and don't worry about making it perfect).
- Return to the draft later and revise it several times, perhaps after getting the reactions of other people. Add new ideas. Try to improve the organization.
- Produce a clean copy when you are reasonably satisfied with your work.
- Edit this copy, and make another if you find errors.
- Check your corrections and proofread the copy again until your final copy is ready for your instructor.

2 Planning and Drafting a Paragraph

Now that you've seen how the writing process works as a whole, we'll examine it in more detail. This chapter shows you the elements of a paragraph and shows you how to plan and draft one. The process will also work for planning and drafting essays, but let's start with paragraphs—the building blocks of essays. Unit II of this book will give you practice in writing specific types of paragraphs and essays; this chapter introduces you to the general practices you need to know:

- focusing the subject
- developing the topic sentence
- planning and drafting supporting sentences
- drafting the paragraph's beginning and end

What Is a Paragraph?

Throughout your college and working career, you will occasionally need to write single paragraphs—for homework assignments, short essay answers, simple memos, and reports on various subjects. More importantly, however, learning to write effective paragraphs is an important first step in learning to write an effective essay, which we'll examine in Chapter 4. Paragraphs discuss the main idea of the essay in smaller, easily understood parts. And each paragraph develops its main idea through supporting explanations, details, and examples.

In fact, you might think of the paragraph as a little essay. Just as an essay is a group of paragraphs that discuss one large idea, a **paragraph** is a group of sentences that discuss a smaller idea. All paragraphs are alike in these ways:

1. A paragraph looks like a unit. It begins with the first line indented (usually about a half-inch, or about five spaces on a typewriter or computer). And each new sentence follows the preceding one *on the same line,* not on a new one.
2. A paragraph *is a unit.* That means each sentence is related to and develops the central idea.
3. A paragraph holds together. That means each idea leads clearly and logically into the next.

Furthermore, like an essay, the paragraph generally contains an introduction, a body, and a conclusion.

- The **introduction** attracts your readers' interest, and it states the paragraph's main idea in a topic sentence.
- The **body** supports the main idea with specific details and explanations in three, four, ten, or even more sentences.
- The **conclusion** often summarizes or ties together the ideas of the paragraph and ends strongly.

Here's a diagram of the main elements of a paragraph.

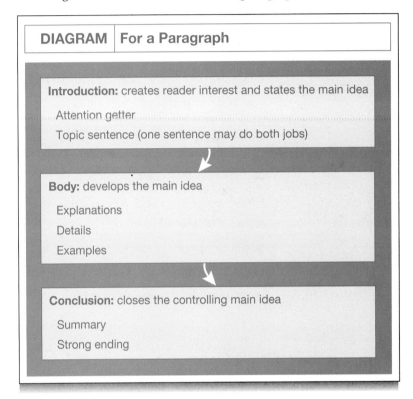

DIAGRAM	For a Paragraph

Introduction: creates reader interest and states the main idea

Attention getter

Topic sentence (one sentence may do both jobs)

Body: develops the main idea

Explanations

Details

Examples

Conclusion: closes the controlling main idea

Summary

Strong ending

We'll be looking specifically at each part of the diagram in the rest of this chapter. This diagram applies to the arrangement of elements in all sorts of paragraphs, as you'll see in Unit II.

Focusing the Subject

Remember that the first step in writing is to explore ideas on your subject. You will probably need to limit the focus of the subject, or you'll have too much to say and too short a space to say it in.

For example, suppose you are assigned to write about "the influence of television." This subject could fill a long book. Brainstorm for a minute: You could discuss television quiz shows, daytime talk shows, late-night talk shows, police dramas, cartoon shows, situation comedies, documentaries, children's shows, movies, soap operas, news broadcasts, sports events, music videos, or commercials. And you could discuss the influence of any one of these on preschoolers, older children, teenagers, adults, or the elderly.

Clearly you need to narrow down the subject. Choose one idea: children's shows. This is your **topic.**

But what will you say about the topic of children's shows? Consider your *attitude toward this topic*. And then write it as a question that you will answer in your paragraph:

> *Are children's shows good or bad?*

Then perhaps you can narrow down the topic further by writing increasingly more specific questions:

> *More specific:*
> *Are children's shows good for young children?*
>
> *Still more specific:*
> *Are children's shows good for teaching young children?*

Remember that the first step of the writing process explores *subject, purpose,* and *audience*. Your attitude toward your subject will help you determine the purpose (probably to inform) and the audience (probably parents of young children). Now that you see how these elements work together, you can turn your question into a statement of your topic idea.

> *Children's shows on television are good for teaching young children.*

Circle the key elements in the topic: *good, teaching,* and *young children*. These are the ideas to explore in the next step of the writing process—prewriting—by brainstorming or freewriting.

EXERCISE 1	Brainstorming Ideas

Have you seen any children's shows on television? If you have, brainstorm ideas about how these shows might teach young children important skills or concepts. If you haven't seen any of these shows, brainstorm ideas about the best ways for adults to learn and improve their English.

_____

_____

_____

_____

_____

_____

| EXERCISE 2 | Focusing a Subject |

Narrow each of the following broad subjects down to a topic that can be developed in a single paragraph.

1. Popular music *How hip-hop music may be disrespectful to women*

_____

2. Living in the city, the suburbs, or a new country _____

_____

3. Women's roles and men's roles _____

_____

4. A favorite activity _____

_____

5. A family custom (or a custom from your native country) _____

_____

6. Cell phones _____

_____

Collaborative Activity

Examining Your Topic
Choose a subject you would most like to write about from Exercise 2. With a classmate, discuss your focus, purpose, and intended audience. Brainstorm a list of limited or focused topics that could be developed in a single paragraph.

Developing the Topic Sentence

Most paragraphs contain one key sentence that presents the main idea and suggests how the remaining sentences will develop that idea. This is called the **topic sentence.** It's usually, but not always, at or near the beginning of the paragraph. The topic sentence helps readers understand your ideas. Then readers can *predict* what comes next based on what you've written. For example, suppose you see this sentence at the beginning of a paragraph:

> Television greatly influences the way we perceive human relationships.

What else would you expect to find in the rest of the paragraph?_____

_____

You'd probably expect an explanation, with examples, of how television influences our perceptions of human relations.

Because the topic sentence gives your paragraph direction, you must compose and revise it carefully. A strong topic sentence

1. is the most general statement in the paragraph
2. makes a claim about the topic
3. can express an opinion or judgment
4. suggests (or even previews) the support of the topic idea that will follow in the paragraph

The Topic Sentence States the Most General Idea

A topic sentence is usually the most general statement in the paragraph, and each of the other sentences develops it specifically.

- General ideas are the largest ones.
- Specific ideas are smaller and fit within the general ones.

For example, when you compare these two sentences, which is more general?

1. There are many popular children's shows on television.
2. *Sesame Street* is the most popular children's television show in the world.

Of course, the first sentence is more general. It discusses many shows, while the second sentence discusses just one of those shows. The second sentence develops the idea of the first sentence.

However, which of the following sentences is more general?

1. *Sesame Street* is the most popular children's television show in the world.
2. It has over 120 million viewers in more than 130 countries.

In this case, the sentence beginning with *Sesame Street* is more general. The sentence that follows it develops the idea.

Therefore, *general* and *specific* are relative terms; one idea is more general when compared to others that develop it. However, the general statement of the topic sentence and its specific development must fit together. For example, a topic sentence such as "There are many popular children's shows on television" is too general for a paragraph about the worldwide popularity of only one show: *Sesame Street.* Likewise, a statement such as "There is a popular Spanish language version of *Sesame Street*" is too specific. It limits the topic to only one version of *Sesame Street* but ignores the other versions of the show throughout the world.

EXERCISE 3	Identifying General and Specific Statements

Circle the letter of the more general sentence.

1. a. The United States declared its independence from England on July 4, 1776.
  b. The United States has been an independent country for more than two centuries.

2. a. Mt. Everest is 29,035 feet (8,850 meters) tall.
  b. Mt. Everest is the tallest mountain in the world.

3. a. Many nationalities live in the big cities of the United States.
  b. Many nationalities live in New York City.

4. a. I want to get a good job after I graduate.
  b. I want to become a lawyer after I graduate.

5. a. The population of my hometown is 11,508.
  b. My hometown is very small.

6. a. George Washington was the first president of the United States.
  b. George Washington was a very important figure in the history of the United States.

The Topic Sentence Makes a Claim

The *topic* of a paragraph is different from its *topic sentence*. The topic is what the paragraph is about—for example, the children's television show *Sesame Street*. However, the topic sentence usually makes a **claim** about the topic—a statement that needs some proof, explanation, or both. Look again at this topic sentence:

> *Sesame Street* is the most popular children's television program in the world.

It *claims* that *Sesame Street* is enormously popular. But it doesn't back up that claim with any evidence or proof. And it doesn't explain why the show is so popular. We can predict that the body of the paragraph will provide that evidence and explanation—and it does. Here's the full paragraph:

> *Sesame Street* is the most popular children's television program in the world. It has over 120 million viewers in more than 130 countries. But the program is popular in part because it reflects the cultures of the countries in which it is seen. Children view versions of the program that have been developed by local producers and educators. Altogether, there are 20 international adaptations of *Sesame Street*. These coproductions combine culturally relevant material with elements of the long-running series from the United States. Consequently, *Sesame Street* is an educationally effective learning tool for young children almost everywhere.

The claim states the **main idea** of the paragraph; the body of the paragraph proves or explains it. In the example you've just read, the proof is facts and figures on the number of viewers, the number of countries, and the number of adaptations of *Sesame Street*. But you can back up a topic sentence in many ways: with descriptions, examples, stories, comparisons, explanations, analyses, or definitions. We'll look at all of these and other ways to develop paragraphs in Unit II.

The Topic Sentence Can Express an Opinion or a Judgment

The type of claim that the topic sentence makes is often an opinion, a judgment, or conclusion. Compare these sentences:

No claim:	Mr. Williams teaches chemistry. (This states only a fact, not an opinion or judgment about Mr. Williams.)
Claim:	Mr. Williams is an excellent chemistry teacher. (*Excellent* expresses an opinion. The body of the paragraph will probably explain *why he is excellent.*)

Most topic sentences include an opinion word or phrase that the remainder of the paragraph can develop specifically.

No opinion or judgment	Judgment
Many high school graduates go on to college.	College often prepares people for *the best* jobs.
No opinion or conclusion	**Opinion or conclusion**
The topic I want to discuss is my cat.	My cat is *very smart*.

Many topic sentences follow this pattern: *subject + stated or implied opinion, judgment, or conclusion*. Here are examples:

Subject	Opinion or judgment
Our soccer team has some	*very talented players*.
Mathematics courses	*challenge* me.
Subject	**Conclusion**
Riding a motorcycle without a helmet	*is dangerous*.

EXERCISE 4 | Identifying Topic Sentences

Underline the topic sentences in the following paragraphs. Be careful: Not every topic sentence comes at the beginning.

What's the Name of That Street?

* * * *

Paragraph A. (1) *Sesame Street, the most popular children's show in television history, was the bright idea of one person.* (2) In 1966, Joan Ganz Cooney worked for a television station in New Jersey. (3) One evening, she and a psychologist friend were sitting around in her apartment after dinner, discussing TV. (4) They had just read a report that very young children watched an average of 27 hours of television a week. (5) Cooney and her friend agreed that if kids were going to spend so much time in front of a TV set, it made sense to teach them something while they were there. (6) But how could she do it?

Paragraph B. (1) Shortly afterward, Cooney thought she had found the answer. (2) She left her job and started the Children's Television Workshop. (3) Her plan was to create an entertaining and fast-moving educational show for young children. (4) Actually, she based her ideas for the show on commercials and the popular comedy show *Laugh-In*. (5) Cooney remembers, "Back then, kids were singing beer commercials. (6) We decided to use the idea of commercials to teach."

Paragraph C. (1) A show that introduces preschool children to numbers and the letters of the alphabet might not seem unusual today, but back then hardly anyone believed it would work. (2) Carroll Spinney, who plays Big Bird on the show, says that teachers "assumed preschoolers weren't ready to read. (3) So we seemed crazy, proposing to sell kids the ABCs, like other shows sold . . . breakfast cereals."

Paragraph D. (1) The major television networks, NBC, CBS, and ABC, didn't want to produce the show because they feared it would be too expensive. (2) So Cooney looked for another way to pay for it. (3) She was lucky. (4) The federal government had created an education program for very young children called Head Start. (5) The government felt Cooney's idea would fit right in, so it contributed $4 million. (6) Cooney raised the rest from the public and from private foundations. (7) She needed every cent. (8) *Sesame Street* would in fact become the most expensive program on television.

Paragraph E. (1) Cooney and the show's producer, Jon Stone, wanted to create a setting that very young children from the poor neighborhoods of the inner city would recognize. (2) The producers didn't want the action to happen in a tree house. (3) That was because, as Stone says, "Kids learn best in a setting similar to their daily lives." (4) However, no one could think of a good location for the show's activities. (5) Then one day, Stone saw a commercial asking college students to be tutors in the inner city. (6) The brick and stone buildings in the commercial gave him the idea for the setting of *Sesame Street*.

Paragraph F. (1) Choosing a name for the show was a much more difficult job. (2) The writers suggested *104th Street, Columbus Avenue* (names of streets in New York) and several other names, including *Sesame Street*. (3) Stone hated them all—especially *Sesame Street,* which reminded him of the old expression used by magicians: "Open sesame!" (4) "Besides," he argued at one meeting, *"Sesame Street* will be too hard for little kids to pronounce." (5) As the time arrived to publicize the show, Cooney asked the writers what name they had come up with. (6) They hadn't thought of one. (7) "I guess we'll have to go with *Sesame Street,"* Stone sighed.

Paragraph G. (1) Perhaps Cooney's most important decision was hiring Jim Henson. (2) He was a brilliant young man whose Muppets (part *marionette*—puppets on strings—and part *puppet*) starred in a Washington, D.C., TV show called *Sam and Friends.* (3) They had also been in commercials and had appeared on television elsewhere. (4) His first (and most famous) Muppet was Kermit the Frog. (5) When Henson was a college freshman, he made the creature by cutting up his mother's old green coat, sewing it into a puppet, and adding the halves of a table-tennis ball for eyes.

Paragraph H. (1) When *Sesame Street* first appeared on November 9, 1969, it wasn't clear that it would succeed. (2) The program received both praise and criticism from the media. (3) Some critics liked it. (4) Many critics said that its fast pace would make kids impatient, so they wouldn't pay attention. (5) But studies showed that preschool kids who watched *Sesame Street* were better prepared to enter school than kids who didn't. (6) Within a year, *Sesame Street* had more than 7 million regular viewers. (7) It has continued to be the most popular children's show in history, not only in the United States, but also throughout much of the world.

EXERCISE 5 | Revising Topic Sentences

None of these topic sentences makes a claim or states an opinion, judgment, or conclusion. Rewrite each one so that its opinion, judgment, or conclusion is clear.

1. This paragraph will compare living on campus with going to a commuter college.
Living on campus offers students advantages that going to a commuter

college cannot.

2. The topic that I want to discuss is popular music. _____

_____

3. Many people have pets. _____

_____

4. An issue in the modern world is the spread of AIDS. _____

_____

5. There are many different kinds of sports in the United States. _____

_____

6. The subject of my paragraph is my flight to the United States. _____

_____

EXERCISE 6 | Writing Topic Sentences

Read each paragraph and write its opening topic sentence. Be sure that your topic sentence is neither too general nor too specific for the paragraph it introduces.

Paragraph A. *The dog has had a long and important relationship with humans.*

The dog became the first trained animal and the only creature that lived with human beings. Stone Age cave paintings in Spain show that people hunted together with trained dogs as early as 10,000 B.C. Many thousands of years before then, however, dogs were working with men and women in Europe. The creatures stayed around the campfires, ate garbage, and guarded their human "pack."

Paragraph B. _____
_____

The ancient Egyptians used their big dogs to hunt antelope. Some Egyptian kings and wealthy people kept dogs as pets. These dogs were the first nonworking animals. In fact, one Egyptian ruler made 2,000 slaves take care of his dogs. Later, the early Greeks used powerful dogs to track lions in Africa. Then, with the development of agriculture, dogs were taught to guard and herd livestock.

Paragraph C. _____
_____

Oddly enough, both dogs and cats came from the same ancestor, which lived 60 million years ago. There is plenty of evidence of the early taming of dogs. Strangely, however, there are no cave paintings or rock carvings of domestic cats. Cats did not appear in written and historical records until 2000 B.C.

Paragraph D. _____
_____

The Egyptians worshipped cats. In fact, one of their goddesses, Bast, had a cat's head. But the Egyptians also put these gods to work, protecting the food supply from rodents. In fact, the cat prevented starvation and disease so well that the punishment for killing a feline—even by accident—was death.

Paragraph E. _____
_____

In fourteenth-century Europe, cats killed many rats that were spreading the bubonic plague. Unfortunately, however, Europeans didn't understand or appreciate the work of their feline friends. As superstition overcame good sense, people associated cats with witchcraft and other evils. They tortured and killed the cats, which resulted in a dramatic increase in the rat population—and a dramatic increase in the plague.

The Topic Sentence May Suggest Its Support

A good topic sentence not only introduces the topic but also indicates the main support that follows in the body of the paragraph. Consider, for example, the topic sentence, "There are *three important reasons* why Mr. Williams is an excellent chemistry teacher." The remainder of the paragraph will explain the three reasons why he is so excellent.

Here is another topic sentence that indicates supporting ideas:

> Mathematics courses challenge me to *study, analyze, and apply what I've learned.*

Topic sentences like these not only help you organize the support. They also help your readers predict the support. These topic sentences therefore serve as outlines—both for you and for your readers.

You don't have to include this outlining language when you first write the topic sentence. If you can see this outline only after you've developed the whole paragraph, go back and revise your topic sentence. The outline isn't always necessary, but it's often useful in shaping a long, complex paragraph.

Keep adjusting your topic sentence and its supporting details until they clearly fit together.

EXERCISE 7	**Writing Your Own Topic Sentences**

Return to one of the topics you listed in Exercise 2. Or, if you don't like that topic, list five or more lessons you have learned or have been taught outside school. Think about some small truths about childhood or parenthood, sportsmanship, working, dating, studying, being disciplined, succeeding or failing, or saving or spending money.

Look over your list and choose the topic you want to explore. Then limit its focus, and draft a preliminary topic sentence. Be sure that your sentence is general (not too specific). Be sure that it makes a claim or expresses an opinion or judgment. And be sure that it suggests or outlines the support that will follow.

Planning the Body

You've selected a topic. You've examined your opinion about it so that you can make a claim. You've drafted a topic sentence that should help you develop your ideas. Now generate that development through brainstorming, clustering, or freewriting.

Types of Development

Support your topic sentence by backing it up with evidence. That evidence can include explanations, details, or examples—or some of each.

Explanations. Because the topic sentence of a paragraph usually expresses an opinion or judgment, you might need to explain the reasoning behind your opinion. Suppose, for instance, that your topic sentence claims that children's shows are a great way for adults to learn English. You could explain that the language on the shows is simple and that the shows emphasize learning the alphabet, the names of numbers, the names of colors, and so on. You could also explain that, even though the programs are simple, adults find them very entertaining.

Specific Details. Specific information makes ideas easier to understand and discuss. If you have researched the topic of children's shows, you could supply data on the number of children who watch them, the effects the shows have on young children's learning when they enter school, and even the effects they have had on school curriculum. (The Internet may be a good place to start searching.)

Examples. You can often explain or strengthen ideas by using an example. You can support an opinion that children's shows are good for teaching young children by using examples from the characters on *Sesame Street*. The Count counts cookies for the Cookie Monster. Ernie and Bert try to pronounce a letter of the alphabet. Grover and Betty Lou eat a nutritious snack together.

Arranging Ideas

After you've finished generating ideas for the body of the paragraph, choose only the ideas that support your main idea, and arrange them in a logical way. Consider these questions:

- Does your topic sentence mention *reasons, ways, methods,* or some similar labeling word? If so, explain several reasons, ways, or methods.
- Would these explanations be clearer or more convincing with examples? If so, supply the examples.
- Do the examples clearly relate to the reasons, ways, or methods? If not, then explain how they relate.

Then organize your material in an appropriate way. You'll learn more about specific types of organization in each of the chapters in Unit II.

Drafting an Introduction

The introduction should attract your readers' interest; it should invite your readers to read the rest of the paragraph. So consider a way to invite them to read on. In some cases, you may simply begin the paragraph with your topic sentence, especially when the topic itself will clearly interest your readers. In other cases, you may need to create that interest. Here are some possibilities:

- Begin with a specific detail: *Big Bird taught me the alphabet last week.*
- Begin with a statement you wish to contradict: *Some people think that children's shows are just for children, but they're wrong.*
- Begin with a question: *What can adults gain from watching children's programs such as Sesame Street?*

Don't rely on a formula, though. Experiment with different openings, and consider how your audience will react to them.

Drafting a Conclusion

A paragraph's closing sentence often summarizes your main idea. Sometimes that means returning to the idea of the topic sentence, but you should change the language so that you don't bore your readers by simply repeating yourself.

Not every conclusion has to summarize, however. You might conclude with a quotation, a joke, a powerful example, a question, or a surprise. For example, you might end the paragraph on children's television shows by saying, "Parents should look carefully at children's shows—not only for what their children can learn, but for what they can learn, too."

And, as with all parts of the first draft, expect to revise later.

EXERCISE 8	Planning Your Paragraph

Brainstorm, cluster, or freewrite the supporting material for the topic sentence you wrote in Exercise 7. Then organize all the materials in an informal outline. The diagram of the outline should include all of the following:

- a preliminary topic sentence that is general enough to cover the whole paragraph, and which states your main idea and perhaps outlines the body of the paragraph

- explanations, details, and examples that clarify or expand on the main idea

- a discussion of the examples when necessary

- a conclusion

Fill in the diagram below, or, if you need more room, make your own on a separate sheet of paper.

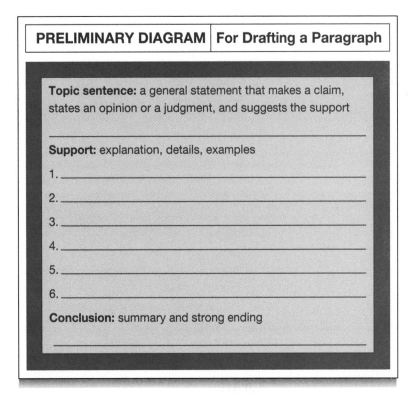

PRELIMINARY DIAGRAM	For Drafting a Paragraph

Topic sentence: a general statement that makes a claim, states an opinion or a judgment, and suggests the support

_____

Support: explanation, details, examples

1. _____

2. _____

3. _____

4. _____

5. _____

6. _____

Conclusion: summary and strong ending

_____

EXERCISE 9	Drafting Your Paragraph

Now write the first draft. Select the strongest and most relevant explanations, details, and examples you've numbered. You don't have to use all of them. Assume that your audience will be your classmates. Your purpose, however, will depend on the subject matter, which could be to inform, to entertain, or to persuade. The first draft should be about one handwritten page or half a computer-generated, double-spaced page.

EXERCISE 10 | Revising Your Paragraph

Chapter 3 will provide specific help in revising your work, but you can begin the revision process now. Put the first draft aside for a few hours (or a day or two), and then read it over carefully. Try to react to the draft as its reader, not its writer. Is anything unclear? Is the organization logical? Are more explanations needed? Are the details and examples convincing? Rewrite the draft, making whatever additions or changes you feel are necessary. Prepare a clean copy for your instructor.

IN SUMMARY | A Paragraph

- is focused on a topic that can be developed fully in a short space
- begins with an introduction that attracts the readers' interest
- includes a topic sentence that makes a claim or states an opinion, a judgment, or a conclusion about the topic
- may outline the body in the topic sentence, allowing readers to predict what will follow
- develops the topic idea in the body with supporting explanations, details, and examples
- arranges the supporting information in some logical way
- concludes with a summary or strong statement

3 Revising and Editing a Paragraph

Revision (*re* = again + *vision*) literally means seeing your work again. If you have set your writing aside for a day or more, you should be refreshed and able to see it differently. Then you can focus on improving it through revision. This chapter will introduce you to the revising practices you need to make those improvements:

- developing the content
- improving the unity
- making the ideas flow better
- editing and proofreading

What Is Revising?

Revising means improving what you have already written. When you revise, you examine how well your first draft makes its point and achieves its purpose for its audience. That may require rearranging ideas, developing ideas further, cutting out ideas that don't support your point, and changing the wording of your sentences. Try to respond to the draft as a reader, not its writer. Does the writing accomplish its goal? Is it clear? Is it interesting?

You want your readers to understand, appreciate, or be convinced by your message. That means its point should be well developed; each sentence should relate logically and smoothly to the others. And, of course, it also means that word choice, word forms, and grammar should be correct and appropriate.

Revision is different from editing, which focuses on correcting grammar, spelling, punctuation, and word choice. Don't worry too much about these things in the early stages of revision. Right now, your most important goal is to improve the content of your paragraph. Then you can polish up that content.

This chapter will show you a number of matters to consider as you revise. But don't think of them as separate steps in the revision process. You may consider all of these matters at the same time—or separately. In either case, however, you will probably revise your paragraph more than once. Most writers do.

Revising to Develop Content

Almost every paragraph can be improved by adding more specific content. The claim in a topic sentence is clearer and more convincing when supported by explanations, details, and examples. Look closely at your paragraph. Are any statements too general? Do any ideas need more support? There is no rule about how much additional content to include. The decision depends on your answers to three questions:

1. How complicated is the topic idea? The more complicated it is, the more you must explain and illustrate the idea.
2. How entertaining should the paragraph be? Examples often help provide that entertainment.
3. How much do your readers know about the topic? The less they know, the more information you must supply.

Notice that the three questions relate to the three questions you should ask yourself at the very beginning of the writing process:

- What is my subject?
- What is my purpose?
- Who is my audience?

The answers will shape your writing from start to finish.

Here's a first draft that the writer realized was weak in development:

> Probably one of the biggest and most expensive meals of all time took place in 1905, when "Diamond Jim" Brady gave a party. Brady spent a lot of money to feed his guests, but, as usual, he ate the largest meal himself. Everyone agreed that it was a very nice party.

Clearly, this paragraph is too general. Although it claims that the party was big and expensive, it does not say how big or expensive. It backs up its claims with more claims (for example, "Brady spent a lot of money") but it doesn't explain or illustrate them specifically. In revising the paragraph, then, the writer thought about the questions a reader might ask, such as "How much money did Brady spend?"

Here's the revision, with the general ideas now developed through explanations, specific details, and examples:

> Probably one of the biggest and most expensive meals of all time took place at a hotel in New York City in 1905, when the famous millionaire and the world's greatest eater, "Diamond Jim" Brady, gave a party in honor of his racehorse, Gold Heels. Brady invited only fifty guests, but the food bill was over $40,000. That was $800 per person! Since nobody could ever eat more than the 250-pound Brady himself, Diamond Jim's own meal probably totaled several thousand dollars. Here, for example, is what he ate—which, for him, was a typical meal. He started with three dozen oysters, followed by a half dozen crabs and two bowls of soup. Next, he ate seven lobsters, two ducks, two huge portions of turtle, a sirloin steak, and large helpings of

> assorted vegetables. For dessert, he consumed a platter of cakes, pies, cookies, and tarts. Finally, he topped it all off with a two-pound box of chocolates. Of course, all that food made him thirsty, so he drank a gallon or two of orange juice. When the meal was over, his guests said that they couldn't recall a nicer party given for a horse.

Notice, too, that the revised paragraph is much longer than the first draft. But the *quantity* of words doesn't improve the paragraph. The *quality* of the information provides that improvement. A strong paragraph supports its main point through clear, persuasive, and lively explanations, details, and examples.

EXERCISE 1	Identifying Development in a Paragraph

In revising the paragraph on "Diamond Jim" Brady, the writer had to consider the questions a reader might ask. Return to the revised paragraph and find the answers to these questions. Write the number of each question in the margin, and underline the words or sentences that answer it.

1. Who was "Diamond Jim" Brady, and why did he give the party?

2. How big and expensive was the party?

3. Where was it?

4. How many people attended?

5. What did Brady himself eat?

6. How much did Brady weigh?

Revising to Improve Unity

Be sure to examine your paragraph for **unity.** Every sentence should develop the main point or claim. So begin by looking carefully at the topic sentence to see if its point is clear. Then examine the remainder of the paragraph to see if any ideas go off the point.

The Topic Sentence as a Guide

Key words in the topic sentence can help you test for unity. Here, for example, is an informal outline of the revised paragraph on Brady. The underlined words in the topic sentence provide a guide to the specific explanations, details, and examples that follow. Notice, too, that the details lead to further layers of specific development.

Topic Sentence: Probably one of the biggest and most expensive meals of all time took place . . . when the famous millionaire and the world's greatest eater, "Diamond Jim" Brady, gave a party in honor of his racehorse, Gold Heels.

biggest and most expensive

1. ... the food bill was over $40,000. That was $800 per person!

2. ... Diamond Jim's own meal probably totaled several thousand dollars.

world's greatest eater

1. Here, for example, is what he ate—which, for him, was a typical meal.
    a. He started with three dozen oysters, ...
    b. Next, he ate seven lobsters, ...
    c. For dessert, he consumed a platter of cakes, pies, cookies, and tarts. ...
    d. Finally, he topped it all off with a two-pound box of chocolates.

2. ... he drank a gallon or two of orange juice.

racehorse

When the meal was over, his guests said that they couldn't recall a nicer party given for a horse.

This outline suggests that the paragraph is well unified. The body sentences follow the guidelines of the topic sentence and support or relate to it. The writer doesn't mention Brady's collection of diamonds, his close relationship with the actress Lillian Russell, or his success as a businessperson. These details may be interesting, but they are off the point.

Predicting as a Guide

Readers don't merely receive information; they actively attempt to find meaning for themselves. They **predict** what will follow from the opening sentences. You can improve the unity of your own paragraph from predicting, too. Here's how to do it:

- Read the topic sentence.
- Stop and think about what your readers would expect to follow the topic sentence.
- Decide if the rest of the paragraph satisfies those predictions.
- Make notes on what to add, remove, or move around to satisfy those expectations.

Predicting is a valuable tool and should become a regular part of your revision practices. It's especially effective when you have someone else read your draft and test it for unity.

✔ **TIPS**

For Determining Unity

Look at the beginning and ending sentences of the paragraph. Is the relationship between them clear and logical? Do all the sentences support or relate to the topic sentence?

Collaborative Activity 1

Predicting

With a partner, exchange the paragraphs you wrote in Chapter 2. Have your partner read your topic sentence aloud and then predict the support that will follow. Was the prediction correct? If not, you will need to revise the topic sentence, or the support, or both. Now read your partner's topic sentence and repeat the process.

EXERCISE 2 | Unifying a Paragraph

One sentence in each group does not relate to the topic sentence. Underline the words in the topic sentence that suggest the type of support you'd expect to find. Then circle the letter of the sentence that doesn't belong.

1. *Topic sentence:* Before the fork was widely used in seventeenth-century Italy, people picked at their food <u>in a variety of ways</u>.
    a. They speared it with an eating knife.
    b. They scooped up their food in a spoon and lifted it to their mouths.
    c. They ridiculed men who used forks and called them unmanly.
    d. They held food with three fingers because using five was considered impolite.

2. *Topic sentence:* The origins of nursery rhymes explain why some lyrics might not be suitable for young children.

   a. For centuries, the rhymes were known only as "songs" or "ditties" and were intended mainly for adults.

   b. For example, some rhymes were taken from common folk songs.

   c. In the 1820s, however, the lyrics of the rhymes were changed because morals had changed.

   d. Also, many nursery rhymes started as songs people sang in taverns, or as jokes, or as the lyrics of romantic songs.

3. *Topic sentence:* The custom of shaking hands may have started not as a greeting, but as a way of protecting oneself.

   a. If a man from a village met another man he didn't recognize, he reached for his knife.

   b. The second man grabbed his knife, too, and then both circled each other.

   c. When they were satisfied that they did not need to fight, they put their knives away.

   d. Each man held out his right hand—the weapon hand—and grabbed the other's hand as a way of showing friendliness.

   e. A different meaning of the handshake originated in ancient Egypt, where pictures show a god transferring power to a ruler by grasping his hand.

4. *Topic sentence:* The Mediterranean is the most polluted sea on Earth.

   a. About one-fifth of the world's oil pollution occurs there, although the sea's volume is only 1 percent of the world's water.

   b. In addition, 120 cities pump their sewage, much of it untreated, into the waters.

   c. The Mediterranean is one of the most popular vacation spots in the world.

   d. The great rivers feeding the Mediterranean—the Rhone, Po, and Nile—are themselves so polluted that they only contribute to the problem.

Revising to Improve the Flow of Ideas

An effective paragraph must also have **coherence.** The ideas in the paragraph must cohere, which literally means "stick together." The first sentence must lead logically into the second sentence, and so on. Look closely at your paragraph again. Is there a smooth flow between ideas? If there isn't, try to strengthen the coherence of the paragraph. Here are some ways to do so.

Logical Arrangement. Arrange your ideas in the most logical order. For example, the paragraph on Diamond Jim Brady first backs up its claim that the meal was big and expensive. Then it illustrates the claim that Brady was the world's greatest eater by describing each stage of Brady's meal, from the appetizers through the chocolates following dessert. The support doesn't jump back and forth between ideas.

In revising, carefully examine your organization. Have you grouped together similar ideas? Should one idea come before another or follow it? What should you say first—or last?

Pronouns. Clear use of pronouns can also help you establish a clear connection between ideas. **Pronouns** replace nouns and refer back to them:

Noun	←	Pronouns
The man		he, him
The woman		she, her
The car		it
Philosophy		it
The men		they, them

These references tie together the ideas between and within sentences. But be careful. A pronoun like *he* can sometimes refer to more than one idea in a sentence:

"When my *brother* told my *father* the news, *he* was excited."

In this case, you may need to repeat the noun to avoid confusion:

When my brother told my father the news, *my father* was excited.

Reinforcement. Repeat key words or ideas in different ways as you move from sentence to sentence. For example, in the paragraph on Diamond Jim Brady, the claim *world's greatest eater* appears in one sentence, and the verbs *ate* and *consumed* appear throughout the description of his meal. Readers can see that description supports the claim.

Transitions. Use transitional words and phrases to explain relationships. A **transition** shows the logical relationship between one idea and another. For example, in the description of the meal in the Brady paragraph, the words *started, next, for dessert,* and *finally* label the stages of the meal. The longer transition, *Of course all that food made him thirsty,* introduces the details about what he drank. And the transition at the beginning, *For example,* introduces the description of the meal.

Here's a list of other transitions. Consult the list often as you write and revise:

Transitions

For Counting: first, second, third, next, then, after that, finally

For Space Relationships: above, around, behind, below, beneath, beyond, close by, farther away, inside, outside, next to, over, under, underneath

For Time Relationships: afterward, after that, then, finally, later (on), next, soon, the next day, tomorrow, yesterday, a year ago, as, during, immediately, meanwhile, last night, in March, in 2004, on July 8

For Addition: additionally, also, furthermore, in addition, moreover, too

For Comparison: in the same way (manner), likewise, similarly

For Contrast: however, nevertheless, on the other hand, yet, despite, still

For Emphasis: above all, especially, in fact, most important

For Illustrations: for example, for instance, in particular, such as

For Reasons: because of, due to, for

For Summary: and so, in other words, in short, in summary, to sum up, to summarize

EXERCISE 3 | Predicting Transitions

Read each passage, and then list four or five transitions you would probably include in the remainder of the passage.

Passage A: The steps involved in registering for classes are rather complicated. First, you must request a set of materials from the office of admissions.

Second, Third, Fourth, Finally

Passage B: After playing on the muddy ground and in the wet leaves, the six-year-old boy was filthy. First, his shoes were covered with mud. Second, his pants were ripped and covered with grass. _____

Passage C: Friday was very busy for Juanita Baxter. In the morning, she had to prepare for a meeting. _____

Passage D: The new three-story auditorium is large and beautiful. On the ground floor, the seats close to the stage are covered with a soft red velvet material, and the space between the rows is wide. Farther from the stage, the seats are just as comfortable, but the rows are closer together, leaving less room for the legs. _____

_____

Passage E: Although born in different countries, Tina and Gloria have a lot in common.

_____

Passage F: Although Bruno and Claudio are twins, they are different in many ways.

_____

Passage G: [Write your own topic sentence and then add the transitions you would probably include in the remainder of the paragraph.]

_____

_____

_____

_____

_____

| EXERCISE 4 | Analyzing a Paragraph for Coherence |

Read the following paragraph, and answer the questions about it.

A Dark, Sweet History

* * * *

(1) Although history does not prove where the chocolate chip cookie began, the cookie certainly wasn't around in 1847. (2) Before then, chocolate existed only as a liquid or a powder, not as a solid. (3) The long road to the chocolate chip cookie began in Mexico around 1000 B.C., when the Aztecs made a ceremonial drink, *xocoatl,* meaning "bitter water," from crushed cocoa beans. (4) Xocoatl later became *chocolatl* in other Mexican dialects. (5) After the Spanish had conquered Mexico about 2,600 years later, they introduced this drink to Europe, where the recipe remained unchanged until 1828. (6) That year, a candy maker in Holland tried to make a finer chocolate powder but instead created a creamy butter. (7) This discovery led to the world's first solid chocolate, produced by a British company in 1847. (8) Hard chocolate therefore became a reality, and the chocolate chip cookie a possibility. (9) From that point on, the origin of the cookie is less certain. (10) According to legend, the first chocolate chip cookie was baked around 1930 at the Toll House Inn, near Whitman, Massachusetts. (11) Ruth Wakefield, the inn's owner, was also its cook and baker. (12) One day, she added chocolate pieces to her butter cookies, creating the Toll House Inn cookie, which she sold nationally. (13) For chocolate bits, Mrs. Wakefield cut up the Nestle Company's large semi-sweet chocolate bar. (14) Nestle was impressed with her recipe and asked permission to print it on the wrapper of the bar. (15) Her reward would be a lifetime supply of free chocolate. (16) The cookie was so popular that in 1939 the company finally introduced Morsels, the packaged chocolate chips. (17) From a bitter drink of the Aztec Indians to the household delight of today, chocolate has come a long way.

1. The paragraph does not begin with the topic sentence. Where is the topic sentence? Underline it.

2. What expressions mark the passage of time? What other transitional expressions give coherence to the passage? Underline them twice.

3. What key words or ideas are repeated to provide coherence? Circle them twice.

4. What pronouns establish coherence? Put them in brackets. Look at the adjectives *this* and *that* before nouns. How do these expressions add coherence to the paragraph?

   _____

   _____

5. How many groups or individuals were involved in discovering, transmitting, manufacturing, and producing the ingredients of chocolate chip cookies? _____

What words or phrases identify the groups?

_____

_____

6. Which incident does the paragraph develop most specifically? Why?

_____

_____

| **EXERCISE 5** | Arranging a Paragraph |

The following sentences are not in the correct order. Number the sentences in the most logical order. (There may be more than one way to order the sentences.) Then write a topic sentence for a paragraph that includes the information in the sentences.

_____ Most humans are right-handed.

_____ The practice began in the fifteenth century.

___*1*___ By studying portraits and drawings of clothes with buttons, historians have traced the reasons why men's clothes button from right to left while women's button from left to right.

_____ Most men found it easier to have clothes that buttoned from right to left.

_____ Men usually dressed themselves at home, on trips, and on the battlefield.

_____ Wealthy women had female servants who dressed them.

_____ Most maids were right-handed.

_____ It was easier to fasten their mistresses' clothes if the buttons and buttonholes were reversed.

_____ Maids faced the buttons head on.

_____ The practice has never been changed.

_____ Topic Sentence: _____

_____

| **EXERCISE 6** | Improving Coherence of the Paragraph |

Collaborative Activity 2

Improving Coherence
With a partner, compare the paragraphs you wrote in Exercise 6. Then write one paragraph that includes the best ideas from both of you.

Now take your revision of the paragraph in Exercise 5 one step further. Rewrite the paragraph, beginning with the topic sentence and following with the supporting information as you rearranged it. But don't stop there. Add transitions and repeated key terms to strengthen the coherence of the paragraph.

EXERCISE 7 | Revising Your Own Paragraph

Collaborative Activity 3

For Exercise 7, write the sentences in the paragraph out of order. Trade them with a partner. Put the sentences in the best order, and suggest transitions to improve coherence.

Use the following checklist as a guide for revising the paragraph you wrote in Chapter 2. If you answer *no* to any question, then revise the paragraph to correct the problem. First, make changes above the lines or write notes in the margin. Then rewrite the paragraph.

REVISION CHECKLIST

		YES	NO
PARAGRAPH	• Does my paragraph have a clear topic sentence that makes a claim?	☐	☐
	• Does the paragraph include enough explanations, details, and examples to support the claim?	☐	☐
	• Does the paragraph have unity, with all the information supporting the topic idea?	☐	☐
	• Does the paragraph have coherence, with the ideas introduced in a logical order?	☐	☐
	• Do pronouns and repeated key words make the ideas flow smoothly?	☐	☐
	• Do transitions show the logical links between ideas?	☐	☐

Using Peer Review in the Revision Process

Working with a classmate, who becomes an audience for your writing, can also help you revise your papers. A friendly reader can often see ways to improve a writer's draft. However, this peer review addresses revision only—not editing. Focus on the content of the draft—not its grammar and mechanics. If you rely only on someone else to correct your errors, you may not learn to correct them yourself. And, in fact, the "corrections" may not be correct.

The following guidelines for revision should help you conduct a peer review.

Guidelines for Peer Review

Collaborative Activity 4

Using Peer Review
Exchange the paragraph you are now revising with a partner. Following the guidelines for Peer Review revise the paragraph, taking your partner's comments into consideration.

1. Begin by saying something positive. For example, you might say, "This opening sentence is really clear" or "I really like this transition."
2. Look at the paper carefully. Is the topic idea clear? Does the draft stick to the point? Is the organization logical? Are any sentences or ideas unclear? Could any parts be explained more specifically? Could examples or better examples be added? Are the transitions between ideas clear?
3. Be specific but polite in suggesting improvements. Don't say, "This part is really bad." Say, "I couldn't understand this part because . . . " Explain why—and, if possible, how—something needs to be improved.

4. Don't interrupt your partner as he or she comments. And take notes as you hear your partner's comments. This way you can decide whether and how to revise the paper later. You don't have to agree with everything your partner says, but you ought to consider it.

Editing the Paragraph

After you've revised your paragraph, you can edit your work. Units III and IV of this book will provide you with specific help in editing for grammar, mechanics, punctuation, and spelling. Consult the checklist at the end of Unit IV (pages 396–397) for a quick survey of the concerns you should attend to in editing.

Proofreading the Paragraph

The final stage in the revision process is proofreading. That means carefully reading your draft more than once to check that your revisions and editorial changes were made correctly.

EXERCISE 8	Editing and Proofreading Your Paragraph

Return to the paragraph that you revised in Exercise 7. Look it over carefully. Are the grammar, mechanics, punctuation, and spelling correct? Make final changes and corrections before writing a clean copy or printing a new computer copy. Then proofread. Submit the final copy to your instructor.

IN SUMMARY	A Revised Paragraph

- is well developed through explanations, specific details, and examples
- has unity, with all statements developing the topic idea
- is coherent, with a smooth flow between ideas
- has been edited and proofread to ensure that grammar, mechanics, punctuation, and spelling are correct

4 Planning and Drafting an Essay

Although you often need to write single paragraphs for school or work assignments, you'll write essays far more often. This chapter builds on the processes involved in planning, drafting, and revising a paragraph (see Chapters 2 and 3). It covers

- the difference between a paragraph and an essay
- developing the thesis statement
- writing the essay

What Is an Essay?

An **essay** is an organized discussion of a subject in a series of paragraphs. A paragraph and an essay actually share many traits.

- The **paragraph** discusses a limited topic, which it introduces in a topic sentence and then supports *in separate sentences*. The topic sentence helps determine and shape the content of the paragraph.

- The **essay** explores a broader topic, which it introduces in a **thesis statement** and then supports *in separate paragraphs*. The thesis statement helps determine and shape the content of the entire essay.

An essay is not simply a longer version of a paragraph. The content of the essay is more complex and needs more development. However, the essay is similar to the paragraph in structure, for it contains three parts:

- The **introduction**—that is, the first paragraph of the essay—attracts the readers' interest, makes the primary claim of the essay in a thesis statement, and may introduce the ideas of the body paragraphs. The introduction should help readers predict the ideas you will develop in the remainder of the essay.
- The **body**—at least three paragraphs and often more—develops and supports the thesis by breaking it down into smaller ideas. In a well-organized essay each body paragraph
  1. introduces its supporting idea in a topic sentence
  2. develops the idea in the body
  3. then concludes with a transition to the next paragraph
- The **conclusion**—the last paragraph of the essay—ties all the essay's ideas together and includes a strong ending.

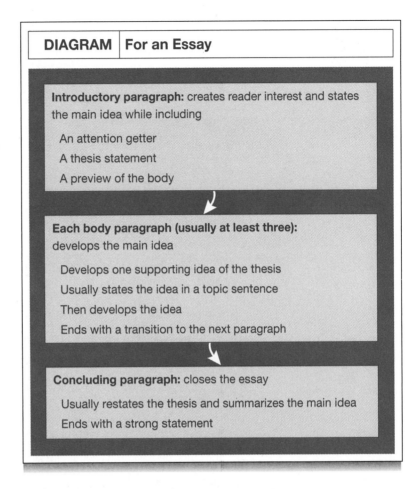

DIAGRAM	For an Essay

Introductory paragraph: creates reader interest and states the main idea while including

An attention getter
A thesis statement
A preview of the body

Each body paragraph (usually at least three): develops the main idea

Develops one supporting idea of the thesis
Usually states the idea in a topic sentence
Then develops the idea
Ends with a transition to the next paragraph

Concluding paragraph: closes the essay

Usually restates the thesis and summarizes the main idea
Ends with a strong statement

EXERCISE 1 | Analyzing an Essay

Here's a final draft of an essay written by Linder Anim, a student from Ghana. Linder attended Truman College in Chicago when Michael Jordan was the best basketball player in the world. Read it carefully, paying attention to the parts, which are identified for you in boldface. Then answer the questions at the end.

Michael Jordan, Superstar
Linder Anim

* * * *

1   Michael Jordan has played for the Chicago Bulls for years, and everyone cheers for him. Fans have filled the seats at the United Center ever since he led the team to six NBA championships, and many millions have watched each of his games on TV. However, it is no wonder that he has attracted such admiration and fame. **[Thesis statement]** *Jordan possesses all the qualities of an athletic superstar: extraordinary attractiveness, incredible physical talent, and exemplary character.*

2   **[Topic sentence]** *First of all, Jordan is a fine physical specimen of a man.* He is not only handsome, but he has a magnificent body on his six-and-one-half–foot frame. He always shaves his hair, which seems to symbolize his commitment to the

game. With his broad shoulders and rippling muscles, he looks strong and formidable in his number 23 jersey.

3   **[Topic sentence]** *Second, Jordan is a talented athlete who has developed a game of speed, agility, and intelligence.* He quickly dodges the opposing team's defense and makes spectacular shots, sometimes as he falls away from the basket, other times when he drives toward it. As a result, he always scores a lot of points, which makes him the top scorer on the Bulls and also within the rest of the NBA. Most amazing of all are his "Air Jordan" moves, which rely on agility and leaping ability. He jumps up in the air and can stay there for a long time before coming down. He is also smart, and as the team captain he tries to keep his teammates as disciplined as he is on the court. Without Michael Jordan, the Chicago Bulls would not be where they are today.

4   **[Topic sentence]** *Finally, Jordan is not only a great athlete, but also a gentleman on and off the basketball court.* As the team captain, he shows cool and controlled leadership and gentility. He never fights, and if any one of his teammates does fight, he immediately calms that person down. After each game, he always puts on a beautiful suit and his earring and politely answers questions from the press. He also donates money to charity for a variety of good causes. Jordan sponsors community services, too, such as basketball camps for kids.

5   **[Conclusion]** *Michael Jordan is a one-of-a-kind superstar.* That is why people look up to him.

1. How many points does the thesis statement in the first paragraph introduce?

    _____ What is the function of the opening sentences of the paragraph

    that lead up to the thesis statement? _____

    _____

2. How are the topic sentences in the body paragraphs related to the thesis statement?

    _____

    Which words or phrases in these paragraphs are transitions? Circle them.

3. Identify the supporting details in the body paragraphs. How many details does each

    paragraph contain? Paragraph 2 _____ Paragraph 3 _____

    Paragraph 4 _____

4. The concluding paragraph consists of only two sentences. Why?

_____

_____

Comparing the Paragraph and the Essay

Reread the essay on Michael Jordan, and pay special attention to its structure. The structuring elements—the thesis statement, topic sentences, and conclusion—shape the whole essay. In fact, if you combined all these framing elements and removed the supporting material, you'd be left with a coherent paragraph:

> Michael Jordan possesses all the qualities of an athletic superstar: extraordinary attractiveness, incredible physical talent, and exemplary character. First of all, Jordan is a fine physical specimen of a man. Second, Jordan is a talented athlete who has developed a game of speed, agility, and intelligence. Finally, Jordan is not only a great athlete, but also a gentleman on and off the basketball court. Michael Jordan is a one-of-a-kind superstar. That is why people look up to him.

Is this paragraph effective? Only as a summary. You can't develop its primary claim very well in so short a space. A large topic such as Michael Jordan requires a multi-paragraph essay to explain and illustrate all parts of the claim:

> **Paragraph 1 thesis:** _Michael Jordan has all the qualities of a superstar._
>
> **Paragraph 2 topic sentence:** _Jordan is a fine physical specimen._
>
>   **Support:** _muscular, 6'6" tall, shaved head, handsome_
>
> **Paragraph 3 topic sentence:** _He is a talented athlete who is quick and smart._
>
>   **Support:** _fast, great jumper with "Air Jordan" moves, best scorer, always thinking_
>
> **Paragraph 4 topic sentence:** _Jordan is also a gentleman on and off the basketball court._
>
>   **Support:** _leader on court, never fights, dresses in suit, polite to press, supports charities and community groups_
>
> **Concluding paragraph:** _Michael Jordan is one of a kind, and everyone looks up to him._

An essay is long enough to give a writer the space to explore ideas fully, so there's room for Linder to develop topic sentences that fully predict the support that will follow—and to make them interesting. Notice how she varies the word choice of her topic sentences, instead of simply repeating the language of the thesis statement. Compare the versions of topic sentences on page 42.

> **Thesis:** *Michael Jordan possesses all the features of an athletic superstar: extraordinary attractiveness, incredible physical talent, and exemplary character.*
>
> | Mechanical topic sentence | Varied and interesting topic sentence |
> |---|---|
> | 1. First, Jordan is very attractive. | First of all, Jordan is a fine physical specimen of a man. |
> | 2. Second, he has incredible physical talent. | Second, Jordan is a talented athlete who has developed a game of speed, agility, and intelligence. |
> | 3. Third, Jordan also has an exemplary character. | Finally, Jordan is not only a great athlete, but also a gentleman on and off the basketball court. |

How did Linder create her essay and vary the wording? She explored and organized her ideas, probably by brainstorming, clustering, and/or freewriting. Then she outlined her ideas, including a preliminary thesis statement, preliminary topic sentences, and possible supporting details. After she drafted the essay, she adjusted her thesis statement and topic sentences to make them more interesting.

Developing the Thesis Statement

As you've seen in Linder Anim's essay, the thesis statement is much like the topic sentence of a paragraph, which was discussed and illustrated fully in Chapter 2. Like the topic sentence, the thesis statement should

- be general enough to cover everything in the essay
- make a claim (that is, state an opinion, judgment, or conclusion)
- allow the reader to predict the support that follows in the body of the essay

One way to guide readers in their predictions is to include an overview, or preview, of the body paragraphs that will follow. You can attach that preview to the thesis statement through linking words such as *because, since,* or *by,* or with a colon [:]. Or you can write an entirely separate sentence.

Linder's essay on Michael Jordan evolved in this way. She began by quickly jotting down a claim in an initial thesis statement:

> *Michael Jordan has all the qualities of a superstar.*

She later expanded the thesis by adding the preview:

> *Michael Jordan possesses all the qualities of an athletic superstar: extraordinary attractiveness, incredible physical talent, and exemplary character.*

When should you write your preview? That depends on when you see the shape of the whole essay most clearly. It may be in the planning stages, or it may be in the revision stages. Don't worry if your first thesis statement isn't perfect. You can revise it many times and at various points in the writing process.

EXERCISE 2	Predicting Supporting Ideas

Examine each of the following thesis statements, and predict the main supporting ideas you'd expect to find in the full essay—and the order in which they might be introduced. Report your findings to the whole class.

1. The methods of choosing the president and vice president of the United States have undergone three major changes throughout the country's history:

   Paragraph 1. _A discussion of the original method of choosing the president and vice president_

   Paragraph 2. _____

   _____

   Paragraph 3. _____

   _____

2. The Japanese elementary and secondary educational system differs from the American system in the length of the school year, in the subjects emphasized in the curriculum, and in the expectations placed on the students by both teachers and parents.

   Paragraph 1. _____

   _____

   Paragraph 2. _____

   _____

   Paragraph 3. _____

   _____

3. Despite what many people think, I believe pets are a waste of time, money, and affection that would be better directed toward our children and family.

   Paragraph 1. _____

   _____

   Paragraph 2. _____

   _____

   Paragraph 3. _____

   _____

EXERCISE 3	Revising and Supporting Thesis Statements

Revise each thesis statement to include a claim that could be developed in an essay. Underline the key words of the claim. If possible, include a preview of the support in the body paragraphs.

1. Our college offers an introductory computer course. Revision: _Our college's_ _introductory computer_ _course offers valuable instruction_ in basic word

   processing, database management, and Web searching.

2. My family has several pets. _____

   _____

3. I live in a big (small) city. _____

   _____

4. I want to major in business administration. _____

   _____

5. Many people study English. _____

   _____

EXERCISE 4	Generating Ideas for Your Essay

Begin work on an essay about why you admire a particular person: a public figure, a relative, a friend, a teacher, or anyone who's had a positive influence on your life or the lives of others. Draft a preliminary thesis statement—just something to get you focused. Then do some brainstorming, clustering, and/or freewriting to discover and produce ideas that develop the thesis. Remember: You're writing an essay, which is much longer and more complex than a paragraph, so generate as many ideas as you can—perhaps two pages' worth.

EXERCISE 5	Selecting Details and Outlining

Now organize your ideas. Using the diagram on page 45, include a preliminary attention-getting opening, a preliminary thesis statement, topic sentences for each body paragraph, support for the topic sentences (which you can simply list), and a concluding statement.

```
PRELIMINARY DIAGRAM | For Drafting an Essay

Preliminary attention getter: _____
_____
Preliminary thesis statement: _____
_____

Preliminary topic sentences:
1. _____
_____
_____
Support: _____
_____
_____
2. _____
_____
Support: _____
_____
_____
3. _____
_____
_____
Support: _____
_____
_____

Preliminary conclusion: _____
_____
_____
```

EXERCISE 6 | Drafting the Essay

Write a first draft of your essay based on materials you've generated and listed in Exercises 4 and 5. Don't worry about writing a perfect draft; you'll be revising it later. Pay attention to the following guidelines.

1. Experiment with different attention-getting openings, perhaps merely listing four or five of them. You can decide which one to use later.

2. State a thesis and, if possible, include some language that predicts the support. You can add or refine this language later, after you've written the body paragraphs and then more clearly know the supporting ideas they contain.

3. In each body paragraph, include a topic sentence, which you may wish to make more varied and interesting during revisions.

4. If any body paragraphs contain only a few sentences, plan on adding content to them later, perhaps after you've gotten more ideas through brainstorming or freewriting.

5. Include a summary in your final paragraph, but don't simply restate the opening thesis statement. Vary the wording, now or when you revise.

| EXERCISE 7 | Revising Your First Draft |

After a break, return to the essay and read it critically. Then revise the essay one or more times, according to the following checklist.

REVISION CHECKLIST

		YES	NO
Essay	• Does the essay have an effective attention-getting opening?	☐	☐
	• Does the thesis statement make a claim and predict the supporting ideas?	☐	☐
	• Is the essay unified, with each body paragraph supporting the thesis idea?	☐	☐
	• Are the body paragraphs arranged in some logical way?	☐	☐
	• Is the claim of each body paragraph stated in a clear topic sentence?	☐	☐
	• Is each paragraph unified and well developed, with all explanations, details, and examples supporting the topic sentence?	☐	☐
	• Are the transitions between ideas clear, both within and between paragraphs?	☐	☐
	• Does the final paragraph summarize the main ideas and end strongly?	☐	☐

| EXERCISE 8 | Making the Final Changes in the Essay |

Collaborative Activity

Peer Review

With a classmate, exchange drafts of your essays. Use the Revision Checklist in Chapter 3.

After revising your essay, edit it for clarity of ideas and for correct grammar, mechanics, punctuation, and spelling. You may want to consult the Revision Checklist above. Then make a clean copy and proofread your essay carefully. Correct for errors, and submit the essay to your instructor.

IN SUMMARY	An Essay

- begins with an introductory paragraph that attracts the readers' attention and states the main idea in a thesis statement, often including language that predicts the supporting ideas that will follow
- continues with body paragraphs that discuss the supporting ideas, each stated in a topic sentence, followed by its support
- concludes with a restatement of the thesis and a strong ending sentence

WRITE, WRITE, WRITE!

The Writing Process

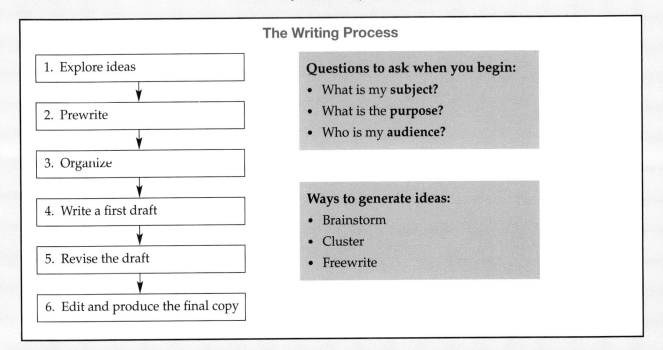

1. Explore ideas
2. Prewrite
3. Organize
4. Write a first draft
5. Revise the draft
6. Edit and produce the final copy

Questions to ask when you begin:
- What is my **subject**?
- What is the **purpose**?
- Who is my **audience**?

Ways to generate ideas:
- Brainstorm
- Cluster
- Freewrite

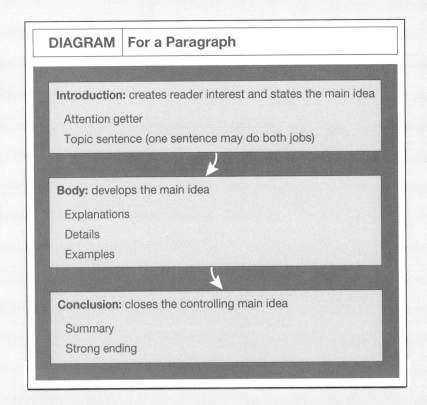

DIAGRAM	For a Paragraph

Introduction: creates reader interest and states the main idea

Attention getter

Topic sentence (one sentence may do both jobs)

Body: develops the main idea

Explanations

Details

Examples

Conclusion: closes the controlling main idea

Summary

Strong ending

THE MORE YOU DO IT, THE BETTER YOU GET!

The Revision Process

1. Locate the topic sentence
2. Study the body sentence
3. Examine the organization
4. Look at the language
5. Recall your purpose
6. Reflect on the conclusion

The aims of revision:
- Unity
- Coherence

What a topic sentence does:
- States the main idea
- Makes a claim
- Can express an opinion or a judgment
- May suggest its support

How to develop the body of a paragraph:
- Explanations
- Specific details
- Examples

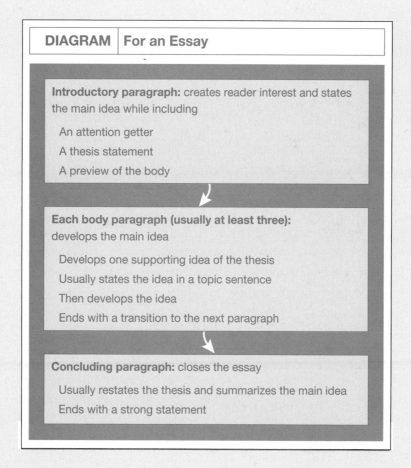

DIAGRAM	For an Essay

Introductory paragraph: creates reader interest and states the main idea while including

An attention getter
A thesis statement
A preview of the body

Each body paragraph (usually at least three): develops the main idea

Develops one supporting idea of the thesis
Usually states the idea in a topic sentence
Then develops the idea
Ends with a transition to the next paragraph

Concluding paragraph: closes the essay

Usually restates the thesis and summarizes the main idea
Ends with a strong statement

II

Different Modes of Writing

Unit I introduced you to the writing process and applied that process to composing both paragraphs and essays. You saw that you write for many different purposes and audiences. You explored and practiced the six steps in the writing process and learned to develop your ideas clearly and convincingly.

Unit II looks at the writing process in more detail. It examines ways to apply the process to different purposes and audiences. You'll learn how to write an effective narrative, description, report, process analysis, cause-and-effect analysis, classification, comparison and contrast, definition, persuasive argument, and summary and response. Each type of writing is different because each aims at accomplishing a different goal. ■

5

Writing Narration

Narration is one of the most powerful ways of communicating with others. A well-written story lets your readers respond to some event in your life as if it were their own. They not only understand the event, but they can almost *feel* it. The action, details, and dialogue put the readers in the scene and make it happen for them.

Moreover, because narration often engages readers' emotions so powerfully, it can play a large role in other types of writing. A strong narrative paragraph can support a persuasive argument or illustrate an explanation or a report. It gives life to your ideas.

This chapter will help you to write a strong narrative by

■ examining a model of narration

■ analyzing what makes a narration effective

■ thinking through ways to organize a narration

■ giving you practice writing narrations

A Model of Narration

Narration is telling a story. And to be interesting, a good story must have interesting content. It should tell about an event your audience would find engaging. You might even think of your narrative as a movie in which readers see people in action and hear them speak. Therefore, it should be detailed and clear, with events arranged in the order in which they happened or in some other effective way. You should aim for a narrative that achieves all of the following goals:

1. It's unified, with all the action developing a central idea.
2. It's interesting; it draws the readers into the action and makes them feel as if they're observing and listening to the events.
3. It introduces the **four Ws** of a setting—*who, what, where,* and *when*—within the context of the action.
4. It's coherent; transitions indicate changes in time, location, and characters.
5. It begins at the beginning and ends at the end. That is, the narrative follows a **chronological order**—with events happening in a time sequence.
6. It builds toward a **climax.** This is the moment of most tension or surprise—a time when the ending is revealed or the importance of events becomes clear.

A diagram of such a paragraph on narration might look something like the one on page 53.

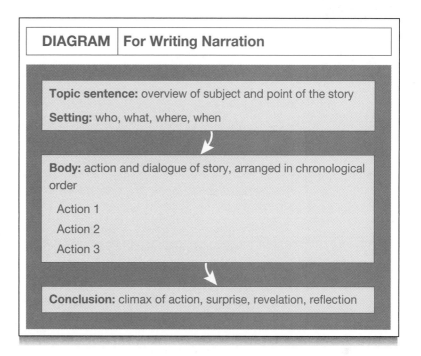

The following narration is taken from James McBride's The Color of Water, the remark-able story about his white mother, who raised twelve black children in New York—all of whom received college degrees and became highly successful adults. In the four-paragraph excerpt you're about to read, young James is fourteen years old, and his stepfather, Hunter Jordan, has just had a stroke. As you read the excerpt, notice how the four Ws of setting are introduced within the context of the action. Notice the specific detail. And notice how McBride handles the conversations between the characters.

Excerpt from *The Color of Water*
James McBride

* * * *

1   [Daddy] came home from the hospital about a week later and seemed to get better. His speech, though slurred, returned. He sat in his basement headquarters, recuperating, while we crept around the house and Mommy walked about silently, eyes still red-rimmed, on edge. One day he summoned me downstairs and asked me to help him dress. "I want to take a drive," he said. I was the oldest kid living at home by then, my other siblings be-ing away at school. He put on his sweater, wool pants, hat, and blue peacoat. Though ill and thin, he still looked sharp. Slowly, he mounted the stairs and stepped outside. It was May and brisk, almost cold outside. We went into the garage and stepped into his gold-colored Pontiac. "I want to drive home one more time," he said. He was talking about Richmond, Virginia, where he grew up. But he was too weak to drive, so he sat there be-hind the wheel of the car, staring at the garage wall, and he began to talk.

2   He said he had a little money saved up for Mommy and a little land in Virginia, but it was not enough. He said that since I was the oldest living at home, I had to watch out for Mommy and my little brothers and sisters because "y'all are special," he said. "And just so special to me." It was the only time I ever heard him refer to race in any way, however vaguely, but it didn't matter, because right then and there I knew he was going to die and I had to blink back my tears. I wanted to tell him that I loved him, that I hoped with all my heart that he would get better, but I could not formulate the words in my mouth. We had never spoken that way to one another. We joked and talked, but

his chief concern had always been my "schoolin" and "church raising" as he called it. He was not a man for dialogue. That was Mommy's job.

3 Two days later he suffered a relapse. An ambulance came and got him. About four in the morning the phone rang. My sister Kathy and I lay upstairs and listened, and through what seemed to be a fog, I heard my older brother Richie telling Mommy, "It's all right, Ma. It's all right."

4 "It's not all right! It's not all right!" Ma cried, and she wailed and wailed, the sound of her cries circling the house like a spirit and settling on all the corridors and beds where we lay, weeping in silence.

Questions for Analysis

1. Look for the four Ws. Where and when does the action take place? What month was it? What are the names of the people in the story? How are these people related?

2. The story moves chronologically through several "scenes." Number each scene in the left-hand margin. Then underline the transitional phrases that show the chronological progression of the action.

3. Movement between scenes often involves more than a change in the time of the action. It also includes changes in location or participants in the action. Circle the transitions that show changes in location or participants. Look especially at the beginning of each paragraph.

4. McBride handles dialogue in two ways: by quoting and by indirectly reporting what people say. Where does he place the beginning and end quotation marks? How are the words in the quotations capitalized? How are the words identifying the speaker punctuated and capitalized?

5. How does this story build toward a climax? What is the climax? Where is it first hinted at?

The Process of Writing a Narrative

Even if we think our own lives have not been dramatic, tragic, or funny, all of us still have personal stories worth telling. Write a paragraph, or more than one paragraph, about an event that affected you greatly and would probably interest your classmates. Your main purpose will be to entertain, but you may also wish to make a larger point about a lesson in life.

If you have trouble describing the event, try a "first": your first day at school, your first date, your first job, the first time you drove a car, or the birth of your first child.

Generating the Materials

If you choose too large a story to tell, one of two problems might result.

1. You'll find yourself writing a book.
2. You'll write a short paragraph filled with generalizations because you can't possibly develop each one.

You should therefore begin by choosing a story that is small enough for you to tell in one or more paragraphs. Start by listing three, four, or more details that occur to you. If possible, consider the point your story will make. That will help you decide which details to include. For example, don't describe your uncle and aunt's little store if that information doesn't develop the point of the story. But if you want to emphasize how your uncle and aunt suffered when the store burned down, then take your readers on a short tour of the store.

Specific details create the realism and drama of a story. And often the best details include dialogue. The words people speak in a story often create more of a sense of realism than their actions. So consider whether to quote the speech of someone and the response that follows.

Explore your topic through freewriting or brainstorming, and then arrange your ideas chronologically. A revised brainstorming list about a first day at school, arranged in chronological order, might look like this:

> *Arrived at school, holding Mom's hand*
>
> *Met lady who said she was my teacher*
>
> *Cried when Mom told me good-bye*
> *"Mom, please don't leave me," I said.*
>
> *Ran after her, but teacher stopped me*
>
> *Told me that I would meet many new friends*
>
> *Led me into a classroom filled with toys, bright posters on the walls, desks, and chairs*
>
> *Became interested in everything*
>
> *Maybe school wouldn't be too bad*

Writing the First Draft

Now write a first draft of the story. Aim to include all of the following elements:

1. A clear, unifying idea. Perhaps you can state that idea as a claim in the topic sentence, such as: "My first day at school was frightening." But the best narratives often omit the topic sentence because it may reveal the climax of the story and detract from the readers' enjoyment. It's OK to begin with a topic sentence, especially if it helps *you* stick to the unifying idea, but be careful not to spoil things for your readers.
2. Information to establish the setting: *who, what, where,* and *when.*
3. Enough detail to develop the unifying idea interestingly and clearly.
4. An arrangement of the details in chronological order.
5. A progression to a climax or dramatic conclusion.

If the first draft of your story turns out to be only five to seven sentences long, you're probably summarizing events rather than developing them specifically. Try to generate more details:

- Close your eyes and put yourself back into the experience. What did you do first, next, and then after that? What did other people do, and how did they respond to each other's actions? What did they say? As events enter your mind, write them down quickly so that you capture them. When you revise later, you can eliminate unnecessary details and smooth out your language.
- Be specific. Look for expressions such as *always, usually, often,* and *sometimes.* These expressions introduce habitual actions—that is, generalizations. Omit them if you can. Then compose sentences beginning with phrases such as *once, one day, one evening,* or a specific hour or day. These sentences should lead you through a sequence of more specific actions.

✓ **TIPS**

For Transitions Showing Chronological Order
Say words such as *first, second, third* or *next, then, afterward* aloud as you explore the sequence of actions. You don't have to include these words in the paragraph if the sequence is clear, but use them if they add coherence.

Revising the First Draft

Return to the paragraph after a few hours or days and revise it further. Often the best idea that unifies the story won't occur to you until you've written the first draft. In that case, examine the draft carefully and consider how to reshape it. Consider these issues:

1. Should you state the unifying idea of the story at the beginning?
2. Should you eliminate some details because they don't support your unifying idea?
3. Should you add more details and dialogue that develop the unifying idea?

Rewrite the story or parts of the story with those questions in mind. Check and improve your use of dialogue. These are the general rules:

1. Begin and end each quotation with **quotation marks** [""], whether the quotation is a single word, a sentence, or several sentences.
2. Capitalize the first word of the quotation.
3. Use a **speaker tag** such as *he said* or *she asked* after the quotation ends. If the speaker tag follows a statement, end the statement with a comma. If the speaker tag follows a question, end the question with a question mark. But place the end punctuation inside the quotation mark, like this:
   ," he said.
   ?" she asked.
4. Begin a new paragraph each time you change speakers.

See Chapter 29 for help in how to use quotations properly.

Finally, work on clarifying your ideas and improving coherence. Let the following checklist guide you in revising your paragraph. Answer the questions yourself or work with a classmate. If you answer *no* to any question, then revise the paragraph to correct the problem. Make changes above the lines or write notes in the margin. Then rewrite the paragraph.

REVISION CHECKLIST

NARRATION		YES	NO
	Does the story have a clear unifying idea? If not, what could that idea be?	❏	❏
	If the story doesn't include a topic sentence, is the unifying idea of the story clear without it?	❏	❏
	Does the setting cover the four Ws?	❏	❏
	Is the story unified, with all the details contributing to the central idea?	❏	❏
	Is the story arranged chronologically? If not, is the organization of ideas and events still effective?	❏	❏
	Do the transitions show the movement from idea to idea and scene to scene?	❏	❏
	Are there enough details?	❏	❏
	Is there dialogue at important moments?	❏	❏
	Is there a climax to the story—a moment at which the action is resolved or a key idea is revealed?	❏	❏

Take notes of these responses to guide your revision. Pay special attention to word choice, clarity, and the use of dialogue.

Further Revising and Editing

Review and revise your story again. Then edit and proofread, checking for misspelled words, words accidentally left out (or left in—especially if you've composed and revised your paper on a computer), and any other errors you notice. Be sure questions are correctly punctuated. Hand in a clean copy of your work.

Additional Writing Assignment 1: Tell a Family Story

When many families get together for yearly holidays or special occasions, they hear the same stories repeated. Write about one of these legends from your family, especially if it's funny. (You may wish to write a story of perhaps four or five paragraphs in length.)

Assume that your audience is a group of people who don't know you, and shape the story so it reveals something important about your family or one of its members. If you can't recall a family legend, write a story about a pleasant or amusing event from your childhood, perhaps one that you'll pass on as a legend to the next generation. Assume again that your primary purpose is to entertain. At the beginning or end of the story, make the unifying idea of the story clear.

A Student Model Essay

Bozena Budżyńska was born and educated in Poland (and elsewhere, as you'll see) before becoming a student at Truman College in Chicago. As you read her story, pay attention to the opening sentence, which serves as the thesis statement; it hints at what is going to happen without revealing the specific events. Notice how the story introduces information about the setting (who, when, what, and where) as the action unfolds. Notice, too, how dialogue carries much of the narrative. And notice how small details near the beginning of the story become important at the end.

The Time of Living Dangerously
Bozena Budżyńska

* * * *

1   The love of photography can be a dangerous affair. So I found out one beautiful day in the tiny West African village.

2   Visiting Ghana as a college exchange student, I met, among other international students, Lisa from Norway. We liked each other instantly and became friends. I enjoyed her wicked sense of humor, adventurous nature, and easygoing personality. We shared a room at the Accra campus and many days full of local delights as well as evenings full of laughter. We also shared an interest in photography. She had her always-working Canon; I had my temperamental Zenith, a Russian camera, which became the theme of many jokes.

3   One day, encouraged after an interesting and relatively trouble-free trip to Togo, we decided to hitchhike through Ghana. Our backpacks ready, cameras loaded, and spirits excited, we said good-bye to our fellow students. Two weeks and many beautiful memories later, we arrived at our destination, a small village in North Ghana just a couple of miles away from Burkina Faso.

4   It was supposed to be our last evening before heading back, when we met two teenage boys who told us how easy it is to cross the border to Burkina Faso even without visas. Wanting to experience yet another African country and maybe to impress the students back in Accra, we decided to take the risk.

5   "We will just take couple of photos, look around, and go back the same day," Lisa said, her voice full of excitement.

6   "You will have to take the pictures since my camera is having a bad day," was my response, as if that was the only problem we should worry about.

7   The warm sunshine coming through the window screen woke us up that morning. Aromas of the street-cooked breakfast wafted in. Delicious grilled plantain never tasted so good. All we needed was a drink of coconut juice. We were ready for the day.

8   The road to the border led through woods. The mild wind tingled our bare arms and faces. The ever so colorful African earth painted our shoes red with each step.

9   Two sleepy border patrol guards smiled as we crossed the border and greeted the little boy who followed us from the village on his yellow bike.

10   "I don't even know what language they speak in this country," Lisa said.

11   "We don't even have the right currency of this country," I added, realizing that this was not a well-planned affair.

12   Just then we came upon a tiny village with men dressed in long embroidered shirts and women in colorful skirts.

13   "Oh my, have you ever seen anything like it?" exclaimed Lisa, pointing to an enormous flag posted in the middle of the village square. It was indeed extraordinary in its design and bright patterns.

14   She reached for her camera and started shooting.

15   Suddenly, a tall man with a hat grabbed Lisa's hand and said in English, "Taking pictures is not allowed here!" His voice was harsh and angry.

16   "Let go!" she screamed.

17   "Give me your camera!" he shouted.

18   "Leave me alone!" Lisa yelled louder.

19   They were both wrestling with the camera.

20   Meanwhile, more people gathered around us, their voices and their faces clearly showing us that we were not welcome there.

21   "They come here to take pictures and later to laugh at us," someone said loudly.

22   "Take the camera away!"

23   "Destroy the film!"

24   I don't like crowds, let alone angry ones, and the situation was getting worse by the minute. "This is dangerous," I thought, realizing that we were no longer in our beloved Ghana with its friendly people. The stories of kidnapped foreigners flashed through my mind. The villagers must have had a bad experience with foreigners to react in such a resentful way.

25   "Just give them the film," I murmured to Lisa.

26   "Over my dead body!"

27   "That might just be, Lisa. Don't be silly."

28   "This is the film with the crocodiles. Don't you understand!"

29   Ah, she mentioned the crocodiles, yet another of our brilliant ideas! We had a local guard let us see the crocodiles up close and feed them chicken. We barely escaped before too many of them came out of the swamp. Lisa snapped a couple of pictures before we had to run.

30   "We will visit them again on our way home and you will take the whole roll." I was trying to be funny.

31   Just then the crowd parted and a serious looking village official approached us. Everyone was trying to explain what was happening.

32   "You must give me the film or I will take you to prison," he demanded.

33   "I am not giving you my film!!!"

34   Prison was more like a mud hut; nevertheless, there we ended up. We could hear the angry crowd outside.

35   "Give me your passports!" the one with the hat demanded.

36   "How do you like your crocodiles now?" I whispered.

37   Suddenly there was some commotion outside and voices raised in a local dialect. Two Ghanian guards we met earlier that day burst in.

38   "You are coming with us!"

39   Lisa looked at me and winked. Outside, next to the soldiers' motorbikes stood the little boy and his yellow bike.

40   Safely across the border, and after the lecture from the guards, we kissed the little boy's cheeks and showered him with treats.

41   And no, I don't have the photograph of the crocodiles on my wall. Lisa's camera and the film were stolen on our way back to the campus. My Zenith, though, is one of my cherished possessions.

Questions for Analysis

1. What is the function of the first two paragraphs of the story? What is the function of the third paragraph?

2. What transitions in the story signal the passage of time or change in location? Underline them.

3. Much of the action and humor of the story are revealed through the dialogue. Look at how the dialogue is handled mechanically: note the punctuation, placement of quotation marks, use of capitalization, paragraphing of dialogue, and identification of the speakers.

4. Notice that in some dialogue, the speakers are not identified. How do you know who is speaking?

5. A lot of the enjoyment and tension in a story comes from oppositions—conflicts, surprises, and contrasts. List some of the most important oppositions.

6. What do the two main characters—Bozena and her friend—have in common? But, more important, how are they different, and how do those differences contribute to your enjoyment of the story?

Additional Writing Assignment 2: Tell a Personal Story

Write about a time when you found yourself in a surprising, unpleasant, or even dangerous situation. Perhaps you had an adventure that would be fun to write about. Establish the circumstances (*who, what, where,* and *when*) at or near the beginning, and then let the action unfold. You may wish to include a bit of dialogue as Bozena did.

Although your narrative may not be as long as Bozena's, you will probably find that it will need more than a single paragraph.

6 Describing a Scene

Description is a useful tool in many kinds of writing. In narration or storytelling, it creates a sense of realism. In reports or explanations, it clarifies and makes ideas more specific. And in persuasive writing, it can clarify arguments and appeal to the reader's emotions. You can describe many things, including people, but in this chapter we'll practice with one kind of description—of a scene.

A clear and lively description depends on close observation. You must pay attention to what you see and hear, and to specific word choices that will make those observations vivid for your readers. Description also demands that you pay attention to the whole writing process. You'll work on that process in this chapter, by

- examining two models of effective description
- analyzing what makes a description effective
- thinking through ways to organize a description
- giving you practice writing descriptions of a scene and a place

Two Models of Description

A **description** of a scene allows your readers to see, hear, or even feel the subject matter clearly. Through careful word choice, strong details, and clear organization, you create a mental picture for your readers. Instead of just *telling* them that a place is pretty, unusual, or horrible, you *show* them the place so that they can see its beauty, uniqueness, or ugliness for themselves.

A good description therefore has a unifying idea, and everything you include must support the idea. Sometimes the idea may simply be that the scene is breathtakingly beautiful or ugly. Other times, the idea may be larger and more complex. For example, you might argue that our government should do more to eliminate poverty and back up that claim with a description of poor, homeless children on a street corner.

Some scenes are simply views of a lake, a building, or a room. But most descriptions include the actions of people, animals, or things. The details you provide often call upon several of the five senses: sight, sound, touch, smell, and even taste. And those details must be arranged logically so that the description is clear.

One common arrangement is **spatial order,** or arranging details in space in some orderly way. Usually this organization involves presenting an overall visual picture of the scene, then locating the specific details in a consistent pattern:

from top to bottom, right to left, center to sides, or nearest to farthest. And within this spatial organization, there may be movement as people or even animals engage in various activities.

A diagram of a spatially organized descriptive paragraph might include most or all of these elements:

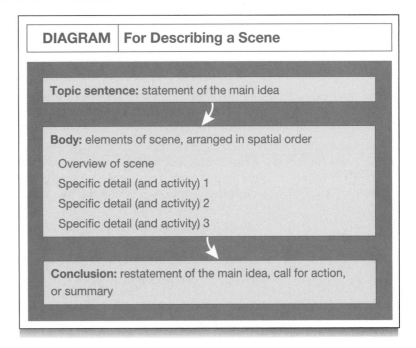

| DIAGRAM | For Describing a Scene |

Topic sentence: statement of the main idea

Body: elements of scene, arranged in spatial order

Overview of scene

Specific detail (and activity) 1

Specific detail (and activity) 2

Specific detail (and activity) 3

Conclusion: restatement of the main idea, call for action, or summary

Here's a model paragraph based primarily on firsthand experience and some research to find supporting data. It is a description of the Grand Canyon that is arranged spatially. As you read it, look for the specific details that support the topic sentence.

A View of the Grand Canyon

* * * *

On my visit to Arizona, I saw one of the Earth's greatest natural wonders, the Grand Canyon. It is a massive hole in the ground covering much of the northwestern part of the state. In all, the canyon is over 270 miles in length (although Grand Canyon National Park includes only 100 miles) and between 4 and 18 miles in width. It is also monstrously deep, over a mile in spots, but a visitor can see all the way to the bottom. The walls are far from flat; they are filled with cliffs, ridges, hills, and even valleys. The multicolored rocks ring the canyon walls in layers, beginning at the top with a sand color, then red, then lavender, then blue-brown, then bright red, and then black at the very bottom. These colors change according to shifts in light; at noon they blend into a bright red, but at sunset they turn dark red and brown. Finally, at the bottom is the Colorado River, which looks like a tiny snake winding through the canyon, although the roar of its current can be heard in places even at the top. In fact, that powerful current has carved out much of the canyon over a 2-billion-year period, and it has left huge towers of rock, like Aztec temples, that rise from the middle of the canyon floor. This massive natural excavation project has also exposed fossils of prehistoric people, dinosaurs, and the earliest forms of plant and animal life that lie within the canyon's walls.

Questions for Analysis

1. What is the topic sentence? Underline it. What is the main idea?
2. What sentences provide general information about the canyon?
3. Where are the specific details introduced? How many of the five senses are used in the description?
4. Circle every transitional word that serves to locate things in the canyon. Look carefully at the placement of these words. What kind of spatial organization do they develop—right to left, top to bottom, center to sides?
5. Is there any movement in the description—either in space or in time? If so, why?
6. The end of the paragraph seems to depart from a pure description of the canyon. Why?

Not every description is organized spatially, especially ones that attempt to give an impression of a scene rather than a specific visual picture. These impressions often employ several of the five senses.

The following description is from a novel by the Chinese American author Amy Tan. In the description, the adult narrator recalls her perceptions as a small child exploring what to her was an exciting environment. As you read it, note how many of the five senses it employs.

Excerpt from *The Joy Luck Club*
Amy Tan

* * * *

dim sum: traditional Chinese food consisting of a variety of small items, including dumplings

1   We lived on Waverly Place, in a warm, clean, two-bedroom flat that sat above a small Chinese bakery specializing in steamed pastries and **dim sum**. In the early morning, when the alley was still quiet, I could smell fragrant red beans as they were cooked down to a pasty sweetness. By daybreak, our flat was heavy with the odor of fried sesame balls and sweet curdled chicken crescents. From my bed, I would listen as my father got ready for work, then locked the door behind him, one-two-three clicks.

husks: shells
gurgling: making low sounds

pungent: strong smelling
eluded: escaped

2   At the end of our two-block alley was a small sandlot playground with swings and slides well shined down the middle with use. The play area was bordered by wood-slat benches where old-country people sat cracking roasted watermelon seeds with their golden teeth and scattering the **husks** to an impatient gathering of **gurgling** pigeons. The best playground, however, was the dark alley itself. It was crammed with daily mysteries and adventures. My brothers and I would peer into the medicinal herb shop, watching old Li dole out onto a stiff sheet of white paper the right amount of insect shells, saffron-colored seeds, and **pungent** leaves for his ailing customers. It was said that he once cured a woman dying of an ancestral curse that had **eluded** the best of American doctors. Next to the pharmacy was a printer who specialized in gold-embossed wedding invitations and festive red banners.

Questions for Analysis

1. Which of the five senses does Amy Tan use? Why would all of these sensory perceptions be important to a child?
2. Why does Tan listen for her father to leave in the morning?
3. In what order are details in the first paragraph presented? What is the order of the second paragraph?

4. In the second paragraph, Tan takes us into the playground—and beyond. Trace the movement by underlining each place that she enters. What words or phrases establish the locations of the places? Circle them.

5. What point does Tan seem to be making in her description in the second paragraph? Circle the key words that seem to make the point. What kind of physical details involving several of the five sentences support that point?

6. There are a number of specific adjectives regarding color in the description. Underline them.

The Process of Writing a Description

Perhaps you haven't seen the Grand Canyon, but you have been to places that other people might want to visit. Write a paragraph for an advertising booklet that would interest people in visiting your town, your college, or any other place that you find interesting, attractive, or exciting. Describe one area—a pretty, unusual, or lively place, and, if it's relevant, include some description of the typical activity occurring there. Make clear to the audience why this place would be worth visiting.

Gathering the Materials

The best way to gather material for the paragraph is to visit the place for about half an hour. Take notes on what you see and hear—and even smell. Record as much information as possible. You probably won't use it all, but it's better to have more than you need than not enough when you compose the first draft.

The following four questions should guide your note taking:

1. Where is the location? (And what is its name?)

2. What are its dimensions and most important features? Where is each feature—on the right, in the middle, above something else, close, or far away?

3. How large or small are the objects you see? How are they shaped? What are their colors?

4. What are people doing in the scene, and where are they? What do they look like?

Here is an example of the kind of brainstorming notes someone might gather in a half-hour visit to the student center at his or her college:

> located on Wright Avenue in the center of the campus
>
> one-story building, modern, lots of glass
>
> hundreds of students inside
>
> pool tables on the north end—six of them
>
> room on the south end with large-screen TV, maybe 50 chairs, busy during soap-opera time
>
> lots of sofas and upholstered chairs
>
> lots of noise

> *students reading, talking, eating doughnuts, drinking sodas*
>
> *table-tennis room next to the pool room, four games at once*
>
> *music room with radio on*
>
> *a lot of tables in the music room*
>
> *some card games at the tables*
>
> *some students on the east side of room sitting in circle talking about an assignment*
>
> *two or three couples talking, laughing, etc.*
>
> *a lot of coming and going throughout the center*
>
> *guys greeting each other*
>
> *size and shape: a square building, large open area in the center filled with tables, sofas, and chairs*
>
> *four rooms—one on each end of center: pool and table tennis, music, TV, study areas*

Arranging the Materials

Now think about the claim you can make based on the information. Your materials would probably fill more than one paragraph, so you need to *select the most important details that directly support your claim or main idea.* You can accomplish this task in one of two ways—or both of them:

1. Write a topic sentence and then select the materials to develop and support it.
2. Select and arrange material through additional brainstorming, clustering, freewriting, or perhaps an informal outline. Then write the topic sentence.

The final draft of the topic sentence might look like this:

> *At almost any time of the day, you will find the student center a place where you can relax, meet people, or study in pleasant surroundings.*

TIPS

For Transitions Showing Spatial Order

Here are some typical transitions:

on the north side . . .

to the right of the fence . . .

a hundred yards to the west . . .

near the main building . . .

in the middle . . .

farther down . . . and still farther . . .

next to the trees . . .

The rest of the paragraph would probably be organized as follows:

1. A general description of the setting, including its location (and probably the time of the scene)
2. Details that support the topic sentence; in the example above, those details would show what is relaxing and pleasant, as well as how people are meeting each other
3. More specific details about the scene, arranged in a logical order—probably spatial or thematic (that is, supporting the main point or claim)
4. Transitional sentences or phrases that introduce the activities in the scene
5. A description of those activities, including a few specific examples

Writing the First Draft

After arranging your material, write a first draft. Don't assume that your arrangement is final. You'll probably shift around details each time you revise.

Revising the First Draft

Don't revise your first draft immediately. Let it sit for a few hours or even days. Then you can view it with a clear mind and probably with better judgment. Look at the arrangement of details. Is it consistent and clear? Also, look at the beginning of each sentence. Does it relate logically to the previous sentence so that the ideas flow smoothly? If not, consider ways to rearrange the materials and add transitions.

Let the following checklist guide you in revising your paragraph. Answer the questions yourself or work with a classmate. If you answer *no* to any question, then revise the paragraph to correct the problem. First, make changes above the lines or write notes in the margin. Then rewrite the paragraph.

REVISION CHECKLIST

		YES	NO
DESCRIPTION	• Does the paragraph include a clear topic sentence that states a claim or main idea?	❏	❏
	• Does the paragraph have unity, with all the details contributing to the main idea?	❏	❏
	• Does the paragraph employ several of the five senses?	❏	❏
	• Is the organization consistent, moving from front to back, left to right, top to bottom, or some other way?	❏	❏
	• Do transitions show the locations of objects and activities within the scene?	❏	❏
	• Is there a clear transition between the description of the place and the people?	❏	❏
	• Are there enough—or too many—details?	❏	❏
	• Are the nouns and verbs specific?	❏	❏

Take notes of these responses and let them guide your revision.

Further Revising and Editing

Return to your paragraph and revise it again, this time paying special attention to specific details and strong word choice. Then edit and proofread your description, checking for misspelled words, words accidentally left out (or left in—especially if you've composed and revised your paper on a computer), and any other errors you notice. Hand in a clean copy of your work.

Additional Writing Assignment 1: Describe a Scene in a Picture

Assume you're writing a booklet for visitors to an exhibit at an art museum. Write a description of the picture below, making clear why visitors should stop to see this work of art. For example, your topic sentence might say that the picture shows a shocking or humorous scene. Compose, revise, and edit the paragraph following the advice provided throughout this chapter.

William Hogarth, *The Enraged Musician,* 1741, British Museum

A Student Model Paragraph

The paragraph that follows was written by Tuyet-Ahn Van, a Vietnamese student living in Chattanooga, Tennessee. Like Amy Tan's description you read earlier in the chapter, this scene conveys the affection that Tuyet-Ahn has for her childhood home. She has traveled back in her mind to capture the sights, sounds, and activities of that place. And like Tan, Tuyet-Ahn puts herself into the scene through her memory.

The description begins with a general discussion of the larger setting, moves to a specific location, and then describes places and activities within it.

The Happiest Place of My Life
Tuyet-Ahn Van

* * * *

The place that I love the most is in the small country where I was born and spent my childhood. I lived in a small village in the middle of a rather large area surrounded with green bamboo hedges. In front of the village was my house with a yard where wet clothes were dried and which was also storage for the rice crop in harvest time. Not far from there was a beautiful garden full of pretty flowers and fruit trees. It was my favorite place. In the afternoon, I used to run merrily along its flower-bordered walks, chasing gorgeous butterflies or catching shining beetles. In doing so, I sometimes trod on a flowering plant, and I was scolded by my mother for being so careless. At the corner of the garden, there was a small arbor with a seat where I spent much time reading some fairy tales or doing my homework. Every morning, I also watched the farmers go by with their horses on their way to the fields. Now and then, their merry laughter broke the momentary silence of the countryside. From some cottages nearby, a slender thread of smoke curled upward, announcing the first activities of the hamlet. Certainly, my home was only a humble village, but I still love it very much. It was the place where I had the happiest memories of my life.

Questions for Analysis

1. What is the topic sentence of the paragraph? What general details about the village does Tuyet-Ahn provide? What place within the village does she focus on most specifically?
2. What words and phrases establish the location of things? What words or phrases establish the times of activities? Underline all the transitions.
3. Aside from visual description, where does Tuyet-Ahn call on other senses, either directly or indirectly?
4. What main impression does the writer wish you to take from her description?

Additional Writing Assignment 2: Describe a Familiar Place

Think about a place that you loved or hated when you were younger, or visit a place that you love or dread now. Put yourself back into the scene and remember what it was like. Focus on specific sights, sounds, activities, or even smells. Then describe it in writing so that your classmates can experience the feelings it creates in you: excitement, affection, fear, disgust, calmness—or any other reaction. Make the main idea clear in your topic sentence, and support it with relevant physical details and actions. Be sure to include transitions that show movement or location in space.

7 Writing a Report

In college and beyond, the results of meetings, discussions, laboratory experiments, and research need to be communicated clearly and accurately. Managers, teachers, scientists, students, businesspeople, and community leaders want to know these results so that they can evaluate and act upon them. These people are often busy, however, so they want a brief report that summarizes what happened, how it happened, and perhaps why.

This chapter will show you how to write one type of report by

- examining a model of a report
- analyzing what makes a report effective
- thinking through ways to organize a report
- giving you practice writing reports

A Model of a Report

A **report** is an organized summary of information; it clearly and accurately relates the decisions, actions, or conclusions involved in an event, an activity, or an investigation—but it does not include every fact and detail.

There are many kinds of reports: formal reports (called *minutes*) on discussions and votes taken in a meeting; reports on the main ideas of a lecture or presentation; reports on the results of an experiment or some research, and so on. Each kind follows its own particular format, but they do have some things in common.

A report typically begins with a statement of its purpose, its central idea, or its conclusions. Then the report presents the supporting information, usually in chronological order or in categories. However, as you'll soon see, the supporting information includes only the main ideas or actions, omitting many of the explanations, details, or examples found in other kinds of writing.

Many reports are entirely **objective:** they do not include any opinions of the writer. But some reports also make recommendations based on the information they present. We'll look at both types of reports in this chapter, beginning with the objective report.

Look at the diagram of a typical report on page 69.

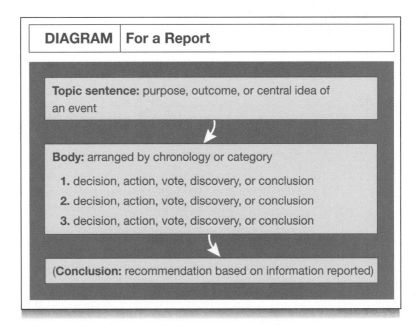

The following is an informational report appearing in a newsletter addressed to the residents of a small suburban city. As you read it, notice that the writer summarizes the facts objectively, offering no opinions or interpretations.

Budget Challenges

* * * *

1   The City Council has taken a number of steps in its attempt to solve the city's $2 million budget deficit. On July 12, the Council held a public meeting to hear a variety of suggestions from residents. A number of residents offered opinions on possible cuts in services identified in the survey conducted the previous month. However, many residents objected to any cuts in services. Instead, the residents suggested ways that the city could increase revenues. Those suggestions included raising the sales tax from 8.5 percent to 8.75 percent or creating new taxes, such as a tax on hotel rooms.

2   Following the open meeting, the City Council discussed the issues at its Financial Review Meeting on July 31. Members of the Council explored ways to save money by cutting or reducing services. Among the possibilities were a cutback in garbage collection from three times a week to twice a week and a reduction in the number of days scheduled for picking up the leaves during the fall. After a lengthy debate, the Council agreed not to make any immediate changes in services at this time and to explore the effects of new taxes suggested by the residents at the July 12 meeting. One member of the Council estimated that an increase in the sales tax would result in an additional $1.5 million in revenue. However, residents would have to vote on this increase in a general election, which could not be scheduled until November 7.

3   The Council instructed members of its staff to investigate the possible results of any cuts in services, tax increases, or new taxes and to report its findings to the Council at the August 5 meeting. No further action will be taken until then.

Questions for Analysis

1. Which sentence states the main idea? Underline it.
2. What is the purpose of the report?
3. Is this report organized chronologically or by category?
4. How many meetings does the report discuss? What words or phrases identify those meeting times and purposes? Circle them.

5. The report summarizes the meetings and doesn't mention the names of any participants. Why?
6. When the staff reports its findings to the City Council in August, how will its report probably be organized—chronologically or in categories? Why?

The Process of Writing a Report

Attend, participate in, or observe some event. Take notes on what you see and hear, and then write a report summarizing your observations for someone who wasn't there. Here are some possible events to report on:

- a lecture in one of your classes
- a lecture or presentation you attend
- a meeting (for a club, an organization, a committee, even a gathering of friends)
- a television show that presents important or interesting information
- an experiment in a laboratory course
- a celebration, a holiday gathering, or other joyous event you participate in or witness

Bring along a notebook or laptop computer to record your notes. Don't worry about writing complete sentences. No one will read the notes but you.

Gathering the Materials

A report is a **summary:** a discussion of the main ideas or most important information, arranged in a way that makes the information easy for the reader to grasp. In a summary, almost all the specific details are omitted. A report on a meeting, for example, includes the decisions agreed to, the votes taken, or the activities completed. It doesn't include what each person said at the meeting, but only the outcomes of the discussion. It doesn't include every fact, but only those facts that lead to decisions, votes, activities, or actions. Therefore, as you take notes on the event, focus only on the central activities or ideas.
Consider these guidelines when taking notes:

1. Record the time and date, the place, and the names of the important participants.
2. Record everything that happens in very brief notes, which don't have to be complete sentences. Think of the summary as a series of topic sentences. Omit smaller ideas that explain or support the topic sentences, unless the details clarify important ideas.
3. As the event progresses, you will see the results of a discussion, the outcomes of votes, the decisions agreed to, or the central ideas emerging. Highlight those in your notes by underlining or by drawing arrows or stars in the margins.

Selecting and Arranging the Materials

After the event, rewrite your notes, focusing on the essential information you've highlighted in your notes. Aim for writing a summary of the event. Omit most of what was said leading up to the outcome. And omit the names of the participants unless they are important (for example, the name of the instructor delivering a lecture). If a number of statistics are provided, cite those that give totals, not those that contribute to the totals. The information you select may be only one-tenth of what you recorded in your original notes, but it should be sufficient for your readers to understand what happened.

Then organize your notes. These questions should serve as guidelines:

1. What was the purpose of the event?
2. What was the outcome (or what were the outcomes) of the event?
3. What main ideas were expressed? Or what important decisions were made?
4. What details are needed to explain or illustrate those ideas or decisions?

Use these questions as the basis for your organization, and arrange the report chronologically, stating what happened first and continuing to the end of the event. Then compose an informal outline of the report. Here's an example:

July 12 meeting
    service cuts suggested
    objections to service cuts
    suggestion for increasing sales tax
    suggestion for hotel tax
July 31 meeting of City Council
    reducing garbage pickup
    reducing leaf pickup days
    increase in sales tax
    decision to consider increase in sales tax
    requires vote by the residents
Staff asked to investigate and report at August 5 meeting

TIPS

For Organizing a Report

If there is a printed outline of a lecture or a printed agenda for a meeting, be sure to use it. The outline will guide you toward the main points.

Writing the First Draft

Now write a draft of the report. State the result or central idea first, followed by the most important supporting ideas or actions. If necessary, include some details that clarify or illustrate important ideas.

Remember that the information you include must be **objective:** you cannot state opinions or interpret events. Compare the following statements. The first directly expresses an opinion, while the second presents a conclusion without interpreting it:

Not objective:	The committee made a good decision. (The writer has interpreted the decision to be good.)
	The group argued over the issue. (The writer has interpreted the discussion as an argument.)
Objective:	The committee decided to delay the vote until the following meeting.
	Members of the group expressed different views on the issue.

Revising the First Draft

Let the following checklist guide you in revising your report. Answer the questions yourself or work with a classmate. If you answer *no* to any question, then revise the paragraph to correct the problem. First, make changes above the lines or write notes in the margin. Then rewrite the paragraph.

REVISION CHECKLIST		YES	NO
REPORT	• Does the topic sentence clearly state the main activity covered by the report?	❏	❏
	• Does the topic sentence indicate the purpose or outcome?	❏	❏
	• Is the body of the report limited to a summary?	❏	❏
	• Does the summary follow a clear organizational pattern?	❏	❏
	• Is the information presented objectively?	❏	❏

Take notes of these responses to guide your revision. Rewrite the report later when you can examine it with fresh eyes and a clear mind. Make sure it's objective and complete.

Further Revising and Editing

Return to the report and revise it again. Edit and proofread your work, checking for misspelled words, words accidentally left out or left in, and any other errors you notice. Hand in a clean copy of your work.

Additional Writing Assignment 1: Report on a Decision-Making Process

Write a report of a discussion you were involved in that led to a simple decision. It could have taken place within your family, among your friends, at work, in a club, or in a class. Limit the topic to a discussion that you can examine specifically in one paragraph. Begin by stating the decision you reached, and then explain how you reached it. Be sure to include who was involved (although you don't have to use everyone's name) and when and where the decision was made.

A Student Model Report

The following report was written several years ago by Veronica Fleeton, a former member of the armed forces and a student at Truman College in Chicago. The purpose of the report is to recommend improvements in the cleanliness of the washrooms of the college. As you read the report, notice that it summarizes the results of a plan devised by the students themselves. Notice that it explains how the plan was carried out, as well as what each part of the plan revealed. In addition, notice that it concludes with a recommendation, which—in this case—was actually accepted.

Let's Keep It Clean
Veronica Fleeton

* * * *

1   A student committee has examined the washrooms throughout the college over the semester. We have concluded that there is very little evidence that they are being cleaned often enough. During several visits to various washrooms on different floors this semester, members of the committee found the doors propped open and the maid carts in the washrooms, but no one actually cleaning the rooms. At other times, we have checked the trashcans, sinks, commodes, floors, corners, and soap and towel dispensers. We found that trashcans were overflowing and the towel and soap dispensers were empty. As a further test, we intentionally planted objects in conspicuous areas such as corners or stall areas. We revisited the washrooms the next day to see if they had been removed. In most cases, they were right where we had planted them.

2   We recommend that this situation be immediately addressed. The college has a large population, and the washrooms are constantly being used. Since they are receiving heavy usage, they should be cleaned at least twice a day to accommodate students in both day and night classes.

Questions for Analysis

1. Who is the probable audience for this report?
2. What is the topic sentence of the first paragraph—the sentence that summarizes the conclusions of the report? Underline it.
3. According to the report, what specific problems were found in the washrooms?
4. What did the group of students do to uncover these problems? Name each action the students took. Notice that the report is organized by categories of action.
5. Although the report is not arranged in chronological order, some transitions make references to time. Circle them.
6. Read the conclusion. Restate the recommendation in your own words.

Additional Writing Assignment 2: Evaluate a Facility

Make a simple plan to observe and evaluate a facility in your school or surrounding community. Does it function well or badly? Would you recommend any improvements? You might evaluate the cafeteria or parking facilities at your school (if the school has them). You might evaluate the service and food at a local restaurant, the facilities in a recreation center or health club, or even a child-care center for small children. You don't have to uncover a scandal or file a complaint. In fact, your report may discuss how well the facility operates. You may wish to collaborate with other students on this report, especially if it involves observations happening at different times. Divide the visits among the members of the collaborative group.

Your plan shouldn't require a lot of time or frequent visits, and you shouldn't disturb the people in the facility. Take notes of your findings.

If you collaborate, each person in the group may write a separate report, or the group may collaborate on a single report. The audience for the report should be the person or persons who would find it most useful. End the report with praise for the facility or recommendations for improvements, if either seems appropriate.

8

Describing a Process

When you write a process analysis, you explain how to do something or how something works. This type of writing is especially informative because it tells readers something they want or need to know. A recipe in a cookbook is a process analysis. Instructions for operating DVD players and appliances are process analyses. So are descriptions of how an egg develops into a mature chicken or how an automobile's motor mixes gasoline with air.

This chapter will help you write a process analysis by

- examining a model of a process analysis
- analyzing what makes a process analysis effective
- thinking through ways to organize a process paragraph
- giving you practice writing process analyses

A Model of a Process Analysis

A **process analysis** explains how something works or how to do something. When it explains how something works, it *observes* the process and describes it in the third person. ("The egg begins to hatch in a week.") When it explains how to do something, it *instructs* the reader in imperative sentences. ("Mix the eggs, flour, and milk in a large bowl.")

In either case, your explanation or instructions must be clear. You must consider what readers already know and what they need to know. You must include all the information necessary for them to understand or perform the process. You must define technical terms. You must present the information logically—breaking down the process into a series of steps. And you must label those steps clearly with transitional expressions.

The organization of a process analysis typically includes two parts:

1. An introduction of the process and a list of the materials (tools, parts, or ingredients) that the process requires

2. An explanation of each step in the process, presented in **sequential order**—that is, moving consecutively from first to last—so that readers can visualize the process or perform it themselves

A diagram of a process analysis is on page 75.

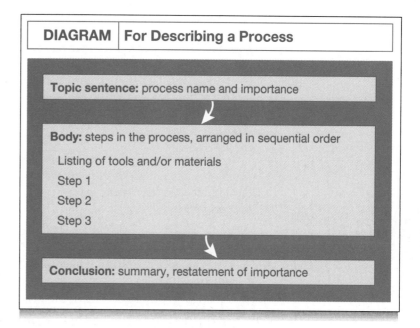

The following example of a process analysis is taken from an article in the "Hers" column of the New York Times *in 1984 by Sue Hubbell. Ms. Hubbell, a graduate of Swarthmore College, moved to the Ozark Mountains of Missouri, where she kept bees for twenty-five years. The example describes her experiences in teaching a young man how to tolerate bee stings. Her goal is to help readers understand the process, not perform it.*

The Beekeeper
Sue Hubbell

* * * *

1   The time to harvest honey is summer's end, when it is hot. The temper of the bees requires that we wear protective clothing: a full set of overalls, a zippered bee veil and leather gloves. Even a very strong young man works up a sweat wrapped in a bee suit in the heat, hustling 60-pound **supers** while harassed by angry bees. It is a hard job, harder even than haying, but the jobs are scarce here and I've always been able to hire help.

2   This year David, the son of a friend of mine, is working for me. He is big and strong and used to labor, but he was nervous about bees. After we had made the job arrangement I set about desensitizing him to bee stings. I put a piece of ice on his arm to numb it and then, holding a bee carefully by its head, I put it on the numbed spot and let it sting him. A bee stinger is **barbed** and stays in the flesh, pulling loose from the body of the bee as it struggles to free itself. The **bulbous** poison sac at the top of the stinger continues to **pulsate** after the bee has left, pumping the **venom** and forcing the stinger deeper into the flesh.

3   That first day I wanted David to have only a partial dose of venom, so after a minute I scraped the stinger out. A few people are seriously sensitive to bee venom; each sting they receive can cause a more severe reaction than the one before—reactions ranging from **hives,** to breathing difficulties, accelerated heart beat and choking to **anaphylactic** shock and death. I didn't think David would be allergic that way, but I wanted to make sure.

4   We sat down and had a cup of coffee and I watched him. The spot where the stinger went in grew red and began to swell. That was a normal reaction, and so was the itching that he felt later on.

supers: containers of honey

barbed: hooked
bulbous: round
pulsate: beat
venom: poison

hives: bumps on the skin
anaphylactic: severe, with accelerated heart beat, dramatic drop in blood pressure, and difficulty breathing

5   The next day I coaxed a bee into stinging him again, repeating the procedure, but I left the stinger in place for 10 minutes, until the venom sac was empty. Again the spot was red, swollen and itchy but had disappeared in 24 hours. By that time David was ready to catch a bee himself and administer his own sting. He also decided that the ice cube was a bother and gave it up. I told him to keep to one sting a day until he had no redness or swelling and then to increase to two stings. He was ready for them the next day. The great amount of venom caused redness and swelling for a few days, but soon his body could tolerate it without reaction and he increased the number of stings once again.

6   Today he told me he was up to six stings. His arms look as though they have track marks on them, but the fresh stings are having little effect. I'll keep him at it until he can tolerate 10 a day with no reaction and then I'll not worry about taking him out to the bee yard.

Questions for Analysis

1. What tools or clothing are needed to perform this process? Why is the process difficult?
2. What is the first main step in the process of desensitizing David to stings? What actions are involved in this step? Why are those actions necessary?
3. What is the second step, and which parts of the actions are different from the ones in the first step? What leads to the next step in the process?
4. At what point does David take over the process? Why?
5. What does Hubbell assume the reader doesn't know about the effects of bee stings? What does she therefore explain?
6. Hubbell does not define technical terms, but see the explanations in the margins of the reading.

Writing a Process Analysis

Write an entertaining description of the steps you or a friend or a relative goes through in performing some daily, weekly, or less frequent ritual. Keep the topic simple so that you can describe it in one paragraph. For example, you could describe dressing for a date or formal event, getting ready to write a paper, doing stretching and warm-up exercises, studying for a big exam, combing hair over a bald spot, or straightening up the mess in a bedroom. Assume your readers are adults who might find your article in a popular magazine.

Gathering the Materials

After choosing a topic, brainstorm or cluster several lists of details to include in the paragraph. You may even want to do a trial run to get ideas. Add to these lists as more ideas occur to you. Include the following:

1. All the materials needed to perform the task. For instance, in a paragraph on fixing your hair: *shampoo, conditioner, towel, blow dryer, comb, brush, hair spray, curlers, curling iron, wall mirror, hand-held mirror, and a lot of patience*
2. Any terms that need to be defined and explained: *mousse, gel, or tantrum*
3. All the steps in the process: *washing, drying, setting, combing, further combing, crying—and then resetting, combing out, and so on*

Arranging the Materials

Now make an outline in which you list all the steps in the order in which you will present them. Include explanations of each step. The outline might look like this:

    I. Topic idea: *Teenage daughter spends hours preparing hair for a date*

  II. Preliminary information

      A. Tools needed: *brush, hair spray, curlers*

      B. Definitions of terms: *mousse, gel*

 III. Steps in the process

      A. *Washing hair*

      B. *Drying hair*

      C. *Styling hair*

      D. *Styling hair again*

 IV. Conclusion: *Daughter looks great*

Writing the First Draft

Now write a first draft of the paragraph that includes all of these elements:

1. A topic sentence that identifies the process and suggests or outlines the steps, such as "My teenage daughter spends a very long time preparing her hair for a date."
2. One or more sentences that list the materials used in the process and define any specialized terms.
3. A step-by-step description of the process, arranged in sequential order.

Revising the First Draft

Let the following checklist guide you in revising your paragraph. Answer the questions yourself or work with a classmate. If you answer *no* to any question, then revise the paragraph to correct the problem. First, make changes above the lines or write notes in the margin. Then rewrite the paragraph.

REVISION CHECKLIST		YES	NO
PROCESS ANALYSIS	• Does a topic sentence identify the process and then outline or suggest the steps involved in performing the process?	☐	☐
	• Is the importance of the process clear?	☐	☐
	• Does the paragraph identify the tools or materials needed to perform the process?	☐	☐
	• Does the paragraph clearly define any unusual or specialized terms?	☐	☐
	• Are all the important steps in the process clearly explained and presented in sequential order?	☐	☐

Take notes of these responses to guide your revision. Rewrite the paragraph later when you can examine it with fresh eyes and a clear mind. You might ask a classmate to try the process you describe, or at least try to follow it, and to let you know if any instructions or steps are not clear.

✓ **TIPS**

For Making the Steps Clear

Transitions in a process analysis need to be very obvious so that readers recognize each step. Here are some useful transitions:

first, to begin, at the start

second, next, then, after that, following that, later

third, fourth, fifth

finally, last, to finish

If some steps in the process occur at the same time, you can introduce them with these transitions:

meanwhile, during, at the same time, while

Further Revising and Editing

Return to the paragraph and revise it again. Edit and proofread it before handing in a clean copy of your work.

Additional Writing Assignment 1: Explain a Diagram

Write instructions that accompany the following diagram to explain and clarify the process it illustrates. Assume that your purpose is to instruct readers in performing the process. They'll be looking at the diagram as they read your instructions.

Begin by clustering or by making several brainstorming lists. Then write a full description of the process, explaining each step or series of related short steps. Revise the paragraph until it clearly follows a logical format such as the following:

1. An opening sentence that introduces the subject, summarizes the process, and mentions the materials or parts involved
2. A middle section that describes each step in the process
3. A final paragraph that summarizes the process or restates its importance

Be sure to include appropriate transitional words to show the movement between steps. Revise and edit your paper, and hand in a clean final draft

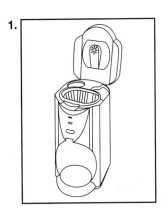
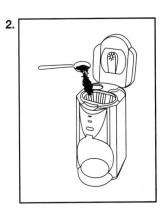
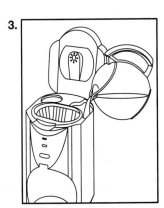
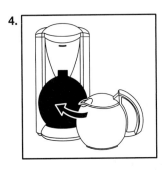

A Student Model Essay

Here's a process analysis by Erica Teal, a student at Truman College in Chicago. As you read it, notice her goal in writing the essay—that is, what she wants readers to do with the information. Pay special attention to the first paragraph, noting why she feels that the process she describes is important and the way she introduces the three major steps of the routine.

Stretching for the Long Run
Erica Teal

* * * *

1　　I never thought warming up and stretching were important before and after a long run, until I pulled a muscle in my thigh, and that was just part of the pain. Isn't running supposed to be good for you? I was having too much fun to worry about such details. Warming up and stretching might possibly be the most crucial part of your workout, so don't skip it. To get the best out of running from both performance and enjoyment, adopt a routine that includes an effective warm-up, stretching, and cooldown.

2　　Warming up is often overlooked, but should be part of your injury prevention routine. After my injuries, I decided to warm up five minutes each day before my run. The benefits of a warm-up before running include increasing your body temperature and getting your blood flowing. The increased blood flow in the muscles gives you flexibility, which reduces the likelihood of injury. To warm up, you could pedal for a few minutes on a stationary bike or jump rope a few turns.

3　　After you have warmed up, you are ready to stretch. Stretching gives flexibility, and without it, you are an injury waiting to happen. Stretching is not the same as warming up. A good stretching routine will enhance your performance through elasticity. When you stretch, move slowly and gradually into each position and hold it for ten seconds before relaxing again. Repeat each stretch several times. After stretching, your muscles are warmer and more elastic. Never stretch a muscle to the point of pain. Pain indicates that you are stretching too hard or that you have an injury that needs some attention—a doctor's attention, that is.

4　　Cooling down is just as important as warming up. After a run, it's important to recover gently. A cooldown brings your muscles back to a resting state and decreases the likelihood of your getting hurt. A cool-down period is at least three minutes long and is followed by stretching the muscles to avoid soreness and, once again, injury.

5　　A good warm-up, stretching, and cooldown are especially important before and after a run. The more you prepare for a run, the more you will enjoy yourself. You'll be injury free and happier in the long run.

Questions for Analysis

1. Which sentences in Erica's first paragraph serve as the introduction? Underline them. Which sentence states the thesis? Circle it.
2. What three steps in the process does Erica list in the first paragraph?
3. Underline the topic sentences in the three body paragraphs.
4. Briefly summarize the benefits of each step in the process.
5. What words in the conclusion restate (but vary) the main points of the body paragraphs?

Additional Writing Assignment 2: Give Advice

As Erica Teal does, write a paragraph of advice to people your age about the process involved in succeeding at some task. Your audience should be people who want or need this advice.

The subject matter could relate to a job, to schoolwork, or to family or social life. You might, for example, discuss how to prepare for a job interview. You might discuss how to share responsibilities at home or how to resolve a typical conflict between siblings or roommates. In any case, choose a process you know well and feel confident explaining.

Your instructor may ask you to make an oral presentation, followed by a question-and-answer period, to your collaborative group (or the whole class) prior to submitting your final draft of the paragraph. Explaining the process aloud and hearing responses or questions from others often reveal steps or instruction that need clarification.

9 Writing about Causes and Effects

We analyze causes and effects every day. We need to know the reasons why something happened. Why won't my car start? Why do I have a sore throat? Likewise, we need to know the results of some action or event. If I have the car repaired, how much will it cost? If a take a new antibiotic, will it cure my sore throat?

Writing about such causes or effects is also an important part of academic and professional life. In science courses—and in scientific professions—you may investigate the causes of a chemical reaction or the effects of a new chemical. In a nursing course, you need to know the causes of a fever and the results of a treatment. In a history course, you may need to know the causes—and results—of a war. In a business course—and in actual businesses—you may examine the effects of a new method of accounting or of advertising.

This chapter will show you how to write a paragraph or essay on causes or effects by

- examining a model of causal analysis
- analyzing what makes an effective analysis on causes or effects
- thinking through ways to organize the paragraph or essay
- giving you practice writing cause or effect paragraphs and essays

A Model of Causal Analysis

A **cause** is the reason an event happens, while an **effect** is the result of the cause. So, for instance, the cause of passing a course may be studying hard, while the effect of passing the course may be earning a degree.

Many things, however, have more than one cause. For example, a person may become ill from lack of sleep, too much stress, poor nutrition, and exposure to a virus. Likewise, many things can have more than one effect. A violent storm may destroy trees, flood streets, blow down power lines, and even tear the roofs off of houses.

If you trace several causes or effects in your paragraph, you may organize it somewhat like you'd do with a narration or a process analysis. You can tell a story of why something happened in **chronological order.** You were late this morning because the alarm didn't go off, you missed your bus, and the traffic arranged in **climax order**—moving from the weakest to the strongest reason. The restaurant is popular because the location is good, the prices are low, the service is fast, and the food is terrific.

Diagrams of a paragraph discussing causes and a paragraph discussing effects might, therefore, look like these:

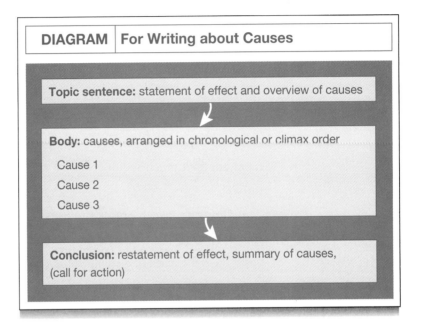

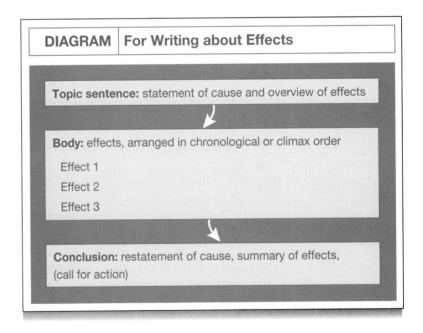

Here's an example of a short essay that explains the probable causes of an event. Because the causes need to be explained in detail, the essay devotes an entire paragraph to each. As you read the essay, notice that the first paragraph introduces the event while the body paragraphs explore its possible causes, or the reasons that it happened.

The Mystery of Custer's Last Stand

* * * *

last stand: traditional name for the battle in which Custer was killed

1   Probably no other battle in U.S. history has created more controversy than the Battle of Little Bighorn River. On June 25, 1876, General George Armstrong Custer made his famous **last stand** against members of the Great Sioux Nation. After dividing the 700 troops of the Seventh Cavalry into three groups that would surround and attack a Native American village, he took command of one group and rushed them into the battle alone. As a result, 3,000 Sioux, led by their chief, Sitting Bull, killed Custer and every one of his 250 men. No one will ever know why Custer ordered his men into such a one-sided fight in which they had no chance for survival. No one will ever know why he didn't retreat once the battle had begun. No one will know the answers because no one from Custer's side lived to tell the story. However, some information about the battle—gathered from scouts, messengers, and the members of the other two groups—suggests four reasons.

2   First, Custer ignored the orders of his commanding officer. He was supposed to bring his troops to the valley of the Little Bighorn River and wait there until another army division could join him. But Custer decided to attack alone. He rode his troops all night and well past dawn, and his men and horses were exhausted when they entered the valley.

3   Second, Custer apparently ignored the advice of his own Native American scouts. The two men, Mitch Bouyer and Bloody Knife, warned him that there were too many Sioux warriors to be captured. Custer probably thought that his Seventh Cavalry could easily defeat any Native American fighters and didn't take the warnings of the scouts seriously.

4   Third, Custer probably misinterpreted the movements of the Sioux. After one of the three groups into which he divided his men, led by Major Marcus Reno, charged the village, a messenger told Custer that it contained far more warriors than they had expected. Custer apparently assumed that the number of Sioux didn't matter because they were running away. He and his group therefore rushed to the far end of the campsite to cut off the escape. He rode hard and fast, further wearing down his men and their horses.

5   Fourth, after the three groups of Custer's men had separated, they probably soon lost communication with each other. Major Reno attacked the campsite, expecting Custer to follow him from the rear. But Custer was trapped at the far end of the camp. Reno finally retreated to the woods near the village, where he was forced to stop and fight. His Native American opponents not only outnumbered him, but they also had better weapons. By the time the third group of the Seventh Cavalry arrived, many of Reno's men were dead, and this last group was trapped as well. Meanwhile, Custer and every single one of his men were being killed.

6   To this day, when people think of Custer, they think of headstrong behavior and stupidity. Although no one knows exactly why Custer and his men lost their lives, headstrong behavior and stupidity are the likely reasons.

Questions for Analysis

1. What is the function of the first paragraph of the essay? What specific details do you learn from it? What is the function of the last paragraph?
2. How many causes for Custer's defeat does the essay suggest? What in the organization makes these causes easy to locate?

3. What words and phrases show a lack of certainty? Why are they necessary?

4. When does the essay depart from past-tense explanation? Why?

5. Is the final paragraph a logical conclusion, based on the evidence presented? Why or why not?

The Process of Writing a Causal Analysis

TIPS

For Transitions Showing Cause and Effect

To guide your readers through a paragraph on causes or effects, the following transitions might be useful.

For identifying causes: *reason, cause, because, since*

For labeling causes or effects: *first, second, finally*

For qualifying causes or effects that aren't definite: *maybe, possibly, probably*

Write a paragraph analyzing the reasons behind an important decision you've recently made—for example, to major in a particular subject, to work part time, to move, or to buy a car. Assume you're writing to explain your decision to an academic adviser, your parents, or a friend.

Generating and Arranging the Materials

Explore your ideas by clustering or brainstorming a list of the causes. Then choose at least three reasons for your decision—the most important, clearest reasons—to develop in your paragraph. List the reasons either (1) chronologically if they happened in a time sequence, or (2) in climax order, moving from the least to most important if they happened at or near the same time:

"Finally, and most importantly, I realized . . ."

"But these reasons alone wouldn't have been enough. The strongest reason came . . ."

Using a simple chart may help you organize ideas:

Causes

1. _____

Example: _____

2. _____

Example: _____

3. _____

Example: _____

Writing the First Draft

As you begin work on your first draft, write a topic sentence or thesis statement to introduce or summarize the causes you'll discuss:

"I decided to major in computer sciences *for several reasons*."

OR

"I decided to major in computer sciences *because of my interest in business, my good grades in computer classes, and the great job opportunities in this field*."

Explore the reasons in the body of the paragraph, but don't just list them. Explain them, and, if you can, support them with specific examples. Consider introducing them through narration, description, or process analysis:

> **Narration:** I wasn't very interested when I began my first computer class. But that changed the day a guest lecturer from one of the large firms downtown came to speak to the class. . . .
>
> **Description:** The company where I had my summer job occupies a large, modern brick building. I worked in a spacious office with a marble floor, polished metal furniture, a wall of windows overlooking the river, and the latest computer equipment. My PC had a 19-inch flat paneled monitor and wireless keyboard and mouse. . . .
>
> **Process:** My expertise in Web design developed in three stages. . . .

Revising the First Draft

Let the following checklist guide you in revising your paragraph. Answer the questions yourself or work with a classmate. If you answer *no* to any question, then revise the paragraph to correct the problem. First, make changes above the lines or write notes in the margin. Then rewrite the paragraph.

REVISION CHECKLIST

CAUSAL ANALYSIS		YES	NO
	• Does the topic sentence state the event (the decision) and clearly introduce or summarize the causes (reasons)?	❑	❑
	• Is each reason presented in a clear chronological or climax order?	❑	❑
	• If the paragraph uses climax organization, is the strongest cause or effect presented last?	❑	❑
	• Is the analysis of the causes and effects specific enough to be convincing?	❑	❑
	• Are the transitions between ideas clear?	❑	❑
	• Is the conclusion logical or reasonable?	❑	❑

Take notes of these responses to guide your revision. Rewrite the paragraph later when you can examine it with fresh eyes and a clear mind. Pay special attention to clarity.

Further Revising and Editing

Revise the paragraph again. Edit and proofread it, and hand in a clean copy.

Additional Writing Assignment 1: Describe the Effects of an Event

Choose another important event in your life, one that resulted in three or more important effects—changes in your living conditions, changes in your behavior, or changes in your attitudes. Here are a few examples:

gaining a younger sibling

losing a loved one or caregiver

losing a job

being involved in an accident

moving to a new neighborhood, city, or country

Assume that your audience is a group of people who know you now but didn't know you at the time of the event. Your purpose is therefore to let these people understand you better. If you prefer not to write about yourself, choose an event in the life of someone you know well.

List at least three effects of the experience, perhaps by brainstorming. Then arrange the effects from weakest to strongest. Support each effect with explanations, details, or examples. Then compose a preliminary topic sentence or thesis statement that makes the point of your analysis clear. For example, it might claim, "The birth of my younger sister changed my life," or "Coming to the United States involved many sacrifices." You can revise this sentence after writing the first draft if your ideas change or if your focus changes.

A Student Model Paragraph

Sara Sebring, a student at Chattanooga State Community College, wrote the following paragraph. She describes an allergic reaction to a medicine—in other words, the effects of an event. As you read it, notice the reason she took the drug, the immediate results of taking it, and the longer-term results.

A Reaction to Medicine
Sara Sebring

* * * *

Some people can take medicines without having a problem. Others react mildly to some medicines. However, I had one terrible reaction to an antibiotic, one that taught me that I would never take it again. I went to the doctor to get treatment for my right eye, which had been swollen shut for the previous two days. He told me my eye was infected and gave me a prescription for Duricef and Polymeral. I then left the doctor's office, had the prescription filled, and went home to take the medicine. I took the Polymeral and had no problems; however, after taking the Duricef, I experienced an allergic reaction. First, I fell asleep and slept for fourteen hours. When I finally woke up, my speech was slurred; I couldn't catch my breath; my neck broke out in a rash; and my face was swollen all over. In addition, I kept running into walls because my balance was off. As a result, I called the doctor's office and reported my condition to the nurse, who said the doctor would return my call in two minutes. Four hours later, the doctor returned my call and said he would phone the drugstore and order a new prescription to stop my swelling. To my dismay, the new prescription was never called in, and three days later my symptoms were still present. Finally, after four days of misery, the symptoms disappeared, and I found out that Duricef was a type of penicillin to which I have an allergic reaction. From this entire episode, not only did I learn that I cannot take Duricef, but I also learned that some doctors do not respond quickly enough to their patients' medical needs. This was truly the worst experience I have ever had.

Questions for Analysis

1. What is the topic sentence of this paragraph? Underline it.
2. What was Sara's first reaction to the medicine? Following that, what symptoms did she exhibit? What was the last allergic reaction she mentions, and what transition introduces it?
3. The allergic reaction caused her to take additional actions. What were they? What results did they bring?
4. What transitional expressions show time relationships? How much time passed between Sara's initial infection and her recovery from the allergic reaction?
5. Two changes in Sara's attitude and behavior occurred as results of this experience. What were they? What transition introduces them? How—and why—do these changes relate to the topic sentence?

Additional Writing Assignment 2: Describe the Effects of an Illness

Like Sara Sebring, you or someone you know has probably suffered from an illness or had a medical emergency. Write a paragraph or an essay in which you describe what happened and analyze the causes or the effects. Or, like Sara Sebring, you might decide to cover both the causes and the effects.

10 Classifying Information

We classify all the time: busy streets and quiet streets, easy classes and hard classes. And usually we think of more than two categories. For example, we store information in a computer database by categories, or types: accounts paid, accounts unpaid, new customers, and so on. We can learn about animals in a biology course by examining them in categories: reptiles, mammals, fish, and so on. And we often write about these findings in reports, memos, and school assignments.

This chapter will show you how to write a classification paragraph or essay by

- examining a model of classification
- analyzing what makes a classification effective
- thinking through ways of organizing a classification
- practicing writing classification paragraphs and essays

A Model of Classification

Classification is a way of dividing a group of people, objects, or ideas into categories based on some **criterion,** or standard for judging them. In fact, you've already seen an example of a paragraph that places people into categories. The model paragraph in Chapter 1 is a classification of pizza customers.

There are many ways to make classifications. You could divide cars into categories based on the criterion of size: full-size cars, mid-size cars, compact cars, and subcompacts. But you could just as easily classify cars by cost, gas mileage, or color. You could classify college students into categories according to the number of credit hours they've completed: freshmen, sophomores, juniors, and seniors. But you could just as easily classify students by age, grade-point average, or major.

In classifying, it's important to make sure your categories are clear and consistent. Here are two guidelines:

1. *Use only one criterion for classifying.* You can group people according to their income, intelligence, or ambition—but not according to income *and* intelligence or intelligence *and* ambition. Otherwise, you might discover that a person fits into more than one category. A rich student can also be bright; a bright student can be lazy or hardworking.

2. *Create categories that allow room for everyone or everything you are classifying.* Suppose, for example, that you are grouping your classmates according to age. If the youngest category includes people between the ages of eighteen and twenty, it excludes a classmate who is only seventeen. A better category might be students younger than twenty and students twenty years old and older.

Above all, don't oversimplify. There are too many negative and misleading simplifications of complex issues in the world already, and they tend to create and reinforce prejudices.

A diagram of a typical paragraph of classification might look like this:

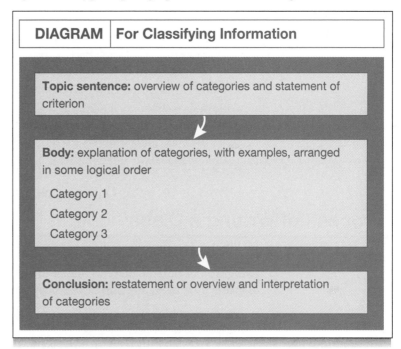

| DIAGRAM | For Classifying Information |

Topic sentence: overview of categories and statement of criterion

Body: explanation of categories, with examples, arranged in some logical order

Category 1

Category 2

Category 3

Conclusion: restatement or overview and interpretation of categories

Here's an example of a paragraph that classifies people into three categories. As you read it, notice the criterion for determining the categories. Notice the explanations of each category. And notice the examples that support each explanation.

Every Body Has a Place

* * * *

If you are looking for ways to describe fat, muscular, and wiry bodies, William H. Sheldon has created a useful vocabulary for doing so. In 1940, he invented a system of classifying body types that corresponds to the three layers of cells in an unborn child: endoderm—the inner layer, which later becomes the stomach and intestines; mesoderm—the middle layer, which forms the skeleton, muscles, and veins; and ecto-derm—the outer layer, which develops into the skin, hair, nails, and nervous system. He believed that these layers emerge differently in each adult. In some people, the layers are evenly balanced, but in many people, one layer dominates the others and forms one of Sheldon's three main body types. The first is the *endomorph,* a person with a soft body and many bulges. He or she may have strong muscles, but they are hard to find beneath the body fat. You can find plenty of examples of endomorphs in any ice cream or pizza parlor. The second body type is the *mesomorph,* a person with big bones and solid neck, shoulders, chest, stomach, buttocks, arms, and legs. You see mesomorph body types often in ads for health clubs or as action heroes—like, for instance, the movie star and former Mr. Universe, Arnold Schwarzenegger (elected governor of California in 2003). The third type is the *ectomorph,* a person with a wiry body, small bones, thin chest, a flat stomach, and small buttocks. An ectomorph may have long arms and legs and is generally very active. Just about every marathon runner is a typical ectomorph. Although Sheldon's classifications aren't perfect, they provide a useful way to describe the hulks, hunks, and scarecrows who populate the planet and compete in the rings and on the fields, courts, and tracks of the world.

Questions for Analysis

1. Which sentence introduces Sheldon's classifications of body types? Why isn't it the first sentence in the paragraph?
2. What criterion determines the classifications?
3. What is the stated purpose for classifying body types?
4. In what order are the categories introduced?
5. What examples of each body type does the writer provide? What words or phrases identify them as such?
6. Examine the conclusion. What attitude toward Sheldon's classifications does it express?
7. Based on the information body of the paragraph, what do you think the words *hulks, hunks,* and *scarecrows* in the last sentence mean? After you have speculated, consult a dictionary.

The Process of Writing a Classification

For a popular magazine that specializes in entertainment and humor, write a paragraph of classification on one of these topics. They'll be familiar to your audience (your classmates), so have some fun and try to be entertaining.

- types of people on a crowded bus, in a library, in a department store during a big sale, or at a party
- types of people at movie theaters or concerts
- types of grandparents
- types of customers you serve
- types of dogs or other pets

Gathering the Materials

Begin by thinking of a single criterion for classification—such as the amount of talking that people do at a student government meeting—and then brainstorm or cluster at least three categories, along with examples that fit within each. If you can't think of a criterion, start by generating categories, see what criterion holds them together, and eliminate or reshape the categories that don't fit the criterion.

Arranging the Materials

Organize your ideas into a chart like the one on page 91. Notice that the main categories, on the left, are arranged from most to least talkative. When you write, discuss the categories in a consistent order—most to least or least to most.

Notice that each category in the chart includes subcategories or examples.

Types of people at a student government meeting		
Criterion: Amount of talking they do		
Category	**Example**	
Big talker	The nonstop "expert," the constant interrupter, and the person who talks to show off	
Medium talker	The occasional talker, the groaner, and the frequent question-asker	
Nontalker	The watcher, the silent notetaker, and the sleeper	

TIPS

For Transitions in Classification
Use transitional expressions to introduce each category. Here are some examples:
first, another, still another, in addition, finally, last

Writing the First Draft

Write a first draft of the paragraph. State the categories and the criterion. Give examples of each category so that your paragraph is lively and entertaining, not merely a list. Then put your paper aside.

Revising the First Draft

Let the following checklist guide you in revising your paragraph. Answer the questions yourself or work with a classmate. If you answer *no* to any question, then revise the paragraph to correct the problem. First, make changes above the lines or write notes in the margin. Then rewrite the paragraph.

REVISION CHECKLIST

CLASSIFICATION		YES	NO
	• Is the purpose of the classification clear?	☐	☐
	• Is the criterion for classification clear—and limited to a single criterion?	☐	☐
	• Does the arrangement of categories move from most to least, least to most, or in some other consistent order?	☐	☐
	• Does each category include clear explanations and examples?	☐	☐
	• Does the paragraph include transitions that make clear connections between each category, explanation, and illustration?	☐	☐
	• Does the conclusion interpret the categories?	☐	☐

Take notes of these responses to guide your revision. Rewrite the paragraph later when you can examine it with fresh eyes and a clear mind. Pay special attention to making the categories vivid and distinct.

Further Revising and Editing

Return to the paragraph and revise it again. Edit and proofread it before handing in a clean copy of your work.

Additional Writing Assignment 1: Classify an Activity

Write a classification of any of the following activities:

- types of exercise
- types of dancing
- types of vacations
- types of nighttime activities

No matter what subject you choose, assume again that you're writing for a popular magazine, that your audience is already somewhat familiar with your topic, and that your purpose is mainly to entertain.

Be sure to use only one criterion for classifying, and create at least three different categories. Include at least one interesting or humorous example for each category.

A Student Model Essay

Jane Smith was a student at Danville Community College in Danville, Virginia. As you read her essay, notice that the first paragraph introduces three categories and that each category is discussed in a separate paragraph in the body of the essay. Notice, too, how her concluding paragraph summarizes the discussion and ends strongly.

Chamber Volunteers
Jane Smith

* * * *

1   My first volunteer experience was when I joined the Burnes County Junior Woman's Club twenty-five years ago. Since that time I have become so involved in this activity that a group of my friends has called me a professional volunteer. According to my husband, John, this is defined as any job that offers no pay, demands lots of time, and requires the donation of supplies from our office. Over the years, I have learned a great deal about the different types of people who work in volunteer organizations. Although most organizations consist of similar types of members, as president of the Burnes County Chamber of Commerce, I have observed that the chamber has a unique membership because these people are representing their businesses, industries, and professions. Therefore, they have distinct motives for offering their time and talents. The majority of these volunteers can be divided into three main categories: the bossy executives, the **glory** seekers, and the **backbones.**

2   The bossy executives are always right. If you don't believe it, just ask them! They have grand ideas and are very willing to tell you how to carry them out. The problem is they expect everyone else to do all the work. When someone else comes up with a different idea, the bossy executives will discuss only its negative aspects even if the idea is much better than theirs. If the committee decides to proceed with the new idea, the executives will still do it their way. No matter what the outcome of a project is, you can be sure of one thing: If anything goes wrong, it is not the bossy executives' faults because they are always right.

3   Unlike the bossy executives who like to be heard and obeyed, the glory seekers participate so that they can be seen. They are the first ones to volunteer for a project that is high profile and involves a lot of free publicity. If they happen to think of a good idea, everyone will know because they will be sure to take all of the credit. However, if anything

glory: fame or praise
backbones: the "spines" or main supports

goes wrong, they react like the bossy executives and are never at fault. When the time comes to begin working, they somehow feel that their presence is not necessary. They leave all of the planning and activities to the third type of volunteers, the backbones.

4   In any committee, if you can have at least one backbone, you can be sure that the work will be done because the backbones believe that actions speak louder than words. Whether these backbones are chairing committees or are members of the team, you know that they will follow through with their responsibilities and pitch in to complete the unfinished tasks of the bossy executives and the glory seekers. Their only motivation is the satisfaction they receive from supporting the organization, and their aim is to follow through and complete every project. When the cameras are flashing and the credits are given, the backbones are content to take the pictures and give the credits to the other team members.

5   Even though the backbones are the ideal chamber members, the bossy executives and the glory seekers do contribute in their own special ways to the goal of the Burnes County Chamber of Commerce. That goal is to deal with issues that affect the economic well-being of our community, and, through the unified efforts of everyone, this goal continues to be achieved.

Questions for Analysis

1. Jane Smith begins the first paragraph by discussing her experience in volunteer organizations and her role as president of a local chamber of commerce. How do those experiences qualify her to classify volunteers?
2. What are the three categories of volunteers introduced in the first paragraph? Underline them. How are these words identified and repeated in the three body paragraphs? Underline these sections, too.
3. Examine the first sentence of the third paragraph, beginning with "Unlike the bossy executives." Why does Jane make this contrast? What role does it have in unifying the essay?
4. How are the first two categories similar? How are they different? Which of the three categories does Jane respect the most?
5. Jane doesn't say which category she belongs to. Which one is the most likely? Why?
6. How does the structure of this essay resemble the structure of a single paragraph? How is the structure different? Why wouldn't this essay work as only one paragraph?

Additional Writing Assignment 2: Classify People in a Group

Using Jane Smith's essay as a guide, classify people in an organization into three types—saving the best type for last. You can discuss types of students in a class, members of a club, players on a team, people at a party, or friends. Arrange the categories so the best appears at the end. According to the directions of your instructor, you may write a single paragraph or an essay.

11 Making Comparisons and Contrasts

Each day you make comparisons or contrasts: this lesson was easier than the last one; traffic this morning ran as smoothly as traffic the day before; the test in biology was the hardest yet. Comparisons and contrasts examine the similarities and differences among people, ideas, or things. Sometimes you write comparisons and contrasts in order to evaluate: that is, to argue that something is better, more valuable, or more useful. Other times, you write comparisons and contrasts to clarify ideas. This chapter will show you how to write a comparison or contrast paragraph or essay by

- examining a model of comparison and contrast
- analyzing what makes a comparison and contrast effective
- thinking through ways to organize a comparison-contrast
- giving you practice writing comparison-contrasts

A Model of Comparison-Contrast

A **comparison** shows how people or things are similar. A **contrast** shows how they are different, usually to evaluate them. And a **comparison-contrast** paragraph discusses both similarities and differences. To do so, it must also organize, explain, and illustrate the similarities and differences in ways that make sense.

There are two main strategies for organizing the comparisons and contrasts:

1. **Whole-to-Whole (or Block) Organization.** In this organization, you describe Movie X completely, and then Movie Y completely. You draw the comparisons and contrasts while describing Movie Y, or after describing Movie Y.

2. **Part-to-Part Organization.** In this organization, you describe one part of Movie X, such as its plot, and then compare it to the plot of Movie Y. Then you return to Movie X to describe its acting, followed by a comparison to the acting in Movie Y. You continue in this way until you have drawn all the comparisons and contrasts between the two movies. If you discuss point A about one subject, then your readers must see its relationship to point A about the other.

Keep these additional guidelines in mind as you compose and revise the paragraph:

1. *Don't oversimplify.* Very few issues are as simple as black versus white or good versus evil. So be careful as you evaluate—deciding if something is better than something else. It's fine to say that Movie X is better than Movie Y, but don't automatically assume Movie Y is a waste of time. Movie Y may be entertaining, but not as good as Movie X.

2. *Don't use circular reasoning.* When explaining why Movie X is better than Movie Y, give specific reasons to support your claim. Don't say that Movie X was better because it was better. For example, the statement, "Movie X was interesting because it held my attention" is circular reasoning because "interesting" and "held my attention" mean the same thing. Give specific reasons instead: "Movie X was interesting because it was fast-moving, full of surprises, and well acted."

3. *Be consistent in discussing each point of comparison or contrast.* Make your comparisons and contrasts easy for your readers to understand. If you discuss the acting, directing, photography, and editing of Movie X, you must discuss all these matters in Movie Y. You should also discuss them in the same order for each movie.

A diagram of a paragraph using the whole-to-whole, or block, organization might look like this:

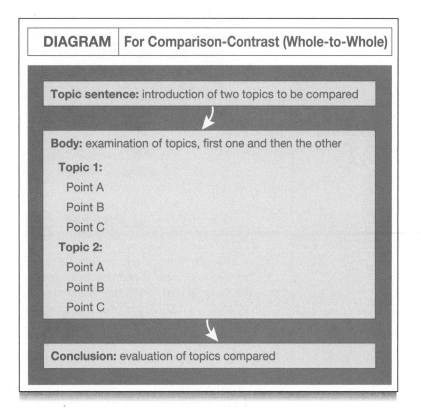

And a diagram of a paragraph using part-to-part organization might look like this:

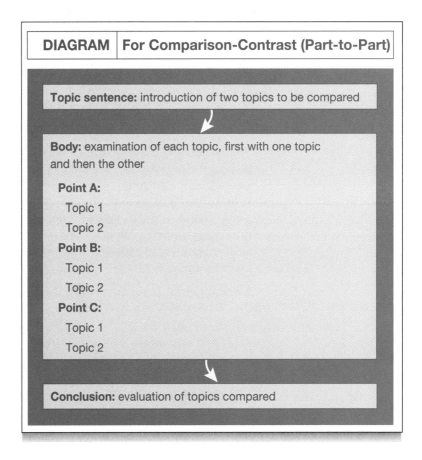

DIAGRAM | **For Comparison-Contrast (Part-to-Part)**

Topic sentence: introduction of two topics to be compared

Body: examination of each topic, first with one topic and then the other

Point A:
　Topic 1
　Topic 2
Point B:
　Topic 1
　Topic 2
Point C:
　Topic 1
　Topic 2

Conclusion: evaluation of topics compared

The following paragraph compares and contrasts two subjects. As you read it, notice that it begins with a contrast of white and dark meat. Then notice that a comparison between two types of birds follows.

The Light and the Dark of It

＊ ＊ ＊ ＊

Why do chickens and turkeys have both dark and light meat, while most other birds we eat (such as quail, duck, or pigeon) have dark meat only? The reason is that there are two types of fibers in the muscles of birds: red and white. The red fibers contain a muscle protein that makes animals able to work for much longer periods than do white fibers, which are designed for short, powerful bursts of activity. You can therefore guess which birds have the most red-fibered muscles—and the most dark meat. They are the creatures that must fly long distances to migrate or to find food—the geese, ducks, and quails. But chickens and turkeys live a less strenuous life. They move around by walking or running, so only their legs and thighs contain dark red fibers. These land birds don't use their wings and breasts very much, so these parts contain light white fibers. In fact, the absence of red fiber in wings and breasts is an advantage. When chickens and turkeys are threatened, their wings and upper bodies must deliver a lot of power quickly, but for only a short time. The next time you pay an extra fifty cents for an order of all-white-meat chicken, remember that these parts of birds racked up fewer trips in the air than you may have taken in an airplane.

Questions for Analysis

1. What is the topic sentence of the paragraph?
2. Is the main purpose of the paragraph to inform, persuade, or entertain?
3. What is the paragraph comparing or contrasting?
4. List the points of comparisons and contrasts in the paragraph. Which does the paragraph mainly discuss—similarities or differences?
5. Is this primarily a whole-to-whole or part-to-part comparison-contrast?
6. Which words show differences among the types of birds? Which words signal similiarities among the types of birds?

The Process of Writing a Comparison-Contrast

Write a paragraph for a feature section of a newspaper or magazine. Compare and contrast two subjects you know well. Conclude by recommending one or both of them to your readers. You might choose two movies, two popular music groups (or songs), two books, two performances, two types of sports (or two games in the same sport), two celebrities, or two cars.

Gathering and Generating the Materials

Begin by reviewing the topic of your comparison and contrast: if possible, see, inspect, listen to, or read about it again—and take notes of what you observe or find.

Use a simple chart to help you generate and organize the points of comparison and contrast. As you list one point about the first subject, you must consider the corresponding point about the second subject. Continue until your chart covers every point. Here, for example, is a chart for two movies:

	College Clowns	**Crash and Burn**
Type	1. comedy	1. action
Actors	2. unknown actors	2. major stars
Plot	3. not much plot	3. suspense leading to a climax
Contents	4. bad humor and silly dialogue	4. action more important than clever dialogue
Rating	5. R	5. R
Length	6. 90 minutes	6. two hours
Cost	7. small budget, no unusual locations, and hardly any special effects	7. large budget, with plane crashes, car chases, and many special effects
Audience	8. appeals to teenagers	8. appeals to teenagers

After you've completed the chart, construct a second chart with the items grouped according to similarities and differences. Create new points to compare and contrast as they emerge from your note taking and thinking.

	College Clowns	Crash and Burn
Similarities		
Rating	1. R	1. R
Audience	2. teenagers	2. teenagers
Dialogue	3. weak	3. weak
Differences		
Type	1. comedy	1. action picture
Actors	2. unknown actors	2. major stars
Plot	3. not much plot	3. suspense leading to a climax
Contents	4. bad humor	4. action
Length	5. 90 minutes	5. two hours
Cost	6. small budget, no unusual locations, and hardly any special effects	6. large budget, with plane crashes, car chases, and many special effects

✔ **TIPS**

For Indicating Comparison-Contrast

Help your readers note comparison-contrast by supplying appropriate transitions. Here's a list:

For comparison (similarities): *like, as, likewise, similarly, also, too, moreover, in a similar way or fashion*

For contrast (differences): *in contrast, on the one hand . . . on the other hand, however, unlike, but*

Arranging the Materials

Then decide on the type of organization to use in your comparison. Read down both columns of the chart for a whole-to-whole approach. Read across the columns for a part-to-part approach. As you continue planning, select examples of each point of comparison or contrast, and consider what explanations or examples to provide.

Writing the First Draft

Now write a first draft. Write a topic sentence that states the major claim of the paragraph, such as: "Although the movies *College Clowns* and *Crash and Burn* both appeal to teenagers, they do so for different reasons." Use either whole-to-whole or part-to-part organization. If the organization you choose doesn't work well when you compose the draft, switch to the other organization. Add transitions to introduce the points of comparison and to emphasize the similarities and differences. Try to conclude with a statement that sums up the main points of the paragraph or that evaluates the topics you've compared.

Revising the First Draft

Let the checklist on page 99 guide you in revising your paragraph. Answer the questions yourself or work with a classmate. If you answer *no* to any question, then revise the paragraph to correct the problem. First, make changes above the lines or write notes in the margin. Then rewrite the paragraph.

REVISION CHECKLIST

		YES	NO
COMPARISON AND CONTRAST	• Is the purpose of the comparison and contrast clear?	☐	☐
	• Does the paragraph include a topic sentence that names the two things to be compared and contrasted and states the central claim?	☐	☐
	• If you have used whole-to-whole organization, are the points of comparison or contrast discussed in the same order?	☐	☐
	• Is each point of comparison or contrast clearly explained and illustrated?	☐	☐
	• Are the transitions between main ideas clear?	☐	☐
	• Is the final evaluation valid? That is, have the points of comparison and contrast prepared readers for it?	☐	☐

Take notes of these responses to guide your revision. Rewrite the paragraph later when you can examine it with fresh eyes and a clear mind. Pay special attention to organization.

Further Revising and Editing

Return to the paragraph and revise it again. Edit and proofread it before handing in a clean copy of your work.

Additional Writing Assignment 1: Evaluating Ideas

Assume you're a newspaper or magazine columnist who often expresses opinions on matters of interest to you and your readers. Write a paragraph of comparison and contrast on one of the following topics:

• families with one or two children or families with five or more children
• studying business or studying art (or music, literature, or liberal arts)
• marrying young or marrying later in life
• working part time to pay for college or borrowing the money
• doing high-impact activities such as running or low-impact activities such as walking

Choose a subject you know well. If you used whole-to-whole organization in the earlier assignment in this chapter, then use part-to-part here—or vice versa. Start with a topic sentence that names the two things you will compare or contrast and makes a claim about them. Tell stories or cite examples to support your main points if possible. Recommend or suggest which of the two things you're comparing is best—or perhaps best for some people, while the other thing is best for other people.

A Student Model Essay

Here's an essay written by Mirham Mahmutagic, a student at Truman College in Chicago who grew up in Bosnia. It compares how Bosnians and Americans think about how to use their time. As you read it, notice how Mirham makes a part-to-part comparison-contrast between time spent in school in the two countries and then, later, between time spent with families.

Examining the Differences: Old Tradition vs. New World
Mirham Mahmutagic

* * * *

1   When I first came to the United States, I remember wondering why Americans have fast-food restaurants, or why they spend so much time eating out, instead of cooking their meals at home, the way we did in Bosnia. Well, after spending six years here in Chicago, I have learned that besides food, everything else also seems to be "on the go" here in the States. That, simply said, is the biggest difference between the "old world" of tradition and history, where I came from, and this "new world" of high rises and big money.

2   In the United States, time, or should I better say the lack of it, has a direct impact on people and their decision on how to use that time throughout the entire course of their lives. People in the States spend a lot of time in their schools, starting as early as the first grade of elementary school. On the average, children here attend eight to nine hours of school every day, five days a week, while children in Bosnia, on the average, attend five to six hours of school every day. After graduating from high school, American youth are facing five to eight years of schooling toward their professional degrees, while in Bosnia that translates into four to five years of college. Finally, at the age of 23, a young doctor starts practicing medicine in Bosnia, while at the same age of 23 the American future physician is finishing the first year of medical school and heading toward the next three. Ironically, the American doctor will spend the rest of his or her life chasing that time "lost" in school by working endless hours and 48-hour shifts year after year, while the doctor in Bosnia will work 40 to 50 hours a week, enjoying most Saturdays and Sundays off.

3   This seemingly simple time grid suggests that children in Bosnia do have more time, outside of school, to spend with their families and their friends, while children in the States don't. Accordingly, children in Bosnia do grow up closer to their families, and as adults they adjust their lives so that they can spend more time in their homes and less time at work. On the other hand, children in America probably grow up with a different set of values, where their career and work will come first and the time for their families and friends will come second. As a result of their dedication to their careers and their work, young Americans appear to be more independent, ambitious, efficient, and prosperous compared to youth in Bosnia. As adults, they seem to have much stronger work ethics than Bosnians do, which ultimately leads to the current immeasurable economic difference between the two countries. Today, those Americans are able to give their children the latest toys and video games, expensive cars, and the latest technological inventions, which is something most of the children in Bosnia grow up without.

4   I can still remember just how beautiful my childhood was growing up in Bosnia. My friends, with whom I have spent endless hours playing games like tag, riding a bike, or playing ball, constantly surrounded me. Unlike many fathers in the States, my father always had time to play with me, help me with the homework, and simply be around whenever I needed him. Now that I think about how important his presence in my life was, I keep wondering if I will have enough time to spend with my child to be able to show him how important the family is, just like my parent showed to me.

Questions for Analysis

1. What sentence or sentences in the first paragraph introduce the comparison? Underline the sentence(s). What are the topic sentences in the remaining paragraphs? Underline them as well.

2. How many comparisons does Mirham make in the second paragraph? Number them, and circle the words that serve as transitions between comparisons.

3. In the third paragraph, and then later in the final paragraph, Mirham begins to discuss how the two cultures he compares seem to have differing values. What differences does he see? Do you agree with his observations? Which values, in his opinion, are most important? Which values, in your opinion, are most important?

4. How does the conclusion relate to ideas earlier in the essay?

5. Construct a grid of the comparisons or contrasts Mirham makes in his essay. Are they consistent and complete?

Additional Writing Assignment 2: Evaluating Values

Like Mirham Mahmutagic, write a paragraph (or an essay) in which you contrast one set of values you have learned with another set that other people seem to think are important. You might consider any one of the following issues: the relationship between parent and child, neatness, study habits, manners, behavior in school, behavior at parties, showing off, the use of language (including slang), or the importance of money or material possessions.

12 Defining Terms

No matter what type of writing you do—whether you're explaining a process, comparing objects or ideas, or writing a report—you may use a term or concept that your audience doesn't understand. In those cases, you need a definition, that is, an explanation of what you mean when you use the term. When the explanation is complex and requires more than a few words, you may have to write a paragraph or an essay of definition. This chapter will show you how to do that by

- examining a model of definition
- analyzing what makes a definition effective
- thinking through ways to organize a definition
- giving you practice writing definitions

A Model of Definition

As you predict your audience's response to your writing, you must think about the times they might ask, "What do you mean?" Suppose, for example, that in a letter to your local school board suggesting changes in the curriculum, you use the term *good students*. The board members might wonder whether you mean quiet students or talkative students, competitive students or cooperative students, students who can recite what they learn or students who can apply it. You need a **definition**—an explanation of how you're using the term.

Your explanation of a term can be a simple matter, and sometimes it is. You can define a term merely with a **synonym**—another word that means the same thing. Or you can cite a short dictionary definition of the term. But at other times defining is not so simple. You may need to explain and illustrate exactly the meaning you intend—or do not intend—in one or more full paragraphs. That definition may include comparisons, contrasts, a classification, and examples.

The diagram on page 103 shows one way a definition paragraph might be organized, assuming that the concept to be defined includes three important ideas. Note that it arranges the ideas in **climax order**—going from the least to the most important.

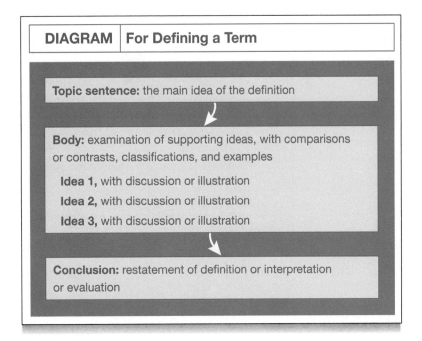

DIAGRAM	For Defining a Term

Topic sentence: the main idea of the definition

Body: examination of supporting ideas, with comparisons or contrasts, classifications, and examples

  Idea 1, with discussion or illustration

  Idea 2, with discussion or illustration

  Idea 3, with discussion or illustration

Conclusion: restatement of definition or interpretation or evaluation

The following definition is taken from a long article in Newsweek *magazine that discusses the growing epidemic of allergies among young people. As you read it, note the formal definition of* allergy *in the first sentence. Then notice how the account increases your understanding of the term by explaining how an allergic reaction works.*

What Is an Allergy?
Jerry Adler

* * * *

1   An allergy is an overreaction by the immune system to a foreign substance, which can enter the body through a variety of routes. [The foreign substance] can be inhaled, like pollen or dander, the tiny flakes of skin shed by domestic animals. It can be injected, like insect venom or penicillin, or merely touch the skin, like the latex in medical gloves. Or it can be ingested. According to the Food Allergy & Anaphylaxis Network, almost any food can trigger an allergy, although eight categories account for 90 percent of all reactions: milk, eggs, peanuts (technically, a legume), tree nuts, finfish, shellfish, soy, and wheat. (Allergies have nothing to do with the condition known as food intolerance; people who lack an enzyme for digesting dairy products, for instance, may suffer intestinal problems, but they are not allergic to milk.)

2   For reasons not fully understood, in some people these otherwise harmless substances provoke the same reactions by which the body attempts to rid itself of dangerous pathogens. These may include sneezing, vomiting, and the all-purpose localized immune-system arousal known as inflammation. The lungs may be affected; allergies are a leading trigger for asthma attacks. In extreme cases, the reaction involves virtually all organ systems and leads to anaphylaxis, a dramatic drop in blood pressure accompanied by extreme respiratory distress that may be fatal without prompt treatment.

Questions for Analysis

1. What is the central definition of *allergy?* Underline it.
2. How many ways may foreign substances enter the body and cause allergic reactions? What words help you identify the number of ways?
3. What examples are given for each of the ways? Underline them. Which of the ways has the most examples? Why?
4. Underline the sentence that draws a contrast. Why was that sentence included?
5. Which sentence in the second paragraph states the topic idea? Underline it twice.
6. Is the second paragraph arranged in sequential order or climax order? What effect does that arrangement create?
7. The definition of *allergy* also includes definitions of additional terms. Circle the words defined. Why are those definitions included?

The Process of Writing a Definition

Assume you are writing a short definition of a term for your classmates. Your choice of a term to define can come from your coursework in school (for example, *mitosis* in biology, *html* in computer science, *socialism* or *capitalism* in social science, *ethics* in philosophy, *thesis statement* in composition, the *Middle Ages* in world history, *counterpoint* in music, *Impressionism* in art, and so on). It can come from your job experiences. Or it can come from your experiences in living in a country other than the United States.

Statement of Definition. Your paragraph or essay should include a sentence that states the definition, followed by a fuller explanation of its meaning. That explanation might include examples that give a full picture of the definition and contrasts with other terms that clarify what the definition is and what it is not. You can state the definition in one of two ways:

* You can express it by a **synonym**—a word with virtually the same meaning as another word. Here are examples of definitions by synonym:

> A CRT (cathode-ray tube) is computer terminology for a *monitor* or *television screen.*
>
> The *aardvark*—or *anteater*—is found in southern Africa.
>
> To *eschew* means to *avoid.*

Note that the synonym and the word it defines must be the same part of speech (noun and noun, verb and verb, adjective and adjective) so that one term can be substituted for another.

* You can express it in a **formal statement of definition,** the method most often used in dictionaries. The statement begins by placing the term into a larger category.

Word	Category
An allergy	is an overreaction by the immune system . . .
A psychiatrist	is a medical doctor . . .

Distinguishing Characteristics. After the statement of definition you add **criteria**—or standards for judging or distinguishing the definition from other words in the same category. These are distinguishing characteristics.

Word	Category or class	Distinguishing characteristics
An allergy	is an overreaction by the immune system	to a foreign substance, which can enter the body through a variety of routes.
A psychiatrist	is a medical doctor	who specializes in the study, diagnosis, treatment, and prevention of mental illnesses.

You may be able to quote the definition from a dictionary or textbook—if that definition fits your meaning and you cite your source. But writers sometimes define a term in a way that doesn't fit the standard dictionary definition. You'll see an example shortly.

Gathering the Materials

Brainstorm a list, or make a clustering chart, of the most important or easily noticed characteristics of the term you're defining. Here's a clustering chart for the definition of *allergy*. It starts with the term and its formal definition in the center. Each branch explores a different characteristic. Further branches list examples.

Selecting and Arranging the Materials

After you've brainstormed or clustered your ideas, select at least three of the most important characteristics to develop further. Make sure each is supported by examples. Include contrasts. Notice, in the clustering chart, that *allergy* is partly defined by what it is not—it is not a food intolerance.

You may wish to outline your paragraph of definition before you start writing.

Writing the First Draft

Look over your outline. Then write a preliminary topic sentence that states the general definition. Continue with sentences that state each of the characteristics you've chosen. Follow each characteristic with an example. Conclude with a restatement or an evaluation.

Revising the First Draft

Let the following checklist guide you in revising your paragraph. Answer the questions yourself or work with a classmate. If you answer *no* to any question, then revise the paragraph to correct the problem. First, make changes above the lines or write notes in the margin. Then rewrite the paragraph.

TIPS

For Transitions in Definitions

Here are some transitions that may help you connect ideas:

for example, that is, that is to say, according to, moreover, in addition, in contrast

REVISION CHECKLIST

		YES	NO
DEFINITION	• Does the topic sentence introduce the term to be defined and the main idea of the term or a formal statement of definition?	❑	❑
	• Is the definition developed through distinguishing characteristics?	❑	❑
	• Do discussions of the characteristics include examples?	❑	❑
	• Is the term defined by contrasts, or by what it is not?	❑	❑
	• Are technical terms further defined?	❑	❑
	• Are the characteristics arranged in climax order?	❑	❑
	• Are the transitions between ideas clear?	❑	❑
	• Does the conclusion include a relevant interpretation or evaluation?	❑	❑

Take notes of these responses to guide your revision. Rewrite the definition later when you can examine it with fresh eyes and a clear mind. Pay special attention to completeness. Is the paragraph of definition complete enough so that readers will know—fully—what you mean by the term? If not, add more explanation.

Further Revising and Editing

After waiting a few hours or days, return to the paragraph and revise it again. Edit your work, and hand in a clean copy.

Additional Writing Assignment 1: Define a Person in a Role

Write your own personal definition of a *good father, mother, teacher,* or *leader.* Include several distinguishing characteristics and examples of each. Your examples can come from your own experiences, the experiences of people you know, or experiences you can imagine.

A Student Model Essay

Amra Skocic, a student at Truman College in Chicago who came from Bosnia, wrote the following definition essay. In it, she defines the term courageous act *by examining the behavior of one person. Note that she begins by citing a formal definition of the term in the first paragraph. Then, in the body of the essay, she gives the definition substance by examining specific distinguishing characteristics and providing extended examples of each. Her final paragraph summarizes the key points.*

True Courage
Amra Skocic

* * * *

1   It is not very often that we hear about, read about, or experience a truly courageous act. Indeed, do we really even understand what a courageous act is? According to *Webster's Dictionary, courage* is defined as "the ability to control fear when facing danger or pain." But there is much more involved. A courageous act is an unselfish gesture taken on a voluntary basis which involves some risk. An example is Oscar Schindler, the real-life hero of the movie *Schindler's List,* who performs a courageous act by saving thousands of Jewish lives during the Second World War.

2   Oscar Schindler is a German factory owner who employs Jewish people and later rescues them from death in the concentration camps. In the beginning, he is primarily motivated by the opportunity to start production and earn a high profit using forced labor. As time goes by, Schindler's motivation changes from greed to selflessness. As he witnesses the mass execution and torture of the Jews in Poland, he realizes that he has the ability to save innocent lives. Gradually this realization overcomes his desire for money. Led by unselfish motivation, his action meets the first **criterion** for courage.

criterion: singular for *criteria*

3   A courageous act must be voluntary, meaning that the person performing the act must have the full opportunity to walk away and avoid risk. Schindler understands his choices, but the one that he makes is to employ Jewish people. He could just as well have employed German workers or used other options without taking any risk. The voluntary nature of employing Jewish people in his factory meets the second criterion for courage.

4   A courageous act involves risk and sacrifice. How much the goal is worth determines the price of risk. From the moment Oscar Schindler decides to save those innocent lives, he is aware of the danger to his own life. If discovered by the Nazis, he will inevitably be killed. This risk completes the third and the final criterion for a courageous act.

5   Is there anything worth risking our own lives for? For most of us, probably not, but for a courageous person like Oscar Schindler, obviously there is. This points out the great difficulty of true courage, which the world rarely sees. Today it is more common for people to act out of selfishness, to avoid any danger, and to let others volunteer. Schindler sets himself apart when he accepts a great risk without potential reward, and without hesitation. Schindler stands as a beacon of courage in a world that still has many dark corners. We would all do well to emulate the courage of Schindler.

Questions for Analysis

1. Amra Skocic includes a dictionary definition in her first paragraph. Underline it.
2. Which sentence in the first paragraph introduces the three distinguishing characteristics of courage that will shape the essay? Underline it twice. Number the three characteristics.
3. In the second, third, and fourth paragraphs, topic sentences refer to each of the three characteristics of the definition. Underline them. Where does Amra place these sentences and why?
4. Amra provides some contrasts in her extended examples. Underline them twice. Why does she provide them?
5. Would the definition be strengthened if she had discussed the actions of more than one person? Why or why not?
6. What ideas are repeated in the summary paragraph? Circle them.

Additional Writing Assignment 2: Define an Abstract Idea

Define an abstract term such as *love, friendship, maturity, beauty,* or *success.* Establish your distinguishing characteristics. Use one person as an example. Narrative paragraphs may help you explain what this person did to show, for example, love or friendship. You may want to introduce contrasts—what this person chose not to do, or what other people often do. You may write one paragraph or a whole essay, such as the one by Amra Skocic.

13 Persuading an Audience

Persuasion is an important part of everyday life. Each day in conversation, you make requests and demands—for example, that a friend lend you some money; that your professor allow you more time to complete an assignment; or that your child, roommate, or spouse put the dirty dishes in the sink. Less often—but far more important—you make written requests that employers consider you for a job, customers buy your products, or a government agency provide you with important documents. In college writing, you must persuade your instructor that your analysis, interpretation, or understanding of an issue is correct or reasonable.

This chapter will show you how to shape a persuasive argument by

- describing the elements of persuasion
- examining a model of persuasion
- giving you practice in shaping ideas into effective arguments
- giving you practice in writing persuasive arguments

A Model of Persuasion

Persuasion is an attempt to convince others that they should accept your views or do what you ask of them. Of course, you cannot persuade everyone to accept every viewpoint, but a well-planned and reasonable argument can often be effective.

The Elements of Persuasion

A persuasive argument should follow a *persuasive strategy* based on an anticipation of the audience response, the reason for persuading, and the type of appeals it includes.

Audience. You cannot ignore your audience's opposing beliefs or feelings about your subject matter. Therefore, you should acknowledge those beliefs or feelings. State them at the beginning of the argument to demonstrate that you're reasonable and fair.

Reason for Persuading. Your goal in persuading may simply be to ask someone to consider an idea, or it may be a **call for action**—a demand or request that your audience do something. State that goal early in the argument. Make your claim in a topic sentence, and then develop the claim in the body of the paragraph or essay.

Type of Persuasive Appeals. The best way to support your claim is with solid evidence: facts, figures, and examples. You may also choose to support a claim by citing an expert or authority on the subject. Appeals to emotions such as sympathy, anger, or even humor can be effective, too. But don't appeal only to emotions. Respect the intelligence of your audience, and tell the truth.

A diagram of persuasive argument might look like this:

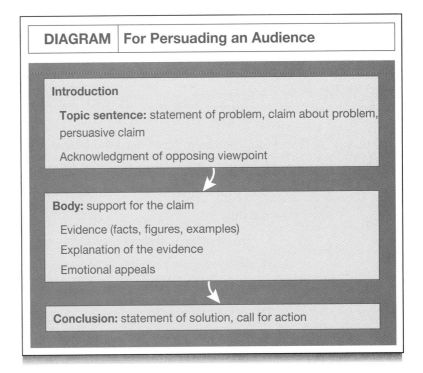

| DIAGRAM | For Persuading an Audience |

Introduction

Topic sentence: statement of problem, claim about problem, persuasive claim

Acknowledgment of opposing viewpoint

Body: support for the claim

Evidence (facts, figures, examples)

Explanation of the evidence

Emotional appeals

Conclusion: statement of solution, call for action

Here's an example of a short persuasive argument. As you read it, note that the author states his claim directly and then supports it. Note the transitions that signal the support.

Why Write on a Computer?

* * * *

Some students may feel most comfortable writing a paper by hand, but there's a better and more productive way. Writing on a computer has many great advantages. First of all, the computer makes it easy to change or rearrange your ideas as you compose a draft. To change an idea, all you need to do is highlight the text and then type in the new material. The original material will disappear as soon as you begin to type. To rearrange an idea, again you simply highlight the text and then use the cut-and-paste commands to place it in a different spot. Second, the computer makes revision much easier. Double-space the text and leave wide margins, and print out your draft so that you can make handwritten notes and changes. Then, instead of copying over the entire paper by hand, you can simply return to the original version in your computer and enter the changes. You can repeat this process as often as you want. Third, the spell and grammar checkers on the computer can help you in editing your work. You shouldn't rely on these tools completely because they can't recognize every error. For example, an incorrect spelling of a word may actually be the correct spelling of another word—but the computer won't know that. And the computer may also label something as a grammatical error when in fact there is no error at all. That's because the computer isn't reading your paper; it's simply scanning the words according to a formula someone designed. Finally, the computer allows you to print out a clean copy of your work so that your audience won't have any difficulty reading your handwriting. Learning how to write on a computer may take some time and effort, but the result is worth it.

Questions for Analysis

1. Who is the audience for this argument, and what purpose does the writer hope to achieve with his audience?
2. In what sentence does the author acknowledge an opposing viewpoint? Underline it.
3. What sentence states his topic idea? Underline it twice.
4. The writer supplies a number of reasons to back up the claim in the topic sentence. How many reasons does he supply? Number them. Circle the transitions.
5. What examples does he use to explain his reasons?
6. What process does he describe to support his claim?
7. Does the writer anticipate any objections to his argument? If so, how does he address those objections?

The Process of Writing a Persuasive Argument

Write an argument about changing (or continuing) some policy of your school. Assume that you are writing to classmates who are familiar with the policy but may not have the same opinion as you do. Here are some suggestions for topics to address:

- the grading system
- required courses
- food services
- tutoring and academic support services
- parking or transportation
- housing

Gathering the Materials

As you begin to prepare a persuasive strategy, consider what the audience knows—and needs to know—about your subject. Consider how to answer or acknowledge the audience's objections or concerns. Think about the goal of your argument, too. Do you want your readers to consider your viewpoint, or are you making a call for action? Write a preliminary topic sentence that states your claim clearly and directly; let your readers know exactly what you want them to believe or do. Since you're recommending or demanding something, the claim will probably include the verbs *should, ought,* or *must.*

Gather and do research on the backing you should provide for your claims. What facts and figures do you know—or where can you find them? What experts or authorities should you cite? You may need to spend some time in the library or on the Internet. Read over the source material more than once to be sure you understand it and can use it accurately.

Organizing the Materials

Once you have gathered your materials, think about the arrangement of your argument. Should your claim appear at the beginning of the argument or, in climax order, at the end? Should you introduce a set of reasons, labeled "first," "second," "third," and so on? Should you support your claim by making comparisons? Or would explaining a process be helpful? Do you need to define any terms or classify ideas? Where would examples be most effective? Should you illustrate an idea with a narrative? Should you quote experts and authorities or paraphrase what they say?

You may wish to outline your argument at this point. Here, for example, is an outline of the model paragraph you read at the beginning of the chapter:

I. Acknowledgment of discomfort students feel writing on computer

II. Topic sentence: Writing on a computer has many great advantages.
    A. Changing or rearranging ideas in first drafts:
       process explained
    B. Revising:
       process explained
    C. Editing with the spell checker and grammar checker:
       process explained
    D. Printing a clean copy

III. Conclusion: Restatement of topic idea

✓ TIPS

For Choosing Transitions in Persuasion

Here are a few transitions signaling different ideas within a persuasive argument:

To concede a point: *of course, surely, naturally, to be sure, no doubt*

To qualify a statement: *perhaps, maybe, possibly*

To predict results or consequences: *therefore, thus, as a consequence, as a result*

To cite an authority: *according to, as . . . says (demonstrates, argues, shows)*

Writing the First Draft

Now, you're ready to write. Draft your argument, with the persuasive claim stated either at the beginning or end, depending on your persuasive strategy. If you use sources written by others, you may either **paraphrase** your source (that is, restate it in your own words) or quote it (that is, use it exactly as it was written, and put it in quotation marks). Acknowledge your source by stating the author, title, date, and page number.

Revising the First Draft

Once again, let the checklist on page 113 guide you in revising your argument. Answer the questions yourself or work with a classmate. If you answer *no* to any question, then revise the paragraph to correct the problem. First, make changes above the lines or write notes in the margin. Then rewrite the argument.

REVISION CHECKLIST

		YES	NO

PERSUASION

- Is the argument directed to a specific audience? ☐ ☐
- Are any counterarguments of the audience acknowledged and addressed? ☐ ☐
- Is the statement of the claim clear? ☐ ☐
- Is the persuasive strategy appropriate for the issue and the audience? ☐ ☐
- Is the evidence convincing and appropriate? ☐ ☐
- Is the evidence presented in climax order? ☐ ☐
- Are the transitions clear? ☐ ☐
- Does the argument end strongly—restating its main claim or calling on readers to act? ☐ ☐

Additional Writing Assignment 1: Make a Recommendation

Recommend a place for your classmates to go—a restaurant, a meeting place, a nightclub, a concert, a library, or any other public place. Argue why they would enjoy or appreciate the place. Assume your readers are neutral toward the subject.

A Student Model Essay

Here's an example of a persuasive essay written by Monica Radu, a former student at Truman College in Chicago. As you read it, notice how it delays its persuasive claim until after a brief introductory story. Notice that its evidence is based primarily on experience.

The Problem with Mathematics
Monica Radu

* * * *

1   "How many sixteenths of an inch are in one inch?" asked the art teacher one day. I sat back, thinking, "What a stupid question to ask! It would be a piece of cake even for a first-grader." Well, maybe for a first-grader, but it did not seem like one for a high-schooler. As the silence persisted, the teacher tried to help: "If you have one dollar and you want to divide it equally among your four friends, how much would you give to each of them?" This was much easier; the students answered right away that it was a quarter. "Very good. Now, why?" The students started to think again. At the very far end, one of them, who figured out that there are sixteen sixteenths of an inch in one inch, was congratulated for being so intelligent.

2   Somebody might ask me: Why did I say this problem would have been easier for a first-grader than for a high-schooler? Because the first-grader still relies on his or her common sense to answer it, while the high-schooler, after a long time of a "scientific approach" to life, loses that skill and replaces it with a bunch of formulas. But as he or she knows no formula for the number of sixteenths in one inch, he or she cannot answer.

3   This is, unfortunately, a true story that happened in my senior year. I never encountered a problem like this in Romania, where I came from less than two years ago. I therefore want to argue that American schools could learn a lesson from the educational system in Europe.

4   During the year I spent in an American public high school, many of my class-mates—especially in my science courses—complained about the difficulties they had in applying formulas to situations not mentioned in class. They said they studied for hours, memorized everything, and did all the problems in the book, and yet, when they came to tests and were faced with new types of problems, they didn't know which formula to apply. So what's the use of a formula if the students don't understand the concept behind it?

5   I learned concepts back in Romania. Consequently, I never studied at home, never forced myself to memorize formulas, and always did my homework in class the day it was due. But I still got easy A's on tests. I'm not saying this to boast. I was not smarter than the other students and maybe even less persevering. It's just that I knew a better method of learning—that of relying on reasoning, not memorizing. And I must say the method has impressive results. In Romania, by the time students graduate high school, about 25 percent of them have passed Calculus II. And mathematics is only one of the many areas of such accomplishments.

6   But how could one expect Americans to use reasoning if they are not taught it? I was amazed to see that teachers here, in America, give hardly any proofs for the the-orems they state. It is as if they were saying, "This was discovered by a great scien-tist, and, as it is written in the book, it is most surely true. The proof is too hard for you, so you don't worry about it." How do the teachers know students will not understand the proof? Why do teachers underestimate them?

7   Let me give you a concrete example. During my junior year of high school in Romania, part of the mathematics course included the limits of functions. It was hard, but not impossible, and I did understand them. Next year, I came to the United States and I was taught limits again. What a difference! We weren't even given the real defi-nition; the teacher presumed it would be too difficult for our level. What we got was a made-up, "easier" formula, based exclusively on intuition, something like "it seems that . . ." or "wouldn't it be nice if. . . ." And maybe everything would have been all right if this new method did not have the special "quality" of sometimes getting the wrong answer.

8   Considering the present situation in many American high schools, it's not a wonder that many jobs in scientific fields are taken by immigrants who started their education in other countries. It is America itself, through its education system, that robs many of its own people of the opportunity to pursue such careers.

Questions for Analysis

1. Who is the likely audience for this argument?
2. Monica Radu doesn't state her persuasive claim at the beginning of her essay. Instead, she chooses to tell a story that illustrates a problem with the way science and mathematics are taught. What is the problem?
3. Later in the essay, Monica states her persuasive claim quite explicitly. Where does she state it? Underline the statement.
4. What examples does she provide to back up her claims? List them.
5. She also bases much of her argument on comparisons. What comparisons does she make? List them.
6. Does she base her argument primarily on appeals to emotion or reason?

Additional Writing Assignment 2:
Argue for a Change in Policy

Like Monica Radu, make an argument for a change in some practice in education, on your job, or in any other area you wish. Assume you're writing to a friendly or neutral audience.

Consider the goal of your argument: Do you want your readers simply to agree with your argument or are you issuing a call for action? Formulate a topic sentence or thesis statement that makes the goal clear. Then consider your persuasive strategy: Should you state the point at the beginning or end of the argument? Decide what kind of supporting information you might include: Should you rely on personal experience, facts and figures, or a combination of the two? Should you back up your claims with examples, comparisons, contrasts, definitions, classifications, and/or short narratives? If necessary, do some research to find facts, figures, and different points of view (indeed, that research might broaden your understanding, modify your ideas—or even change them).

Finally, write and revise your argument.

14 Summarizing and Responding

Summaries and responses play an important role in college writing. In essay examinations and papers, you demonstrate your understanding of material you have read by briefly summarizing its main ideas and explaining them in a condensed form. But you often go beyond merely summarizing the material; you also respond to it. You analyze it, compare or contrast it with other material you've studied, agree or disagree with its ideas, or expand on them further.

This chapter offers you advice on and practice with summarizing and responding by

■ examining a model summary

■ analyzing what makes a summary effective

■ taking you through the process of writing a summary

■ then repeating the process with a response

A Model of a Summary

Before you can respond to something that you read, you need to summarize it so your reader understands the ideas you're responding to or knows that you understand the ideas as well. If your summary of the material isn't accurate, your response may be inaccurate as well.

As Chapter 7 explains, a **summary** is a shorter version of a longer piece of information; it presents the main ideas or the most important information in a brief way. A summary is also objective: It reports what you have read—with no opinions or interpretations. Therefore, a summary should never include the personal pronouns *I* or *me*. You'll state your interpretations and opinions in the response, which follows the summary. Summaries are almost always written in the present tense.

A diagram of a typical summary might look like this:

```
┌─────────────────────────────────────────────────────────────┐
│  DIAGRAM │ For a Summary                                      │
├─────────────────────────────────────────────────────────────┤
│                                                               │
│  ┌─────────────────────────────────────────────────────────┐ │
│  │ Topic sentence: identification of author and title of     │
│  │ reading, and statement of topic or idea                   │
│  └─────────────────────────────────────────────────────────┘ │
│                              ↓                                │
│  ┌─────────────────────────────────────────────────────────┐ │
│  │ Body: supporting ideas, usually arranged in the sequence  │
│  │ of the original                                           │
│  │    Supporting idea 1, with some supporting information    │
│  │    Supporting idea 2, with some supporting information    │
│  │    Supporting idea 3, with some supporting information    │
│  └─────────────────────────────────────────────────────────┘ │
│                              ↓                                │
│  ┌─────────────────────────────────────────────────────────┐ │
│  │ Conclusion: restatement of main idea, or transition into  │
│  │ the response                                              │
│  └─────────────────────────────────────────────────────────┘ │
│                                                               │
└─────────────────────────────────────────────────────────────┘
```

The following is a summary of the student model essay in Chapter 12 (pages 107–108). Note that it identifies the source (author and title), includes only the main ideas of the original, and quotes a partial sentence from the original. It establishes a context for the response, which you will see later in this chapter.

What Is Courage?

* * * *

In "True Courage," Amra Skocic defines *courage* as "an unselfish gesture . . . which involves some risk." The gesture must also be voluntary and involve some personal sacrifice. She cites Oscar Schindler from the movie *Schindler's List* as an example. Schindler is a real factory owner who lives in Nazi Germany during World War II. Schindler acts unselfishly in employing Jewish workers in his factory and protecting them from harm. He voluntarily chooses to protect them and has nothing to gain personally from his action. Furthermore, Schindler risks his own life by protecting the Jews, for he knows that if the Nazis discover what he is doing, they will kill him. Therefore, Skocic argues, he fulfills all the criteria of the definition of courage.

Questions for Analysis

1. Look at the first sentence of the summary. What factual information does it include?
2. How many distinguishing characteristics does Amra list in her definition of courage? List them.
3. Compare the summary to the original. What supporting details are omitted?
4. Is the summary objective? Does it include any opinions or interpretations?

5. Look at the phrase quoted from the original source. How is it used in the summary? How is it punctuated? How does the writer show that he or she has left out some words from the original source?

6. Circle the verbs in the summary. What tense are they?

The Process of Writing a Summary

Choose one of the model paragraphs or student models from an earlier chapter in Unit II and summarize it. Your summary should be much shorter than the original.

Gathering the Materials

An accurate summary must be based on a clear understanding of the material it summarizes. Therefore, you must read the material carefully, and read it more than once. Here's how:

1. **Preview the Reading.** If you're summarizing a chapter of a book or a long article, you may locate main ideas in the headings within a chapter, in the topic sentences of paragraphs, and perhaps in stated summaries at the end of the chapter or article. For shorter readings, look at the opening paragraph, the first sentences of body paragraphs, and the conclusion. These will probably help you identify the controlling idea and the main and supporting points when you begin to read.

2. **Read the Selection Carefully.** Highlight or underline the main ideas and important supporting details. Go over the selection more than once until you're confident you understand it.

3. **Be Thinking about Your Response.** As you plan the summary, you'll probably consider ideas you want to include in your response. Make notes of those ideas.

Arranging the Materials

Now you can select the information to include in your summary. Here's how:

1. **Take Notes and Plan.** Look over the parts you've highlighted or underlined. Then write notes—in your own words—of the ideas you want to include.

2. **Organize Your Ideas Logically.** In most cases, this means following the organization of the original. Begin by outlining the main points in the order in which they're presented.

Here's an informal outline of the summary paragraph you read earlier in the chapter:

DEFINITION OF *COURAGE*

Unselfish

Involves some risk

Voluntary

Involves personal sacrifice

TIPS

For Beginning the Summary

Here are some phrases for introducing the main idea:

1. *In "Title," John Smith states (argues, believes, concludes)* (state the main idea)

2. *According to John Smith in "Title,"* (state the main idea)

3. *John Smith states in "Title" that* (state the main idea)

See Chapter 29 for advice on and practice with using quotations.

EXAMPLE FROM *SCHINDLER'S LIST*

Unselfish in employing Jewish workers in Nazi Germany

Protects them voluntarily

Risks losing his own life, a great personal sacrifice

Writing the First Draft

Now look over your notes and write the first draft. Begin your summary with a **topic sentence** that states the main idea. And, since your reader needs to know what you're summarizing, name the author and title of what you've read.

Write the summary in the present tense since you're explaining what the material *says* now—as you read it—not what the author wrote in the past. Don't copy sentences or parts of sentences from the original. **Paraphrase** the material, using your own vocabulary and sentence structure. Don't imitate the sentence structure of the original, substituting synonyms for a few words. If you do, the summary will be awkward and perhaps ungrammatical, and it won't demonstrate to your reader that you truly understand the material.

It's OK to use short phrases from the original, but you must **quote** those phrases exactly and incorporate them within your paraphrase. Place the quoted material in **quotation marks.** If you leave out words from the original, you can use **ellipsis marks** [. . .] to show where they are omitted.

Revising the First Draft

You'll probably revise both your summary and response at the same time. But we'll focus on the revision of the summary first.

Reread the original material and compare it to the summary. Then use the following checklist as a guide in revising. Answer the questions on the list yourself or work with a classmate. If you answer *no* to any question, then revise the summary to correct the problem. First, make changes above the lines or write notes in the margin. Then rewrite.

REVISION CHECKLIST

		YES	NO
SUMMARY	• Does the summary begin with the author and title of the work you have read?	☐	☐
	• Does the topic sentence state the work's controlling idea?	☐	☐
	• Are all the main ideas of the original included in the summary?	☐	☐
	• Is the summary objective?	☐	☐
	• Is the summary brief and complete?	☐	☐
	• Does the summary avoid copying from the original?	☐	☐
	• If quotations are used, are they incorporated and punctuated correctly?	☐	☐

Take notes of these responses to guide your revision.

Further Revising and Editing

After waiting a few hours or days, return to the summary (and the response) and revise it again.

A Model of a Response

After completing the summary, you can write your response. Unlike a summary, response is **subjective:** It expresses your interpretations, opinions, and arguments.

You may, for example, evaluate how well the writer has achieved his or her goals. You may agree or disagree with one or more claims the writer makes. You may expand on the main ideas of the original reading, comparing it to other readings you've studied in the course. You may relate your own experiences to the material. And because these responses are subjective, you may use the personal pronouns *I* or *me.*

A diagram of a response might look like this:

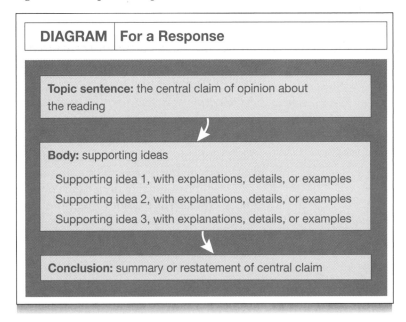

DIAGRAM	For a Response

Topic sentence: the central claim of opinion about the reading

Body: supporting ideas

Supporting idea 1, with explanations, details, or examples
Supporting idea 2, with explanations, details, or examples
Supporting idea 3, with explanations, details, or examples

Conclusion: summary or restatement of central claim

TIPS

For a Smooth Transition between a Summary and a Response
Restate the name of the author of the reading and the reading's main idea as part of your claim about it.

Here's the response that follows the summary of Amra Skocic's essay. Note how the first sentence establishes a transition from the summary and states the central claim of the response. Note that the second paragraph introduces a second, and contrasting, claim.

1   I agree with Amra Skocic's definition of *heroism* and with her selection of Oscar Schindler to illustrate the definition. His actions are especially heroic because of the circumstances in which he chooses to act. When a person risks his or her life to save the lives of others, we surely admire that person's heroism. We applaud the actions of firefighters, police, or ordinary citizens that involve risks to save lives. We call these actions heroic because they fit within our society's shared sense of morality. We know that these people have done the right thing.

2   But I think Schindler's heroism is different and more admirable than the heroism of firefighters and the police. He risks his life within a society that opposes and condemns his actions. The official policy of Nazi Germany is to murder Jews, not to save their lives. Therefore, anyone who tries to protect them is acting immorally and illegally. He is a traitor to his country. Yet Schindler acts according to his belief in a higher moral authority, one that rises above the accepted morality of his society. The example of Oscar Schindler therefore seems to argue for an expanded definition of *heroism.* There are perhaps two kinds of heroism: one that corresponds to the society's moral sense and laws, and a second—and greater—kind that corresponds to a higher form of morality and may directly violate the society's laws. This kind of heroism is rare, but is the kind we tend to admire the most. It is the heroism of Joan of Arc, Mahatma Gandhi, and Martin Luther King, Jr.

Questions for Analysis

1. What is the topic sentence of the first paragraph? Underline it.
2. The writer partially disagrees with Amra Skocic. Does he or she think that Skocic is incorrect? Explain.
3. The writer develops the response through a contrast. What two ideas is he or she contrasting?
4. What examples does the writer cite to support the two contrasting ideas?
5. What words or phrases demonstrate that the response is subjective? Circle them.
6. Circle the transitions. Notice how they tie sentences together.
7. Much of the unity of the paragraphs is achieved through repetition of words and sentence structure. Circle the repetition that most clearly establishes that unity.

✔ TIPS

For Labeling Responses

To help your reader distinguish between the author's ideas and your own, label each with introductions such as the following. Notice that your response may use the personal pronoun *I.*

Author: *According to John Smith . . .*

Smith also states that . . .

When Smith says, . . . he is . . .

When no author is mentioned: *According to [Title] . . .*

Yourself: *I agree with Smith because . . .*

I think that [Title] . . .

The Process of Writing a Response

Now write a response for the summary you wrote earlier in this chapter. It should be at least one paragraph.

Generating and Arranging the Material

Review the original reading—or the notes you've already made about possible responses as you were writing your summary. Consider a central claim to develop in your response, and write it in a preliminary topic sentence. List any supporting ideas or examples. Then develop an organizational plan. An outline might help you get control over your ideas. You'll probably want to use **climax order,** moving toward your most important idea.

Writing the Response

Now draft a response, beginning with a transition from the summary and a statement of your central claim. Refer to the original in your response. Remember that you're talking about the material you read, not telling your own story!

Here's the beginning of another response to Amra Skocic's essay. Notice its transition from the summary and statement of its claim, which leads immediately into an explanation and a comparison. The writer can then develop and illustrate the comparison.

> Amra Skocic defines courageous action well, but this definition doesn't have to be limited to actions involving physical risk. A courageous action can also involve risks to a person's reputation or standing in the community. Both involve potential harm to oneself while benefiting others.

A complete diagram of the summary and response might look like this:

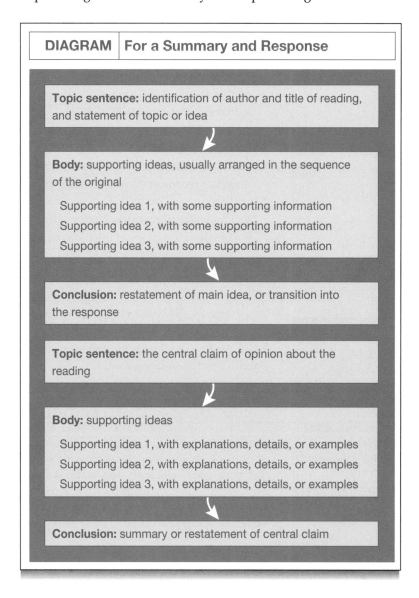

DIAGRAM | **For a Summary and Response**

Topic sentence: identification of author and title of reading, and statement of topic or idea

Body: supporting ideas, usually arranged in the sequence of the original

  Supporting idea 1, with some supporting information
  Supporting idea 2, with some supporting information
  Supporting idea 3, with some supporting information

Conclusion: restatement of main idea, or transition into the response

Topic sentence: the central claim of opinion about the reading

Body: supporting ideas

  Supporting idea 1, with explanations, details, or examples
  Supporting idea 2, with explanations, details, or examples
  Supporting idea 3, with explanations, details, or examples

Conclusion: summary or restatement of central claim

Revising the Response

Now revise the response, using the following checklist as a guide. Answer the items on the list yourself or work with a classmate. If you answer *no* to any question, then revise your draft to correct the problem. First, make changes above the lines or write notes in the margin. Then rewrite.

REVISION CHECKLIST   YES   NO

RESPONSE

- Does the response begin with a clear transition from the summary and statement of claim?   ☐   ☐
- Is the claim well supported with explanations, details, and examples?   ☐   ☐
- Is the organization logical? Are ideas presented in climax order?   ☐   ☐
- Are the transitions from one idea to another clear?   ☐   ☐
- Does the response end by summarizing or tying its ideas together?   ☐   ☐

Take notes of these answers to guide your revision.

Further Revising and Editing

After waiting a few hours or days, return to the summary and response to revise them again. Make sure they tie together.

Additional Writing Assignment: Respond to a Text

Summarize and respond to one of the additional readings at the end of this book.

CONSIDER YOUR WRITING PURPOSE AND AUDIENCE.

Use different modes of writing, depending on your goal.

- Narration
- Description: a scene, a place
- Process analysis
- Cause and effect analysis
- Report

- Classification
- Comparison and contrast
- Definition
- Persuasive argument
- Summary and response

What to include in introductions:
(see pages 38–39)

- Attention-getting opening
- Overview or preview
- Topic sentence (or thesis statement)

What to include in conclusions:
(see pages 38–39)

- General summary or impression
- Call for action
- Climax of action: surprise, revelation, reflection
- Interpretation or evaluation

STRUCTURE THE BODY OF YOUR WRITING EFFECTIVELY!

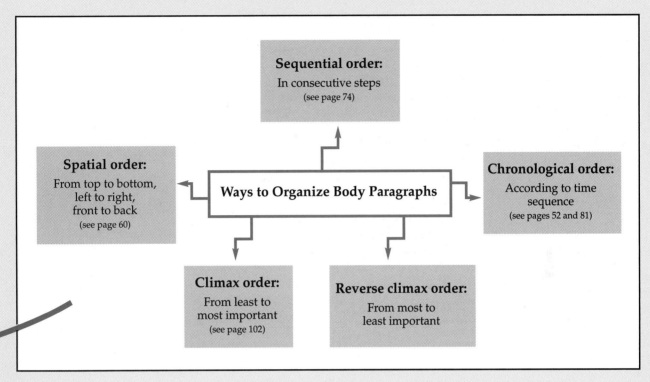

Sequential order:
In consecutive steps
(see page 74)

Spatial order:
From top to bottom,
left to right,
front to back
(see page 60)

Ways to Organize Body Paragraphs

Chronological order:
According to time
sequence
(see pages 52 and 81)

Climax order:
From least to
most important
(see page 102)

Reverse climax order:
From most to
least important

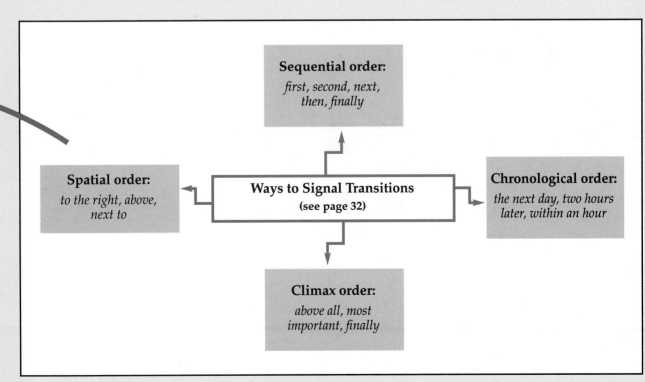

Sequential order:
*first, second, next,
then, finally*

Spatial order:
*to the right, above,
next to*

Ways to Signal Transitions
(see page 32)

Chronological order:
*the next day, two hours
later, within an hour*

Climax order:
*above all, most
important, finally*

III

Gateways to Grammar and Structure

The chapters in Units I and II have taken you through the writing process and through ways of structuring your writing for a variety of purposes and audiences. Unit IV, which follows this unit, takes you through the editing stage of the process. But perhaps you haven't yet developed a complete understanding of the basic grammatical terms and sentence structures. The three chapters in Unit III should help.

Chapter 15 explains the parts of speech, what they mean, and how they work in sentences. Chapter 16 explains and illustrates the basic sentence patterns and how they express meaning. And Chapter 17 looks closely at verbs in all their forms, tenses, and modes. All three chapters help you review or learn these concepts. Together they present basic information about the English language that constitutes a "gateway" not only to understanding English grammar—the focus of Unit III—but to expressing yourself clearly and to writing in English with confidence. ■

15 Identifying Sentence Elements

As you study the chapters in this unit and the next, you may need to become more familiar with some grammatical terms. This chapter will explain and illustrate those terms. You will learn to

- identify sentence elements
- recognize the parts of speech that make up sentences
- examine how the parts of speech function in English

The Basic Sentence Elements

We'll begin by examining the things that make up sentences: the subject and the predicate, clauses, and phrases.

Subjects and Predicates

A **sentence** makes a complete statement or asks a question. It contains a subject and a predicate. The **subject,** which usually begins the sentence, is *who* or *what* the sentence discusses. The subject is a noun or pronoun. The **predicate** completes the statement or question. It begins with a **verb,** which tells what the subject *does* or *is.* You'll learn more about verbs later in the chapter.

Together, the subject and predicate are called a **clause.** In most clauses, the subject comes first and the predicate follows.

Subject + predicate (beginning with the verb) = clause

Here are a few examples:

Subject	Verb	Remainder of predicate
Maria	likes	her job.
I	am working	today.
They	want	to see the movie.
The boys	could have taken	the bus.

EXERCISE 1	Identifying Subjects and Predicates

Underline the subject of each sentence once and the predicate twice.

1. The United States had only thirteen states at its birth.

2. The Declaration of Independence announced that birth on July 4, 1776.

3. Thomas Jefferson was its primary author.

4. Fifty-six men signed the Declaration.

5. The document announced the separation of the United States from England.

6. That separation was not completed until the treaty ending the Revolutionary War in 1783.

Compound Subjects. A subject that consists of two or more nouns or pronouns is called a **compound subject.** Compound subjects are typically joined by *and:*

> Juan *and* I
>
> The men *and* the women
>
> You *and* your friend
>
> Maria, Bozena, *and* Ana

Compound Predicates. Similarly, a predicate can express more than one action about the subject. In this case, there can be two or more verbs, again typically joined by *and:*

> Juan sat down *and* relaxed for a while.
>
> Maria came to the United States in 1999, found a place to live, *and* then got a job.

Types of Clauses

Every sentence must have at least one clause, but a sentence can contain more than one clause. There are two types of clauses:

- An **independent clause** makes a complete statement and can be a sentence by itself.

> The weather is nice today.

Chapter 25 discusses coordinating conjunctions and semicolons in more detail.

When you join two independent clauses, you create a **compound sentence.** The clauses are joined by words such as *and, so,* or *but* (called coordinating conjunctions), or by a **semicolon** [;]. See the box on page 130 for some examples of compound sentences.

Independent clause	Coordinating conjunction	Independent clause
The weather is beautiful,	so	we're going to the beach.
The weather is beautiful now,	but	it might rain later.

Chapter 16 also discusses types of clauses and sentences.

- A **dependent clause** cannot be a sentence by itself and must be joined to an independent clause to complete its meaning. In other words, the dependent clause *depends* on the independent clause. This combination of dependent and independent clauses is called a **complex sentence.** Here are some examples:

Dependent clause	Independent clause
If the weather is nice today,	we will go to the beach.

Independent clause	Dependent clause
We see	that the weather is nice today.

Questions, Commands, and Exclamations

Not all clauses begin with a subject followed by the predicate. There are three important variations of this pattern.

- In a sentence that expresses a **command,** the subject (you) is omitted:

Affirmative:	Be careful.
Negative:	Don't touch that.

- In a **question,** which always ends with a **question mark** [?], the order of the subject and verb is reversed. Often, the verb is split:

Verb	Subject	Verb	Remainder of predicate
Are	you		happy?
Does	Marta	like	her job?
Are	you		working today?
Do	they	want	to see the movie?
Could	your friends	have taken	the bus?

A question can also begin with a **question word.** Here are some examples:

Question word	Verb	Subject	Verb	Remainder of predicate
Where	does	Marta	work?	
When	are	you	working?	
Why	do	they	want	to eat out?
Which bus	could	your friends	have taken?	

- An **exclamation** expresses a strong emotion or reaction. Often it is not a full sentence, so it may omit either the subject or verb. It ends with an **exclamation point** [!].

Wow!	Be careful!
No!	I'm angry!

Phrases

A **phrase** is simply a group of two or more words. It is not a complete thought. Many phrases function as parts of sentences, such as **verb phrases** (*am working, could have taken*) or **prepositional phrases** (*in the evening, across the street*). You'll learn about other types of phrases later in this chapter.

EXERCISE 2 | **Identifying Clauses and Phrases**

Label *C* for clause or *P* for phrase.

_____ *P* **1.** The first president of the United States.

_____ **2.** Who is the current president of the United States?

_____ **3.** There is a presidential election every four years.

_____ **4.** Congress has two parts: the Senate and the House of Representatives.

_____ **5.** Senators serve for six years.

_____ **6.** With one-third of the Senate elected every two years.

_____ **7.** One hundred Senators, two from each state.

_____ **8.** There are 435 members of the House of Representatives.

_____ **9.** Elected every two years.

The Parts of Speech

There are eight **parts of speech,** which make up clauses, phrases, and sentences. We'll look at all eight, beginning with the two most important: nouns and verbs.

Nouns

Nouns name people, places, things, ideas, or actions.

Common and Proper Nouns. Nouns are either

- **proper nouns,** which name specific people, places, things, ideas, or actions and are capitalized
- **common nouns,** which do not name specific people, places, things, ideas, or actions and are not capitalized

TIPS

For Recognizing Some Noun Endings

Nouns can have many endings, but common nouns that name ideas, concepts, or actions typically have these endings:

-tion	election, education, reaction
-ion	fashion, conversion, pension
-ment	government, comment, agreement
-ty	liberty, unity, beauty, ability
-ness	happiness, sadness, hardness
-ance	romance, elegance, appearance
-ence	difference, silence, intelligence
-hood	neighborhood, childhood, motherhood
-ism	socialism, racism, Buddhism

Proper nouns

John Smith, December, Empire State Building, Vietnam, Nigeria, Mexico City

Common nouns

man, month, building, country, city

Singular and Plural Nouns. Most nouns form plurals by adding *-s*. Nouns that end in *-s*, *-ss*, *-x*, *-ch*, *-sh*, or *-z* form the plural by adding *-es*.

Singular	Plural
cat	cats
accountant	accountants
dish	dishes

But some nouns change in other ways. They are **irregular.** Here are some examples:

Singular	Plural
child	children
man	men
mouse	mice
medium	media
foot	feet
criterion	criteria

Some other nouns, especially those that name animals, have identical singular and plural forms, such as these:

Singular	Plural
deer	deer
fish	fish (or fishes)
moose	moose

Count and Noncount Nouns. Some nouns can be counted, and some cannot.

Chapter 18 discusses noun plurals. Chapter 22 discusses count and noncount nouns.

- A **count noun,** as its name suggests, can be counted. You can put a number before it (for example: *one* person, *three* trees). Therefore, it can be **singular** (representing one) or **plural** (representing more than one).
- A **noncount noun** cannot be counted; it can only be singular:

luggage, traffic, furniture, water, air, stuff, coffee, butter, courage, happiness, rain, soccer, grass

Many noncount nouns represent liquids (*water, coffee*), gases (*air, hydrogen*), abstract concepts (*love, courage*), or groups of things (*furniture, homework*).

| EXERCISE 3 | Making Nouns Plural |

Change the singular nouns to plurals. Use a dictionary if you don't know the plural forms.

1. woman _____*women*_____

2. goose _____

3. crash _____

4. window _____

5. tooth _____

6. person _____

7. box _____

8. monkey _____

9. cup _____

10. princess _____

11. nose _____

| EXERCISE 4 | Recognizing Count and Noncount Nouns |

Decide which nouns are count nouns and which are noncount. For the count nouns, write the plural form.

1. chair _____*chairs*_____

2. church _____

3. dollar _____

4. cash _____

5. milk _____

6. liter _____

7. honesty _____

8. ox _____

9. louse _____

10. clothes _____

11. thing _____

EXERCISE 5	Writing Singular and Plural Nouns

Think of five count nouns and write the singular and plural forms. Then think of five noncount nouns and write them.

Singular count noun   **Plural form**

1. _____*rug*_____   _____*rugs*_____

2. _____   _____

3. _____   _____

4. _____   _____

5. _____   _____

6. _____   _____

Noncount noun

1. _____*sleep*_____

2. _____

3. _____

4. _____

5. _____

6. _____

Possessive Nouns. To make a noun possessive, add 's to a singular noun, a noncount noun, or a plural noun that does not end in -s:

Singular or plural without -s ending		
Juan's brother	the dog's tail	my friend's bicycle
the children's room	Mr. Meyers's book	

But plural nouns that end in -s merely take an apostrophe:

Plural with -s ending	
the boys' father	the Wilsons' house

Inanimate objects usually do not take the possessive form with 's.

the girl's hands	BUT	the hands of the clock

EXERCISE 6	Making Nouns Possessive

Form the possessive for each noun by adding an apostrophe or an apostrophe + *s*.

1. Mr. Kim __'s__ brother

2. the girls___ soccer team

3. the bird___ color

4. the Smiths___ house

5. John Keats___ poems

6. Mr. Gonzalez___ brother

EXERCISE 7	Writing Possessive Nouns

Write five phrases using possessive nouns. At least one of them should include a plural possessive form.

1. _____*the horse's back*_____

2. _____

3. _____

4. _____

5. _____

6. _____

The Function of Nouns. Nouns can be the subjects of sentences. Nouns can also be objects, receiving the action the subject performs. Word order—the location of the noun in a sentence—determines its function. In fact, word order is the most important principle of English grammar.

• As a **subject,** the noun generally comes *before* the verb, which begins the statement (or **predicate**) about the subject. The subject performs (or in some cases receives) the action of the verb:

subject	subject
The cat was sleeping.	Mr. Smith was hired as an accountant.

Or the subject can be described by the words following the verb:

subject	subject
The cat looks peaceful.	Mr. Smith is an excellent accountant.

• As an **object,** a noun almost always comes *after* a verb. If the noun receives the action the subject performs, it is a **direct object.**

subject	direct object
The cat ate	the mouse.

If the noun is the person or thing for whom the subject performs the action, it is an **indirect object.**

subject	indirect object	direct object
Mr. Smith gave	John	an accounting book.

Notice that the indirect object can go in two places—(1) before or (2) after the direct object and a preposition (*to, for*).

Subject	Verb	Indirect object	Direct object
Guillermo	loaned	me	his car.
Gladys	made	her children	dinner.

Subject	Verb	Direct object	Indirect object
Guillermo	loaned	his car	to me.
Gladys	made	dinner	for her children.

A noun as an object can also follow a word formed from a verb (a **present participle** or an **infinitive**) or a **preposition,** which usually shows the location of the noun in space or time.

Object of verb	Object of participle	Object of infinitive	Object of preposition
I bought *a car.*	buying *a car*	to buy *a car*	in *the car*

EXERCISE 8 | Identifying Nouns

Underline each noun in the following sentences. Write *S* above each subject and *O* above each object.

1. Many people know about George Washington.

2. He led the Continental Army in the War for Independence.

3. Washington was the first president of the United States.

4. As a boy, young George supposedly promised never to tell a lie.

5. Washington served as a very wise leader of troops and of his nation.

6. However, George Washington had weaknesses like all men.

| EXERCISE 9 | Placing Objects |

Using the groups of words, write sentences that place subjects, direct objects, and indirect objects in the right order. For each sentence, write a second version in which the indirect object appears as the object of a preposition.

1. Juan/mother/flowers/gives *Juan gives his mother flowers. Juan gives flowers to his mother.*

2. I/police officer/my driver's license/handed _____

_____

3. Nicole/her children/bananas/for breakfast/feeds _____

_____

4. Carmen/me/the letter/showed _____

_____

5. Lucy/her parents/dinner/cooked _____

_____

6. George Washington/his father/a lie/never told _____

_____

Verbs

The **verb** begins the statement—or **predicate**—about the subject. A verb

- says what the subject *does* or *is*
- usually follows the subject
- may contain more than one word
- usually has a tense, indicating if the time is in the past, present, or future
- changes form to **agree** with the subject in some tenses

Tense. Verb forms change according to their **tense:** the time of the action indicated by the verb. These times typically refer to the past, present, or future. Here are some examples:

Subject	Verb	Remainder of predicate	
Juan	knows	the answer.	(present)
Natasha	graduated.		(past)
I	will go	to the store	(future)

Agreement. In some tenses (mainly those that refer to the present) verbs change forms to **agree** with their subjects. Typically, these verbs add *-s* or *-es* when their subjects are third person singular, such as *he, she,* or *it.*

First person	Third person singular
I want	he wants
we dance	she dances

However, a few verbs (including the verb *to be*) have irregular forms for agreement:

IRREGULAR VERBS			
First person	Third person singular	Third person plural	
I do	he does	they do	
I go	he goes	they go	(present)
I am	he is	they are	
I was	she was	they were	(past)

Chapters 17–19 discuss changes in verb forms in greater detail.

The irregular verbs *be, do,* and *have* also serve as helping or linking verbs in other verb tenses, which are discussed on pp. 193–196.

EXERCISE 10	Identifying Verbs

Underline the verbs in each sentence.

1. George Washington <u>was</u> a complex man.
2. Sometimes he acted in a warm and friendly way.
3. Other times, he seemed stubborn and unfriendly.
4. These were not bad qualities, however.
5. As a general, he fought and won some important battles during the worst days of the Revolutionary War.
6. As president, he often argued with the members of Congress.
7. Through it all, he had personal problems.
8. Most of those problems came from his troubled relationship with his mother.
9. Though the "Father of His Country," Washington never had any children of his own.

EXERCISE 11	Writing Verbs

Write five sentences. Circle the subject and underline the verb in each.

1. (America's capital) <u>is named</u> for George Washington. _____
2. _____
3. _____
4. _____
5. _____
6. _____

Main Verbs and Helping Verbs. Every predicate contains at least one verb. But a verb can contain two, three, or even four words, which form a **verb phrase.**

- The last word of a verb phrase is the **main verb.** It expresses the basic action or meaning.

- The words that precede it are called **helping verbs.** They help the verb express the meaning, the time of the action, and other circumstances about the action.

Helping verb(s)	+	Main verb	=	Verb phrase
is		going		is going
has		gone		has gone
didn't		go		didn't go
can		go		can go
will be		going		will be going
should have		gone		should have gone
might have been		going		might have been going

Chapters 17–20 further discuss verbs, helping verbs, and modals.

Modal Verbs. Some helping verbs do not change forms. Called **modal verbs,** they express an attitude about ability, possibility, obligation, doubt, or advice. Here's a partial list of modal verbs:

can, could, will, would, shall, should, may, might, must, ought to, had better

Here are a few examples of how modal verbs are used:

Ability:	He can use a computer.
Possibility:	He might have used a computer.
Obligation:	I must use a computer.
Doubt:	My grandfather can't be using a computer!
Advice:	He should use a computer.

EXERCISE 12 | Identifying Kinds of Verbs

Underline all the verbs in each sentence, and label them *HV* (helping verb) or *MV* (main verb).

1. Many of the false legends about Washington *have come* (HV MV) from Mason Locke Weems, the author of *The Life of George Washington.*

2. Historians have judged the biography as largely inaccurate.

3. However, this book would become the source for many later biographies soon after its publication.

4. For example, the "cherry tree story" from the book has been told over and over.

5. According to the story, young Washington had been given a new hatchet and then practiced with it on a cherry tree.

6. After his father had discovered him with the hatchet, the future president confessed: "I cannot tell a lie. I have chopped down the cherry tree."

7. The lesson of the story is simple: All of us should be as honest as George

Washington, the father of our country.

8. Unfortunately, the writer of the story should have been more honest; Weems simply

invented the story.

9. The real moral of the story should be that historians must not make up facts.

EXERCISE 13	Writing Verb Phrases

Write five sentences, each with a helping verb and a main verb.

1. *George Washington has become a legend.* _____

2. _____

3. _____

4. _____

5. _____

6. _____

Transitive and Intransitive Verbs. Verbs can be transitive or intransitive, depending on whether they take a direct object.

- A **transitive verb** usually expresses an action and almost always takes a **direct object** (usually a noun or a pronoun), which receives the action the subject performs and completes its meaning.

Subject	Transitive verb	Direct object
I	ate	dinner.
The dog	has lost	its collar.

Almost all action verbs are transitive: *see, hear, do, make, take, give, cut,* and so on. Transitive verbs that express ideas of transferring something (*give, hand, send, tell,* and so on) or preparing something for someone (*make, create, cook,* and so on) take two objects: a direct and an **indirect object,** which is the person or thing to whom or for whom the action was done.

Subject	Transitive verb	Indirect object	Direct object
Lydia	gives	the children	English lessons.

- An **intransitive verb** cannot take a direct object. Many intransitive verbs express motion: *go, travel, run,* and *fly.* Some intransitive verbs express other types of action: *lie, die,* and *fall.* As shown on page 142, intransitive verbs are often followed by a preposition and its object:

Subject	Verb	Preposition plus object
We	are flying.	
They	drove	to New York.
I	arrived	at work early.
The dog	is sleeping.	

Linking Verbs. A few verbs—called **linking verbs**—do not express an action. They simply say the subject *is* or *was* something. In other words, they give information about the subject that is perceived through the five senses (*sight, sound, touch, smell,* and *taste*). The information is called the **subject complement.** It can be an adjective that describes the subject or a noun that renames it. Here are examples:

Subject	Verb	Subject complement
Henri	is	charming and smart. (adjectives)
Horses	are	terrible house pets. (adjectives and noun)
She	feels / sounds / looks	sick. (adjective)
The chicken	tastes / smells	delicious. (adjective)
Flavia	is	an excellent student. (adjective and noun)

EXERCISE 14　　Identifying Types of Verbs

Underline each verb in the following sentences and label it **T** for **transitive,** **I** for **intransitive,** or **L** for **linking.**

1. George Washington's parents <u>were</u> *L* Augustus and Mary Ball Washington.

2. Young Washington grew up on a farm near Fredericksburg, Virginia.

3. Augustus Washington died when George was very young.

4. After his father died, George would always quarrel with his mother.

5. When he was a teenager, George went to the home of his half-brother, Lawrence.

6. He accompanied Lawrence to Barbados in the West Indies on a business trip.

7. In Barbados, he caught smallpox; as a result, his face looked scarred for the rest of his life.

EXERCISE 15 | **Writing Types of Verbs**

Write five of your own subject + verb combinations. Then label each of the verbs *T* for transitive, *I* for intransitive, or *L* for linking.

1. *After the presidency, Washington retired to his Mount Vernon estate.* [*I*]

2. _____

3. _____

4. _____

5. _____

6. _____

Pronouns

A **pronoun** replaces a noun and functions in the same way a noun does. Therefore, it can be a subject, an object, or a possessive word. The pronoun often refers back to an **antecedent,** a word or phrase that came earlier.

There are seven types of pronouns.

Personal Pronouns. These replace the name of something or someone. They are the only parts of speech that change forms according to function and location:

TIPS

For Remembering Pronouns and Antecedents

Pro means "for," so a pronoun stands in *for* a noun.

Ante means "before," so an antecedent refers to a word that comes earlier.

	Subject pronouns		Object pronouns	
	Singular	Plural	Singular	Plural
First person:	I	we	me	us
Second person:	you	you	you	you
Third person:	he, she, it	they	him, her, it	them

EXAMPLES:

Mark gave *the books* to *Sylvia.*   *Sylvia* got *the books* from *Mark.*

He   gave *them*   to *her.*   *She*   got *them*   from *him.*

Possessive Pronouns. These show ownership or possession. They can function as adjectives before nouns or stand alone to replace nouns:

Possessive pronouns before nouns			
	Singular	Plural	Noun
First person:	my	our	
Second person:	your	your	house
Third person:	his, her, its	their	

EXAMPLE: The house belongs to us. It is *our* house.

Possessive pronouns replacing the noun

	Singular	Plural
First person:	mine	ours
Second person:	yours	yours
Third person:	his, hers, its	theirs

EXAMPLES: Your car is new. My car is old. *Yours* is new, but *mine* is old.

Demonstrative Pronouns. These pronouns identify or refer to a noun:

Singular	Plural
this	these
that	those

EXAMPLE: I want *this* book, but I don't need *those*.

Interrogative Pronouns. These pronouns begin a question:

who, whom, whose, which, what

EXAMPLES: *Who* is the oldest person in the class? *Which* book did you read?

Relative Pronouns. These pronouns relate information back to a noun or pronoun:

who, whom, whose, which, that

EXAMPLE: Annamarie, *who* is from Romania, came here three years ago.

Chapter 21 discusses pronouns further, and Chapters 27 and 28 discuss relative pronouns.

Indefinite Pronouns. These pronouns refer to a category of people or things. They do not refer to a specific person or thing:

Singular

anyone, anybody, no one, nobody, anything, nothing, everyone, everybody, someone, somebody, something, nothing, either, neither, none, another

Plural

all, both, some, a few, many

EXAMPLES: Did *anyone* lose a pen? *Somebody* found one in the classroom.

Reflexive Pronouns. These pronouns repeat the subject as an object (or repeat a noun or pronoun for emphasis):

	Singular	Plural
First person:	myself	ourselves
Second person:	yourself	yourselves
Third person:	himself, herself, itself	themselves

EXAMPLES:

I looked at *myself* in the mirror.

You both can help *yourselves* to some food.

My friend likes big cars, but I, *myself*, prefer smaller ones.

| **EXERCISE 16** | Identifying Types of Pronouns |

Underline each pronoun in the following sentences and label it *PS* for personal subject, *PO* for personal object, *POS* for possessive, *D* for demonstrative, *I* for interrogative, *R* for relative, *ID* for indefinite, or *REF* for reflexive.

I

1. Who was the real George Washington?

2. Physically, he stood six feet tall and weighed a little over 200 pounds.

3. His bones and hands were big.

4. He carried himself with great dignity.

5. He wore a powdered wig, and that wig concealed his reddish-brown hair.

6. His blue eyes were something that everyone noticed about him.

7. According to legend, he never smiled because he had ugly, wooden false teeth.

8. However, Washington was usually a very friendly man who loved attention.

9. He did have false teeth, but they were made from ivory.

| **EXERCISE 17** | Writing Types of Pronouns |

Write eight sentences. Use a different type of pronoun in each. Then label each one *PS* for personal subject, *PO* for personal object, *POS* for possessive, *D* for demonstrative, *I* for interrogative, *R* for relative, *ID* for indefinite, or *REF* for reflexive.

POS

1. *Washington visited his mother in Fredericksburg.*

2. _____

3. _____

4. _____

5. _____

6. _____

7. _____

8. _____

9. _____

Adjectives

An **adjective** modifies (or describes) a noun or pronoun. Adjectives normally appear before the noun they modify, but in sentences with linking verbs they come after the verb. They answer the questions *What kind? Which one?* or *How many?*

> He has a *big* car. (what kind?)   His car is *big*. (what kind?)
>
> The *big* car is his. (which one?)
>
> There are *eight* cars in the parking lot. (how many?)

Occasionally, a noun can function as an adjective before another noun, answering the question *What kind?*

> a *shoe* store   a *geometry* book   a *city* law

Pronouns can be adjectives as well.

> *some* books   *my* book   *another* book

Chapter 24 discusses *-ing* words further, and Chapter 19 discusses past participles.

Verbs can function as adjectives when they take present participle or past participle endings.

> an *interesting* book   a *used* book   a *stolen* book

EXERCISE 18	**Identifying Types of Adjectives**

Underline each adjective in the following sentences and label it *A* for adjective, *NA* for noun functioning as adjective, or *VA* for adjective formed from a verb.

                               VA

1. Washington was a <u>charming</u> man.

2. His great strength and confidence made him a natural leader.

3. His appealing personality attracted women, who loved to dance with him at social events.

4. He loved fox hunting, card playing, and fishing.

5. Although he was a tobacco farmer, he did not smoke.

6. He was calm in the most difficult circumstances.

7. But his unpredictable temper would frighten his political enemies.

EXERCISE 19 | Writing Types of Adjectives

Write four adjective and noun combinations. Use at least one of each type of adjective you identified in Exercise 18.

1. *a sailing ship* _____

2. _____

3. _____

4. _____

5. _____

Articles

The three **articles** (*the, a,* and *an*) are adjectives that determine whether a noun is general or specific.

- *The* is called a **definite article** because it indicates that a noun is specific.
- *A* and *an* are called **indefinite articles** because they indicate that a noun is not specific.
  1. *A* precedes words beginning with a consonant sound.
  2. *An* precedes words beginning with a vowel sound.

Chapter 22 discusses articles more fully.

---

a book (any book)   *an* author (any author)

the book for my geometry class (a specific book)

EXERCISE 20 | Identifying Articles

Underline each article in the following sentences and label it *I* for indefinite or *D* for definite.

    D   *D*
1. <u>The</u> original date of Washington's birth was February 11, 1732, but <u>the</u>

                                                                          I
    date later changed to February 22, when <u>a</u> new calendar was adopted.

2. As an adult, he was a tobacco farmer and slave owner.

3. He was not poor as a child, and he became a very wealthy man.

4. His wife, Martha, was a widow who was a year older than he was.

5. Martha had two children, a boy and a girl.

6. Washington served in the Virginia militia, in the Continental Army, as president of the Constitutional Convention, and then as the first president of the United States.

| EXERCISE 21 | Writing Types of Articles |

Write four sentences that include at least one article. Label each article either **D** for definite or **I** for indefinite.

                                    I   *D*

1. *Washington has been a hero to Americans from Colonial times to the present.*

2. _____

3. _____

4. _____

5. _____

Adverbs

Adverbs modify (or describe) verbs, answering the questions *When? Where? How? How often?*

I got up *early*. (when?)	He speaks English *well*. (how?)
I slept *downstairs*. (where?)	He *usually* speaks Italian. (how often?)

Adverbs can also modify other adverbs, adjectives, and words formed from verbs.

very well (adverb)	*really* good (adjective)	
well dressed	*early* rising	*fast* moving

Many adjectives become adverbs by adding *-ly:*

quick	➡ quickly	careful	➡ carefully

Chapter 23 discusses adverbs more fully.

Some adverbs do not end in *-ly*. Here's a partial list:

For frequency or time: *once, sometimes, always, often, never, now, then, today, yesterday, tomorrow*

For distance or location: *far, near, close, here, there, inside, outside*

For addition: *also, too*

For intensity: *very, well*

EXERCISE 22	Identifying Adverbs

Underline each adverb in the following sentences.

1. <u>Unfortunately</u>, Washington's older brother Lawrence died when George was just twenty years old.

2. George then inherited his famous house, Mount Vernon, from his brother's estate.

3. When Washington was only twenty-one, he trained men for the Virginia militia and bravely fought in the French and Indian War.

4. However, his mother desperately wanted him to stay at home and take care of her.

5. Washington finally returned to Mount Vernon and quickly married a wealthy widow named Martha Dandridge Custis in 1759.

6. He later acquired large amounts of land on which he raised tobacco and racehorses.

7. As a delegate to the Continental Congress, he eagerly supported going to war against Britain.

8. When the Revolutionary War began, Washington was soon given command of the Continental Army.

Conjunctions

A **conjunction** joins one thing with another. There are two types of conjunctions: coordinating conjunctions and subordinating conjunctions.

Coordinating Conjunctions. A coordinating conjunction is a word that joins grammatically equal structures.

Juan *and* I (subjects)	smiling *and* laughing (*-ing* words)
slipped *and* fell (past tense verbs)	large *and* heavy (adjectives)
I arrived early, *but* my friend was very late. (two clauses)	

Chapters 25, 28, and 29 discuss coordinating conjunctions more fully.

There are seven coordinating conjunctions, which you can remember through the expression FAN BOYS, representing the first letter of each conjunction:

For	But
And	Or
Nor	Yet
	So

Here are sentences with two clauses, each joined by a coordinating conjunction:

He was sad, *for* he had lost his favorite pen. (Here, *for* has the meaning "because.")

The pen was expensive, *and* it was very comfortable to use.

He couldn't find it in his book bag, *nor* could he find it at home.

Someone offered to lend him a pen, *but* he didn't want it.

Perhaps he didn't like that pen, *or* the ink was the wrong color.

A new pen would be expensive, *yet* he didn't care.

He wanted the new pen, *so* he bought it.

Subordinating Conjunctions. A **subordinating conjunction** is a word (or words) that joins a dependent clause to an independent clause. The two clauses together form a complete sentence. Here's a partial list of subordinating conjunctions:

Time: *when, while, as, before, after, until, as soon as*
Cause: *because, since*
Condition: *if, unless*

Chapter 26 discusses dependent clauses and subordinating conjunctions more fully.

Here are two examples of sentences with subordinating conjunctions introducing the dependent clauses:

Dependent clause	Independent clause
When our dog is angry,	he barks loudly.

Independent clause	Dependent clause
I did not attend class	*because* I was sick.

EXERCISE 23 | Identifying Types of Conjunctions

Underline each conjunction in the following sentences and label it **C** for coordinating or **S** for subordinating.

1. Washington lost most of his early battles in the war, *C* <u>and</u> he was lucky that most of his men weren't killed.

2. Many of his soldiers deserted the army in 1778 because the winter was so cold.

3. He knew he had to encourage his men, so he fought only in small battles when they were sure to win.

4. After the French joined in the fight against Britain, the course of the war changed in favor of the American colonies.

5. When Washington's 15,000 American and French soldiers defeated the British at Yorktown, Virginia, the British general, Lord Cornwallis, finally surrendered.

EXERCISE 24 | Writing Types of Conjunctions

Write five of your own sentences joined by conjunctions. Then label each conjunction either **C** for coordinating or **S** for subordinating.

1. *Washington's victories at the small battles at Trenton and Princeton*
   $\quad\quad\quad\quad\quad\quad\quad\quad\quad\quad$ *S*
   were important because they boosted his men's morale.

2. _____

   _____

3. _____

   _____

4. _____

   _____

5. _____

   _____

6. _____

   _____

Prepositions

A **preposition** is followed by an object (usually a noun or object pronoun) and indicates the position of the subject in space or time. The preposition and its object form a **prepositional phrase.** Prepositional phrases function either as adjectives or adverbs.

- As adjectives, they generally follow a noun or pronoun:

Noun	Prepositional phrase	Pronoun	Prepositional phrase
the man	*from Thailand* (position in space)	those	*in the window*
the meeting	*in January* (position in time)		

- As adverbs, they often begin sentences or follow the verb:

adverb
prepositional phrase
On July 4, 1776, (time) the Declaration of Independence was signed.

adverb
prepositional phrase
I saw an accident *in front of my house.* (space)

- Some prepositions express other meanings, such as possession:

the top *of* the box
the name *of* the teacher

Here's a partial list of prepositions:

See Chapter 22 and
Appendix C for more
on prepositions.

about	after	before	by		from	like	off	over	toward	up
above	around	below	during	in		near	on	through	under	with
across	at	beneath	for		into	of	out	to	until	without

EXERCISE 25 | Identifying Prepositions

Underline each prepositional phrase and circle the preposition in the following sentences.

1. Washington was always practical (in) business matters, and his practicality became obvious (after) the war.

2. He had not accepted a salary as commander of the army but said that he would simply work for expenses.

3. With the end of the war, he submitted bills for $400,000 worth of expenses.

4. Although Washington eventually was paid, many of his soldiers were not.

5. In 1783, the underpaid officers met with Washington in New York and angrily demanded money.

6. In an emotional speech that brought tears to some officers' eyes, Washington promised them that they would be paid.

7. A week later, Congress gave the officers money that equaled five years' worth of pay.

EXERCISE 26 | Writing Prepositions

Write five of your own sentences, each with at least one preposition. Circle the preposition.

1. *Washington was admired (by) officers and (by) common soldiers who were glad to be (in) his command.*

2. _____

   _____

3. _____

   _____

4. _____

_____

5. _____

_____

6. _____

_____

Other Important Grammatical Forms

Verbs can take different forms and function as other parts of speech: as nouns, adjectives, or adverbs. These grammatical forms are important to recognize.

Infinitives

An **infinitive** combines the word _to_ and the base form of a verb:

to go	to have	to see	to be

Like nouns, infinitives can function as subjects or objects:

> subject
> *To fly from Asia to the United States* takes a long time.
>
> object
> He wants *to major in computer science.*

Participles

Participles, which are formed from verbs, can function as other parts of speech. There are two types of participles: **present participles** (which end in *-ing*) and **past participles** (which end in *-ed* for regular verbs and have other forms for irregular verbs).

Present Participles. Present participles can function as nouns. When they do so, they are called **gerunds:**

> gerund subject
> *Walking every day* is good for your health.
>
> gerund object
> I enjoy *walking in the evening.*

Present participles can also function as adjectives, which can precede or follow the noun they modify:

| a *walking* trip   the man *walking by the shore* |

Past Participles. Past participles can also function as adjectives:

| a *well-known* singer   a singer *admired by many people* |

See Chapters 17 and 19 for more on present participles and past participles.

In general, present participles show a continuing action that the noun performs. Past participles show a completed action that the noun receives:

| *boiling* eggs (they are cooking)   *boiled* eggs (they may even be cold) |

EXERCISE 27 | Identifying Infinitives, Present Participles, and Past Participles

Underline and label each infinitive with *I,* present participle with *P,* and past participle with *PP* in the sentences that follow.

1. Although <u>admired</u> by a whole nation, President Washington had many problems.

2. His mentally disturbed mother was always angry with him.

3. She did not attend his wedding and never came to his house to visit.

4. In spite of her wealth, she constantly asked her son to give her money.

5. Once she even wrote a letter to the Virginia Assembly, complaining that George would not give her enough money to live on and accusing him of neglecting her.

6. When approaching his sixty-eighth birthday, Washington became ill with a virus.

7. He died, not from the virus, but at the hands of his doctors, who treated him by draining half of the blood from his body in less than twelve hours.

8. At the end, he pleaded with his doctors to let him go quickly.

EXERCISE 28 | Writing Infinitives, Present Participles, and Past Participles

Write one sentence with an infinitive (*I*), one with a present participle (*P*), and one with a past participle (*PP*).

1. *Washington was a beloved leader.* _____

2. _____

3. _____

4. _____

16 Recognizing Sentence Patterns

Word order is the most important principle of English grammar, so sentences follow consistent patterns. This chapter will familiarize you with those patterns so that you'll be able to

- recognize the patterns used most often
- recognize other important but less commonly used patterns
- recognize patterns in which the subject acts, and patterns in which the subject is acted upon
- gain practice in writing correct sentences

The terms used in this chapter are all introduced and defined in Chapter 15.

What Is a Sentence?

A sentence makes a complete statement or asks a question.

Statements

All statements consist of two parts:

- the **subject,** the word or words the sentence makes a statement about
- the **predicate,** the word (or, in most cases, words) that make the statement about the subject

Questions

Questions reverse the order of the subject and the verb. Often the verb is split, with the helping verb preceding the subject and the remainder of the verb following the subject. Many questions begin with question words such as *who, where, what,* or *why.*

The Four Basic Sentence Patterns

Although you'll be looking at nine sentence patterns in this chapter, let's begin with the four that are used most frequently.

Pattern 1: Subject + Verb

In this first pattern, the subject is followed by an **intransitive verb,** which cannot take an object. Many intransitive verbs, however, are followed by a prepositional phrase or modified by adverbs:

Subject	Verb	Prepositional phrase	Adverb
Most people	work.		
Rafael	is walking	to the store.	
We	fly		often.

Question

Do your parents work?

Question beginning with question word

Why is Rafael walking to the store?

EXERCISE 1	Writing Sentences in Pattern 1

Write sentences using the verbs in parentheses. One of your sentences should be a question.

1. (went) *I went to the store.* _____

2. (fell) _____

3. (am talking) _____

4. (traveled) _____

5. (is lying) _____

6. (spoke) _____

Pattern 2: Subject + Verb + Direct Object

The second pattern includes a **transitive verb,** which almost always takes a direct object. Descriptive words or phrases may follow the verb and its object:

Subject	Verb	Direct object	Descriptive phrases
We	need	some milk	from the store.
We	saw	the Grand Canyon	last week.

Question

Do we need milk?

Question beginning with question word

When did you see the Grand Canyon?

| EXERCISE 2 | Writing Sentences in Pattern 2 |

Write sentences using the verbs in parentheses. One of your sentences should be a question.

1. (heard) *I heard a loud noise.* _____

2. (gave) _____

3. (took) _____

4. (am making) _____

5. (will do) _____

6. (want) _____

Pattern 3: Subject + Linking Verb + Subject Complement

This pattern includes a **linking verb** (*be, become, appear, seem, feel, taste,* and *smell*), which does not express an action. Instead it *links* the subject to a **subject complement**—an adjective that describes the subject or a noun that renames it:

Subject	Linking verb	Subject complement
Guillermo	looks	sad. (adjective)
Movies	are	great entertainment. (noun)

Question

Does Guillermo look lonely?

Question beginning with question word

Why does Guillermo look sad?

| EXERCISE 3 | Writing Sentences in Pattern 3 |

Write sentences using the verbs in parentheses. One of your sentences should be a question.

1. (sounds) *The music sounds great.* _____

2. (is) _____

3. (became) _____

4. (acts) _____

5. (was) _____

6. (seemed) _____

Pattern 4: Subject + Verb + Indirect Object + Direct Object

In this pattern, the transitive verb is followed by both an indirect object and a direct object. The **direct object** receives the action of the verb. The **indirect object** receives the direct object. It's the person or thing to whom or for whom the action was done:

Subject	Verb	Indirect object	Direct object	Indirect object
You	should give	the waiter	a tip.	
They	bought	her	a present.	
Max	explained		the problem	to me.

Question

Should we give the waiter a tip?

Question beginning with question word

What did they bring her?

Who explained the problem to you?

EXERCISE 4 | **Writing Sentences in Pattern 4**

Write sentences using the verbs in parentheses. One of your sentences should be a question.

1. (made) *I made my friends dinner.* _____

2. (gave) _____

3. (will send) _____

4. (are taking) _____

5. (mailed) _____

6. (served) _____

Other Sentence Patterns

The five remaining sentence patterns are used less often than the first four. Some, but not all, place the verb before the subject.

Pattern 5: *There/It* + Verb + Subject

In this pattern, the word *there* or *it* begins the sentence, and the subject comes after the verb. *There* and *it* are not the subjects but are simply ways of starting the sentence:

Starter	Verb (usually *be*)	Subject	Descriptive phrase
There	are	some pencils	in my briefcase.
It	isn't (easy)	to do the job.	

Question

Is it hard to learn?

Question beginning with question word

Why aren't there any pens in your briefcase?

In the first example, the real subject is *some pencils.* In the second example, the subject is *to do the job* (an infinitive and a phrase).

EXERCISE 5	**Writing Sentences in Pattern 5**

Complete the sentences using the words in parentheses. One of your sentences should be a question.

1. (to sing) It ___*is an easy song to sing.*___

2. (a lot to do) There _____

3. (ten o'clock) It _____

4. (more than one hundred irregular verbs) _____

_____

5. (sad to hear) _____

6. (difficult) _____

Pattern 6: Verb + Remainder of Predicate

This pattern is called a **command** or an **imperative sentence.** Its implied subject (*you*) is omitted, and the verb is the **partial infinitive** (without *to*). The sentence gives advice, directions, or orders. The pattern cannot be used for questions:

Subject	Verb	Remainder of predicate
(You)	Do	your work. (direct object)
	Be	careful. (adjective)
	Don't go.	(intransitive verb)
	Don't send	him the letter. (indirect object and direct object)

EXERCISE 6	Writing Sentences in Pattern 6

Write sentences using the verbs in parentheses. At least one sentence should use a negative.

1. (touch) *Don't touch that hot dish.* _____

2. (sit) _____

3. (go) _____

4. (take) _____

5. (run) _____

6. (swim) _____

Pattern 7: Subject + Verb + Direct Object + Infinitive

In this pattern, which uses verbs such as *tell*, *ask*, *make*, *have*, or *get*, the subject causes the object to act in some way. A partial or full infinitive following the object expresses that action:

Subject	Verb	Direct object	Partial or full infinitive
He	made	her	do it.
They	had	him	do it.
I	got	him	to do it.

Question

Did he make her do it?

Question beginning with question word

Why did they have him do it?

EXERCISE 7	Writing Sentences in Pattern 7

Write sentences using the verbs in parentheses. One of your sentences should be a question.

1. (told) *I told him to finish his homework.* _____

2. (asked) _____

3. (made) _____

4. (will get) _____

5. (had) _____

6. (ordered) _____

Pattern 8: Subject + Verb + Direct Object + Partial Infinitive or Gerund

In this pattern, the subject observes the object as it acts. Some examples of verbs following the subject include *see, hear, notice, feel, look at, listen to,* and *observe.* The action of the object is expressed by a partial infinitive or a gerund:

Subject	Verb	Direct object	Partial infinitive or gerund
He	saw	the turtle	moving.
They	heard	the rain	fall.

Question

Did you see the turtle moving?

Question beginning with a question word

When did they hear the rain fall?

EXERCISE 8 | **Writing Sentences in Pattern 8**

Write sentences using the verbs in parentheses. One of your sentences should be a question.

1. (felt) *I felt the ground shake during the earthquake.*
2. (see) _____
3. (noticed) _____
4. (heard) _____
5. (looked at) _____
6. (is listening to) _____

Pattern 9: Subject + Transitive Verb + Direct Object + Object Complement

In this pattern, the direct object is followed by an **object complement**—an adjective that describes the object or a noun that renames it. Typical verbs for this pattern are *make, name, find, appoint,* and *elect:*

Subject	Transitive verb	Direct object	Object complement
Mohammed	left	his door	unlocked. (adjective)
Margarita	named	her puppy	Frisky. (noun)

> **Question**
>
> Did Mohammed leave his door unlocked?
>
> **Question beginning with question word**
>
> What did Margarita name her puppy?

EXERCISE 9 | Writing Sentences in Pattern 9

Write sentences using the words in parentheses. One of your sentences should be a question.

1. (made) *The class made me a better writer.*

2. (will name) _____

3. (elected) _____

4. (appointed) _____

5. (found/interesting) _____

6. (leave) _____

These nine basic patterns form simple sentences—those with only one clause. You will see how to form compound sentences (with two independent clauses) and complex sentences (with a dependent clause and an independent clause) in Chapters 24–27.

EXERCISE 10 | Writing Questions

Respond to each of the statements with a question. Begin your response with a question word.

1. Wilfredo is working. *Where is he working?* OR *When will he finish?*

2. Maria is leaving tomorrow. _____

3. Amir wants some help soon. _____

4. Silvia gave me something to eat. _____

5. Someone told me a lie. _____

6. He saw something move in the alley. _____

Patterns in the Passive Voice

All the patterns in this chapter have been in the **active voice,** in which the subject *performs* the action of the verb. However, Patterns 2, 4, and 7 can be transformed into the **passive voice,** in which the subject passively *receives* the action of the verb. In these cases, the object becomes the subject, and the verb includes some form of *to be* + past participle.

Generally, we use the passive voice when the object of the action is more important than the person or thing that performs it. Note that the person who performs the action is not mentioned in two of the passive voice sentences in the examples:

Active voice	Passive voice
Pattern 2: s v d.o. Someone stole my wallet.	s v My wallet *was stolen.*
Pattern 4: s v A nurse serves the i.o. d.o. patients breakfast.	s v o The patients *are served* breakfast by a nurse. (The preposition *by* indicates who performs the action.) s v i.o. Breakfast *is served* to the patients. (The indirect object must follow the preposition *to.*)
Pattern 7: s v i.o. Someone told her inf. to be careful.	s v inf. She *was told* to be careful.

Here are examples of the passive voice in a number of tenses:

Simple tenses	Perfect tenses
Present: The course *is offered* every semester.	**Present perfect:** The course *has been offered* before.
Past: The course *was offered* last semester.	**Past perfect:** The course *had been offered* many years earlier.
Future: The course *will be offered* next semester.	
Modals	
The course *should be offered* soon.	
The course *could be offered* soon.	
The course *ought to be offered* soon.	

Chapter 17 discusses the passive voice further.

EXERCISE 11	Writing Sentences in Passive Voice

Rewrite the active voice sentences in the passive voice. Be sure the verb tense is correct.

1. Someone prepares breakfast for the guests every morning.

   Breakfast is prepared for the guests every morning.

2. People speak Spanish in Mexico.

   _____

3. Someone fixed my car last week.

   _____

4. Someone will invite all the students to the meeting.

   _____

5. Someone has already fed the dog its meal.

   _____

6. Juan's boss promoted him to manager last week.

   _____

17 Mastering Verb Forms

In many languages, a verb is limited to a single word or two, and those words have many different forms. But in English, a verb can include as many as four words, which convey a variety of tenses, attitudes, and conditions. We'll look at the majority of those verb forms and tenses in this chapter, from the simplest and most familiar to the less familiar ones.

Specifically, this chapter will give you practice in

- using the various verb tenses
- expressing attitudes through helping verbs
- working with a few special verbs
- expressing actions that the subject receives but does not perform
- establishing conditional relationships among ideas
- using adjectives formed from verbs

The Present and Past Tenses of Verbs

English has two present tenses and two past tenses, and they are formed in similar ways.

Present Tenses

The two present tenses in English communicate entirely different meanings.

Simple Present Tense. This tense discusses habitual actions—actions that happen all of the time, most of the time, or some of the time:

> I *go* to my English class three days a week.
>
> My instructor usually *assigns* a composition on Friday.

It can also discuss current feelings, observations, facts, or statements involving no action:

> I *like* cauliflower, but I *hate* spinach. (feelings)
>
> I *hear* a noise, but I *don't see* anything. (observations)
>
> The Earth *revolves* around the Sun, and the Moon *orbits* the Earth. (facts)
>
> We *don't have* a car. Cars *cost* too much. (statements involving no action)

Present tense verbs have only two endings:

1. verbs that agree with *I, we, you,* or *they* do not end in *-s*
2. verbs that agree with *he, she,* or *it* must end in *-s*

Most present tense verbs require two words to form questions and negatives:

1. the helping verb *do* or *does*
2. the main verb, which never adds an *-s* ending

The one exception to this rule is the verb *to be,* which has three forms and doesn't use a helping verb for negatives and questions:

Subject	Affirmative verb	Negative verb
I	*am*	*am not*
we, you, they	*are*	*are not (aren't)*
he, she, it	*is*	*is not (isn't)*

Questions	
Verb	**Subject**
Am	I
Are	we, you, they
Is	he, she, it

Present Progressive Tense. This tense discusses actions that are happening now or are planned for the future:

> I *am studying* English now.
>
> We *are handing* in our compositions next Monday.

Chapter 18 provides extensive practice with present tense verb forms and subject-verb agreement.

Verbs in the present progressive tense always include two parts:

1. a present tense form of the verb *to be* (*am, is,* or *are*)
2. a present participle

EXERCISE 1	Writing Present Tenses

Rewrite each of the following sentences, changing from the simple present tense (a) to the present progressive tense (b), or the present progressive tense (b) to the simple present tense (a).

1. a. We often walk home after classes.

　b. *We are walking home after classes today.*

2. a. My brother-in-law sleeps fourteen hours a day.

　b. ＿＿＿＿＿＿＿＿＿＿＿＿＿＿＿＿＿＿＿ right now.

3. a. ＿＿＿＿＿＿＿＿＿＿＿＿＿＿＿＿＿＿＿ every week.

　b. My father is washing the car now.

4. a. Adedotun has a party every month.

　b. ＿＿＿＿＿＿＿＿＿＿＿＿＿＿＿＿＿＿＿ this Saturday.

5. a. Mrs. Baxter doesn't watch television.

　b. ＿＿＿＿＿＿＿＿＿＿＿＿＿＿＿＿＿＿＿ now.

6. a. ＿＿＿＿＿＿＿＿＿＿＿＿＿＿＿＿＿＿＿ in the desert very often.

　b. It isn't raining today.

Past Tenses

Like the two present tenses, the two past tenses express different meanings. Their forms are similar to those of the present tenses.

Simple Past Tense. This tense discusses a completed action or event in the past, often at a stated time:

> Stanislav *passed* the test yesterday and *felt* wonderful.
>
> We *didn't see* the movie.

Verbs in the simple past tense end in *-ed*, but some are **irregular** and don't end in *-ed:*

> Regular: *walked, liked*
>
> Irregular: *took, saw, drank*

As with the simple present tense, negative statements or questions in the simple past tense require two words:

1. the helping verb *did*, which signals the tense

2. the main verb

Chapter 19 provides extensive practice with past tense verbs.

Subject	Negative verb	Adverb	Direct object
I	did not walk	fast.	
Sara	did not take		her umbrella.

Questions

Verb	Subject	Verb	Direct object
Did	he	like	the movie?
Did	you	see	it?

Past Progressive Tense. This tense discusses actions in progress at a specific time or period of time in the past. Verbs in the past progressive tense always include two parts:

1. a past tense form of the verb *to be* (*was* or *were*)
2. a present participle

I *was studying* at midnight.

They *were working* all day yesterday.

The past progressive tense often appears in combined sentences joined by *when, while,* or *as:*

I *was taking* a shower *when* the telephone *rang*.

Tomas *tried* to study *while* his sister *was watching* TV.

EXERCISE 2	Writing Past Tenses

Rewrite each of the following sentences, changing the simple past tense (a) to the past progressive tense (b), or the past progressive tense (b) to the simple past tense (a).

1. a. *I studied for the test this morning.*

b. I was studying for the test when you called.

2. a. _____ yesterday.

b. Our telephone wasn't working for several hours.

3. a. _____ every day last week.

b. They were doing the laundry again this morning.

4. a. Phong got a haircut yesterday.

b. _____ when the barbershop

caught on fire.

5. a. They didn't listen to the news during dinner.

    b. _____ last night.

6. a. _____ when

    _____ this morning.

    b. Who was watching the children while you were shopping?

EXERCISE 3	Combining Sentences about the Past

Combine each of the following pairs of sentences, converting the simple past tense to the past progressive tense and using **when** or **while.**

1. Mario had dinner. His cat sat down in his spaghetti.
   Mario was having dinner when his cat sat down in his spaghetti.
   _____

2. I talked to my friend. Several one-hundred-dollar bills dropped from my pocket.
   _____
   _____

3. Mr. Richman admired the scenery. His chauffeur drove the car.
   _____
   _____

4. They fell in love. They danced cheek to cheek.
   _____
   _____

5. Tina washed the dishes. Tim read the paper.
   _____
   _____

6. I took a bath. The house caught on fire.
   _____
   _____

Collaborative Activity 1

Writing in the Present and Past

Write eight sentences that make affirmative statements—two in the simple present tense, two in the present progressive tense, two in the simple past tense, and two in the past progressive tense. Exchange papers with a classmate and do the following:

1. Correct any errors you find.
2. Change each sentence into a negative statement.
3. Change each sentence into a question.

Then check each other's work.

The Future Tenses

Like the two tenses for the past and present, the two main future tenses express different meanings.

Simple Future Tense

In affirmative statements, you use the **simple future tense** to discuss future intentions, expectations, and promises. The simple future tense consists of two parts: *will* + base verb:

I can't talk to you now, but I *will call* you later.

We'*ll come* to the party at 8:30.

Typically, you use its negative form to discuss actions that you cannot do or refuse to do:

I *won't be able* to come to the party.

I *won't lie* to you!

Future Progressive Tense

The **future progressive tense** expresses an action in progress at a later time. It consists of three parts: *will* + *be* + present participle:

I *will be working* at noon tomorrow.

They *will be returning* to Korea next week.

She *won't be taking* the train to work later.

EXERCISE 4	Writing Sentences about the Future

After each of the following statements, write a statement in the simple future tense or future progressive tense.

1. I am working today.

I won't be working tomorrow.

2. We are flying home today.

We will be in Moscow tomorrow.

3. We can't go out tonight.

_____

4. I don't have time to talk to you now.

_____

5. Please don't call me later than 10:00 P.M.

_____

6. He won't drive to work.

_____

7. I hate asparagus!

_____

The Perfect Tenses

A **perfect tense** always links an earlier time to a later time. That later time can be in the present, past, or future. We'll look at all three of those perfect tenses: the present perfect, past perfect, and future perfect.

Present Perfect Tense

The **present perfect tense** can express (1) an action that began in the past but continues into the present, or (2) a completed action in the indefinite (or unspecified) past that relates to the present. The tense consists of two parts: *have* or *has* + past participle:

> I *have studied* English for two years. (The action began two years ago and continues up to the present, when it may end or continue.)
>
> We *have* already *eaten* lunch. (The action was completed at an unspecified time in the past.)
>
> He *hasn't seen* that movie yet. (The negative relates the past to the present.)

Past Perfect Tense

The **past perfect tense** expresses an action or idea in the past that relates to a later time in the past. This tense consists of two parts: *had* + past participle:

> Someone called Ahmad at home after he *had left* for work. (Leaving for work preceded the phone call.)
>
> I told my instructor that I *had been* sick. (The sickness occurred before the conversation with the instructor.)

See Chapter 19 for more on the present perfect and past perfect tenses.

EXERCISE 5 | Writing in the Perfect Tenses

Complete each of the following sentences by including a verb phrase in the present perfect tense or past perfect tense.

1. I don't want to see that movie because *I've seen it before.* _____

2. Bill apologized after he _____

3. I can't take a coffee break now because I already _____

   _____

4. Carmen felt terrible after _____

5. Isaiah couldn't drive a car after _____

6. All the students were happy because _____

7. Mark isn't taking biology this semester because _____

   _____

Future Perfect Tense

The **future perfect tense** expresses an action or event you expect to be completed before a later time in the future. The future perfect tense consists of three parts: *will* + *have* + past participle:

Ten years from now, José
- *will have graduated* from college.
- *will have gotten* a good job.
- *will have married* and (will have) *had* children.

| EXERCISE 6 | Writing in the Future Perfect |

Complete each sentence with a verb phrase in the future perfect tense.

1. By the end of the year, I _will have lost fifteen pounds._

2. Five years from now, I _____

3. By the year 2010, we _____

4. After next week, he _____

5. Once the semester ends, you _____

6. Before the end of the soccer season, Phil _____

Modal Verbs

A **modal verb** expresses an attitude toward what is being said. Modal verbs never change their forms to designate tense or agreement with the subject, but they can refer to the present, future, or past. Modal verbs include:

can, could, will, would, shall, should, may, might, must, ought to, had better

Simple Modals

Simple modals discuss the present or future. They consist of two parts: the modal + main verb. Here are some examples, labeled according to the attitude they communicate:

Ability:	I *can swim* well.
Past ability:	I *couldn't swim* when I was younger.
Doubt:	That *can't be* the answer!
Possibility:	They *might be* late. He *could be* sick.

Necessity:	You *must register* for classes soon. I *don't have to work* tomorrow.
Obligation or warning:	I *must get* a job soon. You *must not touch* that hot stove.
Advice:	You *ought to see* a doctor.
Strong advice:	You *had better take* your medicine.

Progressive Modals

Progressive modals express possibilities, interpretations, or conclusions about present or future circumstances. The progressive modals include three words: modal + *be* + present participle:

| Possibility: | I don't know where Kingsley is now. He | *could be working.*
might be working.
ought to be working.
may be working. |
| Interpretation, Conclusion: | Kingsley isn't home now, so he
Later today, Kingsley | *must be working.*
should be working. |

EXERCISE 7 | **Writing Sentences with Modals**

After each of the following sentences, write a sentence using either a simple modal or a progressive modal. Your sentences can be affirmative or negative. Don't use the same modal verb twice.

1. Juan has a test on Friday. *He should study.* _____

2. Margarita is very sick. _____

3. Tom is taking a nap. _____

4. Tomorrow is a holiday. _____

5. You are driving too fast. _____

6. My friend isn't at work. _____

7. The road is very dangerous. _____

8. There is a wonderful program on television tonight. _____

_____

9. It is raining. _____

10. The car has a flat tire. _____

11. The Wilsons usually have dinner at this time. _____

_____

Perfect Modals

Perfect modals also express possibilities, interpretations, or previous actions or circumstances in relation to a later time. Perfect modals are also built from three words: modal + *have* + past participle:

Possibility, Interpretation, Conclusion:	Kingsley didn't feel well today, so he	*must have been* sick. *could have had* a cold. *might have had* the flu. *may have had* the flu. *should have stayed* home.

Perfect Progressive Modals

Perfect progressive modals also express possibilities, interpretations, or conclusions, interpreting past actions or circumstances in progress. The perfect progressive modals consist of four words: modal + *have* + *been* + present participle:

Possibility, Interpretation, Conclusion:	Manuel wasn't home yesterday. He	*could have been working.* *must have been working.* *might have been working.* *may have been working.*
Interpretation:	However, Manuel was sick yesterday. He	*should have been resting.*

EXERCISE 8	Writing Sentences with Perfect Modals

After each of the following sentences, write a sentence using either a perfect modal or a perfect progressive modal. Your sentences can be affirmative or negative. Don't use the same modal verb twice.

1. Teresa was late for work.
   She should have left earlier.

2. My sister got a perfect score on the examination.

3. You didn't have to walk so far.

4. Henri didn't answer the telephone.

5. Mr. Clark drove all the way from New York to Chicago.

6. Jacob was very sick yesterday.

Special Verbs

Some verbs are used in special ways. We'll look at two commonly used ones: *used to* and *have to*.

Used To

When you describe a habitual action or idea in the past that no longer occurs in the present, use *used to* + main verb:

Affirmative:	I don't swim anymore, but I *used to swim* as a child.
Negative:	I travel by airplane often now, but I *didn't use to* fly.
Affirmative:	Mr. Sampson has lost a lot of weight. He *used to be* heavy.
Negative:	He *never used to exercise,* but he lost weight by running.

EXERCISE 9 | **Writing Statements with *Used To***

TIPS

For Distinguishing Two Kinds of *Used To*

Be careful when writing *used to.* It has two meanings.

1. Without a helping verb, it describes past action that no longer occurs: Juan *used to study* in Mexico. (He studied in Mexico but doesn't study there now.)

2. With a form of the helping verb *to be,* it means "familiar with" or "accustomed" to: Juan *is used to studying* in the United States. (He studies in the United States and is *accustomed to* studying here.)

Complete each of the following sentences using the verbs ***used to, never used to,*** or ***didn't used to.***

1. Dr. Smith listens to classical music now, but *he didn't used to like it.* _____

2. Ms. Gonzalez owns a car now, but _____

3. I don't play the piano now, but _____

4. Since they came to the United States, Amir and Smail haven't seen their parents. However, _____

5. Ms. Lee speaks English well now, but _____

6. Ms. Bozynskaya doesn't smoke now, but _____

Have To

Have to expresses necessity, and in present tense affirmative statements, it means almost the same as statements with *must:*

She *has to study* for her test.	(She must study.)
They *have to study* for their test.	(They must study.)

But negative statements with *had to* and *must* mean different things. The negative of *have to* indicates a lack of necessity:

Today is a holiday, so I *don't have to attend* classes.

The negative *must not* expresses a warning or order:

> That area is dangerous. You *must not go* there.
>
> The test will end at noon. You *must not leave* early.

Past tense statements with *had to* also express necessity or lack of necessity:

> I *had to study* yesterday.
>
> We *didn't have to take* the test on Friday.

EXERCISE 10 | **Writing Statements with *Have To***

Complete each of the following sentences by including a verb phrase with ***have to,
has to,*** or ***had to.*** In these sentences, the verb means **"must."**

1. I couldn't watch television last night because *I had to study for an examination.*

   _____

2. That is a very dangerous intersection, so drivers _____

   _____

3. I have a paper due tomorrow, so _____

   _____

4. When you visit Europe, you _____

   _____

5. Mr. Kim was very sick yesterday, so _____

   _____

6. If you need to pay your tuition, _____

   _____

The Passive Voice

There are two voices in English. In the **active voice,** the subject performs the action of the verb, and in the **passive voice,** the subject is passive—it receives the action of the verb. You can use the passive voice in any tense and with any modal.

Present and Past Tense

All **passive voice** statements include the verb *to be* + past participle. The form of the helping verb *be* determines the tense, and the past participle expresses the action. We'll look at the simple present and simple past first.

Chapter 19 also discusses the passive voice.

Simple Present Tense. Passive voice statements in this tense begin with *am, is,* or *are.* The person or thing performing the action is sometimes identified by the preposition *by:*

> The class *is taught* by an excellent instructor.
>
> The lessons *are presented* clearly.

Simple Past Tense. Passive voice statements in this tense begin with *was* or *were:*

> The class *was taught* by a fine instructor last year.
>
> The new students *were given* an orientation to the college.

Progressive Tenses. You can also express passive voice ideas in the present progressive and past progressive tenses. Here are some examples:

> **Present progressive tense**
>
> The food *is being prepared* now.
>
> **Past progressive tense**
>
> The new employees *were being trained* last week.

EXERCISE 11	Writing in the Passive Voice

Complete each of the following items using a passive voice expression and the verb in parentheses. Compose new sentences, and finish the incomplete ones.

1. You can't drive on Wilson Avenue now. (repair) *It is being repaired.* _____

_____

2. I don't have a watch anymore. (steal) _____

_____

3. Please don't go into the kitchen. (paint) _____

_____

4. The dishes are clean now. (wash) _____

_____

5. The dishwasher was broken, but (fix) _____

_____

6. Did you find your pen, or (lose) _____

_____

Modals in the Passive Voice

Modals in the passive voice interpret, make suggestions about, or draw conclusions about present or past ideas.

Present Ideas. In the present, the pattern is modal + *be* + past participle, as in this example:

The radio doesn't work.	It *should be fixed.*

Future Ideas. In the future, the pattern is *will* + *be* + past participle, as in these examples:

The radio is broken, but it *will be fixed* soon.

Your grades are being processed, and they *will be mailed* tomorrow.

Past Ideas. In the past, the pattern requires a perfect tense, composed of four words: modal + *have* + *been* + present participle. Here are some examples:

The radio didn't work. It	*could have been dropped* on the floor.
	might have been broken earlier.
	must have been broken by someone.
The radio wasn't fixed, but it	*should have been fixed.*

EXERCISE 12 | **Writing in the Passive Voice**

Complete each of the following sentences using an appropriate modal expression in the passive voice.

1. Norma was annoyed that the gym floor was dirty. It *should have been swept* _____

   before her class.

2. I didn't receive my final grades last week. They _____

   _____.

3. Health-clinic employees have a holiday on Independence Day, so the local clinic

   _____ in the afternoon.

4. Main Street was still closed to traffic last week. It _____

   _____ three weeks ago.

5. This song wasn't written by Mozart, so it _____

   _____ by Haydn.

6. Your telephone line was busy all last night. The phone _____

   _____ though it is working today.

CHAPTER 17   Mastering Verb Forms   179

Conditional Sentences

A **conditional sentence** usually includes the word *if*, which establishes a condition that is necessary for an event to occur. We'll examine the four most common conditional sentences: two in the present, one in the future, and one in the past.

Present True Conditional

The **present true conditional** means, "If one circumstance happens, the result also happens." Both clauses are true, and both include present tense verbs. With this type of conditional, you can use *when* in place of *if:*

If clause	Result clause
If (when) the weather *is* cold,	I *wear* my wool coat.
If you *work* more than eight hours a day,	you *receive* overtime pay.

You may use any of the present tenses in the *if* clause:

	Condition	Result
Simple present:	If you *take* good notes during the lectures,	you learn the subject better.
Present progressive:	If I *am feeling* nervous,	I try to relax.
Present perfect:	If *you've already taken* the course,	you don't have to repeat it.

✔ **TIPS**

For *If* Clauses
Place a comma at the end of an *if* clause that begins a sentence. Do not place a comma before an *if* clause that ends a sentence.

The result clause can also precede the *if* clause:

I try to relax if (when) I'm feeling nervous.

You may also use modals in the result clause:

If you're feeling nervous,	you *should relax.* you *can't do* your best work. you *must relax* and *take* your time.

EXERCISE 13 | Writing in the Present True Conditional

Use a clause in the present true conditional to complete each of the following sentences. Begin the clause with *if* or *when*.

1. *If you are a doctor* _____, you work very hard.

2. You should drink plenty of water _____

3. You must drive for a long time _____

4. _____, Mrs. Johnson can go to a hardware store.

5. _____, be very careful.

Future True Conditional

The **future true conditional** means, "If this circumstance happens, the result will probably happen." The result is not certain, of course, because the future is never certain. Since the condition must be satisfied *before* the result, the conditional clause is in the present tense, and the result is in the future tense:

Conditional clause (present)	Future result
If you *get* a nursing degree,	you *will find* a job easily.

Future result	Conditional clause (present)
Tom *won't enroll* for classes this term	if he *doesn't get* a scholarship.

You can also use *unless* to express a condition that prevents a future result:

Result	Condition
We *will* drive to the mountains	unless the roads are too icy. (The icy roads will prevent us from driving to the mountains.)

The future conditional is also used to make predictions or promises:

Prediction:	If Tom *doesn't get* his degree, he *will be* very sorry.
Promise:	I'll *take* you out for dinner if you *help* me paint the kitchen.

Modals that express possibility or probability can be used in the result clause:

If Julia *graduates* in May, she *might take* a long vacation.

I *may call* you tonight if I *have* time.

EXERCISE 14	Writing in the Future Conditional

After each of the following sentences, write a sentence in the future conditional, using either *if* or *unless.*

1. It's raining. *If it stops soon, I'll take the dog for a walk.* _____

2. It takes me an hour to get to school by bus. _____

_____

3. We haven't taken a vacation in a long time. _____

_____

4. I don't have a computer. _____

_____

5. Hector plans to major in accounting. _____

_____

Present Untrue Conditional

The **present untrue conditional** makes a statement that is contrary to the facts: The condition is not true at the present time. The conditional clause uses the simple past, and the result clause uses *would*:

Condition (simple past)	Result (*would* + partial infinitive)
If I *had* a different job, (I don't have a different job.)	I *would be* much happier.
If he *were* ten years younger, (He is not ten years younger.)	*would* he *marry* Patricia?

Notice the verb *were* in the second example above. It's required in the present untrue condition and agrees with all subjects, singular or plural.

You often use the present untrue conditional to give advice and to express dreams or wishes:

| **Advice:** | If I *were* you, I *would be* careful. |
| **Dream or wish:** | If I *were* a millionaire, I *would retire* in Hawaii. |

The result clause can also express a possibility with a modal:

If I lived in Hawaii, I *might learn* to surf.

If you learned Japanese, *could* you *become* a translator?

| **EXERCISE 15** | Writing in the Present Untrue Conditional |

Write a statement in the present untrue conditional after each of the following sentences.

1. Ana is too short to be a flight attendant. *If she were taller, she would get a job with one of the airlines.*

2. I don't have enough money to take a vacation. _____

3. It's very cold today. _____

4. I have to study tonight. _____

5. Mr. Nelson doesn't own a car. _____

6. Mr. Patel is eighty years old. _____

Past Untrue Conditional

The **past untrue conditional** sentence makes a statement that is contrary to the facts: The condition was not true in the past. The conditional clause uses the past perfect tense, and the result clause uses *would + have +* past participle:

Condition (past perfect)	Result (*would + have +* past participle)
If you *had been* careful (You weren't careful.)	you *wouldn't have hurt* yourself.
If Tomas *had left* at 6:00 P.M., (He didn't leave at 6:00 P.M.)	he *would have arrived* on time.

The past untrue conditional is used to apologize, admit mistakes, give advice, or discuss regrets about the past:

Apology: If I *had known* you needed a ride, I *would have picked* you up.

Admitting mistake: If I *had taken* the train, I *would have arrived* on time.

Advice: If you *had studied* harder, you *wouldn't have gotten* such a bad grade.

Regrets: If I *had practiced* more, I *could have been* a concert violinist. (Notice that *could* expresses a possibility.)

You can also use the modals *could* or *might* to express a possibility in the result clause:

Condition (past perfect)	Result
If I had known that Tim was sick, I	*could have taken* him to the doctor. *might have gone* to his house.

EXERCISE 16 | Writing in the Past Conditional

After each of the following sentences, write a statement in the past conditional.

1. Bill didn't do well on the test. *If he had studied, he would have done better.*

_____

2. Juan paid too much money for his new suit. _____

_____

3. I can't play the piano. _____

_____

4. You shouldn't have been late for class. _____

_____

5. They got very wet in the rain. _____

_____

Past Participles and Present Participles

Past participles (such as *spoken, seen*) and *-ing* words, or **present participles** (such as *tiring, exciting*), are formed from verbs. But they often function as adjectives. Here's how to distinguish between the two types of participles.

Present participles express a feeling or action created by the noun they modify:

We heard some *shocking* news. (The news created shock in the people who heard it.)

The book was *interesting*. (The book created interest in me.)

Often that feeling or action is continuing, was continuing, or will be continuing:

Don't touch that pot of *boiling* eggs.

I tried to stay out of the *falling* rain.

Past participles express a feeling or action received by the noun they modify:

The *shocked* man couldn't believe the news. (The man received the shock.)

I am *interested* in the book. (I receive an interest from the book.)

Often that feeling or action is completed, was completed, or will be completed:

These *boiled* eggs are cold.

I picked up some *fallen* rocks by the side of the road.

Collaborative Activity 2

Correcting Sentences

Write five sentences, each of which uses one of the following participles as an adjective: *exciting, baked, married, boring,* and *written*. Exchange papers with a classmate and correct the sentences.

EXERCISE 17 | Writing Present or Past Participles

Complete each of the following sentences with the appropriate past participle or present participle form of the verb in parentheses.

1. The man sounds (irritate) _____*irritated*_____.

2. The movie was very (interest) _____ to me.

3. I always enjoy well-(perform) _____ plays.

4. The (break) _____ branch made a loud noise.

5. The long lecture was very (bore) _____.

6. The (bore) _____ audience fell asleep.

UNDERSTAND SENTENCE ELEMENTS.

What Makes a Sentence?

subject + predicate (beginning with verb) = sentence

Two types of clauses:

- Independent: complete statement
- Dependent: depends on an independent clause to complete its meaning

Four types of sentences:

- Statements
- Questions
- Commands
- Exclamations

Nine sentence patterns:

- Subject + verb
- Subject + verb + direct object
- Subject + linking verb + subject complement
- Subject + verb + indirect object + direct object
- *There/It* + verb + subject
- Verb + remainder of predicate
- Subject + verb + direct object + infinitive
- Subject + verb + direct object + infinitive or gerund object
- Subject + transitive verb + direct object + object complement

MASTER VERB FORMS AND OTHER PARTS OF SPEECH.

Eight parts of speech:
- Nouns
- Verbs
- Pronouns
- Adjectives
- Articles
- Adverbs
- Conjunctions
- Prepositions

Six types of verbs
- Main verbs
- Helping verbs
- Modal verbs
- Transitive verbs
- Intransitive verbs
- Linking verbs

Eight types of nouns:
- Common
- Proper
- Singular
- Plural
- Count
- Noncount
- Possessive singular
- Possessive plural

Seven types of pronouns:
- Personal
- Possessive
- Demonstrative
- Interrogative
- Relative
- Indefinite
- Reflexive

Nine verb tenses:
- Simple present
- Present progressive
- Simple past
- Past progressive
- Simple future
- Future progressive
- Present perfect
- Past perfect
- Future perfect

IV

Editing with Care

Now you can turn your attention to editing—the stage in the writing process when you look carefully at grammar, punctuation, and spelling. The unit begins by showing you how to identify and correct errors in subjects and verbs, verb tenses, word order, pronouns, articles and prepositions, and comparative adjectives and adverbs. Following that, the unit shows you how to edit for complete sentences and how to join sentences correctly in a variety of ways. Finally, the unit helps you edit punctuation and spelling.

In short, this unit shows you how to master the small matters that make a big difference in the way readers respond to your message. ■

18 Making Subjects and Verbs Agree

You want readers to pay attention to your ideas, not to unexpected and confusing word forms. Readers can be confused if the subjects and verbs of sentences don't fit together. With a singular subject, you need a singular verb; with a plural subject, you need a plural verb. This agreement between subjects and verbs is sometimes difficult because some word forms are unusual and some sentences are complicated. This chapter will show you how to overcome the difficulties as you edit. You'll learn

- how to make subjects and verbs work together
- how to recognize exceptions and handle them correctly

What Is Subject-Verb Agreement?

Subjects can be nouns or pronouns. They can be **singular:** representing one person, place, or thing. Or they can be **plural:** representing more than one. Likewise, the verbs that work with subjects can have singular or plural forms. A singular subject goes with a singular verb and a plural subject with a plural verb. That's subject-verb agreement.

Subject-verb agreement occurs only in tenses that deal with the present and with just one verb in the past tense, which we'll discuss in Chapter 19. Right now, we'll focus on the present tense agreement.

Subjects

Since in English sentences the subject generally comes before the verb, the form the verb takes depends on its subject. So we'll begin by looking at the singular and plural forms of nouns. You will need to be able to recognize these forms in order to check subject-verb agreement.

TIPS

For Determining Verb Agreement with Nouns: The Rule of One -s

Plural verbs don't add an -s, but most plural nouns do. Therefore, if the noun-subject ends in -s, the verb usually should not. If the verb ends in -s, the noun-subject usually should not.

Singular:
noun (no -s) + verb with -s
The *student rides* the bus.

Plural:
noun with -s + verb (no -s)
The *students ride* the bus.

Nouns

A *singular* noun, which usually doesn't end in -s, takes a verb that ends in -s:

> A *jaguar is* an animal that runs fast.
>
> One professional *athlete owns* a Jaguar—the fancy, expensive car.

A *plural* noun, which normally ends in -s or -es, takes a verb without an -s ending:

> *Jaguars are* members of the cat family.
>
> Many professional *athletes make* millions of dollars.

The -s or -es ending for plural nouns—whether they're subjects or objects—is important, for it tells readers that you mean more than one. And the -s ending on present tense verbs is important, for it reminds readers that the subject is singular. Both nouns and verbs add -es if they end in –s, -ss, -ch, -sh, -z, or -x.

EXERCISE 1 | Choosing Correct Noun Forms

Some of the nouns in the following sentences should be plural. Correct them by adding -s or -es endings.

Facts about Zebras

1. It's not unusual to see 1,000 zebra ⌃ together at one time. _s

2. They're very social animal.

3. They generally live in short grassy area or open fields.

4. A family group consists of one male (called a stallion), several female (called mares), and many infant.

5. The female are not equal; the principal mare leads the pack and the other follow behind her in single file.

6. And the family stays together, even when they join a large herd.

7. These striped horses are extremely brave, especially when lion and hyenas hunt them.

8. The male often form a semicircle to protect their families.

9. The lions will sometimes escape with severe injuries, because zebras can deliver powerful kick.

EXERCISE 2	Choosing Correct Verb Forms

Decide whether the subject of the sentence is singular or plural. Then write the appropriate present tense form of the verb supplied in parentheses.

Facts about Leopards

1. Leopards normally (hunt) _____*hunt*_____ at dusk and throughout the night.

2. These beautiful cats often (stay) _____ hidden during the day or (lie) _____ in high branches of trees.

3. A male leopard normally (live) _____ alone and (join) _____ a female only for mating.

4. Leopards' spotted bodies (make) _____ wonderful disguises, so the big cats attack their prey by surprise.

5. A single bite from a leopard usually (kill) _____ its prey.

6. Then the leopard (take) _____ its food up into a tree and has a relaxing meal.

Irregular Plurals. Some nouns are irregular and do not form plurals by adding -*s* or -*es* to the base word. Here are a few examples:

Singular	Plural
wife	wives
child	children
woman	women
mouse	mice
tooth	teeth
phenomenon	phenomena
crisis	crises
medium	media

✔ **TIPS**

For Remembering Nouns That Have Identical Singular and Plural Forms

Many (but not all) nouns that have the same singular + plural forms are, the names of fish: salmon, cod, perch, tuna, pike, and halibut.

Some other nouns have identical singular and plural forms, such as these:

sheep	fish	deer	trout	offspring

Still other nouns have only plural forms:

clothes	scissors	pants	shorts	jeans

Finally, a few nouns are singular even though they end is -*s:*

mathematics	physics (and all other nouns ending in -*ics*)	news

EXERCISE 3	Writing Sentences with Irregular Nouns as Subjects

For each subject in parentheses, write a present tense sentence. Make sure the subject and verb agree.

1. (His teeth) *His teeth are very white.* _____

2. (The child) _____

3. (The women) _____

4. (The phenomenon) _____

5. (Several sheep) _____

6. (My clothes) _____

Pronouns as Subjects

A **pronoun** takes the place of a noun. Like a noun, it can be singular or plural and can serve as the subject of a verb:

	Singular + Verb		Plural + Verb	
First person:	I	run	we	run
Second person:	you	run	you	run
Third person:	he	runs	they	run
	she	runs		
	it	runs		

Notice that only the *third person singular* pronouns (*he, she,* and *it*) require a verb ending in *-s:*

he	
she	works, eats, itches, yawns, wiggles, giggles
it	

EXERCISE 4	Choosing Present Tense Verbs

Look at the pronoun subject of each sentence. Then write the present tense form of the verb in parentheses. Make sure the subject and verb agree.

1. We (know) _____*know*_____ how to form plurals of nouns.

2. She (wear) _____ running shoes to class.

3. They (own) _____ a lovely house in the suburbs of Atlanta.

4. He (comb) _____ his hair with his left hand.

5. It often (rain) _____ through my roof in the spring.

6. You (know) _____ how to charm people.

7. I always (write) _____ correct sentences in these exercises.

Subjects Joined by *And*

Any combination of nouns and pronouns joined by *and* also makes a plural subject, which is called a **compound subject.** Note the following examples:

Subject	Verb without *-s*
a pencil and a piece of paper	
Juan and I	go, make, seem
ice cream, cake, and candy	

A compound subject, like a plural noun or pronoun, requires a plural verb.

Only the word *and* joins two subjects. *Or, nor,* and prepositions such as *with* or *in* do not make a compound subject:

The little old lady with seven dogs *is* a grandmother. (Only the woman is a grandmother—not the seven dogs.)

One in a million people *is* talented enough to play professional soccer. (Only one is talented enough—not a million.)

Dark clouds or thunder *is* not a sure sign of rain. (*Or* signals a choice between the two subjects; it doesn't join them. The sentence means "dark clouds *are* not" or "thunder *is* not"—and the verb agrees with the second and last choice.)

Fruit or vegetables are a healthy snack. (Again the verb agrees with the second and last choice.)

Compare these three sentences:

Maria, along with her friend, *works* part time on weekends. (Only Maria is the subject of this sentence.)

Maria and her friend work part-time on weekends. (*And* joins the two subjects of this sentence.)

Neither Maria nor *her friend works* full time on weekends. (*Nor* signals a negative choice, and the verb agrees with the second and last choice.)

✓ **TIPS**

For Remembering about Compound Subjects: The Rule of *And*

When two subjects are joined by *and,* the verb needs to be plural.

Subject *and* subject = verb without *-s.*

EXERCISE 5 | **Forming Agreement with Compound Subjects**

Decide whether the subject of each sentence is singular or plural. Then write the appropriate present tense form of the verb in parentheses.

1. The silver earring and the gold ring (belong) _____ to me.

2. That brown jacket and yellow tie (go) _____ together beautifully.

3. Five scoops of ice cream with two bananas, nuts, and syrup (make)

_____ a delicious treat.

Collaborative Activity 1

Checking Agreement
Write five sentences. Leave blank spaces for verbs. Make the subjects as varied as you can. Exchange papers with a classmate and fill in the blanks with appropriate present tense verb forms. Discuss your answers.

4. After sixty-two years of marriage, Mr. and Mrs. Wilson (look) _____ at each other with great affection—although they can't see too well.

5. The clothes on the bed, on the floor, and on top of the dresser (belong) _____ to my teenage son.

6. The use of compound subjects (become) _____ quite easy to master with a little practice.

Special Present Tense Verbs

The verbs *to be, to do,* and *to have* deserve special attention because they occur so often and take unusual forms. You need to know those forms well to make sure they agree with their subjects.

To Be

To be (is, am, are) is the most common verb in the English language:

> The photographs *are* beautiful.
>
> I *am* beautiful in all of them.

It often serves as a linking verb, preceding an *-ing* word in verb phrases:

> I *am looking* for a good job.
>
> Julio *is looking* for a good place to nap.

Here are the present tense forms of *to be* and their **contractions** (that is, their shortened forms with apostrophes replacing omitted letters):

Subject	Verb	Contractions	Negative contractions
I	*am*	*I'm*	
he, she, it (or singular noun)	*is*	*he's, she's, it's*	*isn't*
we, you, they (or plural noun)	*are*	*we're, you're, they're*	*aren't*

✔ **TIPS**

For Using Contractions
A contraction is a shortened form of a verb. It links to another word with an **apostrophe** ['], which replaces the omitted letters. Examine *be* verbs carefully as you write and edit, especially if your first language does not include *be* or does not use it in the same way as English does.

1. Don't leave off the *'s,* the *'m,* or the *'re.* Change "*He* happy" to "*He's* happy."

2. Don't confuse the contractions with sound-alike or look-alike words: *we're* with *were, you're* with *your, it's* with *its,* and *they're* with *their* or *there.*

EXERCISE 6	Writing *To Be*

Write both the correct full form of the verb *to be* and its contraction with an appropriate pronoun in each of these sentences. When the subject is a noun or a compound subject, change it to a pronoun.

1. Joe _____*is*_____ (___*He's*___) talking to Mr. Williams.
2. I _____ (_____) intelligent, rich, and extremely modest.
3. School _____ (_____) a pleasure and a joy for me.
4. My dog _____ (_____) smarter than my brother.
5. My colleague and I _____ (_____) happy to meet you.
6. You _____ (_____) in the right room.
7. The students _____ (_____) going to be late.

EXERCISE 7	Correcting Errors with *To Be*

Read this draft. There are seven mistakes in the use of the verb *to be*. Correct these mistakes by finding the subjects, making the verbs agree, and fixing errors in the *to be* contractions. The first error has been corrected for you.

More Facts about Leopards

* * * *

(1) A leopard ^*is* a very resourceful hunter. (2) When its hunting in the grassland of Africa, the big cat kills many large animals. (3) In the forest areas, there also small mammals that the leopard eats, such as hares, monkeys, and squirrels, as well as reptiles, such as frogs, and fish. (4) Its typical for a female leopard to give birth to one to three cubs. (5) There kept in isolated areas, like bushes or small caves. (6) Their much darker than adults, which are usually spotted. (7) Female leopards very concerned mothers who leave their infants only when they have to. (8) When the cubs are about two years old, they leave their mother and go out on their own.

Collaborative Activity 2

Discussing Your Editing

Compare your answers to Exercise 7 with a classmate. Were any errors especially difficult to detect? Report your results to the whole class.

To Do

The verb *to do* (*do, does*) serves as a helping verb in most present tense questions and negative statements. The helping verb needs to agree with its subject, as in the following examples:

Do you play the guitar?

He *doesn't* work on Sundays.

Here are the present tense forms of *to do*:

Subject	Verb	Negative verb	Negative contractions
I, we, you, they	*do*	*do not*	*don't*
he, she, it	*does*	*does not*	*doesn't*

The negative forms of *do/does* create the most problems. Many people say and write, "He don't," instead of "He doesn't"—a common but very serious grammatical error. Remember that *does* is the correct form with *he, she,* or *it.*

EXERCISE 8 | **Writing Negative Statements with *To Do***

Write the appropriate negative contraction of **to do** (**doesn't** or **don't**) in each sentence. You will first need to determine whether the subject is singular or plural.

Facts about Lions

1. Lions may attack other animals, but they usually _____*don't*_____ bother each other.

2. They're actually rather social animals. A lion _____ live alone but in a group of two to forty others called a *pride.*

3. However, one male rules the pride, and the rest of the animals certainly

    _____ have the same rights as he does.

4. He is first in mating, and other lions _____ eat until he's finished with his meal.

5. Lionesses are chiefly responsible for hunting for food. The females

    _____ receive this assignment because the male is lazy; his big, furry

    mane is simply too easy for prey to recognize.

6. In the wild, a 350-pound lion will eat 45 pounds of food daily. However, a lion

    _____ eat nearly as much in captivity—usually only 10 to 15 pounds

    a day.

7. The biggest threat to lions _____ come from other animals; it comes

    from human hunters and poachers.

To Have

You use *to have* as a simple verb:

> I *have* homework to do.
>
> Bozena *has* two brothers in Poland.

And you use it as a helping verb, which also needs to agree with its subject:

> I *have worked* on my laboratory report for a week.
>
> Tuyet Ahn *hasn't* ever *failed* an examination.

Here are its present tense forms:

Subject	Verb	Contractions	Negative contractions
I, we, you, they	have	I've, we've, you've, they've	haven't, don't have
he, she, it	has	he's, she's, it's	hasn't, doesn't have

Don't confuse *have* and *has* with *had*—the past tense form of the verb.

EXERCISE 9	Writing *To Have*

Write the appropriate present tense form of *to have*—affirmative or negative—in each sentence. You will first need to determine if the subject is singular or plural.

Facts about Baboons

1. Baboons _____*have*_____ their homes in African forests and mountains.

2. A typical baboon colony _____ as many as fifty members.

3. At night a baboon climbs a tree or cliff, where it _____ a place to sleep.

4. Baboons often travel as much as six miles from their spots, but they usually _____ several sleeping spots within their territory.

5. Baboons (negative) _____ much protection from their enemies, especially leopards—and humans.

6. Therefore, each baboon _____ to be very careful.

7. If an enemy approaches, the baboon (negative) _____ any time to lose as it runs to hide.

8. It _____ to climb a tree; but if no trees are nearby, the male baboons will gather together, scream loudly to scare away their enemies, and fight fiercely if necessary.

9. Baboons _____ a very strong social organization.

Special Problems with Subject-Verb Agreement

Subject-verb agreement is more difficult with certain kinds of sentences or words. We'll examine those situations in this section.

Questions

The subject normally comes before the verb in a sentence, alerting you to the form of the verb that follows. But in questions, the verb comes first. This word order can produce errors in agreement, especially with plural subjects. Here's an example:

> *Incorrect:*   Does Maria and Orlando want to go with us?

You may think that the verb agrees with *Maria,* the word that immediately follows. But this sentence has a compound subject. *Orlando* needs to be included in the verb, too. The sentence needs to be rewritten:

> *Correct:*   *Do* Maria and Orlando want to go with us?

EXERCISE 10 | **Writing Verbs in Questions**

Write the correct present tense form of *to do* or *to be* in each of the following sentences. You will first need to determine whether the subject is singular or plural.

1. ____*Are*____ Luis and Luisa practicing for the burrito-eating contest?

2. _____ seven children, three dogs, four cats, and a slightly confused goat too much to take care of?

3. _____ you know the way to the stadium?

4. _____ Mrs. Smith and Dr. Grant coming to the festival?

5. _____ a woman with triplets have three times the fun?

6. _____ the solution to all the problems difficult to find?

7. _____ these sentences easy to write?

Sentences That Begin with *There*

Expressions that begin with *there* also place the verb before the subject. Use *there is* or *there are,* depending on the subject, or subjects, that follow. These sentences are correct:

> *There's a child* sleeping on our couch.
>
> *There are two children* asleep on our bed. (NOT *There is two children . . .*)
>
> *There are no places* left for us to sleep.

EXERCISE 11 | **Writing Verbs with *There***

Write the correct present tense form of *to be* in each sentence.

1. There ____*are*____ many people who want to study computers.

2. There _____ two things that you need to know: Be smart and be careful.

3. There _____ a soccer ball, a can of deodorant, and a tuxedo in the back seat of the car.

4. There _____ a few rules that no one can break.

5. There _____ a lot of food left from the party.

6. There _____ no more sentences to complete in this exercise.

Collective Nouns

A **collective noun** represents a collection of two or more persons, things, or ideas:

class	orchestra	the United Nations
committee	faculty	the French

Most collective nouns are singular:

The *class is hearing* a lecture on economics.

The *hockey team wins* most of its games.

A few collective nouns are always plural:

The words *police* and *faculty*: The police patrol this area often.

All nationalities: The Dutch are thrilled about playing in the World Cup.

The word *staff*, however, can be either singular or plural, depending on the context in which it is used.

EXERCISE 12 | **Writing Sentences with Collective Nouns**

Write present tense sentences in which the collective noun subject agrees with the verb.

1. The collaborative group *usually reviews the material before moving on to the next subject* .

2. My family _____

3. The police _____

4. The British _____

5. IBM _____

6. The staff _____

Noncount Nouns

Except in a few unusual cases, **noncount nouns** (*water, homework, furniture,* and so on) are always singular. They cannot end in -*s*, and the verb that agrees with them should end in -*s*. Of course, **count nouns** (*one chair* or *six chairs,* and so on) can be singular or plural.

EXERCISE 13	Writing Sentences with Count Nouns and Noncount Nouns

Decide whether each word in parentheses is a count noun or a noncount noun. Make the count nouns plural. Then write a present tense sentence for each noun. Make the noun the subject of the sentence. The noncount nouns, of course, will require a singular verb form. You may wish to place a word like *some* before the noncount nouns.

1. (water) *The water in the bathtub is cold.* _____

2. (homework) _____

3. (parent) _____

4. (money) _____

5. (evidence) _____

6. (fact) _____

7. (furniture) _____

8. (help) _____

9. (idea) _____

10. (advice) _____

11. (information) _____

Indefinite Pronouns

Indefinite pronouns (pronouns that don't refer to a definite person, place, or thing) are always singular. There are four categories of indefinite pronouns:

Some	Every	Any	No
somebody	everybody	anybody	nobody
someone	everyone	anyone	no one
something	everything	anything	nothing

EXERCISE 14 | **Writing Sentences with Indefinite Pronouns**

Complete each sentence, using a present tense verb.

1. Everybody *loves pizza, hamburgers, fried chicken, tacos, and weight-loss diets*

2. Someone _____

3. Anyone _____

4. Somebody _____

5. Nobody _____

6. There _____ no one who _____

Phrases between the Subject and the Verb

A **prepositional phrase** sometimes comes between the subject and the verb. Don't let it confuse you. For example, which verbs should you use in the following sentences?

> The woman with seventeen children (need/needs) a little help.
>
> The shape and size of the ring (is/are) unusual.

Be sure that you aren't distracted by nouns or pronouns in prepositional phrases. The choice of the correct form will be clear when you draw a line through the prepositional phrase:

> The woman ~~with seventeen children~~ needs a little help.
>
> The shape and size ~~of the ring~~ are unusual.

Be aware of potentially misleading prepositional phrases as you edit.

EXERCISE 15 | **Using Correct Subject-Verb Agreement**

Cross out the prepositional phrase between the subject and the verb, determine whether the subject is singular or plural, and then write the appropriate present tense verb form.

1. The reason ~~for all the papers, cans, and other garbage in the park~~ (be) ____*is*____ not difficult to determine.

2. A person with eleven dogs (be) _____ not bored very often.

3. The members of this crew (do) _____ all of the work on board the ship.

4. The hard work of the engineers, drafters, carpenters, and electricians

   (have) _____ contributed to creating a beautiful new campus.

5. An enormous box of pizzas, French fries, garlic bread, onion rings, and nachos usually (disappear) _____ about fifteen minutes after Mario and his friends see it.

6. The cause of most deaths from fires (be) _____ smoke inhalation.

Relative Clauses

In **relative clauses,** the subject pronouns *who, which,* or *that* relate back to the word or words immediately before the clause. That means the verb in the relative clause has to agree with the same word or words:

> I want to introduce you to *the man who owns* this palace.
>
> Be sure to see the movie *Toy Story, which* is playing at the Center Cinema.
>
> My teenage son needs to pick up the *banana peels, apple cores, and hamburger buns that are* rotting on his bedroom floor.

However, *whom, which,* or *that* can also function as the object in a relative clause. In this case, the verb agrees with the subject of the relative clause:

>   o   s v
>
> Here is the young man *whom you are* going to teach English. (That is, you are going to teach *him* English.)
>
>   o   s   v
>
> You'll love the specialty of the house, *which Chef Alberto makes* from fresh tuna and tomatoes. (That is, Chef Alberto makes *it.*)

EXERCISE 16	Writing Verbs in Relative Clauses

Complete each sentence using a present tense verb.

1. I want a car that *looks like a million dollars but costs about a thousand.*

   _____

2. Ludmilla is looking for a man who _____

   _____

3. These are my new friends, who _____

   _____

4. I need a dog that _____

   _____

5. Mrs. Rich has a new eight-carat diamond, which _____

   _____

6. To fix this car, you need a set of tools that _____

   _____

Collaborative Activity 4

Working on Agreement

Prepare ten sentences—two with collective nouns, two with noncount nouns, two with indefinite pronouns, two with prepositional phrases after the subject, and two with relative clauses. Leave the verbs blank. Exchange papers with a classmate and fill in the blanks with present tense verbs. Discuss your answers.

| IN SUMMARY | Present Tense Subject-Verb Agreement |

- Almost all plural nouns end in -s or -es (if the singular form already ends in -s, -ss, -ch, -sh, -z, or -x), but the verbs that agree with them do not; almost all singular nouns do not end in -s, but the verbs that agree with them do.
- The pronouns *he, she,* and *it* and all singular nouns agree with verbs ending in -s.
- All other subject pronouns (*I, we, you,* and *they*) and all plural nouns agree with verbs that do not end in -s.
- All compound subjects (two or more subjects joined by *and*) are plural and agree with verbs that do not end in -s.
- In questions and sentences beginning with *there,* the subject follows the verb and determines agreement.
- All indefinite pronouns and noncount nouns are singular.
- Most—but not all—collective nouns are singular.
- The word or words proceeding subject pronouns *who, that,* or *which* in relative clauses determine the verb agreement. But when *whom, that,* or *which* functions as an object, the subject follows it and determines verb agreement.

EDITING FOR MASTERY

Mastery Exercise 1

Correcting Noun and Verb Errors

The passage contains sixteen errors in subject-verb agreement, noun plurals, missing verbs, and incorrect contractions with *to be*. The first error has been corrected for you. Find and correct the remaining errors.

Some Facts about Cats

(1) Ever since the Egyptian made cats their pets 4,000 years ago, cats always been important to humans as rodent killers. (2) Today some cats still earn their living as rat killers, and a few others works in TV commercials. (3) However, the main job of a cat these days are to be a good companion—and kind owner—of its pet humans.

(4) A cat is very smart, but it don't learn the way a dog does. (5) Some tests of intelligence shows that the cat is smarter than the dog. (6) However, a cat won't allow itself to be trained. (7) As everyone know, a cat will obey its owner only when it's in the mood.

(8) There's thirty-six different breeds of cats, but all the breeds has basically the same physical structure. (9) Cats is the only animals—other than camels and giraffes—that walks by moving their front and hind legs on one side, then the other. (10) And even though humans are fifteen times larger than cats, people have only 206 bones, while cats have 230.

(11) A cat is a very clean animal, and it have a strong sense of balance. (12) The cat's eyesight (especially at night) is its strongest sense, but a cat also hears well. (13) Its the only animal that purrs.

(14) How much like people is the female cat and male cat? (15) A mother cat is tender to her young; unlike a person, however, she can give birth several times a year. (16) On the other hand, a tomcat (male cat) is a terrible father. (17) No matter how many kittens the mother has, he don't stick around to take care of them.

Scorecard: Number of Errors Found and Corrected _____

Collaborative Activity 5

Comparing and Discussing Answers

Compare your answers with a classmate and, if your instructor indicates, report your findings to the entire class.

Mastery Exercise 2

Correcting Noun and Verb Errors

The passage contains sixteen errors in subject-verb agreement, noun plurals, missing verbs, and incorrect contractions with *to be*. The first error has been corrected for you. Find and correct the remaining errors.

Animal Tricks and Traps

(1) Most animals are afraid of other creature ˄. (2) Therefore, many creatures protects themselves from attack by imitating frightening beasts. (3) As a result, their predators think twice before eating them. (4) Certain animals that lives in holes in the ground (such as certain birds) have the ability to hiss like snakes. (5) A group of hissing bees in a hive make a bear wonder if taking their honey is a good idea.

(6) Other animals scare their enemies. (7) Theirs a type of frog that screams so loudly that a predator drop it out of shock. (8) Texas horned lizards inflate themselves like balloon. (9) They also explodes the walls between their sinuses and eye sockets, squirting out fluid from their eyes. (10) An animal that wants to eat the lizards don't find their appearance too appetizing.

(11) Many creatures fool their foes by changing shape. (12) A hawkmoth caterpillar can inflate one end of its body into a "snake head" that move back and forth. (13) A peacock butterfly combine strategies. (14) When its threatened by a bird, the butterfly spreads its wing and exposes large spots that look like eyes. (15) At the same time, it hisses like a snake.

(16) On the other hand, there is those animals that use tricks to get their prey. (17) A snapping turtle has a piece of flesh inside its mouth that look like a worm, which attracts fish who are looking for a meal—but end up as the meal instead. (18) One kind of insect called a praying mantis resembles the petals of a flower, and insects that land on it get a big surprise. (19) And here a final—and rather disgusting—trick. (20) Certain beetles look just like bird droppings; they attract flies, which expect a tasty snack but instead become one.

Scorecard: Number of Errors Found and Corrected _____

19 Using the Past Tense and the Past Participle

You often write about the past, especially if you discuss your own experiences—actions you've done, seen, or heard. In these cases, you use past tense verbs. And you often use a close relation of the past tense: the past participle. These verb forms can be complicated, partly because they come in many varieties and partly because they combine with other verbs in several ways. This chapter will show you how to check verb forms as you edit. You'll learn about

- varieties of the past tense
- the verb forms to select in talking and writing about the past
- other uses of these verb forms

The Past Tense in Its Usual Forms

Like verbs in the present tense, past tense verbs have a long history, and some of their forms changed over many centuries. Most verbs in the past tense share the original past tense ending: -ed, which can be pronounced as /t/ or /d/ or as a full syllable /ɪd/. Although most past tense verbs end in -ed, more than one hundred verbs are irregular. We'll look at both regular and irregular forms in this chapter, starting with regular forms.

Regular Verbs

Here are some past tense sentences:

Subject	Verb	
Ms. Miller	sailed	to Hawaii last week.
I	waved	good-bye to her.
We	packed	some sandwiches for the journey.

Notice that each verb ends in -ed, no matter what its subject. Most verbs in English form the **past tense** in this way. That means they are **regular verbs:**

walk + -ed = walked

seem + -ed = seemed

✔ **TIPS**

For Hearing -ed Endings

When a base word ends with an unvoiced sound (such as /s/, /ch/, /k/, /p/, /th/, /sh/, /f/, or /h/), the final -ed is pronounced /t/.

Examples: *leaped, hiked, reached, raced, missed.*

When a base word ends with a voiced sound (such as /b/, /g/, /m/, /n/, /r/, /v/, /w/, or /z/), the -ed is pronounced /d/.

Examples: *robbed, begged, purred, heaved.*

When a base word ends with the sound /t/ or /d/, the –ed ending is voiced and pronounced as a full syllable.

Examples: *wanted, waited, pleaded, hated, needed.*

> **For verbs that already end in -*e*:**
>
> like + *d* = liked
>
> smoke + *d* = smoked

EXERCISE 1 | Identifying Past Tense Verbs

Circle each verb and then identify its tense. Write *PR* for each present tense verb and *P* for each past tense verb.

_P_ **1.** Ludmilla smiled at the dentist.

_____ **2.** I build houses in my spare time.

_____ **3.** They talk for hours every day.

_____ **4.** He stayed home.

_____ **5.** Lorenzo looked handsome in his new suit.

_____ **6.** I wish you good luck.

_____ **7.** They work downtown.

EXERCISE 2 | Transforming Verb Tenses

The following passage is written in the present tense. Change the passage to the past tense by writing the proper verb form above the line.

The Origins of the Wedding Cake

* * * *

(1) Originally, the bride never *dined* ^dine on the wedding cake; the wedding guests *tossed* ^toss it at her. (2) Until the twentieth century, everyone expects children to come after marriage like night after day—and almost as often. (3) People in ancient times therefore cover the new bride with wheat, a symbol of fertility and wealth. (4) Roman bakers later change the tradition. (5) Around 100 B.C., they start baking the wheat into small, sweet cakes—to be eaten, not thrown. (6) Nevertheless, wedding guests continue to shower the bride with the cakes. (7) Then a new custom develops in which people crumble the cakes over a bride's head. (8) And to increase their chances of having children, the couple swallow some crumbs, a custom known as "eating together."

(9) The practice of eating the crumbs of small wedding cakes extends through-out Western Europe. (10) The English wash down the crumbs with a special ale. (11) They call it "bride's ale," which later evolves into the word *bridal.* (12) Then the cake-eating custom changes even further. (13) Wedding guests bake plain biscuits to bring to the ceremony and place them in one enormous pile. (14) The couple kisses each other over this hill of biscuits. (15) However, in the 1660s, a French chef visits London, watches this ceremony, and considers the practice uncivilized. (16) He therefore decides to change the mountain of ordinary biscuits into a fancy cake with many layers and icing. (17) At first, the British criticize this French creation, but they later adopt the practice as well.

EXERCISE 3 | Writing Past Tense Verbs

Use one of the verbs in the box to complete each sentence with an appropriate past tense verb. You won't use all the verbs, and you shouldn't use the same verb twice.

play	watch	seem	behave	receive
try	look	walk	miss	like

1. Tony _____*received*_____ an award in the weight-lifting class.

2. Your son _____ like a perfect gentleman throughout the ceremony.

3. We _____ the train, so we _____ six miles home.

4. Marie _____ on fourteen pairs of shoes before finding a pair she _____ .

5. The glasses _____ very dirty.

6. Mr. Lim and Ms. Kozinski _____ the film.

To Be

The verb *to be* is irregular. In fact, it's the only past tense verb that changes to agree with its subject. You need to master these forms (see the box on page 208) because they occur so often.

Subject	Verb	Negative contraction
Singular nouns		
I he she it	*was*	*wasn't*
Plural nouns		
we you they	*were*	*weren't*

Notice that the past tense of *to be* acts much like a present tense verb. The verb takes an -s ending (*was*) to agree with *he, she, it,* and singular nouns, as well as with *I.*

EXERCISE 4 | Writing *To Be* in the Past Tense

Write the appropriate past tense form of *to be*.

The Fantastic Mr. Franklin

1. Benjamin Franklin (1706–1790) ___*was*___ an inventor, a scientist, a publisher, an author, a diplomat, and a famous statesman.

2. However, he _____ also the first American international celebrity.

3. While he _____ an ambassador to Paris and London during the American Revolution (1775–1783), no party _____ complete without his presence.

4. He _____ as comfortable with kings and queens as he was with workmen.

5. His accomplishments _____ astonishing, especially since he _____ the tenth of seventeen children from a poor family.

6. His early occupations _____ in printing, first as an apprentice, then a printer, and then a publisher of newspapers and books.

7. He _____ very wealthy when he retired at the age of forty-one.

8. His inventions _____ numerous, including the Franklin Stove, the lightning rod, bifocals, and even the catheter.

9. In politics, he _____ a signer of the Declaration of Independence (1776), the diplomat who _____ in charge of persuading France to support the Revolution, and, later, one of the most important people who _____ responsible for the writing of the U.S. Constitution.

10. Yet, despite being an enemy of the British, Dr. Franklin _____ so respected that he _____ elected to membership in the Royal Society of London.

11. Franklin _____ one of the most amazing people in United States history.

Could and *Would*

Can and *will* are verbs that often appear in your writing as you discuss the present or future. But you use them to discuss ideas in the past, too, although these verbs take different forms. The past tense of *can* is *could*, which discusses ability in the past. Compare these sentences:

> "You *can* kill a man, but you *can't* kill an idea."
> (These verbs refer to present or future abilities.)
>
> —Myrlie Evers, after the killing of her husband Medgar,
> the civil rights leader, in 1963
>
> "No one believed that the great ocean liner *Titanic could* sink."
> (This verb refers to ability in the past.)

The past tense of *will* is *would*, which refers to the future from a point in the past. Compare these sentences:

> "Whether you like it or not, history is on our side. We *will* bury you."
> (This verb refers to the future as it relates to the present.)
>
> —Russian Premier Nikita Khrushchev
> discussing the United States in 1956
>
> "When you first met him, he appeared easygoing, full of humor and nice talking. But if you stayed longer, you'd find he was merciless and *would* destroy anyone and anything blocking his ambition."
> (This verb refers to the future as it relates to the past.)
>
> —The doctor who treated former Chinese dictator Mao Zedong

As you edit your work, check for *can/could* and *will/would*. Are you writing in the past tense? Then use *could* and *would*. Are you writing in the present tense? Then use *can* and *will*.

EXERCISE 5 | **Transforming Verb Tenses**

Rewrite the sentences, changing their tense from the present (a) to the past (b) or the past (b) to the present (a).

1. a. I know that I can pass the test on Friday

   b. I _____*knew that I could*_____ pass the test on Friday.

2. a. He says that he will be late today.

   b. _____ the next day.

3. a. _____

   b. Juan wanted to know if he could borrow your car.

4. a. _____ today.

b. His car wouldn't start yesterday.

5. a. _____

b. Mr. Kim thought that he would graduate in two years.

6. a. No one can answer my question.

b. _____

The Present Perfect Tense

Compare these two sentences:

> Igor lived in Transylvania in 1965.
>
> Igor has lived in Transylvania since 1965.

Put a check next to the sentence that tells you Igor still lives in Transylvania.

You should have identified the second sentence. It is an example of the **present perfect tense,** which in this sentence describes an action that began in the past but relates to the present. The action may continue into the present—or it may end:

> Igor has lived in Transylvania since 1965, { and he is still living there.
>
> but he is moving to Spain today.

Forming the Present Perfect Tense

Circle the verbs in these present perfect tense sentences:

> Sammi Scholar has studied English since 1980.
>
> I have owned my collection of expensive cars for quite a while.
>
> Ralph Reed hasn't come to class in a week.

You should have found two parts to the verb in each sentence: (1) the helping verb *has* or *have* and (2) a verb form called the **past participle,** which for regular verbs ends in -*ed,* just like the past tense form. Notice that the helping verb—*has* or *have*—is in the present tense and changes to agree with its subject, but the past participle does not change:

> *has* OR *have* + past participle = present perfect tense
> (verb ending
> in -*ed*)

Using the Present Perfect Tense

The present perfect tense is used:

1. to describe an action that began in the past but continues into the present.

Often such expressions include *since,* which signals the start of the action, or *for,* which signals the length of the action:

> Rome has been the capital of Italy only *since 1870.*
>
> California has prepared for a major earthquake *for many years.*

2. to describe a completed action in the indefinite past (without mentioning a specific time) that relates to the present.

When you discuss the past in relationship to the present, you usually use the present perfect tense:

Present perfect	Present
Many *have searched* for the Fountain of Youth,	but its location still *remains* a mystery.
I *have* already *received* my driver's license,	so I *don't* need to apply for one now.

Remember that the present perfect tense describes actions in the *indefinite past.* If you describe an action that was completed at *a specific time in the past,* you must use the past tense. Compare these examples:

	indefinite time in past
Present perfect:	I have studied English *for many years.*
	Guillermo has learned to swim.
	specific time in the past
Past:	I studied English *six years ago.*
	Guillermo learned to swim *when he was five.*

Affirmative statements in the present perfect tense often include the adverb *already:*

> I don't have to take calculus. I *have already completed* my mathematics requirements.

Negative statements and questions often include the adverb *yet:*

> I need to take biology. I *haven't registered* for any science courses *yet.*
>
> *Have* you *registered yet?*

| EXERCISE 6 | Transforming Verb Tense |

Change the past tense sentences into present perfect tense sentences.

1. Most Americans loved hamburgers all their lives. _Most Americans have loved_ _hamburgers all their lives._

2. However, hamburgers never contained ham, only ground beef. _____
   _____

3. They continued to be a part of U.S. culture since 1900, when Louis Lassen first
   created them. _____
   _____

4. Buns surrounded hamburgers since the St. Louis Exposition in 1904. _____
   _____

5. The original home of hamburgers, Louis' Lunch in New Haven, Connecticut, served
   hamburgers until the present day. _____
   _____

6. For many years, people all over the world dined on hamburgers at fast-food
   restaurants. _____
   _____

| EXERCISE 7 | Writing Verbs |

Write the appropriate past tense or present perfect form of the verb in parentheses.

1. Americans (consume) _____ _have consumed_ _____ hot dogs for over 120 years.

2. The history of the hot dog (start) _____ 3,500 years ago in
   Babylonia (now Iraq), where people (stuff) _____ animal
   intestines with spiced meats.

3. The practice (continue) _____ throughout European and
   Mediterranean countries for thousands of years.

4. The hot dog, or *frankfurter,* (originate) _____ in Frankfurt,
   Germany, in the 1850s.

5. Because its curved shape (resemble) _____ the shape of a
   German dog called a *dachshund,* it became known as a "dachshund sausage."

6. The name of the popular food (evolved) _____ from these
   German origins.

EXERCISE 8	Writing Sentences in the Present Perfect Tense

After each statement, write a present perfect tense sentence using the verb in parentheses—or use any verb that expresses your meaning.

1. Maria moved to Los Angeles a while ago. (live) _She has lived there for two_

   years.

2. Mr. Smith is looking for a new job. (be) _____

   _____

3. Stephan's mother is in the hospital. (visit) _____

   _____

4. Mr. Wong speaks English very well. (study) _____

   _____

5. Ludmilla is an excellent violinist. (play) _____

   _____

6. I don't need to register for classes. (register) _____

   _____

The Present Perfect Progressive Tense

A variation of the present perfect tense is the **present perfect progressive tense,** which describes continuing actions that started in the past and relate to the present. Verbs in this tense consist of three words: *has* or *have* + *been* + the present participle. Here are some examples:

> They *have been working* hard for a week.
>
> He *has been sleeping* for more than twelve hours.
>
> I *haven't been attending* classes since last week, when I got sick.

EXERCISE 9	Writing Sentences in the Present Perfect Progressive Tense

After each statement, write a sentence using the present perfect progressive tense.

1. Juan is still on vacation. _He has been visiting his family in Venezuela._

2. Mr. Kim has a new job. _____

   _____

3. Ms. Redlinski lost her job a while ago. _____

   _____

4. Mr. Han became a teacher two years ago. _____

_____

5. I got sick last weekend. _____

6. The rain is still coming down hard. _____

_____

The Past Perfect Tense

Compare these three sentences:

> Igor lived in Transylvania in 1995.
>
> Igor has lived in Transylvania since 1995.
>
> Igor had lived in Transylvania before 1995.

Put a check next to the sentence that means Igor began living in Transylvania before 1995.

You should have picked the third sentence. It's an example of the **past perfect tense,** which we'll now examine.

Forming the Past Perfect Tense

Like the present perfect tense, the past perfect tense is formed with a past participle, but the helping verb is *had.*

> *had* + past participle = past perfect tense

Using the Past Perfect Tense

Unlike the present perfect tense, the past perfect tense is purely a *past tense.* It describes an action that occurred before a later time in the past:

> earlier   later
> Columbus *had traveled* to America before Amerigo Vespucci did.
>
> later   earlier
> A German geographer said that Vespucci had arrived first. So the geographer decided to call the New World *America.*

EXERCISE 10	Writing Sentences in the Past Perfect Tense

Using the verb supplied, complete each sentence with a clause in the past perfect tense.

1. (lock) Juan forgot that *he had locked his keys inside the car.* _____

2. (study) Maria told her teacher that _____

_____

3. (receive) Thomas celebrated after _____

_____

4. (close) Mr. Kim remembered that _____

_____

5. (finish) I was very happy because _____

_____

6. (rent) Sylvia told her parents that _____

_____

EXERCISE 11	Writing More Verbs

TIPS

For Distinguishing between the Past Perfect and Present Perfect Tenses

The present perfect and the past perfect tenses are similar, so they are easy to confuse. Remember these differences:

1. The present perfect tense relates the past to the present. Its helping verbs are *has* and *have*.

2. The past perfect tense relates an earlier past action to a more recent one. Its helping verb is *had*.

In each sentence, write the present perfect tense or the past perfect tense, using **been** (the past participle of *to be*).

1. Matthew ____*had been*____ absent a lot, but then his attendance improved.

2. I _____ just _____ to the dentist.

3. We _____n't _____ home to see our parents this year.

4. Anna _____ active in three or four different clubs until she became ill.

5. Working and going to school this semester _____n't _____ easy.

6. Mr. Wilson _____ sick for a week before he finally felt better.

Irregular Verbs

English is full of irregular verbs. More than one hundred verbs don't form their past tense or past participles by adding *-ed*. This section explores seven categories of irregular verbs. You'll find many verbs you already know. But study all the categories, and make a list of the verbs you don't know.

Category 1: -d to -t

In these verbs, the final -d in the present tense changes to -t in the past tense and past participle:

Present tense	Past tense	Past participle
bend	bent	bent
build	built	built
lend	lent	lent
send	sent	sent
spend	spent	spent

EXERCISE 12	Writing Irregular Verbs

TIPS

For Distinguishing *Lend* **from** *Borrow*
In some languages, *lend* and *borrow* are the same verb, but not in English. *Lend* means *giving* something to someone and expecting that the person will return it:

I *lent* my brother ten dollars. (OR I *lent* ten dollars to my brother.)

Borrow means *taking* something from someone, expecting to return it later:

My brother *borrowed* ten dollars from me.

Write the past tense of the verb in parentheses.

**James Buchanan "Diamond Jim" Brady (1856–1917):
The World's Greatest Eater**

1. James Buchanan Brady (build)_____*built*_____ a reputation that no one has ever been able to match: He (be)_____ the greatest eater of all time.

2. Of course, Brady (spend)_____ huge amounts of money in earning the title, for no one (be able)_____ to eat like him on a poor person's income.

3. Born to Irish working-class parents in New York, he first (work)_____ at a railroad station, carrying people's luggage. Then, a few years later, he began to sell railroad equipment, and this job (send)_____ him on his way to becoming very wealthy.

4. By putting together a series of multimillion-dollar railroad deals, he later (build)_____ large fortune.

Category 2: -d and Possible Vowel Change

In these verbs, the final consonant becomes -d. Some have no vowel change before the final consonant:

Present tense	Past tense	Past participle
have	had	had
make	made	made

However, some do have a vowel change before the final consonant:

Present tense	Past tense	Past participle
flee	fled	fled
hear	heard	heard
lay	laid	laid
pay	paid	paid
say	said	said
sell	sold	sold
tell	told	told

EXERCISE 13 | Writing Irregular Verbs

✓ TIPS

For Distinguishing
Say from *Tell*

In some languages, *say* and *tell* are the same verb, but in English they are different:

1. Usually, *tell* is followed by an indirect object (often the person to whom the words are addressed)

   I *told my brother* to rush.

   He *told me* to wait.

   I *told him,* "Don't be late."

2. *Say* is not followed by an indirect object, so the verb often doesn't identify the person addressed:

   I *said,* "Please be on time."

   I *said* that he should be on time.

   To identify the person addressed, use the preposition *to:*

   I *said to him,* "Please be on time."

   I *said* "hello" *to her.*

Write the past tense of the verb in parentheses.

1. Jim Brady (make) _____*made*_____ millions of dollars when he (sell) _____ railroad equipment to large companies throughout the country.

2. He proceeded to spend his money in ways no one (be able) _____ to ever imagine.

3. Each day, he (lay) _____ out his choice of clothing to wear from a selection of over two hundred custom-made suits and fifty silk hats.

4. His collection of jewelry (have) _____ a net worth of at least $2 million.

5. For a single set of buttons and jewels for one shirt and suit, Jim (pay) _____ $87,315.

6. People (say) _____ that his diamond rings (be) _____ the biggest ever seen in New York, and among his more than thirty famous watches, he (have) _____ one that cost $17,500.

7. No one ever (hear) _____ Brady apologize for his fancy jewelry, and he was proud of his nickname, "Diamond Jim."

Category 3: -*t* and Possible Vowel Change

In these verbs, a final -*t* is added, and there is usually a vowel change before the final consonant:

Present tense	Past tense	Past participle
creep	crept	crept
feel	felt	felt
keep	kept	kept
leave	left	left

lose	lost	lost
mean	meant	meant
sleep	slept	slept
sweep	swept	swept

Some verbs show an additional vowel change and add *-ght* at the end of the word:

Present tense	Past tense	Past participle
bring	brought	brought
buy	bought	bought
catch	caught	caught
seek	sought	sought
teach	taught	taught
think	thought	thought

EXERCISE 14 | Writing Irregular Verbs

Write the past tense of the verb in parentheses.

1. Brady (leave)_____*left*_____ none of his possessions alone but added expensive jewelry to them all.

2. He (keep)_____ twelve gold-plated bicycles with diamonds and rubies in the handlebars for his trips in Central Park.

3. For his girlfriend, the singer Lillian Russell, Brady (buy)_____ a special bicycle with pearl handlebars and emeralds and sapphires on the spokes of each wheel.

4. Every Sunday, Miss Russell (catch)_____ the attention of newspaper photographers when, dressed in white, she (bring)_____ this famous machine to the park for a ride.

5. However, although Diamond Jim liked women, he (feel)_____ his strongest affection for another matter: food.

6. Brady's achievements in eating were so amazing that they (sweep)_____ away all competition for greatness.

7. The man never (lose)_____ an opportunity to eat, and stories of his accomplishments (teach)_____ the world what true love for food really (mean)_____ .

Category 4: Single Vowel Change

In these verbs, only the vowel changes, and the past tense and the past participle are the same:

Present tense	Past tense	Past participle
bind	bound	bound
bleed	bled	bled
breed	bred	bred
dig	dug	dug
feed	fed	fed
fight	fought	fought
find	found	found
grind	ground	ground
hang	hung	hung
hold	held	held
lead	led	led
meet	met	met
shine	shone (OR shined)	shone
shoot	shot	shot
sit	sat	sat
slide	slid	slid
speed	sped	sped
spin	spun	spun
stand	stood	stood
stick	stuck	stuck
strike	struck	struck
swing	swung	swung
win	won	won
wind	wound	wound
wring	wrung	wrung

In a few cases, the past participle is the same as the present tense:

Present tense	Past tense	Past participle
become	became	become
come	came	come
run	ran	run

EXERCISE 15　|　Writing Irregular Verbs

Write the past tense of the verb in parentheses.

1. For a typical breakfast, Brady (feed)_____*fed*_____ himself grits, eggs, corn bread, muffins, pancakes, chops, fried potatoes, a steak, and a full gallon of orange juice.

2. This "golden nectar" (win)_____ Brady's love when he was younger, and he never (find)_____ any pleasure in drinking liquor for the rest of his life.

3. Diamond Jim (become)_____ hungry during the midmorning, so this (lead)_____ to a little snack of two or three dozen clams and oysters.

4. After he (sit)_____ down to a real lunch at 12:30, he (swing)_____ into action by eating additional clams and oysters, a platter of boiled lobsters, three deviled crabs, steak, and several kinds of pie.

5. He (fight)_____ off his hunger until afternoon tea, when he (find)_____ time for a platter of seafood and another of his favorite drinks, lemon soda.

6. After that, Jim (hold)_____ his appetite until the evening, when it (come)_____ time for his major meal of the day.

7. He often (wind)_____ up at Charlie Rector's—a fancy New York restaurant—where the owner bragged that Brady (be)_____ "the best twenty-five customers" he (have)_____.

8. Diamond Jim started the meal when he (slide)_____ two or three dozen Maryland oysters down his throat.

9. Crabs (come)_____ next—six of them—and then at least two bowls of green turtle soup.

10. This (lead)_____ into the main courses: six or seven lobsters, two whole ducks, two portions of turtle meat, a sirloin steak, and vegetables—followed by an entire platter of pastries for dessert.

11. Then Brady usually (have)_____ a two-pound box of chocolate as an after-dinner treat.

12. Crowds of people (stand)_____ around the table to cheer on his progress—and to make bets on whether he (will)_____ drop dead before dessert.

Category 5: Double Vowel Change

In these verbs, the vowel changes in each form:

Present tense	Past tense	Past participle
begin	began	begun
drink	drank	drunk
ring	rang	rung
sink	sank (OR sunk)	sunk
spring	sprang (OR sprung)	sprung
swim	swam	swum

EXERCISE 16 | **Writing Irregular Verbs**

Write the past tense of the verb in parentheses.

1. Jim never (drink)_____ any alcohol, but he had a love for

sweets that (spring)_____ as much from a desire for quality as for

quantity.

2. For example, once when visiting Boston, Brady (hear)_____ about a

local factory that (make)_____ fine chocolates.

3. He was impressed after trying a five-pound box of the chocolates. "Best darn

candy I ever ate," his voice (ring)_____ out.

4. As he (begin)_____ to order several hundred boxes of candy for friends

and acquaintances, he was told that there wasn't enough merchandise.

5. "Heck," said Brady, taking out his checkbook, "tell them to build a candy factory

twice the size. Here's the money." The owner nearly (sink)_____ to his

knees when Brady (hold)_____ out a check for $150,000 to be paid

back in candy.

Category 6: No Change

These verbs end in *-t* or *-d* and do not change for the past tense or the past participle:

Present tense	Past tense	Past participle
bet	bet	bet
burst	burst	burst
cast	cast	cast
cut	cut	cut

✓ TIPS

For Checking Irregular Verbs

If you aren't sure you've used the correct past tense or past participle form of a verb, look it up in a dictionary. The entry appears in the present tense, and the past tense and past participle are listed after it. So, for example, if you want to see if *swum* is the correct past participle, look under *swim*. You'll find all of its forms: **swim** vb. / **swam** / **swum** / **swimming**

fit	fit (OR fitted)	fit (OR fitted)
hit	hit	hit
hurt	hurt	hurt
let	let	let
put	put	put
quit	quit	quit
read	read	read
rid	rid	rid
set	set	set
shed	shed	shed
shut	shut	shut
slit	slit	slit
spread	spread	spread
thrust	thrust	thrust

EXERCISE 17 | Writing Irregular Verbs

Write the past tense of the verb in parentheses.

1. Brady was at Charlie Rector's when a friend (tell)_____*told*_____ him about a special sauce for fish prepared from a secret recipe at a restaurant in Paris.

2. Jim (let)_____ Rector know that the owner (have)_____ to serve the dish at his restaurant or Brady (will)_____ take his business elsewhere.

3. The next day, Rector (make)_____ his son George leave college and he (put)_____ the young man on a boat to Paris.

4. Using a false name, the young Rector washed pots in the kitchen of the French restaurant until he (fit)_____ in well enough to learn the secret of the fabulous sauce.

5. After more than two years, George (quit)_____ the job in Paris and returned home.

6. As soon as George stepped off the boat, Brady (thrust)_____ himself forward and demanded, "Have you got the sauce?"

7. That night, as Jim (cut)_____ into the last of his nine portions of fish, he (spread)_____ some sauce on a piece of bread and (shut)_____ his eyes in pleasure.

8. Going back to the kitchen to congratulate George, Brady (say)_____, "If you poured some of the sauce over a towel, I believe I could eat all of it."

Category 7: -*n* or -*en* and Possible Vowel Change

In these verbs, the past participle is formed by adding -*n* or -*en*. Sometimes there are vowel changes as well:

Present tense	Past tense	Past participle
beat	beat	beaten
bite	bit	bitten
blow	blew	blown
break	broke	broken
choose	chose	chosen
do	did	done
draw	drew	drawn
drive	drove	driven
eat	ate	eaten
fall	fell	fallen
fly	flew	flown
forget	forgot	forgotten
forgive	forgave	forgiven
freeze	froze	frozen
get	got	gotten
give	gave	given
go	went	gone
grow	grew	grown
hide	hid	hidden
know	knew	known
lie	lay	lain
ride	rode	ridden
rise	rose	risen
see	saw	seen
shake	shook	shaken
slay	slew	slain
speak	spoke	spoken
steal	stole	stolen
strive	strove	striven
swear	swore	sworn
take	took	taken
tear	tore	torn
throw	threw	thrown
wake	woke	woken
wear	wore	worn
weave	wove	woven
write	wrote	written

Collaborative Activity 1

Learning Verbs

Make a list of the verbs in Categories 1 through 7 that you don't know. Exchange lists with a classmate, and quiz each other on the forms of the verbs.

EXERCISE 18 | **Writing Irregular Verbs**

Write the past tense of the verb in parentheses.

1. For years, medical experts (give)_____ *gave* _____ the 250-pound Brady only a short time to live because he (take)_____ such poor care of his health.

2. Every time a doctor (speak)_____ to him about changing his eating habits, Jim quickly (forget)_____ the advice.

3. However, when his fifty-seventh birthday (draw)_____ near, Diamond Jim (fall)_____ victim to serious stomach trouble.

4. Until then, Diamond Jim (go)_____ on eating whatever he (choose)_____, but he now (know)_____ he (have) _____ to listen to the doctors.

5. Therefore, he (break)_____ his old habits, (swear)_____ off rich food, and never again (overeat)_____ .

6. His body eventually (wear)_____ down, and five years later the stomach illness (take)_____ his life.

7. After doctors (do)_____ an autopsy of his body, they (write)_____ that, over the years, Brady's stomach (grow)_____ five times larger than a normal person's.

8. In his will, Jim (give)_____ much of his fortune to the James Brady Urological Clinic, which he (begin)_____ at Johns Hopkins Hospital in Baltimore before his death.

Collaborative Activity 2

Changing Verb Forms
Write seven present tense sentences, using one verb from each of the seven categories. Exchange papers with a classmate. Turn each sentence into a past tense sentence, a present perfect tense sentence, and a past perfect tense sentence. Then check each other's work.

EXERCISE 19 | **Writing Sentences**

Choose five past tense forms of the verbs in Category 7 and write a sentence using each form. Then rewrite each of these sentences in the present perfect tense, rewording the sentence if necessary.

Other Uses of the Past Participle

The past participle has many uses for expressing ideas. In addition to serving as the main verb in the present perfect and past perfect tenses, the past participle can appear in several other places.

In Three-Word Verb Phrases

Many three-word verb phrases contain a modal + *have* + the past participle to analyze the past:

Modal +	*have* +	past participle
could	have	done
may	have	seen
should	have	gone
might	have	taken
must	have	been
would	have	thought

EXERCISE 20 | **Writing Verb Phrases**

Complete each sentence, using *have* and an appropriate past participle.

1. I didn't do well on the examination. *I should have done better.* _____

2. Yesterday was a holiday, and we could _____

   _____

3. If I had listened to your advice, I would _____

   _____

4. Mr. Fong wasn't at work yesterday. He must _____

   _____

5. I don't know if Dmitri wants to have lunch with us. He may _____

   _____ already.

6. Many people thought that they saw a comet last night, but they might _____

   _____

In the Passive Voice

The past participle is used in the **passive voice,** as in this example:

> This watch *was given* to me by my grandfather.

Note that *the watch* did nothing. The grandfather did the giving. In other words, the subject is *passive;* it does not act but is acted upon. The passive voice always takes this pattern:

> subject + *to be* + past participle

Here are three more examples of the passive voice in three different tenses:

Present tense:	The awards *are* always *presented* by President Gray.
Future tense:	Your grades *will be mailed* to you.
Past tense:	My keys *were lost.*

The passive voice often sounds awkward, so don't overuse it. Use it only (1) when the action is more important than the person who performs it or (2) when we don't know or care who performs the action.

Passive voice:	Three goals were scored by Pelé. (This sounds awkward.)
Active voice:	Pele scored three goals. (This sounds much better.)

As an Adjective

Sometimes a past participle doesn't express an action but becomes an adjective describing a noun. For example, a past participle often follows a linking verb (for example, *is, seem, become,* or *sound*) as a subject complement, describing the subject of the sentence:

Subject	Linking verb	Past participle
I	feel	tired.
The eggs	seem	done.
The can opener	was	broken.

Write a word ending in *-ed* to describe the subject of the following sentence:

Yolanda looked _____ when she heard the news.

Did you write *surprised, startled, excited,* or *annoyed?* These words are past participles.
   A past participle can also begin an adjective phrase that follows and describes a noun:

	adjective phrase
A woman	*named Melinda* just asked to see you.
I've always liked plays	*written by Shakespeare.*

Finally, past participles can also be adjectives before nouns:

A *frightened* dog hid under the table.
He's a *well-known* actor.

TIPS

For Distinguishing between Participles

Interesting causes interest: an *interesting* book

Interested feels the interest: I am *interested in* this book.

Look carefully at the words before or after nouns when you edit. An incorrect past participle form can be confusing and distracting, as in this sentence:

That tire man is sitting down for a minute.

Does the sentence say that the man sells automobile tires or that the man is tired? We can't be sure.

EXERCISE 21	Writing Sentences

Read the following model sentences. Using the verbs in parentheses, write sentences that follow the pattern of each model sentence.

1. We *were amazed* at the skill of the hibachi cook.

   (impress) *I was impressed with the service at the restaurant.*

   (annoy) _____

   _____

2. The Ferris wheel ride is perfectly safe, so please *don't be frightened.*

   (scare) _____

   _____

   (bore) _____

   _____

3. I *am accustomed* to getting up at 5:00 A.M.

   (use) _____

   _____

   (commit) _____

   _____

4. He *seems interested* in our book group.

   (involve in) _____

   _____

   (impress with) _____

   _____

EXERCISE 22	Writing Past Participles

Write an appropriate past participle for each of the following sentences.

1. He sells _____*used*_____ cars.

2. Do you know a man _____ Harry Leggs?

3. The police caught the man selling _____ goods.

4. Several players were hurt during the game: Lopez had a _____ nose; Tomei suffered a _____ leg muscle; and Hansen was carried off with a _____ ankle.

5. You can find ice cream in the _____ food section.

6. Try not to go to places _____ by too many tourists.

7. I don't like my steak rare, but I don't want it _____ either.

IN SUMMARY

Past Tense Verbs
- discuss events that occurred before the present
- end normally in *-ed* but include more than a hundred irregular forms
- include *was/were* for *be* and *could/would* for *can/will*

Past Participles
- usually end in *-ed* but include more than a hundred irregular forms, which may be different from the irregular past tense forms
- appear in perfect tenses, which discuss events that occurred before a later time: The present perfect tense uses *have/has* as the helping verb; the past perfect tense uses *had*; the present perfect progressive tense uses *has/have been* + present participle
- appear after *have* in three-word verbs beginning with modals such as *could, should, may, might,* and so on, and that speculate about the past
- appear after *be* in the passive voice, in which the subject receives the action and doesn't perform it
- function as adjectives after linking verbs or before or after nouns

EDITING FOR MASTERY

Mastery Exercise 1   ***Correcting Verb Errors***

The passage contains seventeen errors in past tense and past participle forms. The first two have been corrected for you. Find and correct the remaining errors.

The Fountain of Youth Industry

(1) Long before Walt Disney ∧*has* even thought of opening a park in Orlando,
    had

people ∧*was* paying to see Florida's most popular tourist attraction: the Fountain of
      were

Youth. (2) Supposedly, Juan Ponce de Léon discover Florida while searching for the

fountain back in 1512. (3) But that story was just a legend.

(4) In 1512, Ponce was out of work. (5) The king of Spain has removed him as

governor of Puerto Rico. (6) Soon, however, the king let him explore new lands in

exchange for 10 percent of all the gold he can find. (7) The king didn't mentioned

anything about a fountain of youth, and neither did Ponce. (8) In fact, he had never

looked for magical fountains. (9) In earlier voyages, he had seeked gold and slaves and

had develop a reputation for cruelty.

(10) In 1535, a Spanish historian claimed, without proof, that Ponce had went looking for the fountain. (11) That story reappeared in 1868, when a historian said that Ponce had been searching for a fountain that would make him young again. (12) Other historians accepted this story, added details, and located the fountain in various areas in Florida.

(13) In 1870, a man in St. Augustine, Florida, named a pond on his property Ponce de Léon Spring. (14) The pond drawed a few visitors who drank its water. (15) Then in 1908, Louella McConnell tolded an amazing story about her property in St. Augustine. (16) She claimed that she seen a large stone cross Ponce de Léon had put under a tree to identify a fresh-water spring. (17) She also produced a map of Ponce's from a box bury near the tree. (18) When other people doubted her evidence, the map mysteriously became too faded to read. (19) Then McConnell began to act crazy. (20) She wrote about secret plans to kill women, was arrested for firing a gun, and told the judge that a police officer was trying to feed her poison apples.

(21) Meanwhile, a millionaire name Henry Flagler was building fancy hotels in St. Augustine and encouraging his wealthy friends to visit. (22) They usually visited the Fountain of Youth, where McConnell charge admission and sold bottled water and postcards. (23) McConnell sold her land to a man from Massachusetts in 1919, but then changed her mind and sued him. (24) Even though the man won the suit, he give up his plans for the property.

(25) After McConnell's death in an automobile accident in 1923, a man named Walter Fraser acquired the property, and make the Fountain of Youth into a popular tourist attraction. (26) An early Christian cemetery was discover on the property in 1934, indicating that the first Spanish town in the New World was probably located there—but this was not because of Ponce de Léon.

(27) Today, Fraser's son, John, runs the park. (28) It contains a fountain (where visitors can have a drink), a Native American burial site, and a gift shop.

Scorecard: Number of Errors Found and Corrected _____

Collaborative Activity 3

Comparing Answers

Compare your answers with a classmate. Your instructor may ask you to report your findings to the class.

Mastery Exercise 2

Correcting Verb Errors

The passage contains sixteen errors in past tense and past participle verb forms. The first one has been corrected for you. Find and correct the remaining errors.

The Dolphin Pilot

helped

(1) He was a fourteen-foot dolphin, who, for more than twenty years, ~~help~~ steamships avoid being shipwrecked off New Zealand. (2) He was the first dolphin whose life was protected by a special law. (3) Pelorus Jack, name for Pelorus Sound, become famous in 1888 when he guided steamships through six miles of dangerous water in Cook Strait, New Zealand. (4) He was love by both sailors and passengers who watched him playfully leaping above the waves. (5) He will often scratch his back against the ship's side and then swiftly slide out in front to guide a steamer along. (6) After getting one ship through safely, the dolphin would immediately leave to wait for another.

(7) Passengers aboard ships described him as silvery white, with eyes that looked "almost human." (8) He always traveled alone and easily cutted through the waves. (9) When two ships needed his services at the same time, Pelorus Jack always choose the faster steamship.

(10) In 1903, a drunken sailor on the *SS Penguin* shooted at Pelorus Jack with a rifle. (11) Luckily, the shot missed. (12) Jack didn't showed up again for two weeks, but then he came back. (13) However, he never again accompanied the *Penguin,* which was wreck in 1909 in Cook Strait. (14) In September 1904, the government of New Zealand passed a law to protect Pelorus Jack, for he had became an international celebrity. (15) A movie was make about him. (16) There was postcards that featured his picture. (17) There were many songs wrote about him. (18) A chocolate bar was named after him. (19) Sightseers, including the famous author Mark Twain, came great distances to see him, and when they seen him jumping out of the water toward them, someone would always shout, "Here comes Pelorus Jack!"

(20) In 1912, Pelorus Jack disappeared. (21) A local newspaper printed an article saying that if he died it was a pity, but if he was killed, it was a shame. (22) Pelorus Jack never appear again.

(23) Incidentally, no one will ever know, but he may have been a she.

Scorecard: Number of Errors Found and Corrected _____

20 Keeping Words in Order

Correct word order in English is essential. The location of a word can determine its function, and the word order of a sentence determines its meaning. This chapter will help you place words correctly by showing you

- different ways to express questions
- correct placement of objects, phrasal verbs, and adverbs
- correct use and placement of negative words in sentences

Indirect and Quoted Questions

Questions reverse the order of a subject and verb. But questions can also be contained in statements. This section looks at two types.

Indirect Questions

Some sentences ask a question:

> How can I get to the train station?

But some sentences imply that a question is being asked without really asking it:

> I want to know how I can get to the train station.

This is an **indirect question.** It is actually part of a statement, so its word order and end punctuation follow the pattern for statements, not direct questions. Compare these sentences:

Direct question:	Where is the office?
Indirect question:	I wonder where the office is.

Note these differences:

- A **direct question** uses question word order—a verb before the subject—and ends in a question mark.
- An **indirect question** uses statement word order—the subject before the verb—and ends in a period.

An indirect question can also be included in a statement that makes a request or asks for information. Here are examples:

Request:	Please tell me *where the registrar's office is.*
Information:	I want to know *if the test is on Friday.*

EXERCISE 1	Writing Indirect Questions

Rewrite each direct question as an indirect question, beginning with the words provided.

1. Do you need any help?

I want to know *if you need any help.* _____

2. How are your parents?

I would be interested to hear _____

3. When does the class begin?

Please tell me _____

4. Did you study for the final examination?

I want to know if _____

5. When can I call the doctor?

Let me find out when _____

6. Where is room 814?

I wonder _____

Collaborative Activity 1

Writing Questions

Write six sentences—three with direct questions and three with indirect questions. Exchange papers with a classmate. Change direct questions to indirect questions and indirect questions to direct questions. Check each other's work.

Quoted Direct Questions

For more information on punctuating quotations, see Chapter 29.

Quoted direct questions differ from indirect questions in word order, punctuation, verb tense, and pronoun use. Quotations reproduce the exact words of the speaker—in the same order and tense. But indirect questions change word order, tense, and pronouns to fit within the statement that introduces them. Note the differences in the following examples:

Direct question	Indirect question
He asked me, "Are you all right?"	He asked me if *I was* all right.
He asked me, "Were you working?"	He asked me if *I had been working.*
He asked me, "When will you come?"	He asked me when *I would come.*

He asked me, "Why can't you come with me?"	He asked me *why I couldn't come with him.*
He asked me, "Did you go to the party?"	He asked me *if I had gone* to the party.
He asked me, "Have you finished?"	He asked me *whether I had finished.*

EXERCISE 2	Writing Questions

Rewrite each sentence as a quoted direct question (a) or as an indirect question (b).

1. a. She asked me, "Are you going to the party?"

　 b. *She asked me if I was going to the party.* _____

2. a. She asked me, "Do you want to come with me?"

　 b. _____

3. a. _____

　 b. She asked me when I could come.

4. a. She asked me, "Did you buy a new car?"

　 b. _____

5. a. She asked me, "Where were you when I called?"

　 b. _____

6. a. _____

　 b. She asked me if I had met her sister.

Objects after Verbs

Objects, which receive the action of verbs, can be placed between or after verbs, depending on the type of verbs. We'll look at both patterns here.

Direct and Indirect Objects

Many verbs take a **direct object,** which receives the action of the verb:

Subject	Verb	Direct object
A repairman	fixed	the broken window.
The company	will open	a branch store.

But some verbs take two objects: a direct object, which receives the action of the verb, and an **indirect object.** As shown on page 234, the indirect object indicates *to whom* or *for whom* the action is, was, or will be done:

Subject	Verb	Indirect object	Direct object
The repairman	sent	us	the bill.
The store	should offer	its customers	many services.

Notice that the indirect object is placed *before* the direct object.

There is a second way to place the direct and indirect objects in a sentence. You may write the direct object *first* and then follow it with *to* or *for* + the indirect object.

- Use *to* with verbs that discuss transferring something or some information to someone: *give, send, mail, take, hand, tell, serve,* and so on.
- Use *for* with verbs that discuss preparing something for someone: *make, prepare, bake, cook,* and so on:

Subject	Verb	Direct object	Indirect object
The repairman	sent	the bill	to us.
The store	should offer	many services	to its customers.
Guillermo	made	some appetizers	for his guests.

These are the only two ways to place direct and indirect objects. They should *never* be placed in this order: *to* (or *for*) + object + direct object:

Incorrect:	I lent to Juan my pen.
Correct:	I lent Juan my pen. I lent my pen to Juan.
Incorrect:	Guillermo made for his guests some appetizers.
Correct:	Guillermo made some appetizers for his guests. Guillermo made his guests some appetizers.

EXERCISE 3 | Writing Two Objects

Rewrite each sentence, changing the position of the indirect object and adding (or removing) *to* or *for.*

1. In 1837, the famous showman P. T. Barnum sold the public his first trick.

In 1837, the famous showman P. T. Barnum sold his first trick to the public.

2. Over 10,000 New Yorkers bought tickets for themselves.

_____

3. Barnum showed them a 161-year-old woman.

_____

4. When an autopsy after her death revealed that she was only eighty, the newspapers told her real age to the public.

_____

_____

5. Barnum had told his customers a lie.

_____

6. Naturally, Barnum did not give refunds to anyone.

_____

EXERCISE 4 | **Writing More Objects**

Using the verbs in parentheses, write sentences containing both direct and indirect objects. Be sure to vary the object word order.

1. (give) _Tomas gave me a piece of paper._

OR

Tomas gave a piece of paper to me.

2. (tell) _____

OR

_____

3. (make) _____

OR

_____

4. (sell) _____

OR

_____

5. (send) _____

OR

_____

6. (bring)_____

OR

_____

Objects with Phrasal Verbs

When you write a sentence using an action verb (which tells what a subject *does, did,* or *will do*), the normal word order is subject + verb + object. The object can be a noun or pronoun:

Subject	Verb	Noun object	Pronoun object
We	picked	some grapes	
We	picked		them.
Asmaa	dropped	the plate.	
Asmaa	dropped		it.
I	took	the dishes.	
I	took		them.

Suppose, however, that you change the meaning of a verb by adding another word that looks like a preposition:

picked up	dropped off	took out

These two-word verbs (sometimes they have three words) are called **phrasal verbs,** and with them the placement of the object is more complicated. With many phrasal verbs, a noun + object can precede or follow the second part of the verb:

I *picked up* some grapes at the store. I *picked* some grapes *up* at the store.

Asmaa *dropped off* the book at my house. Asmaa *dropped* the book *off* at my house.

Try writing the sentence "I _____ the dishes _____" in two ways, using *took away* as the verb.

_____

_____

Did you write, "I took away the dishes" and "I took the dishes away"? Then you see the flexibility of noun objects.

Unlike noun objects, however, pronoun objects *must* come between the two words of the phrasal verb:

I *picked* them *up.*   NOT   I picked up them.

Asmaa *dropped* it *off.*

I *took* them *out.*

Some phrasal verbs don't treat objects in this way. In general, the following rules apply.

Separable Phrasal Verbs

A phrasal verb is **separable** when it moves or changes the condition of its object. A noun object can come before or after the second word of the verb:

> We *put* the dishes *away*. We *put away* the dishes. (The verb *put away* moved the dishes.)
>
> I *cheered* my friend *up*. I *cheered up* my friend. (The verb *cheered up* changed the mental condition of your friend.)

A pronoun object *always* comes between the two words of a separable phrasal verb:

> We *put* them *away*.
>
> I *cheered* him *up*.

Inseparable Phrasal Verbs

A phrasal verb is **inseparable** when it *does not* move or change the condition of an object. In this case, the noun or pronoun object must come *after* the complete verb.

> I *ran into* an old friend yesterday.
>
> I always *count on* you for help. (The objects don't move or change in these sentences.)

EXERCISE 5 | Placing Objects with Phrasal Verbs

Rewrite each sentence. In the first rewritten sentence, move the noun object. In the second, replace the noun object with a pronoun.

1. Please clean up the mess.
   a. *Please clean the mess up.*
   b. *Please clean it up.*

2. I need to hand in my homework.
   a. _____
   b. _____

3. Did anyone figure out the solution?
   a. _____
   b. _____

4. Some people couldn't come, so we called the party off.

a. _____

b. _____

5. We fixed up the house before selling it.

a. _____

b. _____

6. You must fill these forms out to register for classes.

a. _____

b. _____

| EXERCISE 6 | Placing More Objects with Phrasal Verbs |

After each question, write a complete answer, replacing the noun object with an appropriate object pronoun.

1. Did you ask for the check?

Yes, I asked for it. _____

A list of common phrasal verbs can be found in Appendix D (page 421).

2. Are you waiting for the bus?

_____

3. Have you talked about your plans?

_____

Collaborative Activity 2

Composing Sentences
Write at least ten sentences using different phrasal verbs from the lists of separable and inseparable phrasal verbs in Appendix D. Then exchange papers with a classmate and check each other's work.

4. Where do I get on the bus?

_____

5. Who came with you to the meeting?

_____

6. What time do you get through with your classes?

_____

| EXERCISE 7 | Writing More Phrasal Vers |

Write a sentence using the phrasal verb and its object.

       verb   object

1. (make up, the examination) *Alicia made up the examination she had missed.*

_____

       verb   object
2. (put off, studying) _____

_____

       verb object
3. (look up, it) _____

_____

       verb   object
4. (throw away, an old dress) _____

_____

       verb   object
5. (try on, them) _____

_____

       verb   object
6. (take out, the lettuce) _____

_____

       verb object
7. (do over, it) _____

_____

       verb   object
8. (find out, the answer to the question) _____

_____

       verb   object
9. (get back, the money) _____

_____

       verb   object
10. (give up, smoking) _____

_____

       verb   object
11. (work on, the assignment) _____

_____

Adverbs

Adverbs tell *when, where, how,* or *how often* an action occurs. Adverbs can be single words (often ending in *-ly*) or longer expressions, which you can place in a variety of places in a sentence:

Single words

Eighteenth-century clock maker Levi Hutchins *strongly* disliked oversleeping.

He awoke *promptly* at 4:00 A.M. each day.

But *sometimes* he would sleep past his normal waking hour.

Longer expressions

As a result, Hutchins combined a clock and a bell *in a unique way.*

Thus, he invented the first alarm clock *in 1787.*

But don't place an adverb between a verb and its object or objects:

Incorrect:	Levi Hutchins *disliked strongly oversleeping.*
Correct:	Levi Hutchins *strongly disliked oversleeping.*
Incorrect:	He *combined in a unique way a clock and a bell.*
Correct:	He *combined a clock and a bell in a unique way.*

EXERCISE 8 | Editing Misplaced Adverbs

Underline the adverb or adverb phrase in each sentence. Then draw an arrow to the spot where the misplaced adverb should be located in each sentence. In some sentences, the adverbs can be placed in more than one correct location.

1. Three men and a giraffe shared <u>cheerfully</u> a bowl of apples.

2. Throw Momma from the train a kiss.

3. The sleepy man turned off quickly the clock radio.

4. The man walked down the block his dog.

5. I sent very promptly the answer he wanted to him.

6. Johnnie kissed on a moonlit night his wife.

Double Negatives

In most languages, a statement can have two, three, or even four negative words. In English, though, a negative statement can have only one negative word. As shown on page 241, the word can be *not,* which makes the verb negative.

I did *not* do anything last night. I did*n't* have any money.

Or a negative word such as *no, nothing, nowhere,* or *no one* can appear elsewhere in a sentence with an affirmative verb:

I did *nothing* last night. I had *no* money.

You *cannot* use two negatives to express a negative idea. That is an error called a **double negative:**

Incorrect:	I did*n't do nothing* last night.
Correct:	I *didn't do anything* last night.
	OR
	I *did nothing* last night.

In fact, two negatives can actually express an affirmative idea:

Correct:	It's *not unusual* to see ducks in the pond. (It's quite common to see the ducks.)
Correct:	I *never* do *nothing*. (I always do something.)

Here's a list of the most common negative words, along with their affirmative versions:

Negatives	Affirmatives
no one	anyone
nobody	anybody
nothing	anything
nowhere	anywhere
no	any
none	any
never	ever

A few other words express a negative meaning: *hardly* and *barely,* which mean "almost no" or "almost none," and *scarcely* and *rarely,* which mean "almost never":

I had *hardly any* homework this week. (almost no homework)

Juan had *barely enough* time to study. (almost no time)

The Wilsons *scarcely ever* go out. (almost never)

Jake *rarely* eats meat. (almost never)

Like other negative words, they cannot be used with another negative:

Incorrect:	We *didn't have hardly any* money.
Correct:	We had *hardly any* money.

EXERCISE 9 | Eliminating Double Negatives

Cross out one of the two negatives in each sentence, and write any changes above the line.

anything
1. Nobody ever says ~~nothing~~ unkind to Big Louie.

Collaborative Activity 3

Correcting Sentences
Write five sentences that intentionally contain double negatives. Exchange papers with a classmate and correct the sentences. Then check each other's work.

2. When Mr. Swift explains something fast, it doesn't make no sense.

3. I've scarcely spent no money this week.

4. I don't like to borrow nothing from other people.

5. You can't hardly find an honest person these days.

6. I didn't notice no difference between those two steaks; I ate them both.

IN SUMMARY | To Keep Words in Order

- Write direct questions using this word order: verb + subject + verb. Write indirect questions with this word order: subject + verb.
- Place direct and indirect objects in either of these patterns:
  —verb + indirect object + direct object
  —verb + direct object + *to* (or *for*) + indirect object
- With a phrasal verb that moves or changes the condition of the object, place a noun object after or between the parts of the verb. *Always* place a pronoun between the two words of the phrasal verb.
- With a phrasal verb that *does not* move or change the condition of the object, place both noun and pronoun objects *after* the verb.
- Do not place an adverb between the verb and its object or objects.
- To make a negative, use *not* with the verb or *no* before a noun or pronoun, but *don't use more than one negative together.*

EDITING FOR MASTERY

Mastery Exercise 1

Editing for Word Order

The passage contains thirteen errors in (1) indirect questions, (2) placement of direct and indirect objects after verbs, (3) placement of objects with phrasal verbs, (4) placement of adverbs, and (5) double negatives. The first error has been corrected as an example. Find and correct the remaining twelve errors.

The Real Discoverers of the "New World"

On October 12, 1492, the

(1) ⌃The natives of a small island in the central Bahamas discovered ~~on October 12, 1492,~~ Christopher Columbus. (2) They came him across on their beach, along with several of his equally pale companions, who had on very strange clothing. (3) If the natives had been able to understand these visitors, they would have been surprised. (4) Although he knew where was he, Columbus was saying that this island now belonged to something called "Spain." (5) And he was giving to the natives the name "Indians."

(6) Columbus didn't discover no "new world" on October 12, 1492. (7) In fact, Columbus didn't even discover the Central Bahamas. (8) The Taino natives who migrated from South America beat him to it by 800 years.

(9) Long before Columbus arrived, early settlers had begun raising for food plants throughout the Americas. (10) The settlers formed villages and cities that turned into great empires. (11) By 1492, more than 600 separate cultures had in the Americas developed. (12) These inhabitants of the Americas were merchants, farmers, hunters, artisans, religious leaders, and warriors.

(13) No doubt, the island natives who greeted Columbus and his crew were impressed by their appearance, but that appearance didn't intimidate probably them. (14) The Taino were much taller than their European visitors. (15) Thanks to a diet of berries, fruit, and fish, the average male Taino stood nearly six feet tall. (16) By contrast, the sailors who came along with Columbus averaged about five feet, three inches in height. (17) Some of the older Taino were in their seventies. (18) But hardly any Europeans of that era did not live to be fifty, because of their poor diets and frequent plagues that swept through for centuries the filthy cities of Europe. (19) In fact, Columbus would be dead at fifty-six after suffering from severe arthritis.

(20) Who were these tan, gentle natives of the Americas? (21) We know that their ancestors had from Asia migrated by crossing the Bering Strait. (22) But we are still trying to solve the mystery of when did they come and how did their cultures evolve. (23) Anthropologists and archaeologists still talk over this.

Scorecard: Number of Errors Found and Corrected _____

Collaborative Activity 4

Checking Your Answers

Compare your answers with a classmate. Your instructor may ask you to report your findings to the class.

Mastery Exercise 2

Editing for Word Order

The passage contains thirteen errors in (1) indirect questions, (2) placement of direct and indirect objects after verbs, (3) placement of objects with phrasal verbs, (4) placement of adverbs, and (5) double negatives. The first error has been corrected as an example. Find and correct the remaining eleven errors.

National Horsefly Day

for over 200 years

(1) No one seems to know how it happened, but ˄the United States has been celebrating ~~for over 200 years~~ its independence from Great Britain on the wrong day: July 4, 1776. (2) U.S. independence was declared actually on July 2. (3) Hardly nothing important took place on July 4, 1776, except for approval of the wording of the Declaration of Independence by the Continental Congress. (4) In fact, the most important event of that day might have grown out of an invasion of giant horseflies in Independence Hall in Philadelphia.

(5) When the Continental Congress met on June 7, 1776, Richard Henry Lee of Virginia stood up and talked about the need for independence from England. (6) Many of the representatives agreed with him, but his demand presented to them a problem. (7) To vote yes would be an act of treason, punishable by death. (8) So the assembly did what politicians traditionally do when faced with a tough decision: They delayed Lee's motion to study it further.

(9) By the time the Congress met on July 2 again, the representatives had changed their minds. (10) Recent actions by the British had angered everyone. (11) They all agreed therefore on Lee's motion for a declaration of independence.

(12) On July 4, the Continental Congress met for only one item of business. (13) Thomas Jefferson had been asked to produce a formal declaration, so he had written down it. (14) The delegates were there to talk over its contents and approve the final wording. (15) They had read already Jefferson's Declaration before the meeting, and it seemed everyone wanted to add some language or take out it.

(16) It was humid in Philadelphia that day, so the delegates opened windows, letting in hundreds of giant horseflies from a nearby stable. (17) As the hungry horseflies attacked the founding fathers, no one seemed to care about the debate no more.

(18) A very uncomfortable delegate said that Jefferson's declaration seemed suitable to him. (19) Most of the others agreed and approved quickly the document. (20) The delegates just as quickly went out of the building.

(21) The actual signing of the Declaration of Independence took place on August 18, 1776, and some members added to it their names later. (22) In reality, then, there isn't no clear date that marks the independence of the states.

(23) Although we managed to get wrong the date, July 4, 1776, remains an important day in American history, and every citizen should be grateful to the horseflies for their contribution.

Scorecard: Number of Errors Found and Corrected _____

21 Using Pronouns

The word *pronoun* literally means "for a noun," and **pronouns** are in fact substitutes for nouns. They help you avoid repetition, create unity, add emphasis, and combine sentences gracefully. You really couldn't write well without pronouns, so checking them as you edit is important. This chapter will help you use pronouns

- to replace nouns
- to make comparisons
- for clarity and unity
- for emphasis

Selecting the Right Pronoun

Like nouns, pronouns perform a variety of roles in a sentence. Let's take a look at those pronouns and the roles they perform.

Personal Pronouns as Subjects and Objects

Unlike nouns, personal pronouns take different forms according to the role they fulfill in a sentence. For review, here are personal pronouns as subjects and objects:

	Subject	Object
First person		
singular:	I	me
plural:	we	us
Second person		
singular and plural:	you	you

Third person (represents people or things)		
singular:	he	him
	she	her
	it	it
plural:	they	them

Subject pronouns, like all subjects, usually come before verbs. All object pronouns follow verbs, words formed from verbs, or prepositions. Here are examples of object pronouns:

As a direct object:	You helped *them.*
As an indirect object:	I gave *them* the present.
As an object of an *-ing* word:	I wrote to Ms. Sanchez before meeting *her.*
As an object of an infinitive:	You must memorize the names to know *them* well.
As an object of a preposition:	This is between *you* and *me.* It went from *him* to *her.*

When a clause has more than one subject or object, determining the correct pronouns to use can be difficult. Are the pronouns in the following examples correct?

Maria and *me* had a great time. (incorrect)

People have been very kind to my friend and *I.* (incorrect)

One way to determine if the pronouns are correct is to remove—but only temporarily—the nouns and leave only the pronouns. Or, if there are no nouns, only pronouns, remove one, then the other:

. . . *me* had a great time. (incorrect)

People have been very kind to . . . *I.* (incorrect)

With the nouns removed, it is easier to see that the pronouns are not correct. In the first sentence, a subject pronoun is needed. In the second sentence, an object pronoun is needed:

Maria and *I* had a great time.

People have been very kind to my friend and *me.*

✔ **TIPS**

To Avoid Overlooking Pronouns

In many languages, the pronoun is included in the verb, but not in English. In Spanish, for example, the verb *está* means "it is." But in English the pronoun must appear separately. Therefore, while editing your work, make sure the pronoun is in place.

EXERCISE 1 | **Using Correct Personal Pronouns**

Some, but not all, of the sentences contain errors in pronouns. Write the correct forms above the lines. If a sentence is already correct, make no changes.

She and I ~~her and me~~
1. ~~Her and me~~ have always said that for ~~she and I~~ nothing is too good.

2. Can you keep a secret between you and I?

3. Only four other students and him scored above 90 percent on the test.

4. Our pet boa constrictor snake is very close to Lorenzo and I.

5. Me and him shared a pizza, a milk shake, and a diet whipped-cream pie.

6. Just write your checks for her and me, but make them out to "Cash."

Personal Pronouns in Comparisons

In statements that make comparisons, choosing the right pronoun is important. When you compare subjects, you need subject pronouns. When you compare objects, you need object pronouns. Notice in the following comparisons that a subject pronoun and a verb come after *than* or *as:*

> Kashif is a better swimmer *than I am.*
>
> But I dive as well *as he does.*

You can often leave out the verbs, but you should keep the subject pronouns:

> Kashif is a better swimmer than *I (am).*
>
> But I dive as well as *he (does).*

If you compare objects instead of subjects, an object pronoun follows *than* or *as:*

> Ms. Blake treats him as well *as (she treats) me.*
>
> Ms. Blake treats him better *than (she treats) her.*

Notice how the meaning of this sentence changes with a subject pronoun:

> Ms. Blake treats him as well as *I (treat him).*

EXERCISE 2	Using Pronouns to Make Comparisons

Write a sentence that makes a comparison based on the information provided. Use *than* or *as* in the sentence.

1. Bruno is 200 pounds, but she is 112 pounds.
   Bruno is heavier than she (is).

2. Marina is very smart. You are also very smart.

_____

3. Zeeshan works hard. We don't work too hard.

_____

4. Mr. Khan has three part-time jobs. I have only one job.

_____

5. The counselor talks to you quite often. She hardly ever talks to me.

_____

6. Alberto ate fourteen hamburgers for lunch. I ate two.

_____

The Relative Pronouns *Who* and *Whom*

Relative pronouns begin relative clauses. When these clauses refer to people, the most commonly used relative pronouns are *who* and *whom*. *Who* serves as the subject:

> relative clause
> Please return this video game to the person *who* lent it to you.
>
> relative clause
> The man *who lent the video game to me* took my favorite DVD in exchange.

Whom serves as the object. In formal writing, many people insist that *whom* appear. But you can usually drop *whom* from a clause unless the pronoun directly follows a preposition:

> indirect object   subject verb
> Mr. Clark was the man (*whom*) you borrowed the DVD from.
>
> BUT
>
> preposition +
> indirect object
> Mr. Clark was the man *from whom* you borrowed the DVD.

EXERCISE 3	Combining Sentences with Relative Pronouns

Combine each pair of sentences into one sentence, using **who, whom,** or no relative pronoun.

1. The identity of the person is unknown. The person created the first bagel.

   The identity of the person who created the first bagel is unknown.

   _____

2. Somebody probably created the bagel by accident. The person dropped a piece of dough into hot water.

   _____

   _____

3. However, we do know the identity of the man. He first called a bagel a "bagel."

   _____

   _____

4. In 1683, the first coffeehouse in Vienna was opened by a Polish man. He introduced a new bread called the *beugel*.

   _____

   _____

5. Americans changed the name of the round bun to *bagel*. The foreign word was too difficult for them to pronounce. (*Hint:* Begin the clause with *for* or *because.*)

   _____

   _____

6. Nowadays bagels are popular with almost anyone. Bread or rolls appeal to that person.

   _____

   _____

Avoiding Pronoun Confusion and Bias

Because a pronoun often replaces—or refers back to—a noun, readers must recognize which noun it replaces. The word or words a pronoun refers back to are called **antecedents.** Here are some examples of antecedents and the pronouns that go with them:

Antecedent	Pronoun
the team	it
a person	he OR she; him OR her
Kwan and I	we
Kwan and me	us

Kwan and she	they
you and she	you
you and her	you
Kwan and she	they
Kwan and her	them

Unclear Antecedents

But suppose a pronoun could have more than one antecedent. The pronoun's reference may be unclear. For example, what does *he* refer to in the following sentence?

Roberto told his father that *he* had been wrong.

The answer can be either *Roberto* or *his father,* so the sentence needs to be revised. Here are two possibilities:

Roberto told his father, "I was wrong."

Roberto accused his father of being wrong.

No Antecedent

If a pronoun doesn't have an antecedent, the meaning of the pronoun may also be unclear. What does *he* refer to in this sentence?

After I honked my horn at the cab that was blocking the intersection, *he* just honked back and refused to move.

The writer apparently means the *cab driver* but doesn't mention one, so the sentence needs to be revised to include the specific noun:

. . . *the cab driver* just honked back and refused to move.

Here's a third common problem. In informal speech, people sometimes use *they* or *we* without an antecedent:

At work, *they* are receiving double-time pay.

Readers expect meanings to be more exact, so the sentence needs to be revised:

At work, *the employees* are receiving double-time pay.

EXERCISE 4	Correcting Problems in Antecedents

In the following sentences, there are errors in the use of pronouns. If the pronoun has an unclear or missing antecedent, replace it with the correct noun.

1. In the last twenty years, the microelectronics industry has made better and less

   Companies
   expertise products. ~~They~~ manufacture cellular phones, digital watches,

   computers, video games, CD-ROM players, DVD, and MP3 players.

2. Pocket calculators used to cost $50 to $100, but now they sell them for $5.

3. Nowadays they don't repair calculators and watches; they just throw them away.

4. Twenty years ago, nobody thought that computers would be in so many homes, but

   they are so inexpensive now that many families own them.

5. They sell DVD players for under $100 now.

6. The electronics industry is changing so fast that you have to wonder: What will they

   think of next?

EXERCISE 5	Correcting Problems in Antecedents

The pronouns in the sentences can refer to more than one antecedent. Underline each problem pronoun, and substitute a noun that will clarify the sentence's meaning.

Facts about Famous People

1. At the beginning of the century, George Eastman wanted to make inexpensive

   these cameras
   cameras for children. He called ~~them~~ Brownies and sold them for a dollar.

2. Six-shot rolls of film sold for fifteen cents, but Eastman made hardly any profit from

   the cameras. They made the most money.

3. Hans Christian Andersen, the famous writer of children's stories, was terrified that he

   would pass out and be found by a policeman. Then he would bury him alive.

4. Andersen almost always carried a note in his pocket telling anyone who might

   discover him unconscious that he must not assume that he was dead.

5. Because Anderson was also embarrassed by his small chest, he stuffed old

   newspapers beneath his shirt so that it would look more manly.

6. King Charles II, the ruler of Great Britain from 1660 to 1685, sometimes took powder

   from the mummies of Egyptian kings and, in hopes of acquiring "ancient greatness,"

   would rub it on himself.

Agreement in Number

Pronouns should also agree in **number** with their antecedents. That is, a singular pronoun must have a singular antecedent, and a plural pronoun must have a plural antecedent. The following sentence, for example, may be confusing because the antecedent and pronoun don't agree:

---

plural antecedent   singular pronoun

No one should smoke cigarettes because *it's* dangerous.

Rewrite the sentence to avoid the confusion: _____

_____

_____

Did you change *it's* to *they're*? If not, note this carefully:

Singular:	one cigarette = *it*
Plural:	cigarettes = *they*

EXERCISE 6	Correcting Pronoun Agreement

Some—but not all—of the sentences contain an error in agreement between pronoun and antecedent. Circle the antecedent and underline the pronoun that refers to the antecedent. Then correct any errors you find.

1. (The first bubble gum) was invented by Frank Fleer in 1906, but ~~they~~ *it*
   ~~were~~ *was* never sold.

2. The gum was so sticky that only hard scrubbing with a brush would remove them.

3. Fleer spent more than twenty years until they could fix the problem.

4. In 1928, stores everywhere began selling a "new, improved" gum named Dubble Bubble gum. They were pink because Fleer had only pink food coloring available in the factory.

5. None of the other penny candies could compete with Dubble Bubble, which outsold it all.

6. Other manufacturers copied Dubble Bubble, including its color.

7. Now pink bubble gum is everywhere; it's the industry's standard color.

Collective Nouns

Like pronouns referring to pronouns, pronouns referring to collective nouns can give you trouble. A **collective noun**—a team, a band, an audience—represents a group of people or things, and almost all collective nouns are singular. Therefore, you should observe the following rules when using collective nouns:

▶ **The verb should agree grammatically with its singular subject:**

The *class has* met for half the term.

The *band* at the football game *is* loud but not very good.

▶ **The pronoun should agree grammatically with its singular antecedent:**

The *orchestra* reaches *its* greatest heights when Rudolfo Parachuti conducts *it.*

The *team* has already won more games than *it* (not *they*) won all last year.

EXERCISE 7 | **Using Collective Nouns**

The collective noun subjects are supplied in these partial sentences. Complete each sentence, referring back to the subject with an appropriate pronoun.

1. The band *plays its best when Elvis P. Diddy is the conductor.*

2. The committee _____

3. A good department store _____

4. The police _____

5. The team _____

6. The class _____

Indefinite Pronouns and Avoiding Bias

Some pronouns don't refer to a specific person, place, or thing. These are called **indefinite pronouns.** Here's a list of indefinite pronouns for people:

> anyone, everyone, someone, no one
>
> anybody, everybody, somebody, nobody
>
> either, neither

For Identifying Singular Indefinite Pronouns

Here's an easy way to remember that indefinite pronouns are singular. These words end in *one* or *body*. It's simple arithmetic: *one* = one and a *body* = one body. If you're writing in the present tense, look at the verb, which should also be singular:

Everybody *has* . . . , no one *does* . . . , someone *is* . . . , and so on.

All these indefinite pronouns are singular, so they present a special challenge when you're trying to chose a pronoun to go with them. For example, which word (*their, his,* or *her*) should refer to *everyone* in the following sentence?

Everyone in the class has done _____ homework.

Did you answer *their?* This plural word is a common choice, but it creates some problems. Remember that *everyone* is grammatically singular (its verb is *does*), even though it seems like a plural.

Another choice for agreement with *everyone* might be *his.* It's certainly singular but seems to leave women out of the discussion. Of course, *his* works fine when an indefinite pronoun represents only males, and *her* would likewise be correct to represent females:

> Everybody in the men's gym class has done *his* exercises.
>
> Each of the women on the tennis team must practice *her* serve.

As you can see, when an indefinite pronoun represents both sexes, there's no easy choice. Sometimes you can use *his or her,* as in "Everyone in the class has done his or her homework." Other times you can rewrite the sentence with a plural subject:

> All of the students in the class have done their homework.

This last solution is probably the best, but it won't work in every situation. As you revise, pay special attention to pronouns. If they suggest a gender bias you don't intend, change them, or revise the sentence until it says what you mean.

EXERCISE 8 | Avoiding Bias in Pronouns

Rewrite the biased sentences by changing the male singular pronouns to plurals, or using *he or she,* or finding another solution. Adjust the remainder of the sentence to reflect your changes. Replace pronouns with nouns, if necessary.

1. It's a common superstition that when a person breaks a mirror, he will have seven years of bad luck.

   It's a common superstition that when people break mirrors, the people will

   have seven years of bad luck.

   (*Note:* For consistency, the word *mirror* also becomes plural.)

2. The superstition about bad luck started in the sixth century B.C., when a person could see his face in a glass bowl filled with water.

   _____

   _____

3. A "mirror seer" would predict the future from the reflection of anyone who held the bowl in his hands.

_____

_____

4. If someone dropped and broke the bowl, that meant he would soon die.

_____

_____

5. In the first century, the Romans called the bowl a *miratorium*. A person could predict his future by looking at his reflection in it.

_____

_____

6. They believed that a person's health changed every seven years and that he could find out his condition from the mirror.

_____

_____

7. Therefore, seven years of bad health and bad luck came to the man who broke a mirror.

_____

_____

Using Reflexive Pronouns

Sometimes the same person or thing is both the subject and the object in a sentence:

I bought *myself* a present.

He likes *himself,* because nobody else does.

The object pronouns in these sentences are **reflexive pronouns,** because they reflect back to their subjects like mirrors. Here's a full list of these pronouns:

	Singular	**Plural**
First person:	myself	ourselves
Second person:	yourself	yourselves
Third person:	himself (NOT hisself)	themselves (NOT theirselves)
	herself	
	itself	

Notice that the singular pronouns end in *-self,* while the plural pronouns end in *-selves.*

A reflexive pronoun can also repeat (but not replace) a subject or object for emphasis:

> Alberto ate seven whole pizzas, but I *myself* had only three.

EXERCISE 9	Writing Reflexive Pronouns

Write a reflexive pronoun in each sentence.

1. I like to carry on intelligent conversations with _____ *myself* _____ .

2. Brian has taught _____ several languages just by listening to the student conversations between classes.

3. You folks should help _____ to some food.

4. We like to spend some time by _____ once in a while.

5. John thinks very highly of _____ .

6. Many students support _____ while going to school.

Using Demonstrative Pronouns

The pronouns *this/that* and *these/those* actually make nouns more specific. They're called *demonstrative* words because they demonstrate what you're discussing. They serve as **demonstrative adjectives** before nouns (*this woman, that story, these women, those stories*) and as **demonstrative pronouns** by themselves (*this* is a nice place, but *that* is not).

Demonstratives have both singular and plural forms:

Singular	Plural
this	these
that	those

This and *these* usually refer to things physically close, and *that* and *those* refer to things farther away—whether they're subjects or objects.

> *These cookies* (close by) look fresh, but *those* (over there) don't look as appetizing. So I'll take *this one*—and on second thought, I'll take *that* one, too.

✓ **TIPS**

For Using Demonstratives
Don't use demonstrative pronouns alone as subjects of sentences. They almost never have clear antecedents. Add a noun to make the demonstrative an adjective: *this solution, these problems,* and so on.

Unclear: This works well.

Clear: This solution works well.

EXERCISE 10 | Writing Sentences with Demonstratives

Read the following model sentences. Using the words in parentheses, write sentences that follow the pattern of each model sentence.

1. *These women* lost their handbags on the bus.

   (people) *These people found a young child in the park.*

   (gorillas) _____

2. Do you want any of *these desserts* to take home?

   (compact discs) _____

   (hundred-dollar bills) _____

3. I'll take some of *this pasta* and a little of *that sauce*.

   (rice/sushi) _____

   (fruit/vegetables) _____

IN SUMMARY | To Use Pronouns Correctly

- Choose subject pronouns for subjects; choose object pronouns for objects.
- Use the proper pronouns for comparisons of subjects or objects.
- Use the relative pronouns *who* for subjects and *whom* for objects.
- Make sure pronouns clearly refer to antecedents.
- Make sure pronouns agree with their antecedents in number.
- Rewrite pronouns that show inappropriate gender bias.
- Use *-self* for singular reflexive pronouns and *-selves* for plurals; do not use reflexive pronouns as subjects.
- Use the demonstrative pronouns *this* and *that* for singular nouns and *these* and *those* for plural nouns. Demonstrative pronouns can also be adjectives.

EDITING FOR MASTERY

Mastery Exercise 1 | ***Correcting Pronoun Errors***

The passage contains ten errors related to pronoun use. The first error has been corrected for you. Find and correct the remaining nine errors.

Thomas Alva Edison (1847–1931): An Unlikely Genius

themselves
(1) People all over the world find ˄themself living better lives because of the

inventions of one man, Thomas Alva Edison. (2) This man created three large laboratories where he invented and patented 1,097 different products—including the

electric light bulb, the phonograph, and the motion picture camera and projector.

(3) However, he wasn't like any other genius.

(4) When Edison was in first grade, his teacher told him to drop out of school

because he was hopelessly stupid. (5) Edison soon did leave school, and at the age of

twelve he was working full-time selling candy and newspapers on passenger trains.

(6) A disease had already harmed his hearing, and when someone playfully lifted him

by the ears, they made his hearing worse. (7) Although he didn't have much formal

education, Edison began educating him self by experimenting with new inventions.

(8) Unfortunately, one of this experiments set a train on fire, and they fired him.

(9) Soon afterward, Edison got a job as a telegraph operator. (10) His first invention,

in 1868, didn't make any money, but Edison soon quit his job to spend all of his time

inventing. (11) In 1871, he built a machine shop in Newark, New Jersey, that eventually

became the General Electric Company. (12) In the next few years, two companies paid

$70,000 to buy the rights to machines that his assistants and himself had invented.

(13) Soon another of his inventions—the phonograph—were making him famous.

(14) Everyone was buying one for themselves. (15) After this sudden change in his life,

Edison built another laboratory in Menlo Park, New Jersey. (16) There he invented some

of his most important products, including the electric light bulb. (17) In Menlo Park,

many more of Edison's dreams became reality—for he and the rest of the world.

Scorecard: Number of Errors Found and Corrected _____

Collaborative Activity

Comparing Answers
Compare your answers
with a classmate and, if
your instructor indicates,
report your findings to the
class.

Mastery Exercise 2

Correcting Pronoun Errors

The passage contains ten errors related to pronoun use. The first error has been corrected as an example. Find and correct the remaining nine errors.

Edison's Electric Light

(1) For years, Thomas Edison never stopped working, until *he* ~~him~~ and his family finally

took a vacation in the summer of 1878. (2) They traveled to Wyoming to view a total

eclipse of the sun, but it was hardly relaxing. (3) Edison spent the entire time talking with a friend about electrically produced light. (4) When he returned to his laboratory, they put aside all their other projects and began working on a practical and dependable light bulb.

(5) Edison needed money to pay for the project, so he went to New York. (6) There on Wall Street, an important conversation took place between he and the banker J. P. Morgan. (7) Edison told him that the company could produce a reliable electric light in six weeks. (8) As a result, Morgan persuaded other bankers to form the Edison Electric Light Company. (9) The bankers issued 3,000 shares in the company, but they did not sell. (10) Therefore, to encourage business, Edison lied to the newspapers, saying that his company had already perfected the invention. (11) Everyone quickly bought stock for theirselves, and Morgan gave Edison $50,000 to do research.

(12) For the next year, Edison's five assistants and himself worked twenty hours a day. (13) One of the most difficult problems was that the filament (the part that glowed) inside the bulb always burned up or melted after only a few minutes. (14) Edison tried to solve it by putting the filament in a glass bulb and creating a vacuum inside of it. (15) He also tested a variety of materials as filaments, including several types of bamboo.

(16) Finally, Edison manufactured a cotton thread that was coated with carbon and used them as a filament. (17) This kind of filament worked, and Edison turned on his light bulb on October 21, 1879. (18) The bulb glowed with a reddish light for over forty hours and quit only when Edison increased the voltage to test the filament's strength. (19) That small piece of thread in Menlo Park, New Jersey, turned night into day throughout the world.

Scorecard: Number of Errors Found and Corrected _____

22 Mastering the Little Words: Articles and Prepositions

Articles and prepositions are little words, but they play a big role in expressing ideas clearly. This chapter will give you practice in using articles and prepositions correctly. You'll learn

- when to use *a/an*, *the*, or no article
- when to use prepositions for time, place, and other special meanings, and which prepositions to use.

Articles

Articles determine whether a noun is general or specific. The **indefinite article** *a/an* precedes an indefinite or nonspecific noun such as *a door* (meaning "any one door"). The **definite article** *the* precedes a definite or specific noun such as *the front door to my house.*

Articles entered English long ago simply as different pronunciations of the words *one* ("an") and *that* ("the"). So in actual usage, *a/an* replaces *one*, and *the* replaces *that*.

We'll be looking at the main rules for using these articles. Although the rules don't explain all the uses of the articles, they explain most of the uses.

The Indefinite Articles *A* and *An*

The initial sound—not the spelling—of a word determines whether *a* or *an* precedes it.

Vowel Sounds. The article *an* goes before a noun or an adjective modifying a noun if the word begins with a *vowel sound*:

an elephant	*an* awful experience
an enormous task	*an* overcharge

Some words begin with a silent *h*, and the first sound you hear is a vowel. Therefore, *an* precedes these words:

an hour	*an* honor	*an* heir
BUT		
a happy moment	*a* humorous story	*a* holiday

Consonant Sounds. The article *a* goes before words that begin with *consonant sounds:*

a lesson	*a sh*oe
*a ch*air	*a* doctor

Watch out for words that begin with *u*. The letter *u* can stand for several sounds. In the word *university*, for example, the initial *u* stands for the sound /yoo/. When a word begins with the sound /yoo/ spelled *u*, place the article *a* before the word. (Check a dictionary if you're unsure of the pronunciation).

*a u*nit	*a u*nique experience	*a u*seful product
BUT		
*an u*ncle	*an u*nusual experience	*an u*gly mess

EXERCISE 1	Writing *A* or *An*

Place *a* or *an* before each word or phrase.

1. ___*a*___ child
2. _____ horse
3. _____ elm tree
4. _____ humid day
5. _____ uniformed workers
6. _____ honest person

7. _____ union of writers
8. _____ historic event
9. _____ urban setting
10. _____ ironing board
11. _____ ugly scar
12. _____ human being

Singular Count Nouns: *A/An* versus *The*

There are two main types of nouns in English:

- **count nouns** (these can be counted and made plural): *one day, three apples,* or *five people*
- **noncount nouns** (these cannot be counted or made plural): *water, music, honesty,* or *luggage*

Since *a/an* means *one*, it can be used only with a singular count noun. With singular count nouns, use *a* or *an* to mean "any one." Here are some examples:

Take *a* pencil. (any one pencil; there are many choices)

I just ate *an* apple. (one of many possible apples)

A robin built its nest in that tree. (not *a* specific robin; it could be *any one* robin)

Do not use *a/an* before noncount nouns. Instead, use phrases such as *some, any, most, little, much, a lot of, a great deal of*—or nothing at all. See the examples on page 263.

TIPS

For Using *A* or *An*
In many languages, you can write "I am student," but in English you must include the *a* because you mean "I am one of many students." Here are further examples:

He is *a* lawyer.

It is *an* adjective.

She is only *a* little girl.

We don't have	much			a little	
We need	any	milk.	There's	a lot of	work to do.
	some			a great deal of	
Milk is expensive.			I have *work* to do.		

Unlike *a*, which means "any one," *the* means a "specific one" or a "particular one." Note that the phrase or clause after the noun makes it specific in the following examples:

Where is *the* pencil that I just used?
(specifies and distinguishes it from other pencils)

The apple on the table is rotten.
(specifies and distinguishes it from other apples)

The robin you saw yesterday built its nest in that tree.
(specifies and distinguishes it from other robins)

EXERCISE 2 | **Writing *The***

Make each noun in parentheses specific by changing *a/an* to ***the*** and adding a descriptive phrase or clause after the noun. Use several different structures throughout.

1. (a red book)   *the red book on the table*

OR

the red book that I bought yesterday

OR

the red book sitting on my desk

2. (a new car) _____

3. (an old woman) _____

4. (a gardening tool) _____

5. (a large table) _____

6. (an oddly shaped pear) _____

Sometimes, there is *only one* of something in a room, a house, or the whole world. In such cases, the noun is specific—because there is no other choice. So the article *the* precedes the noun:

The roof of this house leaks. (The house has only one roof.)

What time does *the clock* say? (There is only one clock in the room.)

The sky is cloudy today. (There is only one sky.)

After you've mentioned a noun, you've specified which one you mean. Therefore, use *the* if you discuss it further:

Would you buy *a used car* on the Internet?

Yes, but only if *the car* [now specified] had a five-year guarantee.

| EXERCISE 3 | Adding Articles |

Write the missing articles *a/an* or *the* above the lines in the following sentences. Do not place articles before proper nouns.

1. In 1843, ^*a* gentleman from Abbeville, South Carolina, refused ^*a* challenge to ^*a* duel. As ^*a* result, his neighbors were so happy that they gave him ^*a* barbecue.

2. In 1849, Elizabeth Blackwell was first woman doctor to practice in the United States.

3. In 1862, twenty-three-year-old man invested $4,000 of his life's savings in oil refinery. His name was John D. Rockefeller, who became richest man in the United States.

4. In 1865, children's book *Alice's Adventures in Wonderland,* by writer named Lewis Carroll, was published.

5. In 1870, Mississippi sent new senator to the U.S. Congress in Washington, D.C. He was Hiram R. Revels, first black man ever to serve in Senate.

6. In 1871, fire started in barn on West Side of Chicago. It swept through city, destroying $200 million in property. It became known as the Great Chicago Fire.

Collaborative Activity 1

Adding Articles

Write ten sentences, leaving out the articles. Include examples of all the rules about articles. In a small group, pass papers to the left, and add articles where they are needed. Then pass papers again to the left for a third student to check.

Plural Count Nouns and Noncount Nouns: Using *The* or Nothing

TIPS

For Omitting Articles

Many languages (Spanish, French, Portuguese, Italian, and German, for example) require articles before every noun. If your native language demands articles before all nouns, be careful to distinguish nouns used in a general sense in English.

You cannot place *a/an* before a plural noun. So use *the* before a specific plural noun; use no article before a nonspecific (or general) plural noun. Compare these examples:

The three birds on the window sill (specific) are pigeons.

BUT

Birds (in general) are interesting to watch.

The people in my English class (specific) are friendly.

BUT

People (in general) are studying English.

Likewise, don't place the article *the* before a nonspecific noncount noun. Compare these examples:

The water in our swimming pool (specific) is cold.

BUT

Water (in general) covers most of the Earth.

EXERCISE 4 | **Adding *The***

Write *the* above the lines where needed in each sentence.

       the
1. I loved ˄movie I saw this weekend.

2. Beginning of movie was particularly exciting.

3. I went to theater near my apartment.

4. You should read newest book on fat-free cooking.

5. You ought to try new high-protein diet mentioned in today's newspaper.

6. Dogs make good pets.

EXERCISE 5 | **Transforming Sentences**

Rewrite each sentence so that it uses the article *the*.

1. People are very friendly. *The people in my English class are very friendly.*

2. Apartments are expensive. _____

3. Homework is usually interesting. _____

4. Mr. Bulge loves cakes and pies. _____

5. Movies are very popular. _____

6. I often listen to music. _____

Additional Advice about *A/An* and *The*

Use *the* before the names of countries that end in *-s* or contain the words *Republic, Union,* or *Kingdom:*

the Netherlands (but just Holland)

the People's Republic of China (but just China)

the Hashemite Kingdom of Jordan (but just Jordan)

the European Union (but just Western Europe)

Use *the* before the names of rivers, oceans, and seas (but not lakes):

the Nile River	*the* Mediterranean Sea
the Atlantic Ocean	Lake Superior
EXCEPTION: *the* Great Salt Lake	

Use *the* before college names that begin with the words *College* or *University:*

the University of Illinois	*the* College of Liberal Arts and Sciences
BUT	
Boston College	Indiana University

Use *the* before the names of most buildings:

the IBM building	*the* Empire State Building
EXCEPTIONS: Sears Tower, Rockefeller Center	

Use *the* before the names of regions of a city or country—but not before directions:

the Southwest,	*the* West Side (of a city)
BUT	
You must travel west.	

Use *the* before the names of newspapers, but not most magazines:

The New York Times	*The St. Louis Post-Dispatch*
BUT	
Time (magazine)	*People* (magazine)

Do not use *the* before the names of states, cities, or languages:

Indiana	New Orleans
Spanish	

✓ **TIP**

On Capitalizing Names of Newspapers and Magazines
Capitalize *The* only when is part of the actual name of the newspaper or magazine; but do not capitalize *the* when it is not.

EXERCISE 6 | Adding Missing Articles

Write *the* where it is needed.

1. ___*the*___ Caspian Sea

2. _____ University of Pittsburgh

3. _____ Lake Ontario

4. _____ Germany

5. _____ Northwestern University

6. _____ Mandarin Chinese

7. _____ North Side

8. _____ *Washington Post* (newspaper)

9. _____ Canada

10. _____ Republic of Bolivia

11. _____ Atlantic Ocean

12. _____ College of DuPage

13. _____ United Arab Emirates

14. _____ Chrysler Building

15. _____ southwest (direction)

16. _____ *Newsweek* (magazine)

When you place one of the following words or phrases before a noun, you cannot use an article:

For singular count nouns:	every, each, no
For plural count nouns:	many, a few, several, all two, forty-six, one hundred (and so on)
For count nouns indicating two:	both, either, neither, a couple of
For noncount nouns:	much, little, less
For noncount or plural nouns:	enough, some, plenty of, more, all
Possessive adjectives before any noun:	my, our, your, his, her, its, their
Possessive nouns before any noun:	Bill's, the man's, the boys' (and so on)

Articles usually precede adjectives before a noun:

the large, round bowl
a dirty, old T-shirt

And the following five words or phrases precede articles:

both of (*the*)	half (*the* or *a*)	all (*the*)	many (*a*)	such (*a*)

EXAMPLES: *Both of the* men are here.

Half the pie is gone.

Mary ate *all the* cherries.

Many a problem can be solved.

I never saw *such a* fight before.

| EXERCISE 7 | Transforming Sentences |

Revise each sentence, using the word in parentheses and omitting or shifting articles where necessary.

1. I knew the answers.

(every) *I knew every answer.* _____

2. They don't have the books.

(many) _____

3. The food was delicious.

(all) _____

4. I'd like the pie for dessert.

(some) _____

5. It was a long journey.

(such) _____

6. Do you have the money to buy dinner?

(enough) _____

Prepositions

A **preposition** is a short word such as *in, on, off, under, at,* and *through.* It goes before a noun or pronoun (*pre-* means "before") to show the *position* of the noun or pronoun in time or space. Together, the preposition and a noun or pronoun make a **prepositional phrase.** Notice how prepositional phrases added to the sentence "I saw a fire" can locate the position of the fire and the time the action occurred:

I saw a fire *in* the attic *on* Wednesday.

There are many prepositions and thousands of expressions that use them. We'll look at some of the most common prepositions and their uses.

To Indicate Time

Prepositions indicate time in the following ways:

1. *At* a specific or precise time:

Class ends *at* 3:50 P.M.

At midnight, the next day begins.

2. *By* a specific time (means "no later than that time"):

Jill said she might be ready as early as 4:30 but certainly *by* 6:00.

3. *Until* a specific time (continuing up to that time):

Last night Juanita studied *until* 11:00.

4. *In* a specific time period (usually measured in hours, minutes, days, months, or years):

I will be leaving *in* five minutes.

World War II ended *in* 1945.

in the morning, *in* the afternoon, or *in* the evening (but *at* night)

5. *For* a duration of time:

I have been a student *for* thirteen years.

I studied *for* two hours.

6. *Since* a starting date or time:

They have been living next door to us *since* 1991.

No one has eaten *since* 8:15.

7. *On* a specific day or date:

Most people are paid *on* Friday.

The doctor can see you *on* June 12.

8. *During* a continuing time period (or within the time period):

I was ill *during* the night.

We often go to the park *during* the summer.

9. Miscellaneous time expressions:

on time (that is, promptly)

in a while

at the beginning or end (of a day, month, or year)

in the middle (of a day, month, or year)

from time to time (that is, occasionally)

EXERCISE 8 | Writing Prepositions

Complete each sentence with the appropriate prepositions.

1. ___On___ August 1, 1903, a car arrived in New York, completing the first cross-country automobile trip. It had been traveling _____ July 11, when it left San Francisco.

2. _____ June 1905, the Pennsylvania Railroad opened its route between New York and Chicago. The first train made its trip _____ eighteen hours. The next week, New York Central Railroad started its own eighteen-hour train service. Both trains operated _____ only two weeks, and _____ then they had both crashed, killing nineteen people.

3. Most cars produced _____ the first years of the twentieth century were expensive, costing as much as $2,800. Then came Henry Ford's "universal car," the Model T. _____ several years his cars were priced at $850, but later, the Model T sold for $290.

To Indicate Place

Prepositions indicate place in the following ways:

1. *In* a country, area, state, city, or neighborhood:

in France	*in* Michigan	*in* Boston	*in* Lincoln Square

2. *In* (inside of) a place or space:

He has been running *in* the gym; he hasn't gone outside.
The answer is *in* the book.

3. *On* a surface:

The book is *on* the table.
The portrait is hanging *on* the wall.

4. *On* a street or block:

We live *on* Wells Avenue.   They work *on* Main Street.

5. *Off* a surface:

I took the book *off* the table.   The painting fell *off* the wall.

6. *At* a specific address, particular location, or intersection of two streets.

We live *at* 1621 Wells Avenue.	We work *at* the mall.
Let's meet *at* Main Street and Madison.	
Idioms: at work, *at* home, *at* school	I'll be *at* work all day.

EXERCISE 9 | **Writing More Prepositions**

Complete the passage with the appropriate prepositions. There may be more than one preposition that works in a sentence.

The Origin of a Song

* * * *

In 1939, the Montgomery Ward store, located ____*on*____ State Street

(1) _____ Chicago, was looking for something unusual for its Santa Claus to give

to parents and children. Robert May, who worked (2) _____ the store

(3) _____ the advertising department, suggested an illustrated poem, printed

(4) _____ a booklet, that families would want to keep (5) _____ their homes

and reread each holiday season. May recommended a shiny-nosed reindeer, a Santa's

helper; and an artist friend of May's spent hours (6) _____ a local zoo creating

sketches of reindeer. May thought about names for his character everywhere he went:

(7) _____ work, (8) _____ home, even while standing (9) _____ the

corner waiting for a bus. Finally, one day his four-year-old daughter said that she

preferred Rudolph.

That Christmas, 2.4 million copies of the "Rudolph" booklet were handed out

(10) _____ Montgomery Ward stores everywhere (11) _____ the country. In

1949, a song about Rudolph became so popular that the red-nosed celebrity also

became a familiar image (12) _____ Germany, Holland, Denmark, Sweden,

Norway, England, Spain, Austria, and France.

For Vehicles and Chairs

The following prepositions are used to indicate various positions.

1. *In(to)* and *out of* for small vehicles (like cars) and chairs with arms:

I got *in(to)* the cab as someone else was getting *out of* it.
My father likes to sit *in* his big, comfortable chair.

2. *On* and *off* (*of*) for large vehicles (such as planes, trains, buses, and boats) and armless chairs or any long seat (such a bench or a sofa):

We rode *on* the subway and got *off* at our stop.

He's sitting *on* that bench over there.

The man *on* the wooden chair is his brother.

| EXERCISE 10 | Writing More Prepositions |

Complete each sentence with the correct prepositions. There may be more than one preposition that works in a sentence.

1. Years ago, people came to the United States _____*on*_____ ocean liners. Now almost everyone comes here _____ a plane.

2. We took a ride _____ our new car. We got _____ it at the park and walked around for a while.

3. Some of the people are sitting _____ the couch, and some of them are sitting _____ armchairs.

4. Where do you usually get _____ the bus?

5. They were _____ a small boat when it turned over.

6. Would you please get _____ that table and sit _____ a chair?

On and *In*

You may confuse the prepositions *on* and *in* with each other. Note these differences.

1. To show place relationships:

- *On* generally means "on the surface of" or "on top of":

---

on the floor, *on* a street, *on* (top of) a bed (without sheets over one's body), *on* (OR *at*) a street corner, *on* a bicycle (or motorcycle), *on* (top of) a desk

---

- *In* generally means "inside of" or "within":

---

in a room, *in* the water, *in* a bed (with the sheets over one's body), *in* (side) the corner of a room (the walls enclose the person or object), *in* a container, *in* a desk drawer

---

2. To show time relationships:

- *On* refers to a day or a date:

on Saturday, *on* July 5, 2005, *on* Thanksgiving

- *In* generally means "within a period of time," including a month or a season:

in January, *in* summer, *in* an hour or a minute, *in* a while

3. To express idiomatic ideas, whose literal meaning is not clear:

on foot, *on* time, every hour *on* the hour, *in* charge, *in* the mood

EXERCISE 11	Writing *In* or *On*

Complete each sentence with *on* or *in*.

1. You will find the book _____*on*_____ the desk and the papers in the drawer.
2. I will meet you _____ the corner of Fifth and Main.
3. The new table is _____ the corner of the room.
4. I think I left my book _____ my bed.
5. Bill isn't feeling well; he is staying _____ bed today.
6. We haven't gone to a movie _____ a month.
7. Sue is usually _____ time, so she should be here _____ a few minutes.
8. Who is _____ charge of this department?
9. _____ the Fourth of July we sat _____ a hill _____ the park and watched the fireworks.

Other Prepositions

Here are some other prepositions that show a variety of logical relationships.

1. *For* a reason, or *for* someone who benefits:

Bill went to the barber *for* a haircut.

I bought a present *for* my sister.

2. *About* a subject (or *on* a subject):

We were talking *about* our plans for next week.

I recently read an article *about* (or *on*) space travel.

3. *Between* two; *among* three or more:

> We shared the sandwich *between* the two of us.
>
> The five members of the board discussed it *among* themselves.

4. *From* a starting point; *to* a destination:

> We drove *from* Kansas *to* Alaska.

5. *Toward* (in the direction of) a place:

> I walked *toward* the beach but turned south before I arrived there.

6. *Into* (entering) a place or space:

> He just went *into* that room through the back door.

7. *By* someone or something (in passive voice), or *by* means of (meaning "how"):

> The painting was done *by* Rembrandt.
>
> We traveled *by* bus (how we traveled).
>
> *Idiom:* written *by* hand   He wrote his homework *by hand* instead of
>   using the computer.

Collaborative Activity 2

Adding Prepositions

Write twenty sentences, leaving out the prepositions. Include examples of all the prepositions explained in this chapter. Exchange papers with a classmate and add the missing prepositions. Then check each other's work.

EXERCISE 12 | Writing Still More Prepositions

Complete the passage with the appropriate prepositions. There may be more than one preposition that works in a sentence.

The First Major Movie: *The Great Train Robbery*

* * * *

"Moving pictures" were first shown _____*in*_____ the United States _____*on*_____

April 23, 1896, at Koster and Bial's Music Hall (1) _____ New York City. No

one was excited (2) _____ the subject matter: a man walking his dog

(3) _____ one place (4) _____ another, a train arriving

(5) _____ a station, and a balloon floating (6) _____ the air.

(7) _____ a while, no one cared, and motion pictures didn't seem to have much

chance of success.

That changed with *The Great Train Robbery,* which created the classic western, with

believable heroes and villains. Although only ten minutes long, it established filmmaking

techniques that would be used (8) _____ many years afterward. The filmmaker,

Edwin S. Porter, moved the camera around, going back and forth (9) _____

different characters as the action progressed. The story ended dramatically, with the robber turning (10) _____ the audience and shooting straight

(11) _____ them.

The film first opened (12) _____ late 1903 (13) _____ three

locations (14) _____ New York City, but (15) _____ a few months, it

was showing all over the country. Porter thus changed the movie industry

(16) _____ an uninteresting medium (17) _____ a lively new one.

Prepositions That Repeat the Meanings of Prefixes

A **prefix** is a word part that is added to the beginning of a word or word root. Knowing the meaning of prefixes sometimes helps you figure out a word's meaning and decide which preposition is typically used with that word. Take, for example, the word *sympathize*. The prefix *sym* means "with" and the word root *pathize* comes from the Greek word *pathos*, meaning "emotion or feeling." When you sympathize with someone, you share their feelings or literally feel with them.

Many times—but not always—a word with a prefix also repeats the meaning of the prefix in a preposition following the word:

Prefix	Meaning	Examples
ad-, ac-, ap-, a-	to	*ad*mitted <u>to</u> a school *ac*ceptable <u>to</u> me
con-, com-	with	*con*versed <u>with</u> me *com*municated <u>with</u> a friend
ex-, e-	from	*ex*cused <u>from</u> class *e*migrate <u>from</u> a country
in-, im-	in	*in*volved <u>in</u> a crime *im*plicit <u>in</u> his statement
sym-, syn-	with	*sym*pathize <u>with</u> your position *syn*chronize watches <u>with</u>

EXERCISE 13 | Writing Prepositions That Repeat Prefix Meanings

Complete the passage with the appropriate prepositions. Use the meanings of the prefixes in the sentence to help you.

William Collins Whitney's Big Ballroom

* * *

The rich often compete _____*with*_____ one another, and William C. Whitney

(1841–1904) was no exception. Whitney became a multimillionaire by investing

(1) _____ many profitable businesses. Not wishing to be excluded

(2) _____ New York City's high society, he had to own a house that was

acceptable (3) _____ the "right" people. Therefore, he bought a brick mansion at 871 Fifth Avenue and involved himself (4) _____ furnishing it fashionably. He spent four years in Europe, looking for furniture, stained-glass windows, and fireplaces that he and his guests would be comfortable (5) _____ . However, in addition (6) _____ gathering these furnishings, he did a thorough job of destroying palaces. Not concerned (7) _____ the expense, he exported an entire ballroom (8) _____ Bordeaux, France. Because Whitney was always a perfect host, he expanded his facilities (9) _____ these modest beginnings and kept a staff of servants who could serve one hundred people on an hour's notice. His friends came to expect surprises (10) _____ him, and at one of Whitney's dinners, which cost $20,000, each guest discovered an expensive black pearl in one of his or her oysters.

Common Expressions Using Prepositions

See Appendix E, Common Expressions Using Prepositions, page 422.

Many uses of prepositions are idiomatic. In Appendix E, you will find a list of these expressions. You may wish to memorize them, perhaps in groups of ten at a time. Or you may use the list for a reference as you write and edit your papers.

IN SUMMARY   Mastering the Little Words

To use articles with singular nouns
- Place *a* before consonant sounds, including long *u*.
- Place *an* before vowel sounds and silent *h*.
- With singular count nouns, use *a/an* when you mean "one of many."
- Use *the*
  —to point out a specific or particular one;
  —when you mean the only one;
  —to refer to nouns you have already mentioned.

To use articles with plural and noncount nouns
- Place *the* before specific nouns.
- Use no article before nonspecific nouns.

To use articles with names
- Use *the* with country names ending in *-s* or containing the words *Republic, Union,* or *Kingdom.*
- Use *the* with river, ocean, or sea names—but not names of most lakes.
- Use *the* with the names beginning with the words *College* or *University.*

To use prepositions
- Consult the guidelines in this chapter.

EDITING FOR MASTERY

Mastery Exercise 1   ***Supplying Articles and Prepositions***

Complete the passage with the appropriate articles and prepositions. Consult Appendix E, Common Expressions Using Prepositions, when necessary.

The Ford Model T (1908–1928)

The Model T Ford was a fragile-looking automobile, but it became _____*the*_____

most popular car in American history. Henry Ford sold almost 16 million Model Ts

(1) _____ the years 1908 and 1928. (2) _____ Model T was

introduced (3) _____ 1908 and cost $850. It was (4) _____ immediate

best-seller, not only because of its low price, but because it was (5) _____

powerful car, dependable, and simple enough to make it practical (6) _____

the average American to own and drive.

The Model T, whose nickname was the "Tin Lizzie," sold well (7) _____

farms and (8) _____ small towns, where half (9) _____ the country

lived. Furthermore, people could drive it (10) _____ the rough roads

(11) _____ rural America (12) _____ the early 1900s. And people

could depend (13) _____ the Model T. As (14) _____ popular joke

expressed it, (15) _____ Model T owner wanted to be buried

(16) _____ his Tin Lizzie. When friends asked why, he replied, "Oh, because

(17) _____ thing pulled me out of every hole I ever got into, and it ought to pull

me out of this one."

Henry Ford didn't invent the Model T; it was developed (18) _____ a team of

engineers (19) _____ his Ford Motor Company plant. But he brought together

brilliant people who found ways to mass-produce (20) _____ car on

(21) _____ moving assembly line. He cut costs by building only one model and

developing new methods (22) _____ production. He would then lower

(23) _____ price of his cars, which increased sales. In 1924, Americans

Collaborative Activity 3

Checking Your Answers
Compare your answers with a classmate. Your instructor may ask you to report your findings to the class.

bought as many Tin Lizzies as all other cars combined, and next year the Model T sold for (24) _____ all-time low price of $290. Ford told Americans: "I am going to democratize the automobile, and when I'm through, everybody will be able to afford one and about everybody will have one." (25) _____ the time he died in 1947, he had fulfilled his promise.

Scorecard: Number of Correct Articles and Prepositions _____

Mastery Exercise 2

Supplying Articles and Prepositions

Complete the passage with the appropriate articles and prepositions. Consult Appendix E, Common Expressions Using Prepositions, when necessary.

Cornelius Vanderbilt (1794–1877): A Rich American

Cornelius Vanderbilt, who later became known as _____*the*_____ "Commodore" because of his success in shipping, was born in New York, on May 27, 1794. As a young man, he was very interested (1) _____ making money fast. He quit school (2) _____ the age of eleven and was working (3) _____ himself at sixteen. He bought (4) _____ small boat using money he borrowed (5) _____ his parents and took passengers (6) _____ Staten Island (7) _____ Manhattan daily. He quickly succeeded (8) _____ this business and bought three sailing boats. But he sold (9) _____ boats in 1817 to take advantage of the opportunity to learn the steamboat business.

For several years, Vanderbilt took care of (10) _____ steamboats of another man. But he started his own steamboat business (11) _____ 1829. By 1835, he was earning $60,000 a year, and by 1846 the Commodore was (12) _____ millionaire. (13) _____ main reason (14) _____ his success was that he destroyed his competitors. He cut his fares and offered better service to force (15) _____ competition out of business. He soon owned more than a hundred boats.

When gold was discovered in California in 1849, Vanderbilt quickly increased his wealth. He established the Accessory Transit Company, which took gold hunters to California (16) _____ boat and on land. His company charged $300 for (17) _____ entire trip, by far the cheapest rate available. Soon Vanderbilt was making (18) _____ million dollars yearly, and he bragged in 1853 that he was worth $11 million.

In 1860, Vanderbilt lost interest (19) _____ boats and decided to enter the railroad business. Looking (20) _____ a bargain, he bought two railroads and then made them into one profitable company. He also purchased the New York Central Railroad (21) _____ spite of efforts to stop him, and he eventually began (22) _____ first route (23) _____ New York and Chicago.

When he died (24) _____ January 4, 1877, the eighty-two-year-old Vanderbilt was the richest man in the United States. He left a fortune to Central University in Nashville, Tennessee, which later changed its name (25) _____ Vanderbilt University. His son William Henry Vanderbilt inherited more than $90 million.

Scorecard: Number of Correct Articles and Prepositions _____

23 Using Comparative Word Forms

Whenever you compare people or things, you use words like *taller, tallest,* or *more gracefully, most gracefully* to describe them. The forms of these expressions show the comparisons. This chapter will help you check for correct use of these comparative forms as you edit. You'll examine

■ ways to compare people and things that are alike

■ ways to compare people and things that are different

■ special forms of comparative and superlative words

Comparing with Adjectives

One way to compare people or things is with **adjectives.** Adjectives describe nouns or pronouns. They usually go before the word they describe or after a linking verb:

Preceding a noun:	a long movie	a generous man
After a linking verb:	The movie was long.	Mr. Jones is generous.

Present or past participles can also function as adjectives:

Present participle:	an interesting movie
Past participle:	an excited child

There are three methods for making comparisons with adjectives: in equal degree, comparative degree, or superlative degree.

Comparisons of Equal Degree

When you say that two people or things are similar in some way, you make an **equal degree comparison.** It always follows the pattern: *as* + adjective + *as:*

Stanley is *as short as* Tina [is].

Mario was *as excited as* a young child [is].

Negatives: Charlie *isn't as tired as* I [am].

                   Suzanna *wasn't as happy as* William [was].

> ✔ **TIPS**
>
> **For Distinguishing *As* from *Like***
>
> If your first language is Spanish, in which *si* means both "as" and "like," you may confuse the two words in English. You cannot write *the same like* but must write *the same as:* "The pen looks *the same as* the one I lost."
>
> Use *like* as a preposition, meaning "similar to," as in these examples: "The pen looks *like* the one I lost." "My son looks *like* me."

Note that when you compare equals in this way, you don't change the form of the adjective. Note, also, that you may omit the verb at the end of the comparison.

EXERCISE 1 | **Comparing Equals**

Complete each sentence with a comparison using *as . . . as* and the adjective in parentheses.

1. Bill (tall) *is as tall as his brother.* _____

2. Judy (smart) _____

3. The book (good) _____

4. Ms. Kim (hardworking) _____

5. The test (difficult) _____

6. Jill is (excited) _____

The Comparative Degree

When you want to explain that two people or things are different in some way, you use the **comparative degree** of an adjective.

There are two patterns for this comparison:

- A short adjective takes the ending *-er.*
- A long adjective is preceded by the word *more.*

With either pattern, you usually need to complete the statement with *than:*

Adjective ending in *-er*	+ *than*	Bill is *taller than* his brother.	
more + long adjective	+ *than*	A house is *more expensive than* a condominium.	

Here are the rules for using either *-er* or *more.*

▶**Add *-er* to one-syllable adjectives (or *-r* to adjectives ending in silent *e*):**

Equal	Comparative
bright	brighter
cute	cuter

▶**If the adjective ends in a single vowel plus a consonant, you usually double the consonant before adding *-er:***

Equal	Comparative
thin	thinner
big	bigger

TIPS

For Distinguishing *Then* and *Than*

Don't confuse *than* after a comparative adjective with *then,* which means "at a later time." (First, he asked her father's permission. *Then* he proposed to her.)

One way to remember the difference is to remember that *then* is like *when*—and both refer to time.

▶ Add -er to two-syllable adjectives ending in -ow or -y, while changing the -y to -i:

Equal	Comparative
narrow	narrower
pretty	prettier (-y becomes -i)

▶ Place *more* before most other two-syllable adjectives and all adjectives of three or more syllables:

Equal	Comparative
awful	more awful
beautiful	more beautiful
interesting	more interesting

▶ Place *less* before any adjective, no matter what its spelling or number of syllables:

less tall	less intelligent
less thin	less pretty

✓ TIPS

For Avoiding Double Comparatives

Some languages form all comparatives in only one way: by adding a word. But in English, you cannot use *more* and *-er* with the same adjective:

Incorrect:

Bill is more bigger than I am.

Correct:

Bill is *bigger* than I am.

EXERCISE 2 | Writing Comparisons

Write the correct form of each adjective in parentheses.

Some Notable Noses

1. Michelangelo was (talented) _____*more talented*_____ as an artist than as a fighter. A fellow artist broke Michelangelo's nose in a fistfight one day, and as a result, he had a (flat) _____ nose than he had had before.

2. A popular entertainer named Jimmy Durante had a (profitable) _____ nose than any other person in show business. Durante had a long, hooked nose that made him (recognizable) _____ and (rich) _____ than most other comedians.

3. The sixteenth-century Danish astronomer Tycho Brahe had a (shiny) _____ nose than anyone else. He lost the tip of it in a sword fight and replaced it with a gold one—probably an (expensive) _____ nose than anyone else's.

4. Thomas Wedders, who worked in a circus in the eighteenth century, had a (long) _____ nose than anyone else in history. It measured 7½ inches.

Collaborative Activity 1

Looking at Comparative Forms

Divide a sheet of paper into three columns. Then with a group of classmates, list as many adjectives in the first column as you can think of. Try for thirty. (Just think of words before these nouns: *person* and *car*—as in *tall person, beautiful person, new car,* and *red car.*) Then next to each adjective on your list, write the comparative form in the second column. Show which adjectives add *-er* and which need *more*. Leave the third column blank for the moment.

5. Albert Weber's nose was (useful) _____ than most people's noses. He worked as an official smeller for the U.S. Food and Drug Administration.

6. Finally, a Czech composer named Josef Myslivecek had a (noticeable) _____ problem with his nose than other people have. When his nose became diseased, a doctor cut the nose off. That left him (healthy) _____ but a lot (sad) _____ .

EXERCISE 3	Writing More Comparisons

Compose four statements based on the information provided in the chart.

	William Johnson	Brian Thompson
Height	5'6"	6'6"
Weight	140 pounds	330 pounds
Age	45 years old	23 years old
Education	Ph.D.	B.A.
Job	college professor	professional wrestler
Income	$50,000 yearly	$6 million yearly

1. *William Johnson is shorter than Brian Thompson.*

    OR

    William Johnson is less tall than Brian Thompson.

2. _____

3. _____

4. _____

5. _____

The Superlative Degree

When you compare three or more things, you usually use the **superlative degree** of adjectives:

Miles Morgan is the *tallest* player on the basketball team.

Ashif is the *most articulate* person I have ever heard.

These superlative forms differ from comparative forms in three ways: the -er ending becomes -est in the superlative; more becomes (the) most; and less becomes (the) least. Note that the usually appears before the adjective:

Equal	Comparative	Superlative
long	longer	(the) longest
fat	fatter	(the) fattest
pretty	prettier	(the) prettiest
beautiful	more beautiful	(the) most beautiful
generous	less generous	(the) least generous

EXERCISE 4 | Writing Superlatives

Write the correct superlative form of the adjective in parentheses.

1. Most people agree that Michael Jordan is (great) _____*the greatest*_____ basketball player in history.

2. The city with (long) _____ name is probably Krung Thep Mahanakhon Amon Rattanakosin Mahinthara Ayuthaya Mahadilok Phop Noppharat Ratchathani Burirom Udomratchaniwet Mahasathan Amon Piman Awatan Sathit Sakkathattiya Witsanukam Prasit, which is the poetic full name for the capital of Thailand. Foreigners call it Bangkok.

3. Probably (unusual) _____ painting in recent years was done by John Banvard, who covered three miles of canvas with a view of 1,200 miles of the Mississippi shoreline.

4. (small) _____ country on Earth is Vatican City, only sixteen square miles in area, with a population of less than 1,000. It is located inside Rome, Italy.

5. (silly) _____ play ever performed is probably Samuel Beckett's *Breath,* which lasts thirty seconds, has no actors, and contains no dialogue.

6. (large) _____ country in the world in population is the People's Republic of China.

EXERCISE 5 | Writing *Less* and *The Least*

Complete the sentences, using *less* or *the least* and an adjective when necessary.

1. Dan is not very careful, but his brother is even _____*less careful*_____ .

2. Professor Smith never gives a very detailed lecture, but today's was even

   _____ than it normally is.

3. Of all the artists in the world, Thomas is probably _____ .

4. I thought that the second book was _____ than the first book.

5. Mrs. Moody's older children hardly eat a thing, but little Tina eats even

_____ than her siblings.

6. California is the most populated state in the United States, and Wyoming is

_____ .

EXERCISE 6	Writing Statements of Comparison

Collaborative Activity 2

Looking at Superlative Forms

Return to your list from Collaborative Activity 1 and write the superlative forms for each adjective in the third column. Have a classmate check your work.

Write a statement using a superlative form of an adjective to describe one of each group in parentheses.

1. (three fish) *The salmon is the largest of the three fish.* _____

2. (three cards) _____

3. (three birds) _____

4. (three computers) _____

5. (three watches) _____

6. (three professors) _____

Comparing with Adverbs

 TIPS

For Distinguishing Adjectives from Adverbs

Don't confuse adjectives with adverbs in the comparative and superlative forms. An adverb describes a verb, not a noun:

Incorrect:

The roadwork is going *slower* (adjective) than planned.

Correct:

The roadwork is going *more slowly* (adverb) than planned.

Regular adverbs always end in *-ly* and don't change form in the comparative or superlative. Use the same patterns for comparing *-ly* adverbs that you use when comparing three- and four-syllable adjectives:

Equal (*as . . . as*)	Juan writes as quickly as Julio (does).
Comparative (*more than*)	Silvia revises more thoroughly than Juan (does).
(*less than*)	Juan revises less thoroughly than Silvia (does).
Superlative (*the most*)	Maria writes the most clearly.
(*the least*)	Julio writes the least carefully.

| EXERCISE 7 | Comparing Adverbs |

Supply the correct comparative or superlative form of the adverb in parentheses.

1. With more than 160 biographies published about him, William Shakespeare has been written about (often) _____ *more often* _____ than any other person.

2. The nineteenth-century heroine of the Old West, Calamity Jane (Martha Jane Canary), with twelve husbands, was married (frequently) _____ than the famous Mexican revolutionary, Pancho Villa, with nine wives.

3. The name Johnson appears (commonly) _____ than the name Jones in the United States.

4. Of all the flavors of ice cream to choose from, people in the United States buy vanilla ice cream (often) _____ .

5. The (commonly) _____ ordered fast foods are pizza, hot dogs, and hamburgers.

6. The (fast) _____ growing city in the United States is Las Vegas.

Collaborative Activity 3

Looking at Adverbs in Comparisons

Divide a sheet of paper into three columns. Then with a classmate, list as many adverbs in the first column as you can think of. Try for twenty. Next to each adverb on your list, write the comparative form. In the third column, write the superlative form.

Irregular Adjectives and Adverbs

So far, you've seen the regular, comparative, and superlative forms of adjectives and adverbs—the forms that follow consistent rules. But several adjectives and adverbs don't follow these rules; they have irregular forms.

Adjectives and Adverbs with the Same Forms

A few words can serve as both adjectives and adverbs. Here's a partial list:

early	hard	low
fast	late	straight

EXAMPLES:

The *early* bird arrives *early*.

Fast Eddie runs really *fast*.

The comparative and superlative forms of these words are the same whether you use them as adjectives or adverbs:

Equal	Comparative	Superlative
early	earlier	(the) earliest
fast	faster	(the) fastest
hard	harder	(the) hardest

Note how they function as adjectives or adverbs:

> adverb
> The first train *came earlier* than I thought, so I missed it and had to take *a*
>
> adjective
> *later train.*
>
> adjective
> My little brother is *the slowest eater* I've ever seen.
>
> adverb
> Everyone *finishes dinner much faster* than he does.

Good and Well, Bad and Badly

Good is an adjective, and *well* is usually an adverb (or an adjective when it means "in good health," such as "I feel well"):

Adjectives	Adverbs
Francisco did a *good* job.	Francisco did the job *well.*
It's a *good* car.	The car runs *well.*
I feel *well.*	

However, the comparative and superlative forms of *good* and *well* are the same:

Equal	Comparative	Superlative
good	better	(the) best
well	better	(the) best

Adjectives: The salad is *good.* The soup is *better.* But the dessert is *the best* of all.

Adverbs: Juan sings *well.* Lourdes sings *better.* But Sixta sings *the best* of the three.

Likewise, *bad* is an adjective and *badly* is an adverb:

Adjectives	Adverbs
Frederico Falsini is a *bad* actor.	Frederico Falsini performs *badly*.
Tony felt *bad* about losing his teeth.	Tony took a *badly* needed vacation.

Bad and *badly* also share identical comparative and superlative forms:

Equal	Comparative	Superlative
bad	worse	the worst
badly	worse	the worst

Adjectives: The soup is *bad*. The salad tastes *worse*. And the fish tastes *the worst* of all.

Adverbs: Tomas sings *badly*. His brother sings *worse*. But their father sings *the worst* of anyone in the whole family.

EXERCISE 8 | Writing *Good/Well* and *Bad/Badly*

Circle the correct adjective or adverb in parentheses in the left-hand column. Then supply the correct comparative or superlative form of that word in the right-hand column.

1. a. Kim swims (good/well).

b. But Maria swims _____*better*_____.

2. a. His painting looks (good/well).

b. But Renoir's painting looks _____ of all.

3. a. Nobody does it half as (good/well) as you.

b. Nobody does it _____.

4. a. I have seen some (good/well) -trained dogs.

b. But Prince is _____ -trained dog that I have ever seen.

5. a. The light in this room is (bad/badly).

b. In fact, of the light in all the rooms, it is _____.

6. a. The old schoolhouse looks (bad/badly).

b. But it looks _____ than it actually is.

7. a. He fell and broke his arm (bad/badly).

b. It was _____ -looking break that the doctor had seen.

IN SUMMARY	To Make Comparisons

With regular adjectives

- Between equals (equal degree): use *as* + adjective + *as*.
- Between two unequal adjectives (comparative forms):
  —Add *-er* to short adjectives and place *more* (or *less*) before long adjectives.
  —Follow the adjective with *than* (not *then*).
- Among three or more unequals (superlative forms):
  —Add *-est* to short adjectives or place *most* (or *least*) before long adjectives.
  —(Usually) place *the* before superlatives.

With regular adverbs

- Between equals (equal degree): use *as* + adverb + *as*.
- Between unequals (comparative form): place *more* (or *less*) before the adverb and follow the adverb with *than*.
- Among three or more unequals (superlative form): place *(the) most* (or *least*) before the adverb.

With irregular adjectives and adverbs

- For *good/well:* use *better* and *(the) best.*
- For *bad/badly:* use *worse* and *(the) worst.*

EDITING FOR MASTERY

Mastery Exercise 1

Correcting Adjective and Adverb Errors

The passage contains thirteen errors in the use of adjectives and adverbs. The first error has been corrected for you. Find and correct the remaining twelve errors.

The Passenger Pigeon's Rise and Fall

(1) One of the *saddest* ~~most saddest~~ stories of modern times is the story of the extinction of the passenger pigeon in North America. (2) Never have so many animals disappeared so quick. (3) The story is filled with incredible statistics and eyewitness descriptions that are even more harder to believe.

(4) Very few birds were as attractive and graceful like the passenger pigeon, with its light blue feathers and pink breast. (5) However, its most greatest distinction was the giant size of its populations; there might have been more passenger pigeons than any

other bird in history. (6) In fact, the birds got their name because they "passed" overhead in such tremendous numbers. (7) Indeed, the numbers are amazing. (8) One expert on birds watched for two days as one 150-mile-long flock passed over his home. (9) The famous naturalist John James Audubon said that 300 million birds blocked the sun for three days as they flew overhead. (10) Another flock of perhaps 2 billion birds caused a completer solar eclipse than the moon could achieve. (11) A single rifle shot into a flock could supposedly kill at least 200 birds.

(12) For centuries the passenger pigeon lived happy and created no problems for humans. (13) In fact, the bird saved the early North American settlers from starvation when a terrible winter hurt their crops bad in 1648. (14) And the bird became one of the mostest important parts of the diet of the settlers. (15) The pigeon tasted about the same like chicken but was a little more tough.

(16) During the 1700s and early 1800s, hunters found clever ways of killing the birds. (17) One method involved waiting until a flock of pigeons roosted in tree branches for the night. (18) The men set the grass on fire, and its dense smoke killed the pigeons. (19) Another plan that worked good was to attract the birds through a decoy—a live passenger pigeon whose eyes had been sewn shut. (20) When it was placed on a perch called a stool, the bird called very loud and attracted an enormous flock, which the hunters then shot. (21) The term *stool pigeon*—for one person who betrays another—comes from this practice.

Scorecard: Number of Errors Found and Corrected _____

Collaborative Activity 4

Comparing Your Answers
Compare your answers with a classmate and, if your instructor indicates, report your findings to the class.

Mastery Exercise 2

Correcting Adjective and Adverb Errors

The passage contains eleven errors in the use of adjectives and adverbs. The first error has been corrected for you. Find and correct the remaining ten errors.

The Extinction of the Passenger Pigeon

(1) The most ~~mostest~~ remarkable part of the disappearance of the passenger pigeon was how it happened. (2) A number of factors caused the extinction. (3) As the human population grew more large, the people cut down forests and shrunk the pigeons' food

supply. (4) The railroad brought hunters to the West, and they killed the birds and sent them back east to be served as food. (5) Passenger pigeons also became live targets in shooting galleries at city and county fairs. (6) By the 1880s, the baddest damage had been done. (7) There were no more passenger pigeons on either coast and only a few flocks in other places.

(8) The passenger pigeon's most big flock was in Michigan, where the latest great pigeon hunt took place in 1878. (9) Hundreds of people began shooting as many as a billion pigeons in an area about five miles long by a mile wide. (10) Some pigeons flew away but then returned to the same trees, where the hunters killed them easy. (11) It took the hunters thirty days to wipe out the entire pigeon population. (12) Every day, they packed the birds into five railroad cars for shipment to Boston and New York.

(13) The hunters did their job good—so good that the passenger pigeons were being killed off very quick. (14) On the morning of March 24, 1900, a teenager in Ohio shot the lastly passenger pigeon in that state. (15) Maine reported that its only remaining bird was shot by a hunter in 1904. (16) Arkansas recorded the end of the species in 1906.

(17) The pigeons that a hundred years more early had represented about 35 percent of birds in the United States were now reduced to a total of three, all in the Cincinnati Zoo. (18) When two of the birds in the zoo died, a pigeon named Martha was the only one left. (19) Martha lived to be very old—twenty-nine years—but died on September 1, 1914. (20) Its body was sent to the Smithsonian Institution in Washington, D.C., where it was stuffed and mounted. (21) It can be viewed today in the Smithsonian's collection of the most rarest birds.

Scorecard: Number of Errors Found and Corrected _____

24 Identifying Sentences and Fixing Fragments

Every sentence makes a complete statement. But if the statement is incomplete— if it's only a fragment of a sentence—readers will find its idea confusing or even impossible to understand. This chapter will show you how to write complete sentences. It explains

- ways to identify and fix simple sentence fragments
- ways to identify and fix complex sentence fragments

The Structure of the Sentence

Every sentence contains a **subject**—*who* or *what* the statement or question is about. And it must contain a **verb**—stating what the subject *does* or *is.* The verb begins the **predicate.**

The subject and verb usually go together at the beginning of a group of words called a **clause.**

Most often, the subject comes first, and the verb follows the subject. Here are some examples:

Subject	Verb	Remainder of predicate
President Abraham Lincoln	loved	animals.
He	saved	a turkey's life.
The turkey	was	a gift for Christmas dinner.

Taken as a whole, a *subject + verb and remainder of the predicate* is called an **independent clause.** It creates a full sentence. (Sentences can also have two or more clauses, as you'll see in the following chapters.) Right now, however, we'll concentrate on identifying the main elements of a single clause: first the subject and then the verb.

Identifying Subjects

The easiest way to identify the subject and verb is to look for both at the same time. Let's begin, however, with the **subject.**

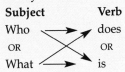

TIPS

For Identifying Subjects and Verbs

One simple question should help you locate the subject and verb of each clause:

Who or *what does* or *is?*

Who or *what,* of course, will identify the subject of the clause. *Does* or *is* will identify the verb.

Subject	Verb
Who	does
OR	OR
What	is

As a reminder, the subject

- tells *who* or *what* the sentence is about
- usually (but not always) appears at or near the beginning of the statement—before the verb, which tells what the subject *does* or *is*

Subject (*who* OR *what*) + verb (*does* OR *is*) = sentence

The following sentence, for example, makes a statement about the subject, *Tad Lincoln.* Notice that the verb *loved* follows the subject:

Tad Lincoln loved a turkey.

EXERCISE 1 | Identifying Subjects

Read the sentences. Ask yourself: *Who* or *what* does this sentence make a statement about? Underline the subjects in the sentences.

1. Tad Lincoln was only ten years old in 1863.

2. He loved a turkey and named it Jack.

3. The bird soon followed young Tad around the White House grounds.

4. Tad and his father agreed not to kill the animal.

5. Pardoning the White House turkey has since become an annual tradition for presidents.

Are these the words you underlined? Each is an example of one type of subject:

1. *Tad Lincoln:* The subject is a **proper noun**—a capitalized name.
2. *He:* The subject is a **subject form of a personal pronoun.**
3. *The bird:* The subject is a **common noun**—which is not capitalized because it does not name someone or something.
4. *Tad and his father:* This **compound subject** is joined by *and.*
5. *Pardoning the White House turkey:* This subject is a verb turned into a noun, called a **gerund.**

EXERCISE 2 | Identifying Subjects

Underline the subject of each sentence. You'll find at least one example of the kinds of subjects explained above.

1. <u>Abraham Lincoln</u> faced attacks from all sides.

2. Southerners hated him.

3. His Republican party was divided over him in the election of 1864.

4. Some Republicans refused to support him.

5. Two of his generals ran against him in elections.

6. Nevertheless, this tall, unattractive fellow from Illinois achieved greatness.

7. He was indeed a self-made man.

8. Studying law on his own, becoming a lawyer, and serving in the Illinois legislature led to his election to the United States House of Representatives in 1846.

9. The future president could also tell a good story or joke—a great asset in campaigning for office.

Identifying Verbs

Now you can turn your attention to the **verbs** in clauses. As a reminder, a verb

- says what the subject *does* or *is*
- usually has a **tense,** indicating if the verb discusses the past, present, or future
- usually follows the subject and begins the predicate
- may contain more than one word

Subject	Verb	Remainder of predicate
Tomás	*needs*	a new hairpiece or a large, floppy hat.
Alberto	*has eaten*	the whole cake and part of the plate.

EXERCISE 3	Identifying Verbs

Circle the complete verbs in the following sentences.

1. Lincoln was controversial throughout his presidency.

2. People might even consider Lincoln a racist today.

3. Lincoln didn't free the slaves at the beginning of the Civil War for a simple reason.

4. He wanted to bring the slaveholding South back into the Union quickly.

5. However, like other great presidents, he grew in office and took courageous positions.

6. In the fall of 1862, he issued the Emancipation Proclamation, freeing the slaves in the areas still in rebellion as of January 1, 1863.

Are these the words you circled?

1. *was:* The verb has a tense. (*Was* is the past tense of *is.*)

2. *might* (even) *consider:* The parts of this two-word verb are separated by *even,* an **adverb.** *Might* is a **modal** verb.

3. *did(n't) free:* This two-word verb is separated by the negative **adverb** *not.*

4. *wanted:* This word again expresses the tense. If you circled *to bring,* this is an **infinitive** and is formed from a verb but doesn't function as a verb. It never has a tense.

5. *grew* and *took:* This **compound predicate** performs *two actions* in *two verbs,* which are joined by *and.*

6. *issued:* This is another past tense verb. If you circled *freeing,* remember this *-ing* word is a **present participle,** and doesn't function as a verb.

Infinitives and *-ing* words, although formed from verbs, normally function as other parts of speech.

Helping Verbs. A verb can include two, three, or even four words. In the examples that follow, *use* is the main verb, and the words before it are **helping verbs**—which help express the complete tense or content of the verb:

Main verb	Main verb with helping verbs		
use	am using	will be using	might have been using
uses	is using	would have used	should have been using
used	has used	might be using	could have been used
	did(n't) use	must be using	must have been used
	may use	may be using	
	will use	could be using	
	had used	will have used	
	can use	should be using	
	does use	must have used	

Note the one exception to the rule about *-ing* words. They are verbs when they follow the helping verb *to be:*

is going, am going, are going, was going, were going, will be going, and so on

Linking Verbs. Linking verbs do not express an action but simply say the subject *is* or *was* something. The most common linking verb is *to be.* The other common linking verbs represent the five senses—*look, sound, feel, smell,* and *taste*—as well as the verbs *become* and *appear:*

Subject	Linking verb	Remainder of predicate
Maria	is seems appears sounded looks felt	happy (adjective).
The food	tastes smelled	good (adjective).
Amir	became was	a doctor (noun).

EXERCISE 4	Identifying More Verbs

Circle the verbs in the sentences. Also, put a box around any infinitives and any *-ing* words that don't function as verbs.

1. Lincoln (won) the election in 1860, [becoming] the sixteenth president of the United States.

2. He was also the first president to die from an assassin's bullet.

3. He would be the second president to die as a result of the "zero curse."

4. From 1840 to 1960, any president winning an election in a year ending in zero did not leave the presidency alive.

5. William Henry Harrison (election of 1840) would die in April 1841 after being in office for only thirty days.

6. President James A. Garfield (election of 1880) was shot and killed by an assassin in 1881.

7. President William McKinley (election of 1900) held office for less than a year before dying at the hands of an assassin in 1901.

8. Warren G. Harding (election of 1920) and Franklin D. Roosevelt (1940) both would not live to the end of their terms, though Roosevelt was elected one more time, in 1944, and died in 1945.

9. And, of course, John F. Kennedy (election of 1960) died from a gunshot coming from the sixth floor of a building in Dallas, Texas.

Abraham Lincoln

EXERCISE 5 | Writing Verbs

Complete the following passage with the past tense of one of the verbs in the box. You won't use all the verbs, and you may use one twice.

ask	be	call	do
face	free	have	hope
know	make	put	win

Lincoln (1)_____*faced*_____ more serious problems than any other president. Therefore, he (2)_____ some very serious and difficult decisions. While the members of Congress were not meeting, he formed an army and (3)_____ thousands of people in jail although he didn't charge them with crimes. Lincoln (4)_____ that this step (5)_____ a violation of the United States Constitution, but it (6)_____ necessary "in cases of rebellion or invasion."

At the beginning of the Civil War, many people in his political party (7)_____ him to end slavery. In 1863, Lincoln (8)_____ the slaves. Still, many people (9)_____ to stop by the war by any means. They (10)_____ Lincoln a dictator. After four long years, the North finally (11)_____ the war.

Collaborative Activity 1

Classifying Verbs

With a classmate, compare the verbs you chose for Exercise 5. Classify your answers into one or more of the following: (1) verbs with two or more words, (2) action verbs, and (3) linking verbs. Prepare lists for each category, and share your lists with the class.

EXERCISE 6 | Identifying Subjects and Verbs

Here's a chance to apply all you've learned about recognizing subjects and verbs. In each sentence, underline the subject(s) and circle the verb(s).

1. After her husband's assassination, Mary Todd Lincoln invited several "spiritualists" (people believed to have special powers) to the White House.
2. They comforted the grieving widow.
3. Years later in Chicago, Mary went to séances (spiritualist meetings) in hopes of communicating with her dead husband.
4. Once, on a trip to Boston, she attended a séance.
5. Mary used the name "Mrs. Tundall" to hide her identity.
6. Her dead husband supposedly appeared before her during the séance.
7. She then visited the studio of William Mumler, a "spirit photographer."
8. Mumler produced a photograph of Mary with Abraham.
9. The president was in the background with his hands on Mary's shoulders.

What Is a Fragment?

A **fragment** is an incomplete statement that's written as if it were a sentence. Fragments occur for many reasons. Here are a few:

- In trying to express an idea, you might not pay attention to where a sentence ends.
- You might place periods where you hear pauses.
- You might be omitting subjects or writing only partial verbs.
- You might be unclear about the uses of joining words such as *although* and *because*.

No matter why fragments occur, however, it's important to identify and eliminate them. And that's what we'll be doing in the rest of this chapter.

Fixing Simple Fragments

A simple fragment is an incomplete clause. Let's take a look at several types:

- fragments missing a subject
- fragments missing a verb or part of a verb
- fragments beginning with infinitives or *-ing* words
- fragments that are only details or examples

Missing Subjects. Suppose you write a statement in which the subject performs *two actions* expressed in two separate verbs. If you end the statement after the first verb, the second verb will be left hanging, without a subject, in a fragment. Here's an example:

Sentence:	In the 1850s, many people went to séances.
Fragment:	And supposedly communicated with their dead relatives.

The fragment contains a verb, *communicated,* but doesn't have a subject. You could fix the fragment in at least two ways:

Combining:	In the 1850s, many people went to séances and supposedly communicated with their dead relatives.
Adding a subject to the fragment:	In the 1850s, many people went to séances. *These people* supposedly communicated with their dead relatives.

Missing or Incomplete Verbs. Some simple fragments result from writing incomplete verbs. Notice the missing helping verbs in the examples on page 299.

For Supplying Verbs in Fragments

Some languages treat the subject before the verb *to be* differently from the way English does, and that can cause some confusion:

- In Spanish, for example, one word—the verb—expresses the subject-verb combination *it is*. Be careful, therefore, not to write fragments such as "Is easy" and "Was a nice day" when the full clauses in English are *"It is easy,"* and *"It was a nice day."*

- Some Eastern European languages omit the verb *to be* entirely from sentences. Be careful, therefore, not to write the sentence fragments "He tall" or "She a doctor" when the full sentences in English are *"He is tall,"* or *"She is a doctor."*

Incomplete verbs	Complete verbs
Spiritualists *putting* people in touch with the dead.	Spiritualists *were putting* people in touch with the dead.
Abraham Lincoln's wife Mary often *gone* to séances.	Abraham Lincoln's wife Mary *had* often *gone* to séances.

The most frequently omitted helping verbs are *to be* (*is, am, are, was, were*) and *to have* (*has, have, had*).

Infinitives and *-ing* Words. Remember that infinitives and most *-ing* words don't function as verbs but only introduce or continue a sentence. If they aren't attached to that sentence, they hang loose as fragments. Look at these examples:

Sentence:	Mary Lincoln's young sons Willie and Eddie had died.
-ing word fragment:	*Sending her into a deep depression.*
-ing word fragment:	*Refusing to accept her children's death.*
Sentence:	Mary told her sister that they visited her each night.
Infinitive fragment:	*To comfort Mary after President Lincoln's death.*
Sentence:	Several spiritualists visited her at the White House.

You can fix the fragments by attaching them to the complete sentences:

Mary Lincoln's young sons Willie and Eddie had died, sending her into a deep depression.

Refusing to accept her children's death, Mary told her sister that they visited her each night.

To comfort Mary after President Lincoln's death, several spiritualists visited her at the White House.

Hanging Details or Examples. Some fragments are simply details that continue the idea of the previous sentence. For instance, the detail fragment that follows this sentence doesn't contain a verb:

sentence	detail fragment
At a séance, people would sit in a dark room.	*With their hands on the table.*

You can fix the fragment by adding it to the sentence:

At a séance, people would sit in a dark room with their hands on the table.

EXERCISE 7 | Fixing Simple Fragments

Locate the fragments in this exercise. Then fix each one by supplying the missing subjects, verbs, or partial verbs, or by attaching the fragment to a complete sentence. Be careful: Some sentences are complete.

1. Lincoln ⋀*was* shot at Ford's Theatre in Washington, D.C., on April 14, 1865.

2. Charles Leale the first doctor to reach the president's box.

3. Mary almost ready to faint. Sat on a couch near her chair.

4. Leale asked a few soldiers to place the president on the floor.

5. Other doctors arrived in the president's box and were able to revive him. Using artificial respiration and some brandy and water.

6. Leale then said that the president was sure to die.

7. From the couch, Mary quietly moaned, "His dream was prophetic."

✔ TIPS

For Identifying and Fixing Fragments

In writing, the punctuation represents pauses that occur with the rise and fall of our voices. The pitch of our voices *drops* at the end of a sentence, and that's where a period belongs.

Say this sentence aloud. Notice how your pitch lowers at the period:

I went to the store.

Now say this incomplete sentence:

If I had gone home first, . . .

Because this sentence is incomplete, the pitch of our voices rises at the comma.

Read your sentences aloud as you edit your papers. If you hear your voice rise at the end of a sentence, look closely at that sentence. It could be a fragment (unless it is a question, which also ends with our voices rising).

Fixing Complex Fragments

You've looked at simple sentences that contain a single independent clause. Now you'll look at **complex sentences** that contain two clauses: a **dependent clause** and an **independent clause**. The dependent clause depends on the independent clause to complete its meaning. If the dependent clause is not joined to the independent clause, the dependent clause is a fragment. There are two main types of these fragments:

- those beginning with words like *although* or *because*
- those beginning with words like *who, which,* or *that*

***Although* and *Because* Types.** Find the subjects and verbs of the following clauses:

> *Because* the doctors were trying to save the president . . .
>
> *Although* Mary Todd Lincoln could not help her husband . . .

Each clause contains a subject and a verb, but these dependent clauses don't make complete statements. After you read them, you want to ask, "What happened?" The **subordinating conjunctions** *because* and *although* link their clauses to a second, **independent clause** that completes the statement:

> *Because* the doctors were trying to save the president, *they took him to the nearest house.*
>
> *Although* Mary Todd Lincoln could not help her husband, she *stayed at his bedside.*

Here is a more complete list of the subordinating conjunctions that create dependent clauses:

after	as soon as	if	until
although	because	once	when
as	before	since	whether
as if	even though	unless	while

When you spot a dependent clause fragment, you can correct it in one of two ways.

1. Join the dependent clause to the sentence that precedes or follows it. This is usually the best and most common solution:

Fragments

When President Lincoln finally died. Mrs. Lincoln was waiting in the front room of the house.

Nearly two hours had passed. *Before she finally felt strong enough to go back to the White House.*

Sentences

When President Lincoln finally died, Mrs. Lincoln was waiting in the front room of the house.

Nearly two hours had passed *before she finally felt strong enough to go back to the White House.*

Punctuation is very important. When a dependent clause begins a sentence, use a comma. When a dependent clause comes at the end of a sentence, don't use a comma.

2. Remove the joining word before the dependent clause, and write the clause as a separate sentence. However, this solution often creates short, awkward sentences. You may choose to keep a subordinating conjunction and use correct punctuation:

Fragments

Nearly two hours had passed. *Before she finally felt strong enough to go back to the White House.*

No joining word

Nearly two hours had passed. *She finally felt strong enough to go back to the White House.*

Subordinating conjunctions

After nearly two hours had passed, she finally felt strong enough to go back to the White House.

Nearly two hours had passed *before she finally felt strong enough to go back to the White House.*

TIPS

For Using *Although*

Don't confuse *although*—a conjunction—with *however*, a transitional word that does not join ideas. (See Chapter 25.) And be careful not to use *although* and *but* together.

EXERCISE 8 | Fixing Complex Fragments

Find the sentence fragments in this exercise. Fix each one either by joining it to the clause that completes its meaning or by rewriting it as a complete sentence. Place commas where they're needed. Be careful: One of the items does not contain a sentence fragment.

Lincoln's Strange Dream

1. On the evening of April 11, 1865, President Lincoln and Mrs. Lincoln were talking with several friends. When Lincoln suddenly began to discuss his dreams.

   On the evening of April 11, 1865, President Lincoln and Mrs. Lincoln were talking

   with several friends when Lincoln suddenly began to discuss his dreams.

2. He said that he had been unable to sleep well. Because he had had a terrible dream ten days earlier. _____

   _____

3. Since he had been waiting for important messages about the war. He went to sleep very late. _____

   _____

4. In his dream, he heard soft sobs. As if a number of people were weeping.

   _____

5. He left his bed and wandered downstairs. When the sobbing grew louder. Although the mourners were invisible. _____

   _____

6. He kept going from room to room. Then he arrived at the East Room.

   _____

Who, That, and Which **Types.** A second kind of complex fragment includes the words *who, that,* and *which.* Look at these examples:

> . . . *who* was a famous actor at the time.
>
> "Voices" that Mary Lincoln began to hear ten years later . . .
>
> . . . *which* was a place for the mentally ill.

These are also dependent clauses—and incomplete statements. You can complete their meaning in two ways:

1. Attach them to the words that make the statement complete:

> **Sentences**
>
> *President Lincoln was assassinated by John Wilkes Booth,* who was a famous actor at the time.
>
> "Voices" that Mary Lincoln began to hear ten years later *were used as evidence of her mental illness.*
>
> *In 1875, she spent four months in a private hospital called Bellevue,* which was a place for the mentally ill.

2. Rewrite the clauses and make them complete by replacing *who, which,* or *that* with a noun or a subject pronoun. Again, this might not be the best solution if it creates short, choppy sentences:

> **Separate sentences**
>
> President Lincoln was assassinated by John Wilkes Booth. Booth was a famous actor at that time.
>
> In 1875, she was spent four months in a private hospital called Bellevue. It was a place for the mentally ill.

Since the handling of *who/which/that* clauses is complicated, we'll return to it again in Chapter 27.

EXERCISE 9 | Fixing More Complex Fragments

Find the sentence fragments in this exercise. Fix each one by joining it to the clause that completes its meaning. Be careful: One of the items does not contain a sentence fragment.

The End of Lincoln's Dream

1. In the East Room, Lincoln saw a platform. That held a body wrapped in funeral clothing. *In the East Room, Lincoln saw a platform that held a body wrapped in funeral clothing.*

2. All around the platform were many people. Who were crying. _____

3. One of the soldiers. Who were acting as guards. Told him that it was the president. Who had been killed by an assassin. _____

Collaborative Activity 2

Comparing Your Solutions

In a small group, share and compare the ways in which you've fixed the fragments in Exercises 8 and 9. If you have different solutions, list them, and then share your lists with the class.

4. The crowd cried loudly with grief. That noise awoke Lincoln from his dream.

_____

_____

5. Mrs. Lincoln was frightened by her husband's story. Which the president reminded

her was only a dream. _____

_____

EXERCISE 10 | **Fixing Fragments**

Road each group of words and label each item either **S** (for sentence) or **F** (for fragment). If a fragment, punctuate it correctly—adding a period or a comma—and add the words to make a complete sentence.

_S_ **1.** If you think the first part of the sentence is complete, you aren't noticing the rise in pitch at the comma.

_____ **2.** When there's a rise in the pitch of your voice. _____

_____

_____ **3.** The result should be that you can tell when a sentence is complete.

_____

_____ **4.** Your ear is a pretty good judge of these matters. _____

_____

_____ **5.** With enough practice and repetition. _____

_____

_____ **6.** This exercise should give you a better idea about how sentences sound.

_____

IN SUMMARY | To Fix Fragments

- Make sure that each statement contains at least one subject and a complete verb.
- Make sure that you do not mistake an *-ing* word or an infinitive for a verb.
- Make sure that there are no hanging details or examples written as complete statements.
- Make sure that a clause beginning with words such as *although* or *because* is attached to a clause that completes its idea.
- Make sure that a clause beginning with words such as *who, that,* or *which* is attached to the words that complete its idea.

EDITING FOR MASTERY

Mastery Exercise 1

Eliminating Fragments

The passage contains thirteen fragments. Find and correct them by following the steps below. The first one has been done for you.

1. Identify the subject(s) and the verb(s) in every clause.
2. Make any changes necessary in sentences that are incomplete, including:
   a. supplying a missing subject or a missing (or incomplete) verb
   b. joining an incomplete sentence to another sentence (by removing a period between the two sentences or by changing the period to a comma)
   c. rewriting the fragment

The Death of Abraham Lincoln

(1) On Friday, April 14, 1865, Lincoln met with his cabinet. (2) ~~To~~ *to* discuss changes in the treatment of the South. (3) Now that the war was over. (4) His mood was happy, and he telling everyone around him to look for a way to make the peace last. (5) By preparing a plan to bring the southern states back into the Union with little punishment.

(6) That evening he and his wife went to see a play at Ford's Theatre in downtown Washington. (7) The policeman guarding the president left his post. (8) To get either a drink or a better view of the play. (9) When a pistol shot rang out. (10) Lincoln fell forward in his chair. (11) A man jumped from the president's box to the stage. (12) In the process breaking his leg. (13) He waved his gun and shouted something. (14) Then he escaped through a back exit and mounted a horse. (15) Which was waiting outside.

(16) Lincoln was taken to a house across the street from the theater. (17) Where he died the next morning. (18) Throwing the shocked nation into grief. (19) Although many groups had criticized him for one reason or another. (20) Abraham Lincoln was finally a hero of the entire nation.

Collaborative Activity 3

Comparing Sentences

Compare your answers with a classmate. Your instructor may ask you to report your findings to the class.

(21) The assassin was soon discovered. (22) John Wilkes Booth, who was an actor. (23) After a huge manhunt, Booth was trapped in a barn on April 26, and shot and killed. (24) A military court sentenced four other conspirators to death. (25) Including Mary Surratt, who was the owner of a boardinghouse.

Scorecard: Number of Fragments Found and Corrected: _____

Mastery Exercise 2

Eliminating Fragments

The passage contains thirteen fragments. Find and correct them by following the steps below. The first one has been done for you.

1. Identify the subject(s) and the verb(s) in every clause.
2. Make any changes necessary in sentences that are incomplete. These changes can include
   a. supplying a missing subject or a missing (or incomplete) verb
   b. joining an incomplete sentence to another sentence (usually by removing a period between the two sentences and sometimes by changing the period to a comma)
   c. rewriting the fragment

So What If His Name Was Mudd?

(1) Dr. Samuel A. Mudd set the broken leg of a mysterious visitor in 1865 and ended up in prison with a life sentence. (2) ^*for* ~~For~~ assisting in the escape of President Abraham Lincoln's assassin. (3) Although four years later the next president pardoned Mudd. (4) In 1992, several of his descendants were still trying to prove he was completely innocent. (5) The Army Board of Correction of Military Records. (6) Considered the Mudd family's appeal.

(7) Some facts about the case are clear. (8) The man who found his way to Mudd's country house on the morning of April 15. (9) He was actor John Wilkes Booth, who was wearing a false beard. (10) Booth had shot Lincoln and broken a leg when he jumped from the president's box.

(11) The government's original interpretation of these facts has always been weak. (12) The original trial appeared to be unfair. (13) The use of false and suspicious testimony, and the refusal to hear evidence that was favorable to Mudd. (14) According to that evidence, Mudd hardly had known Booth. (15) After the assassination, when Booth looked for treatment at Mudd's house. (16) The doctor was unaware that Lincoln had been shot.

(17) Louise Mudd Arehart, the youngest of Mudd's ten surviving grandchildren, was his biggest supporter. (18) Arehart relied heavily on her grandmother's story of what had happened. (19) When Booth came to the Mudds' house. (20) The grandmother became

suspicious of Booth. (21) Especially after his false whiskers fell off. (22) Mudd, who had been out, returned home. (23) He had learned of Lincoln's murder. (24) And the search for the assassin. (25) When soldiers arrived the following week, Mudd told them everything he knew and produced the boot he had cut from the stranger's injured leg. (26) On the boot was the name "J. Wilkes."

(27) Therefore, Arehart and many other of Mudd's descendants appealed Dr. Mudd's case. (28) However, the Assistant Secretary of the U.S. Army. (29) Refused to hear their appeal. (30) Announcing that the Board had no right to "settle historical disputes."

(31) The fight to clear Mudd's name still continues.

Scorecard: Number of Fragments Found and Corrected _____

25 Joining Sentences through Coordination

If you want to keep your readers interested, you need to create some variety in your sentences. If you don't, here's what happens:

> My sentences are short. They are simple. Each contains only one idea.
> They can't express complex thoughts. Short sentences get boring. They are
> all alike. They make me sound like a first-grader. I had better stop now.
> You will be glad to stop reading, too.

Sentence variety comes largely from joining sentences—clearly, logically, and correctly. This chapter will examine one method of joining sentences called **coordination.** You'll learn how to

- join sentences by adding words
- join sentences by using punctuation
- use words and punctuation correctly

Connecting Sentences with Coordinating Conjunctions

The most common way to connect sentences is to use joining words called **conjunctions.** We'll look at how one set of conjunctions both joins and explains the logical relationships between sentences.

The Coordinating Conjunctions

Coordinating conjunctions join grammatically equal structures, as in the following examples:

> Karif *and* I (two people, or subjects)
>
> tripped *or* fell (two actions, or past tense verbs)
>
> a large *yet* athletic man (two describing words, or adjectives)
>
> moved quickly *but* carefully (two words describing actions, or adverbs)

There are seven coordinating conjunctions, which you can memorize by remembering the words *fan boys:*

For	But
And	Or
Nor	Yet
	So

Coordinating conjunctions can also join *two sentences*. An independent clause (which contains a subject and verb) makes a complete sentence. Therefore, when you join two sentences with a coordinating conjunction, you create a single sentence with two independent clauses. That single sentence is called a **compound sentence.**

EXERCISE 1   Identifying Conjunctions

Find and underline the coordinating conjunctions in the sentences. Look carefully. One item does not contain a coordinating conjunction, so the two clauses are not correctly joined. Circle the word that incorrectly joins the two clauses.

1. Male babies often wear blue, <u>and</u> female babies wear pink.

2. Years ago, people wanted to protect their infant boys from evil spirits, so they dressed the boys in blue.

3. People associated blue with good spirits, for those spirits lived in the blue sky.

4. Of course, people cared about their female children, yet people did not care enough to dress them in blue.

5. Many years later, people still dressed the males in blue, but they chose pink for the females.

6. The superstition about evil spirits had disappeared, or people might have dressed their girls in blue also.

7. Very few parents today know the reasons behind these traditional colors, nor do parents care.

8. Some parents choose yellow, then color doesn't make any difference.

9. The color doesn't make any difference to the baby, and even the parents know that.

Coordinating conjunctions not only join two clauses, but they also *explain the logical relationship between the two clauses:*

Conjunction	Purpose
for	shows a reason (The second clause gives a reason for the first.)
and	shows addition
nor	shows a negative alternative (It's the negative form of *or*, and it must follow a clause containing a negative word such as *not*.)

Conjunction	Purpose
but	shows contrast
or	shows an alternative or choice
yet	shows an unexpected contrast (It's similar in meaning to *although*.)
so	shows a result (The first clause results in the second.)

Punctuating Compound Sentences Joined by Coordinating Conjunctions

Not every coordinating conjunction requires a comma. Here are the rules:

▶ **Place a comma before the coordinating conjunction** *that joins independent clauses:*

independent clause	coordinating conjunction	independent clause
Alberto likes ice cream,	*but*	he likes pizza better.

▶ *Don't use a comma* **before coordinating conjunctions that join just two words:**

word	coordinating conjunction	word
Alberto likes *spaghetti*	*and*	*pizza*, but he doesn't like hot dogs.

EXERCISE 2	Completing Sentences

Complete each sentence with an independent clause.

1. The Internet has become very important today, and *many people now rely on it for e-mail and information.*

2. Nowadays, people love the speed and convenience of e-mail, so _____

_____

3. Many people also shop on the Internet, for it _____

_____

4. Companies without computer technology must change, or _____

_____

5. Prices of computers continue to drop, yet _____

_____

6. Ten years ago, hardly anyone used the Internet, but _____

_____

7. Many people don't realize that their cars contain hundreds of computer chips,

nor _____

_____

EXERCISE 3	Writing Combined Sentences

Write your own seven combined sentences. Use a different coordinating conjunction—*for, and, nor, but, or, yet,* and *so*—in each sentence. Be sure to punctuate your sentences correctly. Compare your sentences with those of a partner.

Connecting Sentences with Semicolons

TIPS

For Avoiding Comma Errors

Some languages use a comma to join independent clauses. But in English, commas separate clauses. Be sure to link together independent clauses with either a semicolon or a coordinating conjunction.

Correct: The first living creature to go into outer space wasn't a human; it was a Russian dog named Laika.

Correct: Unfortunately, the Russians chose not to bring Laika back to Earth, so the poor creature died in orbit.

There is only one punctuation mark that can join two sentences into one. This is the **semicolon [;]**. Take a good look at the semicolon; notice that it's a combination of a period and a comma.

- Like a period, it signals the end of a complete statement.
- Like a comma, it signals that the sentence continues.
- But unlike a period or a comma, it joins two clauses into one sentence.

Use a semicolon when the logical connection between the two clauses is obvious and needs no explanation. Here are some examples:

California is the most populous state in the United States; one out of every nine people lives there.

Alaska has very long and cold winters; not many people want to live there.

Follow these guidelines to use semicolons properly and gracefully in your writing:

- Never use a coordinating conjunction with a semicolon.
- Don't capitalize the first word after the semicolon.
- Don't overuse semicolons; your writing will sound too choppy.

EXERCISE 4	Writing Clauses after Semicolons

Using the words in parentheses, write sentences that follow the pattern of each example. Be sure that your sentences join two independent clauses with a semicolon.

1. Living in a big city has many advantages; it provides opportunities to see plays, hear concerts, and visit museums.

   (small town) *Living in a small town has many advantages; it allows you to know your neighbors well and participate in community activities.*

2. Dolphins and whales cannot breathe under water; they must come to the surface for air.

   (fish)_____

   _____

3. The life expectancy of people in the United States is rising; many people live to be over eighty.

   (cost of college)_____

   _____

4. Alaska is the largest state; Rhode Island is the smallest one.

(Russia/Vatican City) _____

_____

5. In horseracing, the average rider is very light; he or she weighs about 125 pounds.

(professional wrestler) _____

_____

Collaborative Activity 1

Discussing Your Combined Sentences
Compare your answers to Exercise 4 with a classmate. Then share your results with the class.

6. College tuition is expensive; many students cannot afford it.

(public transportation/many people) _____

_____

Transitional Words after the Semicolon

Sometimes the logical connection between the two clauses joined by a semicolon isn't clear. Consider this example:

Juan said he was eating too much; he ate a second piece of cake. [Huh?]

You can clarify that logical connection by adding a word directly after the semicolon:

Juan said he was eating too much; *however,* he ate a second piece of cake.

This additional word is called a **conjunctive adverb.** Like a conjunction, it shows a link between two ideas. And, like an adverb, it explains *how* or *in what way* the ideas are related.

It's also called a **transitional word** because it shows the transition (or movement) from one idea to another. Here's a list of common conjunctive adverbs:

Transitional word (conjunctive adverb)	Acts like this joining word (conjunction)	But in this way (adverb)
furthermore, moreover, also	and	in addition
however	but	in contrast
nevertheless	yet	in contrast
therefore, consequently	so	as a result
otherwise, instead	or	as an alternative
meanwhile, then, later, afterward	(none)	shows time relationships

Remember: The conjunctive adverb doesn't join two clauses; *the semicolon joins them.* As with the coordinating conjunctions, punctuation is important.

- The semicolon comes first.
- The conjunctive adverb comes next.
- The comma comes last.

Independent clause	Transitional word	Independent clause
Mario enjoyed quiet;	*nevertheless,*	he worked at the bowling alley.
Claudia studies during the week;	*however,*	she likes to go out on the weekends.

EXERCISE 5 | Substituting Transitional Words

Rewrite each sentence. Replace the coordinating conjunction with a conjunctive adverb. Use the correct punctuation.

The Voyage of the *Kon-Tiki*

1. Thor Heyerdahl was born and raised in Norway, but he is most famous for his travel to Polynesia in the South Pacific. *Thor Heyerdahl was born and raised in Norway; however, he is most famous for his travel to Polynesia in the South Pacific.*

2. In 1936, he learned the legend of a pale-skinned god Tiki, who brought the ancestors of the Polynesian natives from the West across the sea, so he logically concluded that they came from Peru in South America. _____

_____

3. He wanted to prove that such a voyage was possible, so in 1947 he built a raft like the kind he thought the early natives used. _____

_____

4. He made a forty-five-foot long raft, which he called *Kon-Tiki,* out of logs and bamboo, and he used only rope to hold the logs together. _____

_____

5. Heyerdahl and a crew of six had to be incredibly skilled and brave, or they would never have completed their 4,300-mile voyage across the open sea. _____

_____

6. After 101 days, the raft reached the reefs near a Polynesian island, but strong waves smashed the cabin and broke the mast in two. _____

_____

7. The boat was destroyed and the crew thrown into the water, yet they were able to wade their way to the island. _____

_____

8. People said that a fragile wooden raft couldn't possibly cross the Pacific Ocean, yet Heyerdahl proved them wrong. _____

_____

9. Heyedahl's book describing the journey was extremely popular, and his documentary film about the experience won an Academy Award in 1951. _____

_____

_____

EXERCISE 6 | Writing Combined Sentences

Complete the sentences after the semicolon by adding a transitional word, a comma, and a second independent clause. Use a different transitional word each time.

1. In the United States, there is very little difference between "men's work" and "women's work" these days; *therefore, both sexes do a variety of jobs in all sorts of professions.*

2. Many doctors and lawyers are women; _____

_____

3. Most married women are no longer simply "housewives"; _____

_____

4. It's not unusual to see women working at construction sites; _____

_____

Collaborative Activity 2

Trying Out More Combined Sentences

Compare Exercise 6 with a classmate to see if you both found new transitional words that make each sentence interesting.

5. Many men work in what used to be "female" professions; _____

_____

6. Most women and men are probably happy about the changes in our society;

_____

_____

EXERCISE 7 | Combining More Sentences

Combine each pair of sentences using either coordinating conjunctions or semicolons (and transitional words if necessary).

Harriet Tubman (1820–1913): Liberator of Slaves

1. Harriet Tubman was not even five feet tall. She was black. *Harriet Tubman was not even five feet tall, and she was black.*

2. She had been enslaved in Maryland. She became free in 1849 by escaping to Philadelphia, Pennsylvania, where slavery was illegal. _____

_____

3. She was determined to help slaves gain freedom. She returned to the South.

_____

_____

4. She was the woman the slaves called "Moses." She led the slaves to the free states in the North. _____

_____

5. No one knew how it happened. The slaves mysteriously disappeared and followed her on secret trails. _____

_____

6. Tubman wasn't satisfied that only she was free. She had to help her family, her friends, and finally strangers get away, too. _____

_____

7. She knew that she could be captured and made a slave in the South. She returned to the South as many as nineteen times to free her people. _____

_____

8. She was a tender woman. She comforted the men and women who followed her on the long, painful journey by foot. _____

_____

9. She knew that runaway slaves who returned to their masters would endanger the others. Whenever they tried to turn back, she commanded them to continue on or die.

_____

_____

IN SUMMARY	To Join Sentences with Coordination

- Use one of the coordinating conjunctions (*for, and, nor, but, or, yet, so*), preceded by a comma.
- Use a semicolon (;) when the logical connection between two clauses is obvious.
- Add transitional words such as *however, therefore,* and *nevertheless* after the semicolon if necessary.

EDITING FOR MASTERY

Mastery Exercise 1

Combining Sentences

Eleven of the following items contain two independent clauses that are not joined in any way. Join the clauses using either a coordinating conjunction or a conjunctive adverb, if necessary. Use correct punctuation. Be careful: Three of the items shouldn't be changed. (The first item has been done for you.)

Harriet Tubman and the Underground Railroad

1. Harriet Tubman was an expert on the routes to the North $_\wedge$ *, for* she knew every farmhouse and cottage along the way where the escaping slaves could get food and fresh clothing.

2. A farmer asked who was knocking on his door, Tubman would reply that it was a "friend with friends."

3. Her answer was a secret message it was her "ticket" on the Underground Railroad.

4. These messages and her courage led more than 300 slaves to freedom.

5. The railroad had no tracks or trains it took its passengers where they wanted to go.

6. Many people knew the term *Underground Railroad* by the 1830s it actually resembled a real railroad.

7. The "conductors" on the railroad freed the slaves from captivity they guided them at various points on their journey.

8. There were "stations," where sympathetic men and women gave runaways food and fresh clothing.

9. The railroad's journeys even had timetables they showed when slaves would arrive or depart from a particular station.

10. Tubman usually made her trips during the long winter nights the slaves followed her along back roads and through the woods.

11. During the day, she hid them in barns, holes in the ground, swamps, and people's homes.

12. Tubman was a brilliant planner she carried fake passes to fool patrolmen who were looking for runaways, and she paid local blacks to take down the posters identifying the runaways.

13. Once, she had to travel through a town where one of her former masters lived she dressed as an old woman and walked slowly down the street carrying several live chickens tied with a string.

14. She turned a corner and saw her old master walking toward her she quickly released the string, ran after the chickens, and escaped.

Scorecard: Number of Errors Found and Corrected _____

Collaborative Activity 3

Comparing Answers
Compare your answers with a classmate. Your instructor may ask you to report your findings to the class.

Mastery Exercise 2   *Combining Sentences*

Eleven of the following items contain two independent clauses that are not joined in any way. Join the clauses using either a coordinating conjunction or a conjunctive adverb, if necessary. Use correct punctuation. Be careful: Three of the items shouldn't be changed. (The first item has been done for you.)

The Workings of the Underground Railroad

1. No one knows where the term *Underground Railroad* came from *; however,* it might have begun with an event in 1831.

2. That year in Kentucky, the owner of a runaway slave named Tice Davids chased after him Davids jumped into the Ohio River and swam across.

3. The master got into a small boat and followed the slave then he could not find Davids on the shore.

4. Nobody in the nearby town had seen or heard of the slave the master told friends that Davids must have gone off on an "underground railroad."

5. The Underground Railroad was very well planned in some places, in other areas, runaway slaves had to take care of themselves or rely on fellow blacks for aid.

6. For runaway slaves and a person who helped them, every step was dangerous.

7. Harriet Tubman usually led her runaways on Saturday night so that she could be two days ahead of her pursuers, who wouldn't find out about the escape until Monday.

8. Most runaways did not have guides like Tubman they traveled to the North by following the North Star.

9. On cloudy nights, the runaways couldn't see the stars they felt the trunks of trees for the moss that grew on the northern sides.

10. The hardest part of the journey for the slaves was through the South they had almost nobody to help them or hide them.

11. As the fugitives moved north, they might contact a representative of the Underground Railroad he would give them the name of a conductor to help them.

12. At each station, the fugitives would be hidden, given food and supplies, and then sent to the next station.

13. Fugitives reached a new station then they signaled to its conductor by knocking on a window or saying code words.

14. The Underground Railroad was an enormous success it helped as many as 60,000 slaves escape to the North or Canada.

Scorecard: Number of Errors Found and Corrected _____

26 Joining Sentences through Subordination

As you saw in the previous chapter on coordination, joining sentences helps you express logical relationships and achieve sentence variety. However, coordination alone cannot accomplish both these goals. In this chapter, we'll look at how to join sentences in a second way: through **subordination.** This chapter will teach you how to

- join sentences by making one clause dependent on the other
- join sentences by turning one clause into a phrase

What Is Subordination?

Coordination joins equals, but not all ideas are equal. In the following sentence, for example, is the first idea as important as the second?

> I came home from work, and I found an eight-foot cobra snake in my living room.

If you answered *yes,* perhaps you live in a rather strange neighborhood! These ideas shouldn't be joined by *and.* They need to be joined in a way that expresses their inequality. Here are two possibilities:

> *When I came home from work,* I found an eight-foot cobra snake in my living room.
>
> *After coming home from work,* I found an eight-foot cobra snake in my living room.

Now the less important idea is *subordinate* to the more important one. The joined ideas form a **complex sentence,** which contains both an independent and a dependent (or subordinate) clause. This chapter explains, in detail, how you can combine sentences with subordination.

Subordinating with Clauses

One type of subordination creates a **dependent clause**—which, as its name suggests, depends on an independent clause to complete its meaning.

- The dependent clause contains the less important idea.
- The independent clause contains the more important idea.

Like an **adverb,** the dependent clause often tells when, why, or where the idea in the independent clause takes place. So these dependent clauses begin with words like *when, because,* and *where.* Read the following two sentences, for example:

> Alberto sits down for dinner. He can eat seven pizzas.

You could join them by subordinating the less important idea, introducing it with *when:*

> *When* Alberto sits down for dinner, he can eat seven pizzas.

Now the first clause merely says when the second, and more important, action occurs. And this first clause can no longer make a complete statement:

> *When* Alberto sits down for dinner, . . . (what happens?)

The joining word *when* subordinates the clause it introduces. We therefore call it a **subordinating conjunction.**

Combine the following two sentences with the subordinating conjunction *because:*

Alberto had some serious indigestion.
He ate seven pizzas with mushrooms and olives.

_____

_____

And combine these two sentences with the subordinating conjunction *where:*

There is food.
You will find Alberto.

_____

_____

Are these the sentences you wrote?

> Alberto had some serious indigestion *because* he ate seven pizzas with mushrooms and olives.
>
> *Where* there is food, you will find Alberto.

Joining clauses with *when, because,* and *where* gives you more ways to express logical relationships. It also helps you create sentence variety.

✔ TIPS

For Detecting Fragments
A dependent clause beginning with *because* or *where* must be connected to an independent clause to make a complete statement:
(What happened?) . . . *because* he ate seven pizzas with mushrooms and olives.
Where there is food, . . . (what will happen?)

EXERCISE 1 | Identifying Subordination

Each sentence in this exercise contains a dependent clause and an independent clause. Label each clause **DC** or **IC.** Then find and underline the subordinating conjunction that begins that dependent clause.

Jesse Owens

The Triumph of Jesse Owens

1. *DC*
   In 1936, ~~when~~ the Olympic Games began in Nazi Germany, Adolf Hitler wanted the *IC*
   games to prove his theories of Aryan (white) superiority.

2. However, after a twenty-two-year-old African-American named James Cleveland (Jesse) Owens had competed in the track-and-field events, these theories were destroyed.

3. Owens felt tense at the beginning of the track-and-field events because a German had won a gold medal the day before and received Hitler's congratulations.

4. But later the same day, when one of the African-American athletes won a gold medal, Hitler did not shake his hand but hurried out of the stadium.

5. Although Hitler claimed he left to escape a light rain, the meaning of the German dictator's action was obvious.

6. If Hitler felt bad about a black man winning a medal, Jesse Owens would soon make him feel much worse.

7. When the track-and-field events were over, Jesse Owens had won four gold medals, breaking or equaling *nine* Olympic records.

Common Subordinating Conjunctions

The last exercise introduced you to many of the subordinating conjunctions. Here's a more complete list, divided into categories:

For Using *Although*

1. Many people confuse *although* with *however*. *Although* is a conjunction. It joins clauses (notice where the comma goes):

   Although the class was very difficult, I really learned a lot.

   But *however* is a transitional word that doesn't join anything (notice where the semicolon and comma go):

   The class was very difficult; *however,* I really learned a lot.

2. In some languages, *although* and *but* begin both clauses in a combined sentence. In English, however, you may use only one of the conjunctions:

   Incorrect: Although Alberto wasn't very hungry, *but* he ate nineteen cheeseburgers.

   Correct: Although Alberto wasn't very hungry, he ate nineteen cheeseburgers.

   Correct: Alberto wasn't very hungry, *but* he ate nineteen cheeseburgers.

***Time* conjunctions**

after	*After* I left, . . .
as	*As* I was walking down the street, . . .
as soon as	*As soon as* you finish, . . .
before	*Before* the lights go out, . . .
once	*Once* you have finished the cleaning, . . . (*Once* means "after.")
since	*Since* I made my first billion dollars, . . .
until	*Until* the sun sets, . . .
when	*When* the semester is over, . . .
while	*While* the music was playing, . . .

***Reason* or *cause* conjunctions**

because	*Because* you are improving your writing, . . .
since	*Since* the water in the lake is so warm, . . .

***Place* conjunctions**

where	*Where* there is smoke, . . .
wherever	*Wherever* you can find a job, . . .

Other subordinating conjunctions set up a contrast or condition:

Contrasting conjunctions

although	*Although* you look honest, . . .
even though	*Even though* the test was difficult, . . .
whereas	*Whereas* many people thought the world was flat, . . .

Conditional conjunctions

if	*If* I have the opportunity, . . .
unless	*Unless* he stops playing that music so loudly, . . .

Punctuating Dependent Clauses

Here are the rules for using commas with adverb dependent clauses:

▶ **Place a comma after an adverb clause** *that begins a sentence.*

---

sub.
conj.   dependent clause   independent clause
When the alarm clock rings in the morning, I put the pillow over my head.

▶Do not use a comma before an adverb clause that comes later in a sentence (but you may use a comma before a long clause beginning with the words *unless, although, where,* or *since*).

independent clause	sub. conj.	dependent clause

I put the pillow over my head *when* the alarm clock rings in the morning.

BUT

I always get to work on time, *although* my hair may not be combed or my shirt buttoned.

EXERCISE 2 | Joining and Punctuating Sentences

Read each pair of sentences. Then join them with a subordinating conjunction that best expresses the logical relationship between the sentences. The conjunction can come before either the first or the second sentence. Place a comma where it is needed.

Jesse Owens' Most Remarkable Day

1. Jesse Owens' success in the 1936 Olympics was no surprise×. *because he* ~~He~~ had done something even more amazing a year earlier.

2. He competed in the Big Ten Championship on May 25, 1935. He had the greatest day in the history of modern athletics.

3. He didn't think he would even be able to participate. He had hurt his back a few weeks earlier.

4. He could not even jog at the warm-up before the meet. He decided to compete in the 100-yard dash.

5. He got off to a perfect start. He finished the race in 9.4 seconds, matching the world record.

6. Owens took only a single long jump. He leapt almost twenty-seven feet and beat the world record by nearly a half-foot.

7. Owens won the 200-yard dash in 20.3 seconds. He set another world record.

8. Owens finished the 220-yard low hurdles in 22.6 seconds. He broke an eleven-year-old world record.

9. Owens completed four events in 45 minutes. He set three world records and tied another.

| **EXERCISE 3** | **Writing Sentences with Dependent Clauses** |

Collaborative Activity 2

Writing Combined Sentences

Write two dependent clauses. Then, with a classmate, combine the four clauses into a single list. Work independently for a few minutes to add independent clauses and create complete sentences. Compare and discuss your results.

Each of these sentences is incomplete, so complete them. Be sure that your ideas contain both a subject and a verb. Add a comma wherever it is needed.

1. When you are in the neighborhood *, please come to my place and visit me.* .

2. I can give you a place to stay if _____.

3. Before you leave _____.

4. Since California has many earthquakes _____.

5. _____ after an earthquake happens.

6. _____ although everyone knows about the danger.

7. People live in California because _____.

Subordinating with Phrases

You can also subordinate the less important idea by making it a **phrase**—a group of two or more words that don't include a complete subject and verb. Here's an example of a *when* clause changed into a phrase:

> dependent clause
> *After Jim Thorpe became* the most famous athlete in track and field,
>
> independent clause
> *he competed* in the 1912 Olympic Games in Stockholm, Sweden.
>
> phrase
> *After becoming the most famous athlete* in track and field,
>
> independent clause
> *Jim Thorpe competed* in the 1912 Olympic Games in Stockholm, Sweden.

- Notice that the phrase begins with *after,* and the verb *became* converts to an *–ing* word: *becoming.*
- Notice, too, that the subject of the adverb clause, *Jim Thorpe,* moves to the independent clause.

You can't convert every dependent clause into a phrase—just those that begin with the conjunctions *after, while, when, since, before,* and *although.* Also, the subject of the dependent clause must be the same as the subject of the independent clause. Here are a few more examples:

> *After*
> *While* ⎬ *triumphing in the Olympics,* Thorpe became a national hero.
>
> *Before coming into the Olympics,* Thorpe was not well known.

In fact, some phrases can drop the conjunction and begin with an *-ing* word:

Coming into the Olympics, Thorpe was not well known.

▶ **Like a dependent clause beginning a sentence, a phrase that begins a sentence requires a comma.**

EXERCISE 4	Revising Sentences

Each of the following sentences contains a dependent clause and an independent clause. Rewrite each sentence, changing the dependent clause into a phrase.

Jim Thorpe (1887–1953): A World-Class Athlete

Jim Thorpe at a goal-kicking exhibition

1. When people think about the backgrounds of great athletes, people would never expect James Francis Thorpe to have become one of the best in history. *When thinking about the backgrounds of great athletes, people would never expect James Frances Thorpe to have become one of the best in history.*

2. Before Jim Thorpe came to the Carlisle Indian School in Pennsylvania, he lived in Oklahoma Territory as a member of the Sac and Fox Tribe. _____

3. Although Thorpe planned to become a tailor at Carlisle, he attracted attention throughout the country as a track-and-field athlete. _____

4. In 1912, Thorpe won six of seven events while he led the tiny Carlisle team to a tremendous victory over the much larger team from Lafayette. _____

5. While he continued to compete in track and field, he became a nationally recognized runner, place kicker, and defensive player in football. _____

6. After he enjoyed such success in football, he went on to play major league baseball.

EXERCISE 5	Combining Sentences

Combine each of the following pairs of sentences using an *-ing* word with **when, while, although, after,** or **before.**

1. Jim Thorpe won the five events in the pentathlon in the Olympics. He won the decathlon so easily that it shocked the world. *After winning the five events in the pentathlon in the Olympics, Jim Thorpe won the decathlon so easily that it shocked the world.*

2. Thorpe received a bronze bust of himself from King Gustov of Sweden, who called him the greatest athlete in the world. Thorpe said only, "Thanks, King." _____

    _____

3. The world learned that Thorpe's Olympic medals had been taken away from him. The world was astonished. _____

    _____

    _____

Collaborative Activity 3

Comparing Combined Sentences

Compare your answers to Exercise 5 with a classmate. Did you combine sentences in more than one way?

Now combine the sentences by using coordinating conjunctions or semicolons. See how many ways you can find to join the clauses. Report your results to the class.

4. In 1913, the Amateur Athletic Union (AAU) took back Thorpe's Olympic medals. It claimed he had played baseball for money in 1909 and 1910. _____

    _____

5. Thorpe played for only a few dollars. He was considered a professional who should not have competed in the "amateur" Olympic Games. _____

    _____

6. The AAU refused to change its ruling. It finally awarded Thorpe his medals—in 1973, sixty years later, and twenty years after he had died. _____

    _____

IN SUMMARY	To Join Sentences with Subordination

- Use a subordinating conjunction such as *if, when, although,* or *because* to relate a less important idea to a more important one.
- Make the less important idea into a phrase beginning either with a word such as *when, while,* or *after* or with an *-ing* word.

EDITING FOR MASTERY

Mastery Exercise 1

Eliminating Sentence-Joining Errors

The following passage contains twelve errors related to joining sentences. Some sentences are actually fragments. Some sentences contain incorrect punctuation or are missing commas. The first one has been done for you. Find and correct the remaining eleven errors.

Jesse Owens Defeats Hitler

(1) Because Adolf Hitler wanted to turn the 1936 Olympics into a gigantic show of Nazis superiority, (2) ᵪThe German dictator built a huge Olympic center, including a 100,000-seat stadium just outside the city of Berlin. (3) Hitler was thrilled, when the Austrians gave him the Nazi salute in the opening parade. (4) The Bulgarians received loud cheers. (5) When they marched like Nazi troops. (6) But the German crowd booed the Americans; because they didn't salute or dip their flag to Hitler.

(7) Hitler's joy disappeared on the second day of the track-and-field events when the American Jesse Owens took the lead in the 100-meter run. (8) Although his fellow African-American teammate Ralph Metcalfe challenged him strongly, but no one caught Owens as he won the gold medal.

(9) The following morning as the qualifying trials took place for the broad jump. (10) Owens failed on his first and second attempts. (11) He had only one chance left, and he was obviously tired. (12) Because he had just run the qualifying races of the 200-meter dash.

(13) When Owens felt a hand on his shoulder. (14) He turned around to face Luz Long, a tall, blue-eyed German broad jumper. (15) Long suggested that Owens begin his jump a few inches before the starting board. (16) Owens did so and easily qualified.

(17) Later that afternoon, Owens set an Olympic record on his second jump. (18) Although, Luz Long tied it on his next-to-last try. (19) Owens, however, then lengthened the Olympic record on his fifth and sixth attempts. (20) After landing on his final jump. (21) Owens was congratulated by Long.

Collaborative Activity 4

Comparing Corrections
Compare your answers with a classmate's. Your instructor may ask you to report your findings to the class.

(22) While collecting four gold medals in all. (23) Owens didn't receive a single word of praise from Adolf Hitler. (24) Indeed, Owens and his nine African-American teammates outscored every other national team and won thirteen medals, eight of them gold.

(25) Their triumph made Hitler's theory about the superiority of white blood look ridiculous.

Scorecard: Number of Errors Found and Corrected _____

Mastery Exercise 2

Eliminating Sentence-Joining Errors

The following passage contains eleven errors related to joining sentences. Some sentences are actually fragments. Some sentences contain incorrect punctuation or are missing commas. The first one has been corrected for you. Find and correct the remaining ten errors.

"Babe" Didrickson in the javelin event, Xth Olympics, 1932

Mildred "Babe" Didrikson Zaharias: The Greatest Woman Athlete

(1) Although women weren't expected to perform as well as ⋏*men,* ~~men.~~ (2) Mildred "Babe" Didrikson Zaharias could throw, run, and hit better than just about anyone of either sex. (3) While standing at one end of the field; she could throw a baseball all the way to the other end. (4) She was incredibly skilled in tennis, bowling, and basketball. (5) She won more than fifty major golf tournaments, including three women's national competitions. (6) "Babe" Didrikson Zaharias was also one of the best track-and-field

performers of all time. (7) Because she was so talented in so many ways. (8) This native of Beaumont, Texas, was named the greatest woman athlete of the first half of the twentieth century.

(9) After Babe Zaharias became famous nationally in 1930 in Dallas she won both the baseball throw and the javelin throw. (10) Although she finished second in the long jump, but her jump was good enough to top a world record. (11) In 1931, she continued to break records in New Jersey; where she threw a baseball 296 feet and won both the 80-meter hurdles and the long jump.

(12) Zaharias did far better in the 1932 Olympics in Los Angeles. (13) The athlete threw the javelin more than 143 feet for new Olympic and world records. (14) She ran the 80-meter hurdles in less than 12 seconds and set more new Olympic and world records. (15) Although, her high jump was good enough to break another world record. (16) She was penalized for "diving" over the bar and finished in second place.

(17) After winning almost all the women's track-and-field events for a decade. (18) She became a world-champion golfer. (19) Her new sport led to amazing achievements in sports history. (20) Even though Zaharias had a cancer operation in 1953. (21) She took first place in the women's national tournament in 1954. (22) In fact, she triumphed in every contest. (23) Until she finally lost her battle with cancer and died in 1956.

Scorecard: Number of Errors Found and Corrected _____

27 Joining Sentences with Pronouns

The previous two chapters showed you a number of ways to combine sentences. This chapter will introduce you to another option: methods for joining sentences with **pronouns**—words that replace nouns.

We'll be looking at how to

- join sentences with pronouns that make one clause dependent on another
- join sentences by making one clause function as a noun

Relative Clauses

The following two sentences are short and choppy, an example of the problem we've examined in the previous two chapters:

> I talked to a counselor. She was very helpful.

These sentences are begging to be combined—in this instance by replacing the subject pronoun *she* with a different pronoun, *who:*

> I talked to a counselor *who* was very helpful.

We call *who* a **relative pronoun** because it *relates* the information in its clause (*who was very helpful*) to the antecedent, *counselor.* The clause the pronoun begins is called a **relative** or **adjective clause.**

The relative pronouns are:

Subjects	Objects	Possessive
who	whom	whose
that, which	that, which	

Relative Pronouns as Subjects

The relative pronouns *who*, *that*, and *which* can serve as subjects of their clauses:

Dr. Dunn is the professor *who* teaches modern languages.

You have to take a course *that* fulfills the natural science requirement.

Our car, *which is ten years old,* needs to be replaced.

These three relative pronouns relate to different antecedents:

- *Who* describes people (or sometimes animals).
- *Which* describes things.
- *That* describes either people or things.

Clauses beginning with the relative pronouns *who*, *which*, or *that* are therefore called **relative clauses.** They're **dependent clauses** because they cannot stand alone as sentences. And they function like **adjectives** because they describe nouns or pronouns. You will learn how to punctuate relative clauses on page 334.

EXERCISE 1	Combining Sentences

Combine each pair of sentences using *who*, *that,* or *which* to create a relative clause.

The Origins of April Fool's Day

1. Throughout France in the early sixteenth century, New Year's Day was celebrated on March 25. It began the spring season. *Throughout France in the early sixteenth century, New Year's Day was celebrated on March 25, which began the spring season.*

2. People would celebrate for a week by exchanging gifts at parties and dinners. These ended on April 1. _____

3. However, in 1564, King Charles IX moved the date of New Year's Day back to January 1. It was the beginning of the new (and more accurate) Gregorian calendar. _____

4. Nevertheless, for many of the French, gift-giving and parties continued to occur on April 1. They resisted the change. _____

5. Some people made fun of these conservatives by sending foolish gifts and invitations to parties. The parties didn't exist. _____

6. After the French became comfortable with January 1 as the beginning of the year, they continued to play jokes on April 1. It became a tradition. _____

_____

7. Two hundred years later, the English adopted the custom. It then went on to reach the American colonies. _____

_____

Relative Pronouns as Objects

Here are three more examples of sentences that could be combined with relative pronouns:

> Please give this form to the man. You will see *him* at the front desk.
>
> You must fill out several forms. You can get *them* from the receptionist.
>
> This is a form. You need to write your name and address *on it*.

The pronouns *him* and *them* in the second sentences are objects. Therefore, the relative pronouns that replace them must also be objects. The pronouns are *whom, that,* and *which.* They relate to different antecedents:

- *Whom* relates to people.
- *That* relates to things.
- *Which* relates to things and must follow a prepositon.

> Please give this form to the man *whom* you will see at the front desk.
>
> You must fill out several forms *that* you can get from the receptionist.
>
> This is a form *on which* you need to write your name and address.

Notice the word order of the relative clauses. A relative pronoun begins the clause—and the object pronoun in the original sentence is omitted:

> Please give this form to the man *whom* you will see (him) at the front desk.
>
> You must fill out several forms *that* you can get (them) from the receptionist.
>
> This is a form *on which* you need to write your name and address (on it).

In many sentences, you can also omit the object relative pronoun—but not when it follows a preposition:

> Please give this form to the man (whom) *you will see at the front desk.*
> You must fill out several forms (that) *you can get from the receptionist.*
>
> BUT
>
> This is a form *on which* you need to write your name and address.

EXERCISE 2	Combining Sentences with Object Pronouns

Join each of the following sentences by making one a relative clause. You may omit the object pronoun, but be sure the word order of the second clause is correct.

The Origins of Thanksgiving Day

1. Most people in the United States know the story of Thanksgiving. They celebrate it on the fourth Thursday of November. *Most people in the United States know the story of Thanksgiving, which they celebrate on the fourth Thursday of November.*

2. A ship called the *Mayflower* left Holland in 1620, carrying 102 people. People called them Pilgrims. _____

   _____

3. On December 11, 1620, after four months at sea, it landed at a place. We now call it Plymouth, Massachusetts. _____

   _____

4. By the next fall, forty-six Pilgrims were dead from disease. Hundreds of local Indians had died from it as well. _____

   _____

5. The survivors, however, were thankful because food was abundant. They had harvested it. _____

   _____

6. The Pilgrims celebrated for three days with local Indians. The Indians had befriended them. _____

   _____

Placement of Relative Clauses

Most often, a relative clause follows directly after the noun or pronoun it describes—at the beginning, middle, or end of a sentence. Otherwise, the sentence may not be clear:

Poor:	Syed bought a car for his daughter *that cost a fortune.* (What cost a fortune—the daughter or the car?)
Better:	Syed bought his daughter a car *that cost a fortune.*
	OR
	Syed bought a car *that cost a fortune* for his daughter.

Commas with Relative Clauses

The punctuation of relative clauses can determine the meaning of a sentence. Here's why.

Restrictive Clauses. The relative clause is essential to the meaning of the following sentence:

You can't start a car *that has a dead battery.*

If the relative clause is removed, we cannot identity which car the sentence discusses:

You can't start a car . . .

The original sentence with the relative clause *restricts* the meaning of the car to the one with a dead battery—and not any other car. Therefore, we call it a **restrictive relative clause.**

Remember that commas *separate* ideas—but the information of this relative clause shouldn't be separated from the words it relates to.

- Therefore, don't put commas around a restrictive relative clause.

Nonrestrictive Clauses. Many relative clauses are not essential to the meaning of a sentence. Remove the relative clause from the middle of the following sentence, for example:

My new car, *which I bought in October,* started every day in the coldest weather.

My new car . . . started every day in the coldest weather.

In this case, the basic meaning of the sentence doesn't change. The relative clause is a **sentence interrupter.** It merely adds a bit of extra information—the kind of information you might include in parentheses. Because that information doesn't restrict meaning in a particular way, we call it a **nonrestrictive relative clause.**

- Put commas around a nonrestrictive relative clause, in the same place as parentheses would go:

My new car, *which I bought in October,* started every day in the coldest weather.

My new car *(which I bought in October)* started every day in the coldest weather.

The rules for using commas with relative pronouns are simple:

1. The pronouns *who* or *which* often begin a nonrestrictive relative clause. Enclose these clauses in commas.

2. The pronoun *that* always begins a restrictive relative clause. Never enclose a *that* clause in commas.

3. But *who* (and sometimes *which*) can begin restrictive relative clauses, too. So test the meaning of the clauses by temporarily removing them from the sentence. If the meaning is still clear, then use commas around the relative clause.

✔ TIPS

For Using Relative Pronouns: *In Which*

Some writers like to use the expression *in which* because they think it sounds elegant. The result is often incorrect and unclear.

Incorrect: The topic, *in which* we discussed today, was immigration.

Correct: The topic, *which* we discussed today, was immigration.

In which makes sense only when *in* is logically part of the sentence.

Uncombined sentences: I want to discuss a topic. I am interested in it.

Combined sentences: I want to discuss a topic *in which* I am interested. (*In it* becomes *in which.*)

✔ TIPS

For Using Relative Pronouns: Fragments

A relative clause only *describes* a noun; it doesn't make a complete statement. Even if the noun is the subject of a sentence, the action of the verb cannot be completed in the relative clause. A noun plus a relative clause equals only a fragment.

Fragment: The cat that sleeps on top of the TV . . . (*does* or *is* what?).

Fragment: Teachers who give difficult assignments . . . (*do* or *are* what?).

Fragment: The watch, which Tuan gave me . . . (*does* or *is* what?).

When you combine sentences with *who, that,* or *which,* be sure the independent clause keeps both its subject and a verb.

| EXERCISE 3 | Punctuating Relative Clauses |

Underline the relative clauses in the following sentences, and place commas around the relative clauses that need them.

The Blessing after the Sneeze

1. "God bless you" is an expression <u>that people say after someone sneezes.</u>

2. The practice of blessing someone which began in Greece in the fourth century B.C. began with the philosophers Aristotle and Hippocrates.

3. They observed many people who seemed to sneeze just before dying from illness.

4. Therefore, to save sneezing people from dying, they recommended blessings that included "Long may you live!" and "May you enjoy good health!"

5. The Romans who had basically similar ideas continued the practice of the Greeks.

6. However, "God bless you" which is a religious expression began for a different reason.

7. During the sixth century, there was a terrible plague that killed many people in Italy, so the pope asked people to pray for the sick.

8. Therefore when people with the illness sneezed, their friends and relatives replaced "May you enjoy good health" with a stronger prayer which was "God bless you."

9. The meaning of this expression which people use frequently has changed over time.

Collaborative Activity 1

Comparing Combined Sentences

Compare your answers to Exercises 2 and 3 with a classmate's. In Exercise 2, did you combine the sentences in the same way? In Exercise 3, did you agree on the placement of commas? Report your results to the class.

| EXERCISE 4 | Completing Sentences with Relative Clauses |

Complete each of the following sentences. Insert commas where necessary.

1. I want to major in a field *that will help me find an enjoyable career.* _____

2. People who don't eat meat _____

   _____

3. In July, the temperature in Arizona which often reaches more than 110 degrees

   _____

4. _____ which many students major in _____

   _____

5. The older chairs and desks that are falling apart _____

   _____

6. _____ who live in New York _____

   _____

Relative Clauses with *Whose*

Here are two more sets of sentences that could be combined:

> On Thanksgiving Day, we recall the people. Their ship arrived on the shores of North America on December 11, 1620.
>
> That ship carried 102 passengers. Its name was the *Mayflower*.

Their and *its* in the second sentences above are possessive and function as adjectives. Therefore, they must be replaced by the possessive form *whose*, which refers to either people or things:

> On Thanksgiving Day, we recall the people *whose ship* arrived on the shores of North America on December 11, 1620. That ship, *whose name* was the *Mayflower*, carried 102 passengers

---

EXERCISE 5 | Combining Sentences with *Whose*

Combine each set of sentences, making the second one an adjective clause.

1. You're the man. Your car is parked on my lawn. *You're the man whose car is parked on my lawn.*

2. Those are the chairs. Their legs are broken. _____

3. Pardon me, but are you the student? Your books are lost. _____

4. You must be the person. Your daughter just started school. _____

5. Relative clauses will be confusing. Their meaning is unclear. _____

6. I bought a used car. Its tires need to be replaced. _____

Noun Clauses

The following two short, choppy sentences are begging to be combined. Do so by omitting the words *something* and *it* and substituting the pronoun *what*:

I understand something. Mr. Baxter said it.

Combined: _____

Is this what you wrote?

I understand *what* Mr. Baxter said.

Notice that "what Mr. Baxter said" replaces "something"—the *object* of the verb. Since an object must be a noun (or pronoun), the clause beginning with *what* is a **noun clause.**

A noun clause can also be the subject of a sentence. Compare these examples:

Sentence with a noun subject	Sentence with a noun clause
His behavior annoyed me.	*What he did* annoyed me.

Other joining words can begin noun clauses:

He told me	*where* *how* *that* *when* *why*	I should go.
He asked me	*if* *whether*	he should go.

✓ TIPS

For Using *What* and *That*

Don't confuse *what* with *that*.

Incorrect: I see the chair *what* I want.

Correct: I see the chair *that* I want.

What actually means "the thing that" and functions in this way:

I know *what* I want. (I know the thing that I want.)

When you aren't sure whether to use *that* or *what*, see if you mean to say "the thing that" and choose the correct relative pronoun.

EXERCISE 6 | Writing Noun Clauses

Read the following model sentences. Using the words provided in parentheses, write two sentences that imitate the pattern of each model sentence.

1. We know what you want.
   a. (understand/need) *I understand what you need.*
   b. (see/lost) _____

2. I told you that I would be late.
   a. (said/make) _____
   b. (remembered/call) _____

3. Do you have what you need?
   a. (recall/said) _____
   b. (realize/did) _____

4. What concerns me the most is finding a new apartment.
   a. (interests/graduating) _____
   b. (bothers/losing) _____

5. I know when the train comes.
   a. (understand/how) _____
   b. (explained/why) _____

Phrases

How would you combine the following sentences?

> The eight-foot-tall man must be a basketball player. He is wearing Nikes and a jersey.
>
> The Toyota is my second car. It is parked in the alley.

One possibility is to combine them with *who* or *that* clauses:

> The eight-foot-tall man *who is wearing Nikes and a jersey* must be a basketball player.
>
> The Toyota *that is parked in the alley* is my second car.

But the combined sentences would be just as clear (and shorter) if you eliminated *who* and *that* and the verbs that follow them:

> The eight-foot-tall man *wearing Nikes and a jersey* must be a basketball player.
>
> The Toyota *parked in the alley* is my second car.

These shorter versions of combined sentences now use **phrases**—groups of two or more words—instead of clauses.

Try combining these sentences without using *who, that,* or *which:*

1. Many high school students have read *Great Expectations*. It is a novel written by Charles Dickens.
2. The book was made into a movie. The movie was made in 1998.

1. _____

_____

2. _____

Is this what you wrote?

> Many high school students have read *Great Expectations,* a novel written by Charles Dickens.
>
> The book was made into a movie in 1998.

These combined sentences contain four types of phrases—all of which describe or rename nouns:

- phrases beginning with a *present participle* (*wearing* Nikes and a jersey)
- phrases beginning with a *noun* (*a novel*)—technically called an **appositive,** which adds identifying information to the noun that precedes it
- phrases beginning with a *past participle* (*written* by Charles Dickens)
- phrases beginning with a *preposition* (*in* 1998).

Consider these choices when you combine sentences.

EXERCISE 7 | Combining Sentences

Combine each pair of sentences using the methods described in this chapter.

A Sticky Solution

1. The idea for the Velcro fastener began in 1941. It started with an unlucky accident that happened to the wife of Swiss manufacturer George de Mistral. *The idea for the Velcro fastener began in 1941 with an unlucky accident that happened to the wife of Swiss manufacturer George de Mistral.*

2. The zipper on her dress jammed and would not unjam. She was wearing it to a formal affair. _____

3. A few months later, de Mistral thought of a better way to fasten fabrics. He was on a hunting trip with his dog. _____

4. The dog's ear became covered with sticky burrs. They came from brushing against some weeds. _____

5. De Mistral noticed tiny hooks on the ends of the burrs. He examined the burrs under a microscope. _____

6. Sixteen years later, this principle led to the manufacture of Velcro. It was little burr-like hooks on fabric. (*Hint:* Place the second idea after *principle,* and use commas.)
_____
_____

EXERCISE 8 | Combining Sentences

Combine each of the following groups of sentences into one sentence using any of the methods you have learned about in Chapters 25, 26, and 27.

The Origins of New Year's Day

1. Our word *holiday* comes from a word. It means "holy day." All celebrations used to be religious. *Our word "holiday" comes from a word that means "holy day" because all celebrations used to be religious.*

2. New Year's Day is the oldest "holy day." It began in the city of Babylon. It was the capital of ancient Babylonia. Babylonia is now part of Iraq. _____
_____

3. Late in March, Babylonians had a huge festival. They wanted to celebrate the new year at a particular time. It was the beginning of spring. _____

_____

4. They had an enormous parade. It included music, dancing, and performers. The performers wore costumes. _____

_____

5. The holiday began to change with the Romans. They created a calendar. It celebrated the new year on March 25. _____

_____

6. Roman rulers and government officials changed the months and years. They made the months and years longer. They wanted to lengthen time. The time was when their terms of office lasted. _____

_____

7. Members of the Roman Senate met in 153 B.C. They changed the date of the new year to January. _____

_____

8. The holiday changed again during the Middle Ages. The British celebrated it on March 25. The French celebrated it on Easter Sunday. The Italians celebrated it on Christmas day. _____

_____

9. These differences continued until about 400 years ago. The date of January 1 was finally agreed on. _____

_____

| IN SUMMARY | To Join Sentences Using Pronouns or Phrases |

- Use the relative pronouns *who, whom,* or *that* in a relative clause describing a person. *Whom* can function only as an object pronoun.
- Use the relative pronouns *which* or *that* in a relative clause describing a thing or an idea.
- Put commas around nonrestrictive relative clauses.
- Use *whose* as an adjective before a noun in sentences such as "I found a book *whose cover* is torn."
- Use *what* or *that* to create a clause that functions as a noun.
- Whenever possible, change relative clauses into phrases.

EDITING FOR MASTERY

Mastery Exercise 1

Eliminating Sentence-Joining Errors

The following passage contains eleven errors related to joining sentences. The errors include incorrectly used relative pronouns, sentence fragments, incorrectly punctuated relative clauses, and incorrectly used noun clauses. The first one has been corrected for you. Find and correct the remaining ten errors.

The First Thanksgiving: 1621

(1) The Pilgrims ˄*who* ~~which~~ settled in Plymouth in 1620 had suffered through a difficult first year, when more than half of them had died. (2) But after the harvest the following fall, there were many things what they were thankful for. (3) They had plenty of food and they were alive, mostly because of the help of one person: an English-speaking Pawtuxet Indian named Squanto, whom would stay to help them until his death two years later.

(4) As a boy, Squanto had been captured by explorers to America. (5) Who sold him into slavery in Spain. (6) He escaped to England, spent several years working for a wealthy merchant, and returned to his native Indian village just six months before the Pilgrims landed. (7) During the first year what the Pilgrims were in Plymouth, he had helped them build houses and grow crops of corn and barley. (8) In the fall of 1621, the Pilgrims elected a new governor, who's name was William Bradford. (9) He declared a day of thanksgiving in their small town. (10) Which had seven private homes and four public buildings.

(11) According to Governor Bradford's own *History of Plymouth Plantation,* the celebration lasted three days. (12) The day before it began, he sent "four men fowling," and they returned with "a great store of wild turkeys." (13) However, the "turkeys" in which they found may not have been actual turkeys. (14) Although wild turkeys did live in the forests, "turkey" in those days meant any form of bird, who included ducks and geese.

(15) The Pilgrims invited the chief of the Wampanoag tribe, Massasoit, and ninety of his braves. (16) The four Pilgrim women and two teenage girls whom the previous winter had not killed prepared the feast—for ninety-one Indians and fifty-six settlers.

Collaborative Activity 2

Comparing Corrections
Compare your answers with a classmate and, if your instructor indicates, report your findings to the class.

Scorecard: Number of Errors Found and Corrected _____

Mastery Exercise 2

Eliminating Sentence-Joining Errors

The following passage contains eleven errors related to joining sentences. The errors include incorrectly used relative pronouns, sentence fragments, incorrectly punctuated relative clauses, and incorrectly used noun clauses. The first one has been corrected for you. Find and correct the remaining ten errors.

The Birth of the National Holiday

(1) October 1777 was the first time ˄*that* ~~what~~ all the thirteen colonies joined in a common thanksgiving holiday. (2) Which celebrated an important victory over the British during the Revolutionary War. (3) However, the colonies celebrated this holiday only once.

(4) In 1789, that was the year of his inauguration, the first president, George Washington, proclaimed Thanksgiving as a national holiday, but the thirteen states didn't accept the proclamation. (5) For one thing, many Americans felt, that the hardships of a few early settlers weren't important enough to commemorate. (6) Certainly the new nation had bigger events what deserved a celebration. (7) In fact, Thomas Jefferson, which became president in 1801, actually condemned a national recognition of Thanksgiving.

(8) The creation of the day that we now celebrate nationwide it was mostly because of the work of a magazine editor who's name was Sarah Josepha Hale. (9) Mrs. Hale, whom edited the *Boston Ladies' Magazine* in 1827, wrote that the country should observe a Thanksgiving holiday. (10) When *Ladies' Magazine* merged with *Godey's Lady's Book,* Mrs. Hale became the editor of the most popular woman's magazine in the country, with 150,000 readers. (11) She continued to write strong editorials in favor of a Thanksgiving celebration.

(12) Additionally, for almost forty years, she wrote hundreds of letters to governors, ministers, newspaper editors, and each president. (13) She always made the same request. (14) Which was that the last Thursday in November should be a time to "offer to God our tribute of joy and gratitude for the blessings of the year."

(15) Finally, national events turned Mrs. Hale's request into a reality.

(16) By 1863, the Civil War had divided the nation in two. (17) Mrs. Hale's final editorial appeared in September of that year, right after the Battle of Gettysburg. (18) Although the northern states had won the battle, many soldiers on both sides had lost their lives. (19) This persuaded President Abraham Lincoln to issue a proclamation on October 3, 1863, in which set aside the last Thursday in November as a national Thanksgiving Day.

Scorecard: Number of Errors Found and Corrected _____

28 Repairing Run-ons and Correcting Comma Splices

Good writing depends on sentences that are clear, concise, interesting, and easy to read. You therefore need to be aware of all the options open to you for combining sentences. You also need to recognize and avoid combinations that don't work.

This chapter will show you how to correct two common errors in sentence joining:

■ clauses joined by nothing at all

■ clauses joined by nothing but a comma

Run-on Sentences

What joins the two independent clauses in each of the following sentences?

> My friend Juan is very strange he wears six rings in his nose.
>
> We saw an early movie then we had a pizza later at Guido's.

Nothing joins them. The first clause simply runs on into the second. These are **run-on sentences**—two independent clauses with nothing linking them together: a very confusing and serious error.

You can repair run-ons in a number of ways:

1. Add a coordinating conjunction:

> My friend Juan is very strange, *for (so)* he wears six rings in his nose.

2. Add a semicolon:

> My friend Juan is very strange; he wears six rings in his nose.

3. Add a semicolon and a transitional word:

> We saw an early movie; *afterward,* we had a pizza at Guido's.

4. Rewrite the sentence to eliminate a clause:

> My *strange* friend Juan wears six rings in his nose.

5. Rewrite the sentence, adding a relative pronoun to create a dependent clause:

My friend Juan, *who* wears six rings in his nose, is very strange.

6. Add a subordinating conjunction to create an adverb dependent clause:

After we saw an early movie, we had a pizza at Guido's.

7. Convert one independent clause to a phrase:

With six rings in his nose, my friend Juan looks very strange.

8. Rewrite the clauses as separate sentences:

We saw an early movie. Then we had a pizza at Guido's.

See Chapters 25–27 for more discussion of these ways of joining sentences.

If you find a run-on sentence as you edit your work, experiment with different corrections until you find one that best expresses your meaning.

EXERCISE 1	Revising Run-on Sentences

Rewrite each run-on sentence in this exercise to eliminate the error. Use a variety of solutions: coordinating conjunctions, subordinating conjunctions, semicolons and transitional words, relative pronouns, or complete revisions of the sentences.

Canine Convict Number C2559

1. Pep was a male Labrador retriever he belonged to neighbors of the governor of Pike County, Pennsylvania. *Pep, who was a male Labrador retriever, belonged to neighbors of the governor of Pike County, Pennsylvania.*

2. Pep was a friendly dog he went wild and killed the governor's cat one hot summer day.

_____

_____

3. The governor was very angry he put Pep on trial and sentenced the dog to life imprisonment. _____

_____

4. The poor animal went to the penitentiary in Philadelphia the warden gave him an ID number like the rest of the cons. _____

_____

Collaborative Activity 1

Comparing Combined Sentences

Compare your answers to Exercise 1 with a classmate's. Make a list of the different solutions for each item. Report your results to the class.

5. The story has a happy ending Pep's fellow inmates loved him and he could switch cellmates at will. _____

_____

6. Pep spent six pleasant years in prison (forty-two dog years) then he died of old age.

_____

_____

Comma-Spliced Sentences

For Avoiding Comma-Spliced Sentences

In other languages (for example, Spanish), joining two independent clauses with a comma is common practice. In English it's not.

Correct in Spanish: The cook prepared the meal quickly, it was ready in ten minutes.

Correct in English: The cook prepared the meal quickly, *so* it was ready in ten minutes.

What joins the two independent clauses in these sentences?

> Alberto wasn't satisfied with just three pizzas, he ate seven.
>
> Alberto eats six meals a day, however, he never gains any weight.

Commas don't join the clauses, because commas *separate* ideas. And *however* can't join clauses because *however* is a *transitional* word. So nothing joins the clauses. They're **comma-spliced sentences**—two independent clauses with a comma between them but with no joining word.

Comma-spliced sentences occur far more frequently than run-ons. That's because writers try to join sentences with commas instead of separating them with periods. Like run-on sentences, though, comma-spliced sentences often confuse and annoy readers. Repair these damaged sentences in the same way you repair run-ons:

- Insert conjunctions.
- Insert semicolons (with transitional words if necessary).
- Insert relative pronouns to create relative dependent clauses.
- Rewrite the sentences.

EXERCISE 2 | Revising Comma-Spliced Sentences

For Avoiding Misused Transitional Words

Beware of *then* and *also*. They are transitional words, not conjunctions.

Incorrect: I took a quick shower, then I headed off to class.

Correct: I took a quick shower, *and then* I headed off to class.

Incorrect: I have a quiz on Thursday, also I have to finish my math assignment.

Correct: I have a quiz on Thursday, and I also have to finish my math assignment.

Label each item here with **CS** (for comma splice) or **OK** (if it's correct). Then repair each comma-spliced sentence, using a variety of solutions.

The Loyal Dog

__CS__ **1.** Eisaburo Ueno was a college professor at Tokyo University, he had a dog named Hachi. *Eisaburo Ueno, a college professor at Tokyo University, had a dog named Hachi.*

_____ **2.** Every morning he went to a railroad station near his home, his dog always came with him. _____

_____

_____ **3.** Every evening he returned on a train, Hachi was always there to greet him. _____

_____

_____ **4.** One day in 1925 Professor Ueno had a heart attack at school, then he died. _____

_____

_____ 5. Hachi lived for ten more years, he went to the train station every evening and patiently waited for his master. _____

_____

_____ 6. When the professor didn't arrive, the dog sadly went back to Ueno's family. _____

_____

_____ 7. Hachi always met the evening trains, he became a familiar sight to Japanese travelers. _____

_____

_____ 8. Finally, Hachi died at Shibuya station, he was still hopeful that the professor was on the next train. _____

_____

Collaborative Activity 2

Comparing Combined Sentences

Compare your answers to Exercise 2 with a classmate's. For the items that are OK, explain why these sentences are complete and correct. Report your results to the class.

_____ 9. Today a statue of Hachi sits outside of Shibuya station, where people put wreaths around the statue's neck and leave small gifts. _____

_____

_____ 10. In 1987, Japanese filmmakers made a movie about Hachi, the dog that has become a national symbol of loyalty and devotion. _____

_____

EXERCISE 3 | Eliminating Sentence-Combining Errors

Each of the following items contains one or more run-ons or comma splices. Correct the errors above the lines.

The Death of Dian Fossey: The Lonely Woman of the Forest

1. It was a quiet morning at Karisoke Research Station in Rwanda, *but* noises suddenly broke the silence.

2. A group of men stormed into the cabin of Wayne McGuire, he was an American graduate student, they woke him up.

3. They kept on repeating in Swahili that Dian was dead, it was a language he did not know well, he finally understood them.

4. He found Dian Fossey's body lying next to the bed in her cabin, she had been murdered.

5. It was four days later, the 54-year-old woman was buried in the station's animal cemetery, in a spot next to the graves of some mountain gorillas that she loved so dearly.

6. Dian Fossey had spent her life studying the mountain gorillas, also she had saved them from extinction.

7. McGuire was accused of the crime and fled the country, however, there were other, more obvious suspects.

8. Fossey had made friends with the mountain gorillas, at the same time she had made enemies in Rwanda.

Dian Fossey (photo by Peter G. Veit for the National Geographic Society)

IN SUMMARY	To Repair Run-ons and Comma Splices

- Add a coordinating conjunction (*for, and, nor, but, or, yet, so*).
- Add a semicolon and, if necessary, a transitional word (*however, therefore, nevertheless*, etc.), followed by a comma.
- Use a subordinating conjunction (*because, when, if, although*, etc.) to create an adverb dependent clause.
- Use a relative pronoun (*who, which, that*) to create a relative dependent clause.
- Rewrite the sentence.
- Convert one independent clause to a phrase.
- Write the two clauses as two separate sentences.

EDITING FOR MASTERY

Mastery Exercise 1

Eliminating Sentence-Combining Errors

The following passage contains eleven run-on or comma-spliced sentences. The first one has been corrected for you. Find and correct the remaining ten errors.

Dian Fossey's Crusade to Save the Gorillas

(1) Dian Fossey's closest friends praised her as a warmhearted, completely dedicated woman; in fact, they called her "Queen of the Apes." (2) She worked most of her life to save the East African mountain gorillas, consequently, they are a less endangered species. (3) Today there are 650 mountain gorillas alive in the world, there were only 250 in the mid-1970s.

(4) Although people used to think that gorillas were dangerous animals, Dian Fossey's research changed that idea. (5) She began by watching these gentle giants from a safe distance, later on she moved among them. (6) She imitated their grunting sounds and body language, she also chewed on the wild celery they loved and scratched them.

(7) Fossey's desire to live among the gorillas was understandable, she had been a lonely child who loved animals. (8) However, she couldn't have any pets except a goldfish when it died, she cried for a week.

(9) She saw gorillas on her first trip to East Africa in 1963, she described them as "big and imposing but not monstrous at all." (10) She left Africa, then she returned four years later and established the Karisoke Research Station in Rwanda.

(11) Fossey loved the gorillas but constantly chased after poachers, they were killing the animals. (12) When she caught the poachers, she took away their weapons and even whipped them. (13) She also fought the Rwandan government which wanted to make the gorillas' home into a tourist attraction. (14) Fossey said that the gorillas didn't belong in zoos or circuses, she threatened to shoot any tourist approaching her station. (15) She made many enemies among the Rwandans, and her murder has never been solved.

Collaborative Activity 3

Comparing Corrections
Compare your answers with a classmate's and, if your instructor indicates, report your findings to the class.

Scorecard: Number of Errors Found and Corrected _____

Mastery Exercise 2

Eliminating Sentence-Combining Errors

The following passage contains eleven run-on or comma-spliced sentences. The first one has been corrected for you. Find and correct the remaining ten errors.

The Talking Gorilla

                                                                        and
(1) For centuries, people have dreamed of communicating with animals, ^ the most likely candidates for communication have always been apes. (2) It is not a surprise that the first animal to fulfill that dream was a female gorilla named Koko, she was born at the San Francisco Zoo on July 4, 1971. (3) In 1972, a psychology student named Francine Patterson began the gorilla's incredible education. (4) Patterson taught Koko American Sign Language, the friendly 290-pound beast quickly became a good student.

(5) Patterson and her assistants started by teaching Koko the signs for food, drink, and other things. (6) Eventually Koko was able to use language more creatively. (7) For instance, she was taught that *dirty* referred to her bowel movements, soon she used it to describe people and events as well. (8) She later chose her own meaning for certain signs, for example, *good* meant "yes" and *lip* meant "woman." (9) She learned to make jokes, also she was interviewed on television—and even on the Internet.

(10) By 1983, Koko had been studying for more than twenty years, she had learned about 900 different signs. (11) Researchers wanted to see if she could teach her language skills to another ape, therefore they began looking for a mate for her. (12) Koko didn't find a mate until 1994. (13) Then she met Ndume, he was from a Chicago zoo, and they were immediately attracted to each other.

(14) There are critics of Patterson's experiments with Koko, they complain that the gorilla has never learned grammar or how to ask a question. (15) However, there is no doubt that Koko and other gorillas can answer questions, usually with one-word signs. (16) The human dream of communicating with animals started long ago, it has come true with a friendly ape named Koko.

Scorecard: Number of Errors Found and Corrected _____

29 Punctuating Sentences

As you've seen in previous chapters, punctuation marks—commas, periods, and semicolons—are signals that help readers understand your sentences and avoid confusion. Incorrect punctuation can announce the end of a sentence that hasn't ended, join ideas that shouldn't be joined, or separate ideas that shouldn't be separated.

To punctuate correctly, you must know the rules. This chapter will help you

- identify where punctuation is needed
- know which punctuation marks to select: commas, periods, question marks, exclamation points, semicolons, colons, dashes, parentheses, or quotation marks

The Comma [,]

If you tend to place a comma wherever you hear a pause, be careful. You might be mispunctuating. **Commas** have six specific uses—some to separate ideas and others to enclose them.

Items in a Series

▶Separate three or more items with commas.

A **coordinating conjunction**—usually *and*—introduces the last item in a series. A comma before the conjunction is optional; you can include the comma or not. (In this book, we include it.) But be consistent; include it or omit it each time:

Subjects:	Anna, Lidya, *and* I
Verbs:	They came late to the party, threw their coats on the bed, *and* ran for the refreshments.
Adjectives:	The field was wet, muddy, *and* slippery.
Phrases:	They looked on top of the dresser, in the drawers, behind the dresser, *and* under the bed.

EXERCISE 1 | Editing for Comma Use

In each sentence, place commas between items in a series. Add *and* before the last item.

1. Benjamin Franklin was a printer, writer, philosopher, inventor, scientist, politician, *and* diplomat.

2. Franklin was so successful that he was able to retire at the age of forty-four. He had started a newspaper started the first American subscription library become clerk to the Pennsylvania legislature established the first firefighting company become postmaster of Philadelphia begun the American Philosophical Society published his famous *Poor Richard's Almanac*—a collection of humor wisdom and financial advice he continued for twenty-five years.

3. King Henry VIII of England (1491–1547) had six wives: Catherine of Aragon Anne Boleyn Jane Seymour Anne of Cleves Kathyrn Howard Katherine Parr.

4. Henry divorced the first Catherine beheaded Anne lost Jane in a childbirth death canceled his marriage to Anne executed the second Catherine stayed married to the last Catherine.

Independent Clauses

▶Place a comma before the coordinating conjunction joining two independent clauses.

✓ **TIPS**

For Using the Coordinating Conjunctions

To help you recall the coordinating conjunctions, think of the phrase **FAN BOYS**.

For	But
And	Or
Nor	Yet
	So

The Cherokee Indians were an agricultural people, *and* they lived in villages in the southern part of the United States.

Their homes at first were made of mud, *but* later the Cherokee built themselves log cabins.

They established their own courts and schools in the early 1800s, *and* they had a higher standard of living than their white neighbors.

▶Only the coordinating conjunction joining two independent clauses requires a comma. Don't use a comma between two nouns or verbs.

Incorrect: The Cherokee also had a written constitution, and published their own newspaper.

Correct: The Cherokee also had a written constitution and published their own newspaper.

EXERCISE 2	Editing for Comma Use

Place commas where they're needed before any coordinating conjunctions that join independent clauses. The first sentence has been corrected for you. You should add six additional commas.

Sequoyah (c. 1770–1843): Inventor of an Alphabet

* * * *

(1) Young Sequoyah called the white people's books "the talking leaves," and he and his fellow Cherokee of Tennessee were fascinated with the magical power of the books. (2) They had seen the white settlers reading books and writing messages on paper. (3) Sequoyah's friends said that the Great Spirit had given this magic to whites but hadn't given it to the Indian peoples. (4) Sequoyah thought their arguments were nonsense for the white man had himself invented "the talking leaves."

(5) Sequoyah came from the Native American village of Taskigi and his mother was a member of the ruler's family. (6) As he grew older, he became a fine silversmith, a talented storyteller, and a skillful participant in dances, footraces, and ball games. (7) He was illiterate like everyone else in his tribe.

(8) A hunting accident left Sequoyah permanently handicapped or his later life might have been different. (9) After the injury, he had more free time and more chances to think about how his people might also come to get "the talking leaves." (10) He began walking in the woods and there he spent hours alone, avoiding everyone, playing like a child with pieces of wood, or making little marks on the wood with stones. (11) His wife and friends encouraged and sympathized with him for they were sure that he was either going mad or communicating with spirits. (12) Months became years and the sympathy turned to laughter and disrespect. (13) Nevertheless, Sequoyah continued to follow his dream.

✓ **TIPS**

For Avoiding Comma-Spliced Sentence Errors

Speakers of Spanish need to be careful about trying to join two complete sentences with a comma. The practice is correct in Spanish but not in English. Commas don't join—they separate. Two sentences joined by a comma create an error called a *comma-spliced sentence*.

Interrupters

▶ Place two commas around words, phrases, or clauses that interrupt a sentence. These interrupters can be temporarily removed without changing the basic meaning of a sentence.

With interrupter:	A Cherokee newspaper, *The Phoenix*, began publication in 1828.
Interrupter removed:	A Cherokee newspaper began publication in 1828.

With interrupter:	Many Cherokee, who live in Oklahoma and North Carolina today, originally lived in the southeastern United States.
Interrupter removed:	Many Cherokee originally lived in the southeastern United States.

One type of sentence interrupter is called an **appositive,** a word or phrase that renames a noun. Appositives after proper nouns usually need commas, but appositives after common nouns do not:

Will Rogers, *a famous actor,* was a Cherokee Indian.

The famous actor Will Rogers was a Cherokee Indian.

Be sure to enclose an interrupter between two commas, even if you think you hear just one pause. Otherwise, the sentence may be confusing:

Incorrect:	Sequoyah, whom many people have studied was a famous leader of the Cherokee. (This looks like a sentence fragment.)
Correct:	Sequoyah, whom many people have studied, was a famous leader of the Cherokee.

Remember, too, that commas enclose **relative clauses** (*who, whom, that, which* clauses) only when they are **nonrestrictive**—that is, when they don't provide essential information. The clause in the previous example is nonrestrictive. A **restrictive relative** clause provides information essential to understanding the idea, so it isn't enclosed in commas. You may wish to review the discussion of these clauses in Chapter 27.

Introductory or Concluding Expressions

▶Place a comma after most introductory phrases or clauses.

Long introductory (or transitional) phrases require a comma, but many short phrases don't:

For many centuries, the Cherokee lived in the Appalachian Mountain area.

Perhaps the first European contact with the Cherokee happened in 1540.

An introductory dependent clause requires a comma:

When Fernando de Soto came from Spain to the New World in search of gold, he had many clashes with the Cherokee.

A sentence can also end with a transitional word or phrase (see Chapter 25). These are also set off with commas:

He never found gold, *however.*

He died instead, *having searched throughout Florida and along the Mississippi River for three years.*

Don't use a comma, however, when the ending phrase completes the idea of the sentence:

De Soto's body was sunk in the Mississippi *to prevent the Cherokee from mutilating it.* (completing the idea)

His companions continued down the river to the Gulf of Mexico, *from which they returned to Spain.* (a separate idea)

EXERCISE 3	Incorporating Transitional Expressions

Add the transitional expressions in parentheses to the sentences. Decide if the expressions belong at the beginning or the end. Punctuate the sentences with commas where necessary, and correct the capitalization.

Sequoyah's Attempt at Developing an Alphabet

1. (at first) Sequoyah tried to create a symbol for every word of Cherokee. *At first, Sequoyah tried to create a symbol for every word of Cherokee.*

2. (however) He eventually found this approach was too difficult and decided to assign a character to each sound. _____

3. (when his friends and neighbors talked) He no longer heard what they were saying. _____

4. (instead) He carefully listened to their sounds, trying to separate the sounds and identify new ones. _____

5. (with eighty-six characters representing all the sounds of spoken Cherokee) What he finally invented was not so much an alphabet as a *syllabary.* _____

6. (when combined) These characters produced a clear and remarkably effective written language. _____

7. (in all) The task took Sequoyah twelve years. _____

| EXERCISE 4 | Punctuating Interrupters and Transitional Expressions |

Punctuate the passage. The first sentence has been corrected for you. You should add thirteen additional commas.

Sequoyah's Fame

* * *

(1) Many stories, true or false, have been told of how Sequoyah presented his "alphabet" to the Cherokee people. (2) According to one story his little daughter read aloud what the chiefs had privately told him to write on a paper. (3) No matter what the true story was Sequoyah's alphabet was so simple that it could be learned in a few days. (4) Moreover those who learned it then taught it to others. (5) Within a few months a group of almost entirely illiterate people suddenly became literate. (6) Furthermore the odd little man who had been laughed at by his people was now treated as almost a god.

(7) In 1828 Sequoyah and other Cherokee people arrived in Washington, D.C., to discuss a disagreement over the federal government's failure to honor its treaties. (8) Because Sequoyah had already become famous he received a great deal of attention in the capital. (9) Charles Bird King a famous painter asked him to sit for a portrait, and many newspaper reporters asked for interviews.

(10) After their discussions the Cherokee signed another treaty to exchange their lands for new ones in Oklahoma. (11) Although most of the Cherokee refused to leave Tennessee and Alabama Sequoyah's group from Arkansas moved west toward Oklahoma. (12) Sequoyah now over sixty years old built himself a new cabin, took care of his small farm, and traveled through the woods to the river from time to time. (13) He lived there for days or weeks, filling his buckets with water, taking care of his fires, and talking to anyone who came to see and speak with the famous Cherokee philosopher.

Two or More Adjectives

▶ **Place a comma between coordinate (not cumulative) adjectives.**

Coordinate adjectives are adjectives that you do not have to order in a specific way. If you can put the word *and* between them, then they are coordinate:

| a *smart, playful* dog | OR | a *playful, smart* dog | OR | a *smart and playful* dog |
| a *cold, windy* day | OR | a *windy, cold* day | OR | a *cold and windy* day |

Cumulative adjectives do have to be ordered in a specific way and *cannot* be separated by a comma (or the word *and*). For example, you must write *the cool blue water*, not *the blue cool water*. Cumulative adjectives should be placed in the following order, depending on their types and subtypes: (1) opinion, (2) appearance (size, shape and length, condition), (3) age/color, (4) origin (ethnicity, religion), (5) material, (6) noun used as adjective.

opinion	size	origin		
a *beautiful*	*little*	*Haitian* sculpture		

condition	age	material	n. as adj.
a *soft*	*old*	*leather*	*baseball* mitt

EXERCISE 5 | Punctuating Adjectives

Place commas where they are needed in the phrases.

1. a smart, hardworking student

2. a beautiful large birthday cake

3. an old red wagon

4. a torn worn faded pair of jeans

5. a well-known Japanese actor

6. a cool dry climate

Dates, Places, and Addresses

▶**Place a comma between parts of dates, places, and addresses.**

Put commas after the day and year for full dates. Also put a comma between a city and state in a sentence—and after the state, too, if the sentence continues. When you address an envelope, however, don't put a comma after the street name or between the abbreviation for the state and the zip code:

On August 9, 2004, the building should be completed. (No comma separates the month and day, but a comma follows the year.)

Brookline, Massachusetts, is a lovely town. (Note the comma after the state.)

324 W. Juneway Street
Brookline, MA 01506 (No comma comes before the zip code.)

EXERCISE 6 | Punctuating Addresses

Place commas in the dates or places. Some sentences may not need commas.

1. 1522 E. Hartford Street

Elizabethtown, New York 12932

2. Have you been to Columbus Ohio before?

3. After December 5 2008 Corine will be an attorney.

4. We expect 2008 to be a good year—after we pay our income taxes.

5. The Declaration of Independence was signed on July 4 1776 in Philadelphia Pennsylvania.

6. We will meet you on January 15 2008 in San Juan Puerto Rico.

EXERCISE 7 | Editing for Commas

Place commas where they're needed in the passage. The first sentence has been corrected for you. You should add nineteen additional commas.

Sequoyah's Final Deeds

* * * *

(1) Although Sequoyah lived in a peaceful forest around Lee's Creek, Oklahoma, the Great Spirit did not allow him to end his life that way. (2) The federal government which had for so long wanted to take Cherokee land in Tennessee and Alabama decided to remove the Cherokee people from the area. (3) Consequently a large group of soldiers drove some 17,000 Cherokee from their homes. (4) The Native Americans began a long hard journey west and suffered for many months. (5) About 4,000 Cherokee people died before the Native Americans arrived in Oklahoma Territory in the spring of 1839. (6) When the new arrivals met the Cherokee people who were already there problems immediately started. (7) The groups argued over the land over the local government and over many other matters.

(8) Sequoyah who wished to stop the disagreements among his people persuaded them to be reasonable. (9) At a meeting of the entire tribe everyone agreed to live in peace. (10) Consequently the Cherokee of Alabama Tennessee Arkansas and Oklahoma joined together to become the Cherokee Nation.

(11) However Sequoyah still could not rest. (12) He wanted to find a group of Cherokee who had come out west many years before. (13) Where were these lost Cherokee who did not know of his alphabet or the new nation? (14) Sequoyah who was now an old man headed south with nine horsemen. (15) He supposedly found the lost Cherokee and died somewhere in Mexico. (16) Not long afterward in California a type of redwood that included the largest trees in the world was named "sequoiah" after the only man in history to invent an entire alphabet.

Collaborative Activity 1

Looking at Commas

With a classmate, review your answers to Exercises 2, 3, 4, and 7. Discuss areas of disagreement with the class.

Collaborative Activity 2

Correcting Comma Errors

Write ten sentences in which you deliberately omit necessary commas. Be sure to include at least one error representing each of the seven rules presented so far in this chapter. Then exchange papers with a classmate, and punctuate the sentences correctly. Check each other's work.

The Period [.]

Periods have two functions: to signal the end of sentences and to mark abbreviations.

Statements

▶End every complete statement with a period.

Sentences that aren't statements need a different mark of final punctuation. End questions with a question mark and exclamations with an exclamation point:

It looks like a nice day.

BUT

Do you think it will rain?

Get out of here!

Abbreviations

▶Use periods for most abbreviations.

The following abbreviations require periods:

Mr.	Dr.	A.M.	etc.
Ms.	Rev.	P.M.	i.e.
Mrs.			e.g.

Abbreviations require periods, but **acronyms** do not. Each letter of an acronym represents a word. Here are some common examples:

1. government agencies
   CIA: **C**entral **I**ntelligence **A**gency
   FBI: **F**ederal **B**ureau of **I**nvestigation

2. well-known organizations
   Operation *PUSH:* **P**eople **U**nited to **S**ave **H**umanity

3. some television or radio stations
   WGN: owned by the Chicago *Tribune,* which calls itself the **W**orld's **G**reatest **N**ewspaper

4. acronyms that have become so well-known that they are now words
   scuba: **s**elf-**c**ontained **u**nderwater **b**reathing **a**pparatus
   Consult your dictionary when you aren't sure whether the word is an abbreviation or an acronym.

✓ **TIPS**

For Using Abbreviations Correctly

Most words in academic compositions shouldn't be abbreviated. Spell out units of measure, e.g., *pounds, feet, years,* or *hours.* Don't use *lb., ft., yr.,* or *hr.*

Use *and,* not *&.*

Spell out the names of months and days: *February* and *Tuesday.* Don't use *Feb.* or *Tues.*

Don't abbreviate addresses except on envelopes.

Spell out the names of cities and states and words like *avenue* and *street:* Ocean Avenue, Virginia Beach.

EXERCISE 8 | Including Periods

Place periods where they're needed in the following groups of words.

1. I don't care what you say, I am not going to speak in front of all those people,

2. 7028 W Potter Dr
   Glendale, AZ 85308

3. N B C

4. Mr and Mrs Jones

5. The Environmental Protection Agency is called the E P A

6. Get your scuba gear we're going to dive off the coast

The Question Mark [?]

TIPS

For Punctuating Correctly

In Spanish a question begins with an inverted question mark [¿] and an exclamation with an inverted exclamation point [¡]. In English question and exclamation marks come at the end. Don't confuse the different practices, and check for errors in your editing.

▶ Place question marks only after direct questions.

Question marks, like periods, end sentences—in this case, sentences that ask a question.

A **direct question** always ends with a question mark:

| **Direct questions:** | When was the Cherokee War? |
| | Who fought in the war? |

But don't use a question mark with an **indirect question,** which is contained within a larger statement and uses the word order of a statement:

| **Indirect questions:** | I'd like to know when the Cherokee War occurred. |
| | Please tell me who fought in the war. |

EXERCISE 9 | Punctuating Direct and Indirect Questions

Place a period or a question mark at the end of each sentence.

1. When did Sequoyah die?

2. No one knows for sure where Sequoyah died

3. Sequoyah asked his people if they could live in peace with each other

4. I want to know how many letters are in Sequoyah's alphabet

5. How many sequoia trees are in the national forest

6. Where do the Cherokee live today

The Exclamation Point [!]

▶Use exclamation points after expressions of strong emotion.

An **exclamation point** signals excitement, anger, fear, or other strong emotions, whether in a full sentence or simply in a partial sentence:

> This is the last time I'll tell you!
>
> Don't, please!
>
> Help! Police!

Don't overuse exclamation points! Too many of them will annoy your readers! (As do the sentences you have just read.)

EXERCISE 10	Supplying End Punctuation

Punctuate the sentences with a period or an exclamation point.

1. The Cherokee people have survived terrible tragedies.

2. In just a few years after the Spanish explorer Fernando de Soto arrived in 1540, European diseases wiped out at least 75 percent of the Cherokee population

3. During the Civil War, the Cherokee lost 25 percent of their population

4. No other group of Americans suffered as much during the war

5. With as many as 370,000 persons, the Cherokee are the largest Native American group in the United States today

6. The Cherokee are an amazing people

The Semicolon [;]

A **semicolon** is a combination of a period and a comma. Like a period, it makes the reader stop. Like a comma, it urges the reader to go on. The semicolon has two uses: to join independent clauses and to separate items in a series containing internal punctuation.

Independent Clauses

▶Join independent clauses with a semicolon.

A semicolon may join independent clauses whose ideas are closely related:

> The name *Cherokee* comes from a Creek Indian word; it means "people of a different speech."

Don't use a conjunction (such as *and* or *but*) after the semicolon. But you may use a transitional word such as *however* after the semicolon. The transitional word is followed by a comma:

> Most Cherokee today accept this name; *however,* some call themselves *Tsalagi,* which comes from their own language.

EXERCISE 11 | Using Semicolons

Place semicolons and commas where they are needed in each sentence. Be careful: One sentence doesn't require additional punctuation.

1. The early Cherokee lived in small village; each village also had a large meetinghouse.

2. A frame of a Cherokee house was made of branches and vines the outside was covered with mud.

3. The houses of the village were dug into the ground however the council house was usually located on a small hill.

4. The Cherokee had settled on land used by earlier tribes therefore they did not create the hills themselves.

5. Cherokee villages usually had their own democratic governments, although the villages came together for ceremonies or meetings about war.

6. Each member of a Cherokee community was respected everyone participated in the decision making.

Items in a Series

▶ **Use semicolons to separate items with internal punctuation.**

Commas separate three or more items in a series, but if the items themselves contain commas, separate the items with semicolons:

> According to the 2000 census, the only cities in the United States with a population of more than one million are New York, New York; Los Angeles, California; Chicago, Illinois; Houston, Texas; Philadelphia, Pennsylvania; San Diego, California; Phoenix, Arizona; San Antonio, Texas; and Dallas, Texas.

EXERCISE 12 | Punctuating Items in a Series

Place semicolons and commas where they are needed in each sentence.

1. Following the assassination of Martin Luther King Jr., violence erupted in Chicago, Illinois; Baltimore, Maryland; Pittsburgh, Pennsylvania; and Washington, D.C.

2. You will read the following novels by these authors in the American Literature course: *The Scarlet Letter* by Nathaniel Hawthorne *The Adventures of Huckleberry Finn* by Mark Twain *Moby-Dick* by Herman Melville *The Sound and the Fury* by William Faulkner *The Great Gatsby* by F. Scott Fitzgerald and *For Whom the Bell Tolls* by Ernest Hemingway.

3. The winners of the Academy Awards for 2003 were as follows: Best Picture *Chicago* Best Director Roman Polanski for *The Pianist* Best Actor Adrien Brody in *The Pianist* Best Actress Nicole Kidman in *The Hours* Best Supporting Actor Chris Cooper in *Adaptation* and Best Supporting Actress Catherine Zeta-Jones in *Chicago.*

4. If you are going south on your vacation, be sure to visit Bear Wallow Kentucky Pewee Kentucky Bulls' Gap Tennessee Difficult Tennessee Hot House North Carolina Improve Mississippi Scratch Ankle Alabama and Dime Box Texas. (They are all on the map.)

5. Among the most important dates in World War II were September 1 1939 when Hitler invaded Poland December 7 1941 when the Japanese attacked Pearl Harbor Hawaii September 3 1943 when Italy agreed to suspend fighting May 7 1945 when Germany surrendered unconditionally and September 2 1945 when Japan signed formal terms of surrender.

The Colon [:]

TIP

For Full Sentences Following a Colon

When a complete sentence follows the colon, use a capital letter with the first word of the sentence.

Colons are like equal signs. They indicate that the last words of a grammatically complete statement are equal to the words that follow the statement.

▶**Use a colon after a complete introductory statement.**

When you introduce a list or a long quotation, end the introduction with a colon:

> Please bring the following items: a package of doughnuts, a case of soda, a picnic blanket, and five bottles of suntan lotion.

Be sure to place a colon only after a complete statement:

> Please bring a package of doughnuts, a case of soda, a picnic blanket, and five bottles of suntan lotion. (*Please bring* is not a complete statement because the verb requires an object, so don't use a colon here.)

Never place a colon after any form of *to be:*

Incorrect:	Alberto's favorite foods are: tacos, enchiladas, and sushi.
Correct:	Alberto's favorite foods are tacos, enchiladas, and sushi.

EXERCISE 13 | **Using Colons**

Place colons and commas where they are needed in each sentence. Be careful: One sentence doesn't require additional punctuation.

1. For our trip to Central America, we took only some basics items: suntan lotion, some light clothing, and a great deal of money.

2. For any dance at which the Big Band plays you need three important items comfortable shoes comfortable clothes and comfortable earplugs.

3. Sally's appearance follows all the latest fashions a blue T-shirt jeans torn at the knees orange and green hair and seventeen piercings in her left ear.

4. The three winners of the contest were Rolando Rodriguez Lavelle Wilson and John Jacobs.

5. Carl always knows the best restaurants the best movie theaters and the best places to shop.

6. Don't forget to add mustard, mayonnaise, ketchup, tomatoes, pickles, peppers, salt, relish, and onions to make a great hot dog, if you can still find it under all that stuff.

The Dash [—]

Dashes separate—and enclose—items in a sentence. They usually come in pairs.

▶**Enclose an emphasized sentence interrupter between two dashes.**

Use dashes (—) in pairs, just like the two commas that enclose sentence interrupters. Unlike the commas, however, the dashes call attention to the interrupter:

Some—but not all—of the work was easy.

The answer—I think—is obvious.

▶**Use only one dash for an interrupter at the end of a sentence.**

Of course, when an interrupter comes at the end of a sentence, it needs only one dash:

The answer is obvious—I think.

Dashes are especially useful to set off an interrupter that contains commas:

Punctuation marks—commas, periods, semicolons, and the like—help readers understand your sentences.

Parentheses [( )]

Parentheses enclose an item that isn't essential to a sentence's meaning. They always come in pairs.

▶**Enclose a de-emphasized sentence interrupter in parentheses.**

Dashes call attention to a sentence interrupter; parentheses draw attention away from it. They enclose information that's merely incidental to a sentence (usually short explanations, definitions, or examples—such as the material you're reading right now). Think of parentheses as footnotes within a sentence; almost anything that can go into a footnote can go into parentheses, as shown in the box on page 363.

The wallaby (a small- or medium-sized kangaroo) is found only in Australia and New Zealand.

George Washington Gale Ferris (1859–1896) built the Ferris wheel for the World's Columbian Exposition in Chicago in 1893.

The parentheses are part of the sentence in which they appear, so a period follows the second parenthesis mark if it's at the end of a sentence:

The American Civil War lasted four years (1861–1865).

EXERCISE 14	Using Dashes and Parentheses

Punctuate each sentence interrupter with two dashes (or one dash) or with parentheses.

1. Five planets —Mercury, Venus, Mars, Jupiter, and Saturn—are visible to the eye.

2. Uranus the first planet to be observed only by a telescope was discovered accidentally by William Herschel, who thought it was a comet.

3. The best candidate among the planets for having life other than Earth, of course is Mars.

4. Since the moon's gravity is too weak to hold atmosphere, there is no weather at all on the moon in fact, there is no wind, no sound, no life.

5. The surface temperature of the sun is approximately 6,000 degrees Kelvin 11,000 degrees Fahrenheit.

6. The planet with the largest number of moons as many as sixty-one is Jupiter

Quotation Marks [" "]

Use **quotation marks** to record *exactly* what someone said or says. Quotation marks come in pairs, enclosing and identifying the exact words of a speaker or writer.

Quotation marks can also identify the exact words that you've taken from other sources—including titles, words being defined, or words used in a special way. We'll begin with those uses.

Titles

▶Use **quotation marks for titles of poems, songs, articles, and chapters.**

Use quotation marks around the titles of short works or works contained within longer ones:

"Coming of Age" (chapter title within a book)

"Terrible Fire Kills Three" (newspaper headline)

TIP

For Quoting Titles

Don't put quotation marks around the titles of your own writing or writing assignments. But if, in another assignment, you refer to the title of another work (including another of yours), then place the title in quotation marks.

My Summer Vacation (title of assigned essay)

My Reaction to Being Asked to Write about "My Summer Vacation" (journal entry)

"Michelle" (song title contained within an album)

"Ode on a Grecian Urn" (poem contained within a book of poems)

Underline (or set in italics if you're using a computer) the titles of books, the names of magazines, the names of newspapers, and other longer works:

<u>A Farewell to Arms</u> (book title)

<u>Time</u> (magazine)

<u>Chicago Tribune</u> (newspaper name)

<u>The Simpsons</u> (television series)

<u>The Pianist</u> (movie)

<u>42nd Street</u> (play)

EXERCISE 15 | **Punctuating Titles**

Use underlining or quotation marks where appropriate.

1. <u>Life</u> magazine
2. The New York Post (newspaper)
3. Cold Mountain (novel)
4. The Fight against AIDS (title of article) in Newsweek (magazine)
5. The Producers is a very popular Broadway production.
6. My favorite song from the album Rappin' with the Dudes is I Wanna Be Famous.

TIPS

For Handling Definitions

Underlining and italicizing are interchangeable. So if you write on a computer, you may use either device. But choose one or the other and then be consistent.

Definitions

▶Underline (or italicize) words you define, and quote the definitions.

<u>Agnostic</u> literally means "without knowledge" (of God), while <u>atheist</u> means "without belief in God."

Recalcitrant means "unwilling"; it comes from a Latin word, *recalcitrare*, which means "to kick back."

Words Used in a Special Way

▶Use quotation marks for words with unusual meanings or used in unusual ways.

When you want to call attention to a word or phrase used in an original or unusual way, enclose it in quotation marks:

The world's most famous eater, "Diamond Jim" Brady, never touched a drop of alcohol but instead drank his "golden nectar," orange juice.

Don't overuse quotation marks, especially to quote slang words. If you feel you must excuse your word by placing it in quotes, use another word instead:

Poor:	Sam is a real "bum."
Better:	Sam is always in trouble.

Speech

▶**Use quotation marks for the exact words a person says or writes.**

Quotation marks signal a **direct quotation**—the exact words of a speaker or writer. Never use quotation marks with **reported speech**—a retelling in your own words of what the speaker or writer says or said:

Direct quotation:	Harry said, "I need to rest for a while."
Reported speech:	Harry said that he needed to rest for a while.
Direct quotation:	Patty asked, "Are you studying for the exam with anyone?"
Reported speech:	Patty asked if I was studying for the exam with anyone.

Note that the words *that* or *if* (or *whether*) introduce reported speech. Notice, too, that with direct quotes, the words identifying the speaker are not within the quotation marks.

EXERCISE 16 | **Writing Quotations and Reported Speech**

Change each of the direct quotations (a) into reported speech (b), or reported speech (b) into direct quotations (a).

1. a. Tomas said, "I know what I am doing."

   b. *Tomas said that he knew what he was doing.* _____

2. a. My mother always asks me, "What do you want for supper?"

   b. _____

3. a. _____

   b. Martha told me that she had been working late.

4. a. The doctor told me, "You can make an appointment for tomorrow."

   b. _____

5. a. _____

   b. Mr. Joseph asked where the registrar's office is.

6. a. The man asked us, "Have you seen a kangaroo carrying a pogo stick?"

   b. _____

Follow these rules when punctuating and capitalizing quotations:

▶Capitalize the first word of a complete quoted sentence, but don't capitalize the first word of a partially quoted sentence.

▶Place a comma after the introductory words that identify the speaker.

▶Place a comma, question mark, or exclamation point inside the end quotation mark, followed by the words identifying the speaker, which do not begin with a capital letter.

▶Enclose the entire quote—whether one word, one sentence, or more than one sentence—in a single set of quotation marks.

▶However, you may interrupt a quotation to identify the speaker and then resume the quotation.

Note these examples:

> In a letter to a friend, Thomas Jefferson asked, "What country before has ever existed a century and a half without a rebellion?" (A comma follows the identification of the speaker; the quotation begins with a capital letter; and the question mark comes before the final quotation mark.)
>
> "Give me liberty," said Patrick Henry, "or give me death!" (The quotation is interrupted to identify the speaker and then resumes without capitalization. The exclamation point is the end punctuation of the sentence and appears inside the quotation mark.)
>
> Carry Nation was famous for her crusades against alcohol. Once, after she had smashed tables, chairs, and the bar inside a saloon, a police officer came to arrest her for defacing property. She protested, "Defacing? I am defacing nothing! I am destroying!" (The three sentences are treated as a single quotation.)

Collaborative Activity 4

Writing Dialogue

With a classmate, compose a short dialogue between two people on a humorous subject—a first date, a trip to the barber or beauty shop, someone giving advice to a friend, or whatever you wish. Check it over for correct use of quotation marks, punctuation marks, and paragraphing.

When you write dialogue, begin a new paragraph each time you change speakers. Here's an example:

> When author Samuel Clemens, alias Mark Twain, proposed marriage to Olivia Langdon, her upper-class father asked the young man for character references, which Clemens provided. However, the letters that Langdon received all said that Clemens was totally irresponsible and unsuitable for marriage.
>   "Haven't you a friend in the world?" Langdon asked.
>   "Apparently not," Clemens replied.
>   "I'll be your friend myself," Langdon said. "Take the girl. I know you better than they do."
>   His instincts were correct, since Clemens proved a loyal and loving husband to Olivia.

TIPS

For Using Quotation Marks

Speakers of Russian should note that the opening quotation mark goes at the head of the word, not at the bottom of the word, as in Russian.

Incorrect: „Hello."
Correct: "Hello."

EXERCISE 17 | Punctuating Quotations

Punctuate and capitalize the quotations.

Famous Last Words

1. As Ethan Allen, the famous Revolutionary War soldier, lay dying, his doctor
   said to him **,** **"**General, I fear the angels are waiting for you. **"** *He* he answered.
   "Waiting, are they? Well—let'em wait! **"**

2. As he lay in a near coma, Thomas Edison said it is very beautiful over there .

3. Well, I must arrange my pillows for another weary night murmured Washington
   Irving, the famous American author When will this end?

4. As Marie Antoinette, the French queen, was being led to her execution, she stepped
   on the executioner's foot. Monsieur she exclaimed I beg your pardon!

5. Marie Antoinette's husband, King Louis XVI, bravely asked his servants why do you
   weep? Did you think I was immortal?

6. I have a terrific headache complained Franklin D. Roosevelt.

7. Please mumbled Theodore Roosevelt put out the lights.

IN SUMMARY | To Punctuate Sentences

Using commas
- Separate three or more items in a series with commas.
- Separate two independent clauses joined by coordinating conjunctions with a comma.
- Enclose a sentence interrupter with commas.
- Separate introductory words or phrases from the rest of the sentence with a comma, but don't use a comma when the ending phrase completes the idea of the sentence.
- Separate two or more coordinate adjectives with commas.
- Separate elements in dates, places, or addresses with commas.

Using periods
- Use periods after sentences that make a statement.
- Use periods after abbreviated words, except those that stand for government and other well-known organizations, television and radio stations, and acronyms.

Using question marks

Question marks follow all direct questions but not indirect questions.

Using exclamation points

Use exclamation points after all sentences or sentence fragments expressing strong emotion.

Using semicolons

- Semicolons join two independent clauses whose ideas are closely related but are not joined by the coordinating conjunctions *and, but, yet, or, nor, so,* or *for.*
- Semicolons separate items in a series when the items have internal punctuation.

Using colons

Placed after a complete statement, a colon introduces a list or a long quotation. Do not place a colon after any form of the verb *to be.*

Using dashes

Dashes enclose a sentence interrupter that you want to emphasize.

Using parentheses

Parentheses enclose incidental information in a sentence.

Using quotation marks

- Put quotation marks around the titles of short works or works contained within longer works.
- Use quotation marks around definitions.
- Set off words that you use in a special way with quotation marks.
- Use quotation marks around a speaker's exact words (but not reported speech).
    —Capitalize the first word of a complete quoted sentence.
    —Place a comma after words that introduce the quotation, including the words that identify the speaker.
    —End quotations with a period, a comma, a question mark, or an exclamation point. Place all periods and commas inside the final quotation mark. Place question marks and exclamation points inside the final quotation mark if they're part of the quotation, but outside the final quotation mark if they're not part of the quotation.
    —Use quotation marks around the *entire* quotation, not each sentence in the quotation.
    —Each time you quote a new speaker, begin a new paragraph.

EDITING FOR MASTERY

Mastery Exercise 1   *Correcting Punctuation Errors*

The following passage contains sixteen punctuation errors. Some punctuation marks are missing, and others are incorrect. The first error has been corrected for you. Find and correct the remaining fifteen errors.

Creation of the World: A Yakima Indian Legend

(1) In the beginning of the world, everything was water. (2) Whee-me-me-ow-ah, the Great Chief Above, lived up in the sky all alone. (3) When he decided to make the world he went down to the shallow places in the water and began to throw up great handfuls of mud that became land.

(4) He piled some of the mud so high that it froze hard and made the mountains. (5) When the rain came, it turned into ice and snow on top of the high mountains. (6) Some of the mud was hardened into rocks. (7) Since that time the rocks have not changed, they have only become harder.

(8) The Great Chief Above made trees berries, and roots grow on the Earth. (9) He made a man out of a ball of mud, then he told the man to take fish from the waters, and deer and other game from the forests. (10) When the man said, "I am lonely", the Great Chief Above made a woman to be his companion and taught her how to dress skins, how to find bark and roots, and how to make baskets out of them. (11) He taught her which berries to gather for food and how to pick them and dry them. (12) He showed her how to cook the salmon; and the animals that the man brought.

(13) When the woman prayed to the Great Chief. (14) She said, "Please answer my prayer."(15) I need help in having children." (16) He answered her prayer.

(17) But in spite of all the things the Great Chief Above did for them, the new people quarreled. (18) They argued so much that Mother Earth was angry, and she shook the mountains so hard that those hanging over the narrow part of Big River fell down. (19) The rocks, that fell into the water dammed the stream and also made rapids and waterfalls. (20) Many people and animals were killed and buried under the rocks, and mountains.

(21) Someday the Great Chief Above will overturn those mountains and release the spirits that once lived in the bones buried there. (22) Those spirits live in the tops of the mountains; watching their children on the Earth and waiting for the great change that is to come. (23) The voices of these spirits can be heard in the mountains at all times. (24) Mourners who cry for their dead hear spirit voices reply, therefore they know that their lost ones are always near.

(25) We did not know all this by ourselves. (26) We were told it by our fathers and grandfathers, who learned it from their fathers and grandfathers. (27) No one knows, when the Great Chief Above will overturn the mountains. (28) But we do know this: The spirits will return only to the people who kept the beliefs of their grandfathers.

Scorecard: Number of Errors Found and Corrected __________

Collaborative Activity 5

Comparing Answers

Compare your answers with a classmate's. Your instructor may ask you to report your findings to the class.

Mastery Exercise 2

Correcting Punctuation Errors

The following passage contains sixteen punctuation errors. Some punctuation marks are missing, and others are incorrect. The first error has been corrected for you. Find and correct the remaining fifteen errors.

Grandmother Spider Steals the Sun:
A Cherokee Indian Creation Legend

(1) In the beginning, there was only blackness, nobody could see anything. (2) Animals kept bumping into each other and moving blindly. (3) They said, "What this world needs is light. (4) Fox said that he knew that some people on the other side of the world had plenty of light, however, they were too greedy to share it with others. (5) Possum said that he would be glad to steal a little of it. (6) He added, "I have a bushy tail." I can hide the light inside all that fur." (7) Then he traveled to the other side of the world. (8) He found the sun hanging in a tree and lighting everything up. (9) He sneaked over to the sun, picked out a tiny piece of light, and stuffed it into his tail. (10) However; the light was hot and burned all the fur off. (11) The people discovered his theft and took back the light; and Possum's tail has been bald ever since then.

(12) "Let me try." said Buzzard. (13) "I know better than to hide a piece of stolen light in my tail. (14) I'll put it on my head." (15) He flew to the other side of the world and, diving straight into the sun grabbed it in his claws. (16) He put it on his head; but it burned his head feathers off. (17) The people took the sun away from him, and Buzzard's head has remained bald ever since that time.

(18) Then Grandmother Spider said, "Let me try!" (19) First, she made a thick pot out of clay, next, she spun a web reaching all the way to the other side of the world. (20) She was so small, that none of the people there noticed her coming. (21) Quickly, Grandmother Spider snatched up the sun, then she put it in the bowl of clay, and rushed back home along one of the pieces of her web. (22) Now her side of the world had light, and everyone was happy.

(23) Grandmother Spider brought the sun to the Cherokee; and she also brought fire with it. (24) Besides that, she taught the Cherokee people, the art of pottery making.

Scorecard: Number of Errors Found and Corrected _____

30 Checking Spelling, Apostrophes, Hyphens, and Capitals

Small errors can distract your readers from the content of your writing. It is important that you pay close attention to spelling, apostrophes, hyphens, and capitalization as you edit your work. This chapter will help you

■ learn the rules

■ practice applying them

Spelling

You can eliminate many spelling problems if you follow some simple practices:

1. *Check your spelling constantly.* If you compose by hand, circle words whose spelling you aren't sure of, and then look them up as you edit. The dictionary will not only show you how to spell the words, but it will show you how to pronounce them, where to separate them between syllables, and what their forms are in different tenses, as plurals, or as different parts of speech. If you compose on the computer, use the spell checker function, but don't trust it completely. It can't tell the difference between *led* and *lead,* for example, and won't catch the spelling error.

2. *Carefully pronounce words you aren't sure how to spell.* Look them up in the dictionary, and learn the spellings that correspond to those pronunciations. But because English is a combination of several languages, each with its own spelling rules, a sound can be spelled in many ways. So use the dictionary all the time. And don't rely entirely on a computer spell checker. It can give you the "correct" spelling of a word—but not the word you want to use.

3. *Look for root words in longer, more complex words.* For example, *member* is inside *remember* and *differ* is inside *different.* This advice is especially important in words with a silent letter or a hard-to-recognize vowel sound. For example, *finite* is in *definite* and *labor* is in *laboratory.*

4. *Don't confuse words that sound or look alike (their/there/they're, its/it's,* and so on). Check your dictionary repeatedly until you can clearly distinguish one word from the other.

5. *Use memory games to remind you of spellings.* For example, everybody wants to eat two *deSSerts,* but nobody wants to be stranded in a *deSert* more than once. You'll find tips throughout this chapter to help you remember spellings.

6. *Keep your own spelling list of problem words* (preferably on flash cards so that you can study each one separately). Write each word in a sentence. Underline or capitalize the troublesome part of the word: *proBABly, choiCe, studYing.* Consult Appendix B at the back of this book for additional help with commonly misspelled words.

7. *Carefully proofread your papers,* whether you write them by hand or keyboard them into a computer. You should catch a number of careless errors in the process. Use computer spell checker programs, but don't rely on them entirely. They can't think for you, and they won't catch every mistake.

The following rules should also help improve your spelling.

The Long and Short Vowel Sounds

Carefully pronouncing words will help you spell them only if you know which letters represent the various sounds. That's especially true with the **vowels,** which can have a number of sounds and spellings.

The Long Vowel Sounds. When you say the names of the vowels, you're pronouncing the long vowel sounds. But most often when spelling these long vowel sounds, you must *combine two vowels,* either together or separated by a single **consonant.** Here are some examples:

Sound	Spelling	Example
long *a*	*ai*	main, lain, chain
	ay	hay, say, pay
	ei	sleigh, reign
	a consonant *e*	fate, hate, crate
long *e*	*ee*	seem, meet, three
	ea	beat, dream, league
	ie	believe, achieve, brownie
	ei (after *c*)	receive, deceive, conceive
	final *y*	happy, ugly, unity
	e consonant *e*	precede, Chinese, complete
long *i*	*ie*	pie, tie, flies
	igh, ign	light, sigh, sign
	final *y*	sky, fly, cry
	i consonant *e*	nice, cite, line
long *o*	*oa*	boat, coat, roam
	final *o*	piano, auto, potato
	o (followed by *ld*)	sold, scold
	o consonant *e*	chrome, wrote, role
long *u*	*oo*	boot, shoot, food
	ui	fruit, juice
	ew	new, few, crew
	final *ue*	clue, argue, true
	u consonant *e*	cute, huge, refuse

✓ TIPS

For Spelling
Pay special attention to the ways that vowel sounds are spelled in English. Take the words *bit* and *bet,* for example. The letters *i* and *e* stand for short vowel sounds in these words, though in other languages the same letters often represent long vowel sounds. Proofread your work carefully.

The Short Vowel Sounds. A single vowel usually stands for a short vowel sound. Compare these words:

Words with short vowel sounds	Words with long vowel sounds
hat	hate
bat	bait
man	main
bet	beat, beet
pet	Pete
bit	bite
quit (*u* always follows *q* and is not considered a vowel in this position)	quite
hop	hope
hot	hotel
cot	coat
cut	cute
subtle	suit

Although you may not be able to eliminate misspelled long and short vowel sounds completely, the list should help. And each time you hear a vowel sound you aren't sure how to spell, check your dictionary. You'll learn more about spelling long and short vowel sounds later, when the chapter discusses doubling final consonants.

Long vowel sounds spelled *ei* or *ie* are especially confusing. But there is some consistency to their spelling, as explained in the Tips on this page.

> ✓ **TIPS**
>
> **For Spelling Words with *ie* or *ei***
>
> To keep these spellings straight, remember this rhyme:
> *I before e*
> *Except after c*
> *Or when sounded like a*
> *As in neighbor or weigh.*
>
> 1. *i* before *e*: *believe, relief*
> 2. except after *c*: *receive, conceive*
> 3. or when sounded like *a*: *eighty, sleigh*
>
> Some exceptions: *caffeine, either, their, foreign, protein, leisure, weird, seize*

EXERCISE 1 | Writing Long Vowels

Write two or three words for each long vowel sound and its spellings. Don't use any of the words from the list on page 372.

1. long *a*

   ai   claim, bait, train _____

   ei _____

   ay _____

   a consonant *e* _____

2. long *e*

   ee _____

   final *y* _____

   ea _____

   ei (after *c*) _____

   e consonant *e* _____

   ie _____

3. long *i*

ie _____

final *y* _____

igh, ign _____

i consonant *e* _____

4. long *o*

oa _____

o (followed by *ld*) _____

final *o* _____

o consonant *e* _____

5. long *u*

oo _____

ew _____

u consonant *e* _____

ui _____

final *ue* _____

EXERCISE 2	Choosing the Correct Spelling

Circle the correctly spelled word.

1. (brief) / breif   **6.** reciept / receipt

2. field / feild   **7.** percieve / perceive

3. conciet / conceit   **8.** thier / their

4. frieght / freight   **9.** weight / wieght

5. chief / cheif

Plurals of Nouns and Singulars of Verbs

Add *-s* or *-es* to form plural nouns and present tense, third person singular verbs. Both nouns and verbs follow the same spelling rules for taking *-s* or *-es*.

▶ Add *-es* to nouns or verbs ending in *ss, ch, sh, z,* or *x.*

boss, fix, reach, wish = *bosses, fixes, reaches, wishes*

▶ Add *-es* to most nouns or verbs ending in *-o.*

tomato, potato, do = *tomatoes, potatoes, does*

Some exceptions: radios, pianos, stereos

▶ Change final -*y* to -*i* and add -*es* after a consonant.

study, try, sky = studies, tries, skies

... after a vowel; merely add -*s*.

... ys, buys

... rb) endings from -*f* or -*fe* to -*ve* before adding -*s*.

... nives, wives

... hiefs, safes, chefs

EXERC

4. hoof _____

5. shelf _____

6. life _____

... nd verbs.

..., pies, makes, walks

... en, man = men

EXERCIS

... g any changes are that necessary.

7. rose _____

8. switch _____

9. breath _____

10. key _____

11. boss _____

CAPILANO UNIVERSITY BOOKSTORE
2055 PURCELL WAY
NORTH VANCOUVER, BC V7J 3H5
(604) 984-4972
GST # R106871361

Sale
Receipt: C00138038   001 001
Cashier: Glenda   09/18/09 13:14

1 PENCIL MARSMICRO BULK 3,5,7
  10034606
  #775 05 & #775 07   Y $5.10
1 CALCULATOR SHARP SCIENTIFIC
  10071595
  E 581WBBK   Y $17.50
1 RS / GATEWAYS TO ACADEM
  04777
  0-13-140888-7   Y $43.25

          Subtotal: $65.85

                                   $3.29
5% GST $1.23
7% PST

          Total: $70.37

Tender:

DEBIT CARD $70.37

Change Due: $0.00

   Customer Savings: $0.00

      THANK YOU
   CAPILANO UNIVERSITY
   FALLTERM 2009 TEXTS
 RETURN DEADLINE SEPT 30 2009
    WWW.CAPILANOU.CA

        C 0 0 1 3 8 0 3 8

Suffixes

A **suffix** is an ending attached to a **root (or base) word** to form a new word. Here are some examples:

Root word	Suffix	New word
agree	-ment	agreement
grace	-ful	graceful
sad	-ness	sadness

Note the rules for the spelling of words when suffixes are added:

▶ Change -*y* to -*i* if the letter before -*y* is a consonant.

Root word	Suffix	New word
needy	-ness	neediness
happy	-er	happier
pretty	-est	prettiest
angry	-ly	angrily
deny	-al	denial
beauty	-ful	beautiful

NOTE: Never change final -*y* to -*i* before the suffix -*ing*: denying, trying.

▶ Don't change a -*y* that comes after a vowel.

Root word	Suffix	New word
play	-ed, -ing	played, playing
lay	-er	layer
employ	-ment	employment

EXERCISE 5 | **Adding Suffixes**

Combine the root words and suffixes, making any changes that are necessary.

1. destroy + er *destroyer*

2. stay + ed _____

3. apply + cation _____

4. ugly + est _____

5. pay + ment _____

6. witty + cism _____

7. play + er _____

8. fly + ing _____

9. happy + ly _____

►Drop final -e when the suffix begins with a vowel.

Root word	Suffix	New word
ridicule	-ous	ridiculous
argue	-ing	arguing
strangle	-ing	strangling
SOME EXCEPTIONS: hoeing, canoeing		

►With most words ending in -ce or -ge, do not drop the final -e when the suffix begins with a or o:

noticeable	courageous

►Keep final -e when the suffix begins with a consonant.

Root word	Suffix	New word
hope	-ful	hopeful
complete	-ly	completely
time	-less	timeless

SOME EXCEPTIONS: argument, truly, awful
NOTE: Many writers spell acknowledgment and judgment without an e before ment.

EXERCISE 6 | Combining Root Words and Suffixes

Combine the root words and suffixes, making any changes that are necessary.

1. hate + ful *hateful*_____

2. awe + ful _____

3. dance + ing _____

4. sincere + ly _____

5. fame + ous _____

6. amuse + ment _____

7. dine + ing _____

8. admire + ation _____

9. tire + some _____

►The suffix -ly changes adjectives to adverbs without changing the spelling of the root word (except that final -y may become -i).

This rule is especially important for root words ending in -l (making -lly) or root words ending in -e (making -ely):

Root word	New word
real	really
sure	surely
sincere	sincerely
careful	carefully

Exception: true = truly

| EXERCISE 7 | Adding -*ly* to Root Words |

Change the adjectives to adverbs by adding -*ly*.

1. ideal *ideally* _____   **6.** necessary _____

2. bare _____   **7.** real _____

3. usual _____   **8.** true _____

4. sure _____   **9.** happy _____

5. angry _____

▶**For short vowel sounds, double the final consonant.**

As you saw earlier in the chapter, a combination of vowel-consonant-vowel (such as -*ate*, -*ine*, and -*ope*) usually stands for a long vowel sound (which sounds the same as the name of the vowel):

| hate | Pete | bite | hope | cute |

However, a combination of vowel-consonant-consonant stands for a short vowel sound, as in the following examples:

hat	hatter
pet	petted
bit	bitten
hop	hopped
cut	cutting

> **✓ TIPS**
>
> **For Doubling Consonants**
> Speakers of Spanish need to be careful about doubling final consonants. In Spanish you don't double consonants, and all vowels stand for only a single sound. Proofread your work carefully.

▶**Double the consonant for words with a short vowel when you add a suffix.**

If the word's vowel remains long, the consonant does not double. Contrast these words with long and short vowels:

(to cause a scar)	scar	scarring, scarred
(to frighten)	scare	scaring, scared
(to get rid of)	rid	ridding
(to ride, as in a car)	ride	riding
(to hop, like a bunny)	hop	hopping, hopped
(to wish)	hope	hoping, hoped
(to slice)	cut	cutter
(attractive)	cute	cuter

EXERCISE 8 | Adding Suffixes

Combine the root words and suffixes, making any changes that are necessary.

1. win + ing _winning_

2. tune + ing _____

3. write + ing _____

4. stop + ed _____

5. run + ing _____

6. hit + ing _____

7. heat + ing _____

8. stir + ing _____

9. mad + er _____

▶ **Don't double all final consonants of words with more than one syllable.**

A root word can have more than one **syllable**—a grouping of letters containing a single vowel sound. With root words of more than one syllable, double the final consonant only if the accent falls on the syllable immediately before the suffix:

com**mit**ted	oc**cur**red
be**gin**ning	sub**mit**ted
pre**ferr**ed	ex**pel**led

When the accent falls on another syllable, do not double the consonant:

happened	**lis**tened
answered	**coun**selor
preference	**trav**eled

EXERCISE 9 | Doubling Final Consonants

Combine the root words and suffixes, doubling the final consonant of the root word when necessary. Be careful to note where the accent falls.

1. refer + ed _referred_

2. unravel + ing _____

3. parallel + ing _____

4. compel + ed _____

5. prefer + ence _____

6. occur + ed _____

7. transfer + ed _____

EXERCISE 10 | Recognizing Correct Spelling

Circle the correct spelling.

1. runing / running

2. diferent / different

3. stuborn / stubborn

4. regreted / regretted

5. writing / writting

6. gramar / grammar

7. comming / coming

8. biten / bitten

9. sitting / siting

10. dining / dinning

Prefixes

A **prefix**—an addition to the beginning of a root word—usually doesn't affect the spelling of the root. No letters are dropped or doubled:

Prefix	Root word	New word
un-	natural	unnatural
dis-	integrate	disintegrate
mis-	spell	misspell
il-	logical	illogical
in-	accurate	inaccurate
im-	moral	immoral
co-	operate	cooperate

EXERCISE 11 | Identifying Correctly Spelled Words

Circle the correct spellings.

1. misspell / mispell

2. unnable / unable

3. inumerable / innumerable

4. misstake / mistake

5. ilegal / illegal

6. disagree / dissagree

7. missapply / misapply

8. disatisfied / dissatisfied

9. unnatural / unatural

EXERCISE 12 | Correcting Misspellings

Correct each misspelled word. When the spelling rules won't help you, use a dictionary or look at the list of commonly misspelled words in Appendix B.

TIPS

For Using Memory Devices

1. StationERy is papER.
2. Old AGE is a trAGEdy.
3. Bad gramMAR will MAR your writing.
4. The LLs are paraLLel in this word.
5. He is BUSY in his BUSIness.
6. The princiPAL is your PAL.
7. TOGETHER we went TO GET HER.
8. To write ALL RIGHT as one word would be ALL WRONG.
9. AFFECT is a verb that begins with A for ACTION.
10. Strange but true, there is a LIE in beLIEf and beLIEve.
11. Don't let the IR in theIR IRk you.
12. There is an ITCH in wITCH.
13. WhICH one has the sandWICH?
14. HERE is in tHERE and wHERE.
15. FULL loses an L at the end of a word: THANKFUL, GRATEFUL, HELPFUL, etc.

1. accross _across_____
2. adress _____
3. alot _____
4. arguement _____
5. athelete _____
6. basicly _____
7. begining _____
8. beleive _____
9. brillient _____
10. buisness _____
11. carefuly _____
12. childrens _____
13. choosen _____
14. comming _____
15. competion _____
16. definate _____
17. delt _____
18. diffrent _____
19. dinning _____
20. disapoint _____
21. discribe _____
22. dosen't _____
23. eigth _____
24. entrence _____
25. enviroment _____
26. existance _____
27. explaination _____
28. extremly _____

29. finaly _____
30. freind _____
31. goverment _____
32. grammer _____
33. tomatoe _____
34. truely _____
35. trys _____
36. heigth _____
37. hisself _____
38. hopeing _____
39. imediately _____
40. interlectual _____
41. intresting _____
42. jewlry _____
43. knowlege _____
44. localy _____
45. lonly _____
46. mispell _____
47. necesary _____
48. ocasion _____
49. occurance _____
50. perfer _____
51. possble _____
52. potatoe _____
53. preceed _____
54. priviledge _____
55. probly _____
56. recieved _____

57. rember _____

58. sacrafice _____

59. sence _____

60. seperate _____

61. shinning _____

62. sincerly _____

63. studing _____

64. suceed _____

65. suprise _____

66. temperture _____

67. themselfs _____

68. usualy _____

69. writen _____

70. writting _____

The Apostrophe [']

The rules for using apostrophes are actually rather simple. The **apostrophe**—a little hook above the line where a letter (or letters) would normally be—has only three functions: to form possessives of nouns, to form contractions, and to make letters plural.

Possessives

▶ Add 's to make a singular noun possessive.

When something belongs to someone, that person possesses it. There are several ways to express possession or ownership:

> the house that belongs to Kathleen
>
> the car my neighbor owns
>
> the room of my brother

However, a simple apostrophe (') + s added to a noun signals possession in a shorter and more direct way:

> *Kathleen's* house
>
> my *neighbor's* car
>
> my *brother's* room

This form of the noun is called the **possessive**.

Although a house, a car, and a room are concrete and material, a person can also possess abstract, nonmaterial things:

> the idea of my friend = my *friend's* idea
>
> the explanation made by the teacher = the *teacher's* explanation
>
> the ambition that Rafael has = *Rafael's* ambition

EXERCISE 13	Forming Possessives

Rewrite each phrase using apostrophe + -s.

1. the book that belongs to Tom *Tom's book* _____

2. the coat that Toyin has _____

3. the work done by Wilfredo _____

4. the personality of Kareem _____

5. the apartment that belongs to Maria _____

6. the bicycle that the boy owns _____

7. the statement made by Mr. Johnson _____

▶ **Add ' to make a plural noun ending in -s possessive.**

As you know, most plural nouns end in *-s:*

friends	boys	classes	the Smiths
teachers	students	parents	the Gonzalezes

You make these words possessive by adding ' after the *-s:*

> the books that belong to more than one boy = the *boys'* books
>
> the car that belongs to my neighbors = my *neighbors'* car
>
> the attitude of my parents = my *parents'* attitude

The correct placement of the apostrophe is important; it tells the reader whether the possessive noun is singular or plural:

> the *boy's* house (singular—one boy)
>
> the *boys'* house (plural—more than one boy)

All singular nouns should add *'s,* even if they end in s.

> *Carlos's* smile
>
> the *boss's* desk

EXERCISE 14 | Making More Possessives

Rewrite each expression, using 's or '.

1. the lounge for women *the women's lounge*
2. the idea of my coworkers _____
3. the house that belongs to Ms. Jones _____
4. the room that belongs to the children _____
5. the day for every mother _____
6. the schedules of the professors _____
7. the laws of Texas _____
8. the first tooth of the baby _____
9. the daughter of the Wilsons _____

▶ **Use 's or ' to show possession with objects and time.**

Objects can also possess things, as in these examples:

the front tire of the bicycle = the *bicycle's* front tire

the new stoplights of the streets = the *streets'* new stoplights

Even some time expressions use 's or s'. Notice that the phrases with apostrophes sound more graceful than the ones with *of:*

the pay of a week = a *week's* pay

the work of two years = two *years'* work

EXERCISE 15 | Editing for Apostrophes

Insert the missing apostrophes in each sentence.

1. I'm taking a week ʌ vacation soon.   *'s*
2. The rooms air conditioner needs to be repaired.
3. A few hours work should take care of the problem.
4. This years schedule allows more time off than last years schedule.
5. The red cars front tires were damaged in the accident.
6. I won't work on New Years Day.

EXERCISE 16 | Spelling Words Ending in -s

Circle the correct spelling in parentheses.

1. It was the (companies / company's) responsibility.

2. The Cubs scored five (runs / run's) in the ninth.

3. He (runs / run's) a large business.

4. Four people danced in the (movies / movie's) opening scene.

5. I ate at the (cities / city's) best restaurant.

6. The trees have lost their (leaves / leaf's).

TIPS

For Correcting Errors with Apostrophes

Don't put an apostrophe before every final -s. Apostrophes signal possession, not plurals or third person singular verbs:

Possessives

the *cat's* litter box

the *family's* secret

Plurals

Several *cats* use that litter box (not *cat's*).

The building houses eight families (not *family's*).

Verb endings

He *wants* to meet you (not *want's*).

The team *plays* today (not *play's*).

Contractions

▶ **Use an apostrophe to replace the missing letter(s) in a contraction.**

A **contraction** is a joining of two words that requires omitting a letter or several letters from the second word. An apostrophe occupies the spot of the missing letters:

> do not = *don't* (' replaces *o*)
>
> cannot = *can't* (' replaces *no*)
>
> it is = *it's* (' replaces *i*)
>
> they are = *they're* (' replaces *a*)
>
> they would = *they'd* (' replaces *woul*)

EXERCISE 17 | Forming Contractions

Make the following pairs of words into contractions, placing apostrophes properly.

1. he is *he's* _____

2. we will _____

3. it has _____

4. they are _____

5. we are _____

6. has not _____

7. you are _____

8. it is _____

9. does not _____

10. can not _____

11. he would _____

EXERCISE 18 | Editing for Apostrophes

Collaborative Activity 2

Correcting Apostrophe Errors

Write five sentences containing words that need apostrophes, but leave the apostrophes out. Exchange papers with a classmate, add the missing apostrophes, and correct each other's work.

Add apostrophes where necessary.

1. It 's cold today.

2. Were going to get it done.

3. Theyre always getting into trouble.

4. I dont know what youre asking me.

5. Its purpose is clear.

6. Whos there?

Plurals of Letters

▶ **Add *'s* to form the plurals of letters used as letters.**

When you need to make a letter or group of letters plural, add an apostrophe before the final *-s* so that your readers don't mistake the *-s* for one of the letters:

> Watch your *p's* and *q's*.
>
> Billy already knows his *ABC's*.
>
> Maria got all *A's*.

Hyphens [-]

Hyphens always join. They join two or more words to make them one, or they keep words joined when you must break them at the end of a line.

Hyphens to Join Words

▶ **The most popular style is to hyphenate two-word numbers.**

In formal writing, use a hyphen to join all two-word numbers between twenty-one and ninety-nine, as well as all fractions:

thirty-five		one hundred
fifty-one	BUT	321 (Use numerals for numbers that require three or more words to write out.)
two-thirds		

EXERCISE 19 | Hyphenating Numbers

Hyphenate the numbers if necessary.

1. twenty-one

2. three hundred

3. forty six

4. one thousand

5. three fourths

6. eighty two

▶Hyphenate between a prefix and a capitalized noun.

pro-American   trans-African

▶Hyphenate between the prefixes *self-*, *all-*, and *ex-* (meaning "former") and all nouns.

self-confidence   ex-teammate   all-world

▶Hyphenate words with *-in-law*.

mother-in-law   brothers-in-law (Note how the plural is formed.)

▶Hyphenate two or more words acting as a single adjective before a noun.

a three-piece suit   a four-star movie

a ten-foot pole

▶But don't hyphenate these groups of words when they don't precede nouns.

The pole is ten feet long.

The movie received four stars from many critics.

✔ **TIPS**

For Making Hyphenated Adjectives Singular

Unlike the practices in many languages, adjectives in English don't change to show the plural. Therefore, a hyphenated word before a noun (in the adjective position) always takes a singular form:

a two-*star* movie (not *stars*)

a five-*foot* ladder (not *feet*)

EXERCISE 20 | Hyphenating Words

Hyphenate the groups of words as necessary.

1. an ex-officer of the group

2. two sisters in law

3. a self made woman

4. a two man job

5. a pro Russian speech

6. a hard to get out of bed morning

▶Check your dictionary about hyphenating compound words.

A **compound word** is formed from two or more complete root words (like *background*). There are three different ways to write compounds:

1. As one word:

Root word	Root word	New word
house	fly	housefly
through	out	throughout
school	house	schoolhouse

Notice that these compound words do not drop any letters from their root words.

2. As hyphenated words:

Root word	Root word	New word
heavy	duty	heavy-duty
give	(and) take	give-and-take

3. As two separate words (these are called "open" compound words):

heat wave	grand piano	ice cream

Use your dictionary when you're unsure about hyphenating or spelling a compound word.

EXERCISE 21	Writing Compound Words

Create a compound word by adding a second root word after each word.

1. day *daylight* _____

2. run _____

3. under _____

4. house _____

5. ground _____

6. half _____

7. school _____

8. car _____

9. window _____

Syllables

▶Hyphenate words at the end of lines only between syllables.

A **syllable** is a word or word part that contains a vowel. For example, the word *understand* has three syllables: *un-der-stand.* When you must hyphenate a word at the end of a line, break the word only between syllables. You can't hyphenate a one-syllable word such as *go, make,* and *seen:*

ac-cu-rate	in-tel-lec-tu-al	com-mu-ni-ty
BUT NOT		
stra-ight (one syllable)	pict-ure (the syllable break is at *pic-ture*)	

Here are some hints about the best way to break words when it's necessary.

1. Break syllables after complete root words:

do-able	spell-ing	play-er

2. Break syllables after prefixes or before suffixes:

un-fair	sad-ly
trans-port	state-ment

3. Break syllables between two consonants—unless the consonants stand for one sound, such as *-th, -sh, -sc,* or *-ch:*

cap-tain		south-ern
vol-un-tary	BUT	
hus-band		reach-ing

Consult your dictionary if you're unsure of the syllable breaks.

4. Break already hyphenated words only at the hyphen.

Since two hyphens in one word will confuse your reader, break a hyphenated word only at its hyphen:

Poor:	un-Amer-ican
Better:	un-American

In fact, try not to break a hyphenated word between lines.

5. Don't hyphenate a contraction:

Incorrect:	does-n't	is-n't

6. Don't leave only one letter at the end or beginning of a line:

Poor:	a-live	cloud-y
Better:	alive	cloudy

And don't trust a computer to hyphenate for you. It doesn't know the difference, for example, between *pre-sent* (verb) and *pres-ent* (noun) or *pro-ject* (verb) and *proj-ect* (noun).

| EXERCISE 22 | Hyphenating between Syllables |

Use hyphens to divide the syllables in each word, unless the word cannot be divided. A word may need more than one hyphen.

1. unnecessary *un-nec-es-sar-y*

2. repeat _____

3. stepped _____

4. waited _____

5. watered _____

6. seemed _____

7. ex-president _____

8. aren't _____

9. guardhouse _____

10. attention _____

11. strange _____

Capitalization

Capitalize sentences, names, and titles according to the following rules.

▶Begin every sentence with a capitalized word.

In the beginning, the book was slow reading.

He said that he felt fine.

▶Capitalize the pronoun *I*.

I

BUT

he, she, it, you, we, they

▶Capitalize proper nouns—names of people, places, courses, organizations, languages, and words formed from them.

Howard	Fleet Street
the National Audubon Society	English
New York	New Yorker
Main High School (BUT high school)	
China	
Biology 111 (the name of a course) BUT biology (not a course name)	

EXERCISE 23 | Capitalizing Proper Nouns

Underline the letters that should be capitalized.

1. <u>r</u>ussian

2. george herman "babe" ruth

3. the corner of prairie road and
   central street

4. mathematics 101

5. mathematics

6. california wine

7. i, you, he

8. american civil liberties union

9. spanish

▶Capitalize a person's title before his or her name.

Mayor Juarez	BUT	He is the mayor.
Professor Williams	BUT	Who is your English professor?
President Lincoln	BUT	Abraham Lincoln was president.
Dr. Williams	BUT	She is a doctor.

▶Capitalize names of areas or countries.

Don't capitalize these terms when they mean only a direction:

The North won the Civil War.	BUT	We are traveling north.
She is from the West.		Which way is east?

▶Capitalize the names of days, months, and holidays.

Don't capitalize the seasons of the year:

Tuesday		summer
March	BUT	spring
Independence Day		fall

▶Capitalize all major words in titles.

Don't capitalize little words—short prepositions, conjunctions, and articles—unless they're the first or last words in the title or subtitle:

For Whom the Bell Tolls
Life on the Mississippi
Journal of the American Medical Association
"What to Listen For"

EXERCISE 24 | Capitalizing Nouns

Underline the letters that should be capitalized.

1. tuesday

2. winter

3. august

4. I want to visit the west.

5. a reverend

6. do you speak Italian?

7. the wind is coming from the east.

8. webster's collegiate dictionary

9. the president of the United States

IN SUMMARY | Spelling, Apostrophes, Hyphens, and Capitals

Adding final -s or -es
- Add -es to words ending in ss, ch, sh, z, or x or most words ending in o.
- Change -y to -i after a consonant and add -es.
- Change most nouns ending in -f or -fe to -ve before adding -s.

Adding a suffix
- Change -y to -i after a consonant.
- Keep final -e before a suffix beginning with a consonant.
- For words with short vowels, double the final consonant before adding a suffix. Don't double the final consonant if the word has a long vowel sound.

Using apostrophes
- To show possession, add 's to all singular nouns, but add just an apostrophe to plural nouns ending in -s.
- To make a contraction, put the apostrophe in the place of the omitted letter(s).
- To make letters plural, add 's.

Using hyphens
- Hyphenate two-word numbers from *twenty-one* to *ninety-nine* and all fractions.
- Hyphenate a prefix and a capitalized noun.
- Hyphenate prefixes *self-*, *all-*, or *ex-* and a noun, and all words with *-in-law*.
- Hyphenate two or more words acting as a single adjective before a noun.
- If you break a word at the end of a line, hyphenate only between syllables.

Capitalizing
- Capitalize the first word of every sentence or title.
- Capitalize the pronoun *I*.
- Capitalize names of people, places, organizations, courses, languages, and words formed from them.
- Capitalize a title when it is used before a person's name.
- Capitalize areas or countries (but not directions).
- Capitalize names of days, months, and holidays (but not seasons of the year).

EDITING FOR MASTERY

Mastery Exercise 1

Correcting Spelling and Other Matters

The following passage contains twenty-one errors in spelling, apostrophe use, hyphenation, and capitalization. The first error has been corrected for you. Find and correct the remaining twenty errors.

The Origins of the "Happy Birthday" Song

(1) *Believe* ~~Beleive~~ it or not, the song that you hear at most birthday party's is copyrighted, and the copyright owners often recieve royalties when its sung. (2) The melody was writen by two sisters from Kentucky, Mildred and Patty Smith Hill, and was first published under the title "Good Morning to All" in 1893. (3) The song was never meant for birthday celebrations but instead welcomed youngsters enterring a class room each morning. (4) It developed into its current, diffrent role as a result of a theft.

(5) Mildred Hill, who composed the melody, was a church organist, a concert pianist, and an authority on african american spirituals. (6) She died in Chicago at the age of fifty seven. (7) Her sister Patty Smith Hill had writen the original lyric's for the song while she was principal of a kindergarten in Louisville, Kentucky, where Mildred also taught.

(8) The Hill sisters copyrighted their song on October 16, 1893. (9) However, on March 4, 1924, it apeared without thier approval in Robert H. Colemans songbook. (10) Although the song still had its original title, Coleman changed part of the lyrics to say, "Happy birthday to you."

(11) The song was then published sevral times over the next ten years, often with small changes in the lyrics. (12) By 1933, everyone knew the song as "Happy Birthday to You." (13) A year later, when the song was sung every night in a Broadway Musical, another Hill sister, Jessica, went to court and sued. (14) She was angry about the theft of the song and the failure to pay royalty's to her brothers and sisters. (15) She won her lawsuit. (16) The Hill family owned the rights to the melody and had to be payed every time the song was part of a commercial production.

(17) The results of the suit were immediate. (18) The Western Union company, which had deliverred a half-million singing birthday greetings, stoped using the song. (19) It was eliminated from two plays on Broadway. (20) And in another play entitled *Happy Birthday,* it's star, Helen Hayes, spoke the lyrics so the producers could avoid paying royalties.

(21) Dr. Patty Smith Hill died at the age of seventy eight, aware that she and her sister had started an amazing birthday tradition.

Scorecard: Number of Errors Found and Corrected _____

Collaborative Activity 3

Checking Your Answers
Compare your answers with a classmate. Your instructor may ask you to report your findings to the class.

Mastery Exercise 2

Correcting Spelling and Other Matters

The following passage contains twenty-one errors in spelling, apostrophe use, hyphenation, and capitalization. The first error has been corrected for you. Find and correct the remaining twenty errors.

The Ghostly Rhyme (A Chinese Legend)

(1) Long ago, a wise man was sent to the jungle after he complained about dishonesty in the ˄*government* goverment (2) He built a small hut near a stream among the cinnamon trees. (3) He brought the water for his tea in a bamboo diper and ate the fish he caught, the fruit he picked, and the vegtables he grew in a small patch. (4) But usualy he spent his day reading.

(5) When a friend asked him why he lived in such a lonly spot, he was supprised. (6) "But I'm not alone," he said. (7) "My books have told me all about these hills. (8) I have the spirits of the wood's for company." (9) Later when he developed a cough, his friends tried to get him to come down to the city to see a doctor, but he refused. (10) "The smell of Pine is the best medicine," he said.

(11) One day, he picked up a book by his favorite poet, but worms had eatten away the outside edges of the pages. (12) He opened the book to read a poem and found that the last line was missing, which he could not rember. (13) He tryed to recall it by reciting the next-to last line over and over: (14) "The sun on my old garden shine's . . ." (15) He soon forgot to eat and even sleep.

(16) One day, his friend's found him dead inside his hut, with the book in his lap.

(17) Saddly they buried him with the book, but that night the sound of the wind shaking the leafs of the cinnamon trees sounded like someone sighing. (18) The raindrops fell like someone impatiently taping a finger.

(19) Then his ghost appeared reading the poem aloud but stopped just before the last line. (20) At first people were frightened, but they realized that his ghost was harmless. (21) Eventually, though, he began to haunt the main street and shout out the words of the poem. (22) People beged the old man to go away.

(23) At last, a poet went up to the hut in the woods, sat down, and waited for the old man to come. (24) The ghost finaly appeared and read from the book. (25) The poet recognized the poem, and when the wise man ended before the last line, the poet asked him to continue. (26) Once again, he read but stopped at the same place. (27) "The sun on my old garden shines . . ."

(28) "But I am gone," the poet finished. "No flesh confines."

(29) The ghost smiled in releif and closed his book. (30) He dissapeared, and no one ever saw or heard him again.

Scorecard: Number of Errors Found and Corrected _____

CHECK EVERY ASPECT OF YOUR WRITING CAREFULLY!

Twenty Questions

Use the following checklist as you revise and edit your writing.

_____ 1. Are my verb tenses correct? (See Chapters 17–19.)

_____ 2. Are my verb forms correct, especially in verbs that contain more than one word? (See Chapters 17 and 19 and Appendices A and C.)

_____ 3. Do subjects and verbs agree? (See Chapter 18.)

_____ 4. Is the word order of my sentences correct? (See Chapters 16 and 20.)

_____ 5. Have I used the correct forms of pronouns, as subjects and objects? (See Chapter 21.)

_____ 6. Are all pronoun antecedents clear, and do pronouns agree with the nouns or pronouns they refer to? (See Chapter 21.)

_____ 7. Have I used *a, an,* and *the* correctly? (See Chapter 22.)

_____ 8. Have I used prepositions correctly? (See Chapter 22.)

_____ 9. Have I handled comparisons correctly? (See Chapter 23.)

_____ 10. Have I corrected any sentence fragments? (See Chapter 24.)

_____ 11. Have I joined short, choppy sentences? (See Chapters 25–27.)

_____ 12. Have I used coordination and subordination correctly? (See Chapters 25 and 26.)

_____ 13. Have I used pronouns correctly to join ideas in sentences? (See Chapter 27.)

_____ 14. Have I corrected sentences that are run together? (See Chapter 28.)

_____ 15. Have I corrected clauses that are improperly joined with commas? (See Chapter 28.)

_____ 16. Have I used transitions to connect ideas? (See Chapters 3 and 5–14.)

_____ 17. Is my punctuation correct? (See Chapter 29.)

_____ 18. Have I spelled words correctly? (See Chapter 30 and Appendix B.)

_____ 19. Have I used capitalization correctly? (See Chapter 30.)

_____ 20. Have I double-checked all my corrections and proofread my writing one final time?

Additional Readings
and
Appendices

Additional Readings

Every good writer is a good reader. Reading provides you with models of writing, along with inspiration to write, ideas to write about, and information to discuss in writing. The following selections should interest you. The authors are professional writers—many of them famous—and even students like you, who had great stories to tell and worked hard to tell them well. Each selection discusses issues that you face each day—or issues that perhaps you've never considered. But one of the purposes of reading is to learn what other people have learned and wish to share with you in their writing.

Read a selection at home and consider the questions that follow it. The questions—as well as the suggestions for writing—will give you additional practice in building the skills you've been working on throughout this book.

The key to reading well is to *read with a purpose*. You should know what to look for and how to understand a reading. Here's some advice to follow as you read these selections—and any selections, any time:

1. **Preread the Selection.** Skim over the title, the first paragraph, the first and last sentences of the body paragraphs, the concluding paragraph, and any headings in the selection.

2. **Expect to return to a selection after you've read it.** Purposeful reading involves reviewing what you've read to be sure you understand its ideas. That's especially important as you study. You don't have to reread every word, but you have to be able to locate the important ideas.

3. **Highlight or underline main ideas.** Look for thesis statements and topic sentences and identify them, either with a highlighting pen or by underlining. Then, when you return to the selection for further review and study, you can locate main ideas quickly.

4. **Make notes in the margins of the text.** Record your reactions to a sentence or a paragraph: statements of agreement or disagreement ("great!" "yeah, right!"); reactions ("this reminds me of . . ."); objections ("but what about . . . ?"); thoughts about things you could discuss in class or in writing ("how about the issue of . . . ?"). Think of these notes as a dialogue you're having with the author of the text. The purpose of reading is to get you to think, so record your thoughts.

5. **Reread while you're reading.** If you don't understand a sentence or idea, go back and reread the sentence or sentences that precede it. The puzzling passage may then make more sense. But if it doesn't, note the problem in the margin so you can return to it later, or perhaps discuss it with others.

6. **Circle or underline unfamiliar words.** Try to determine their meaning in context—from the sentence and the paragraph they're in. If you must look them up, do so after you finish reading. Then reread the selection. You'll go much faster—and understand much more.

7. **Know how fast you read—and how fast you read different things.** One of the keys to success in school is budgeting your time effectively. So you ought to know how long it takes you to read 20 pages in social science or 20 pages in history. Time yourself with each textbook. How many pages have you finished in 15 minutes or an hour? That way, you can set aside enough time to read carefully and thoroughly so you can plan your week's activities.

8. **Take frequent breaks.** Don't try to read a long, difficult selection straight through. Reading with a purpose can be hard work. Pause and rest every 15 minutes or half hour. But don't take long breaks, or you'll find excuses not to read.

9. **Make journal entries in response to readings.** If the selection raises questions or ideas, capture them in writing. Discuss the questions in class, and collect ideas that you can use later if you write about the selection for homework or a quiz.

10. **After the reading, look up the words you've circled and study them.** Work on building your vocabulary. Write the words and their definitions in a notebook or computer file. Or write each word and definition on a separate note card. Review the words each day and practice using them in sentences.

Needing and Wanting Are Different
Jimmy Carrasquillo

* * * *

We all must decide on our priorities, especially when money is involved. Many teenagers think they will be happy if they can buy a car, have all the latest CDs or video games, or eat out with their friends several nights a week. And many teenagers find themselves working too many hours at part-time jobs while their schoolwork suffers. In the following article, Jimmy Carrasquillo, a high school senior, describes his problems with balancing work, school, and athletics. As you read it, notice how he got into trouble, how he woke up—literally—and saw what the trouble was, and what he has learned from the experience.

1   "Mom, can I have some money?" Those are the words my mother used to hear all the time. In return, I heard, "Why don't you get a job? Not to make me happy, but so you have your own money and gain a bit more responsibility." So last year I got a job with Montgomery Ward's photo studio, working about 25 hours a week. For $5 an hour, I was a telephone salesman, trying to persuade people to come in for a free photograph.

2   All this was during football season and I was on the team as a kicker. To do football and homework and my job at the same time became really hard. I was burning out, falling asleep at school, not able to concentrate. My first class was physics and I hated it. I'd just sit there with my hand on my cheek and my elbow on the desk, and start dozing. One day the teacher asked my partner what I was doing and she said, "Oh, he's sleeping." The teacher came to the back of the class and stared at me. The whole class looked at me for about two minutes and laughed.

3   My third-period history teacher was really concerned. She was cool. A lot of the time, I'd fall asleep in her class. She'd scream, "Wake up!" and slam her hand on my desk. I'd open my eyes for about two minutes, pay attention, and go back to sleep. She asked me if I could handle school, football, and work. I said, "Yeah. I'm doing OK so far." She said, "Why? Why all this?"

4   I told her it was for the things I needed, when actually it was for the things I wanted. Needing and wanting are different. Needing something is like your only shoes have holes in them. But when a new pair of sneakers came out and I liked them, I'd get them. My parents didn't feel it was right, but they said, "It's your money, you learn to deal with it." Within two years I had bought 30 pairs. My parents would laugh. "You got your job, you got your money—but where's your money now?" They didn't realize how much my job was hurting my schoolwork.

screwed up: slang for "incorrect" or "confused"

5   My priorities were **screwed up.** On a typical night I did about an hour of homework. A lot of times it was hard for me to make decisions: Do I want to be at work or do I want to be at practice? Do I want to worry about what I'll have in the future? Sometimes I felt there was no right choice. One week in the winter I had to work extra days, so I missed a basketball game and two practices. (I'm on that team, too.) When a substitution opportunity came at the next game, the coach looked at me and said, "OK, we're running I–5," a new play they had developed during the practice I had missed. I told him I didn't know it, so he told me to sit back down. I felt really bad, because there was my chance to play and I couldn't.

6   I really did resent work. If I hadn't been so greedy, I could have been at practice. But I kept working, and the job did help me in some ways. When you have a lot of responsibilities, you have to learn to balance everything. You just grow up faster. At home, your parents always say, "I pay the bills, so while you're here you're under my rules." But now with my money I say, "No, no no, you didn't pay for that, I did. That's mine."

7   Slowly, I've come to deal with managing money a lot better. At first, as soon as I had money, it was gone. Now it goes straight into my bank account. This year I decided not to work at all during the football season. I have a lot more time to spend with other players after the game and feel more a part of the team. I've only fallen asleep once in class so far. I'm more confident and more involved in my classes. My marks are A's and B's, a full grade better than this time last year. I'm hoping that will help me get into a better college. I don't go shopping as much. I look at all the sneakers in school and think, "I could have those," but I don't need them. Last year I thought that being mature meant doing everything. But I'm learning that part of growing up is limiting yourself, knowing how to decide what's important, and what isn't.

Questions for Analysis

1. Paragraph 1 suggests the reasons that Jimmy Carrasquillo decided to get a job. What were they?
2. Paragraph 2 does not begin with a topic sentence. What is the topic sentence? Underline it. Find and underline the topic sentences in paragraphs 3–7.
3. Jimmy states his thesis in Paragraph 4. What is it, and how does it relate to the title of the article?
4. What, according to Jimmy, is the difference between wanting and needing? What example does he cite to illustrate these differences?
5. This essay essentially describes the trouble Jimmy got into from trying to work so many hours. But, aside from the money he made, did the experience benefit him? If so, what were those benefits, and where does he describe them?
6. Paragraph 7 draws a number of contrasts. List them. Then write in your own words what main lessons they show that Jimmy has learned.

Writing Assignments

1. Discuss an important lesson you've learned the hard way. What happened, and what did it teach you?
2. Discuss a time when someone helped you understand and perhaps correct a mistake you were making. What happened? What was the result?
3. Write your own definition of maturity, and illustrate it with two examples: one of immature behavior and another of mature behavior.

4. Jimmy confesses that at one point he had 30 pairs of sneakers. His situation is probably unusual, but not impossible in the United States. Compare and contrast what a teenager like him needs and wants to buy with the needs and wants of teenagers in another culture you know.

5. Summarize the article and then respond. How, in your own experience, are needing and wanting different?

What a Cat
Erica Teal

* * * *

Pets are often treated like members of the family—and sometimes like spoiled children. In the following essay, Erica Teal describes the family's very fat and very much loved cat. Erica returned to study at Harry S Truman College in Chicago after working in a managerial position in a bank for a number of years. Another of her writings appears in Chapter 8. In this essay, she describes her pet cat. As you read, note the attention to detail in describing the cat's appearance and behavior. Note, too, Erica's obvious affection for the animal.

1   When I was growing up, my sister had an amusing and unusual house cat named Binkey. He was so immense that you had to take a second look to make sure he wasn't a dog. We lived in a large four-bedroom-family **three flat,** which gave Binkey a lot of space to meander. He went from floor to floor terrorizing each household.

three flat: an apartment building with three apartments

2   Binkey weighed in at 38 pounds. He had large round emerald eyes. His body was gray with an all-white underside, and he had a mixture of tan, gray, and black down his back, with a streak of white in the center. He had a lovely tail that fanned out like a peacock spreading its features for display. My sister believed he was so huge due to the love she gave him, but I beg to differ. He was enormous because of the amount of food he consumed.

monstrous: very large

3   Binkey had a **monstrous** appetite. Not only did he eat his three meals of the day, he also ate small pets throughout the building, which consisted of birds, hamsters, and gold fish. We noticed at times that Binkey's belly would be wet. Also, our gold fish were slowly vanishing. But how? We thought he was too large to climb on top of the tank, until one day after we returned from church. We found Binkey lying on his side on top of the fish tank. His belly was so large, it rested in the water, and the fish would come to the top and examine the **conspicuous** object floating in the water. He would slowly stretch his paw into the water, swiping at the fish and eating them like they were **savory** appetizers. This was one of the most amusing acts that Binkey performed.

conspicuous: very easily noticed

savory: delicious

4   There was something unusual about Binkey. He had a passion for water. My sister gave him weekly baths from the age of six weeks. When he heard the sound of water running in the tub, he would make a mad dash for the bathtub and leap in it. Whenever we wanted to take a bath, we usually had to close the bathroom door, or there would be a frisky feline swimming in our bath water.

5   Binkey gave us 12 years of amusement and wonder. The last adventure he had was jumping out the window from the second floor into a tree while chasing a squirrel. He fell two stories and shattered the bones in his two front legs. He has been deeply missed, for he was part of the family.

Questions for Analysis

1. What is the thesis statement in the opening paragraph? Underline it.

2. Each of the three body paragraphs includes a topic sentence. Underline the topic sentences.

3. Erica uses several kinds of support for topic sentences. Where does she use physical description? Where does she use examples? Where does she tell a little story?

4. What evidence does Erica supply to support her claim in the last paragraph that Binkey was part of the family?

Writing Assignments

1. Like Erica Teal, write an essay of at least five paragraphs about a pet you have or had (if you never had a pet, write about a friend's). Describe its physical appearance, and tell about some of its typical or more unusual behaviors.

2. Some Americans may be kinder to pets than to family members. Write about why you think that is true.

3. If you were raised in a culture that seems to treat pets differently than the way they are treated in the United States, contrast the different ways pets are treated in the two cultures.

4. Summarize the story and then respond. Why was the family so fond of this cat? Do you think every family would have been fond of this cat?

The Music of a Place by the Ocean
Giuliano Correia

* * * *

Rio de Janeiro in Brazil is often called one of the most beautiful cities in the world. And in the description that follows, it is easy to see why. Its author, Giuliano Correia, is a student at Harry S Truman College who has traveled widely but still loves the beaches of his native Brazil. In the following essay, he describes his favorite two: Ipanema and Leblon. He first provides an overall view of the scene and then takes you on a tour of the beaches. As you read the description, note how it employs several of the senses, including touch. Note, too, how each paragraph is unified around a topic idea.

situated: located

1   If you have the opportunity to go to the city of Rio de Janeiro in Brazil, you will be enchanted by the magic of Ipanema and Leblon beaches. Those neighborhoods, **situated** on the southeast of the rugged city's coast, are the best examples of what Rio is famous for. The four-mile-long shore is the perfect combination of natural and urban environments. The beaches, hills, and forests blend with the well-preserved buildings and narrow European-style streets surrounded by 300-year-old trees.

cliché: an overused expression or idea

2   It may sound a little like a **cliché,** but when you pace down the sidewalk of those beaches, it really feels as if you were part of a *bossa nova* song. At least, the scenery is exactly the same: a gentle breeze, the smooth sound of the waves and the special way the natives of Rio walk by you, swinging their bodies sensually to the rhythm of the sea and gazing at nowhere. The poetry and melody of the many songs that poets have written about Ipanema are still in the air, making the atmosphere so special.

3   The walking path begins in Ipanema at the *Arpoado*, a gigantic rock that sits between the land and the ocean, in the northern part of the coast. It is common to see couples there, staring at the sea as if they were hypnotized by the sound of the waves crashing on the stone. Heading south, there are traffic lanes, framed by dancing palm trees, connecting this beach to Leblon and separating the wide sand line from the buildings.

mosaic: art made from different colored stones

4   Every Sunday one of the lanes is closed so people can use it for skating, jogging, or just walking. That is when you realize why Brazilians are famous for being so beautiful. They work out and tan their bodies to perfection, and the sight of such beauty is breathtaking. All along the sidewalk, a **mosaic** of black and white rocks in the design of waves,

art deco: a style of art from
the 1920s and 1930s

5   are little sheds, in every mile of the shore. They are refreshment bars where people stop by to have cold coconut juice, take a breath, or rest from the all-year-long warm sun. The people are known for friendliness and will start a conversation for any reason.

   If you look to the right, the continental side, you will see mostly **art deco** buildings, built in the 1960s by rich and traditional families. They have colorful gardens and large glass windows that reflect the color of the ocean. Green mountains frame the city in the background while, on the left side, round rocks stand out in the dark blue sea like huge white whales of a child's dream.

6   Another special distinction of the beach is the sand. It is a sort of a warm white powder that gives the best foot massage you can ever imagine as you dig your feet into its softness. At the end of the day, it is common to see people coming, apparently from work, still in their suits, taking their shoes off for a walk by the beach. For the *Cariocas,* as the local residents are called, going to the beach to pray, relax, and rest from the everyday routine is vital; it is like a religion. You will learn with them that the beach is the solution for any problem.

samba: a popular Brazilian
dance

7   Finally, crossing the channel that separates both beaches, you are at Leblon, a more recent version of Ipanema. The buildings are more modern and there are more hotels and restaurants, though the atmosphere is the same. Famous poets, musicians, and celebrities are usually hanging out at corner cafes, always improvising **sambas,** bragging about being *Cariocas,* and living in the most beautiful city in the world.

paraglide: glide gently to the
ground on a small parachute

8   At the south end of this beach, when your "song" is almost over, stands an enormous double-edged hill called "The Two Brothers." At dusk, people jump off its top to **paraglide.** At the bottom of the hill, you can end your day at a famous observatory that sits out on the ocean, looking over the entire city. With the breeze touching your body, you watch the Ipanema-Leblon Bay getting dark, as the music goes low and the sun sets behind the city, being thankful for the melodic and poetic picture that Rio is.

Questions for Analysis

1. In Paragraph 1, what, according to Giuliano, makes the beaches so unique?
2. Each body paragraph includes a topic sentence. Underline them.
3. Giuliano uses more than the senses of sight and sound in his description. What other senses does he use? Underline the sentences that contain them.
4. What transitional expressions in the body paragraphs locate things spatially? Circle them.
5. The description is also organized according to a time sequence. When does the "tour" begin and when does it end?

Writing Assignments

1. As Giuliano Correia does, write a description of your favorite outdoor place to visit. If possible, go there and take notes of what you see, hear, feel, and even smell as preparation for the writing.
2. Write a description of one place in which different activities occur at different times of the day. Use chronological order to take the reader through the changing activities.
3. Describe your least favorite place. Indicate what makes it so unpleasant or disagreeable.
4. Summarize the description of Ipanema and Leblon and then respond. What activities on the beaches would you find most enjoyable? Or compare or contrast the beaches of Rio to a beautiful place you know.

The Beauty of My Town
Max Rodriguez-Reyes

* * * *

The peace and simplicity of a small town in a small country can be very attractive, as you'll see in this essay by Max Rodriguez, a native of Guatemala and former student at Harry S Truman College in Chicago. As you read the essay, notice how Max describes the town at different times of the day or week. Notice, too, how he includes sounds and tastes in addition to the sights of the town.

1   I come from a small town called Coban, far from Guatemala City, with a population of about 2,000 people, mostly of Mayan Indian descent. The beauty of green villages and mountains and the spiritual culture of the Mayan Indians are preserved almost intact from the region of their birth.

counterpoint: opposing or contrasting point

2   In the morning when I am there, I enjoy the cool mountain breezes and the pure golden sunlight as a refreshing **counterpoint** to the endless ticking of the clock. When I leave my house, the first things that strike my senses are the smell of fragrant wildflowers and the sight of Mayan Indians riding their horses up the mountain on the way to work. In the afternoon, I walk along the woodland trails amid the tall trees and the singing of **innumerable** birds, exchanging endless greetings with the Mayans passing by. Then I wander along the river, where the clear blue water running **serenely** down the mountains never fails to make me yearn for an evening swim.

innumerable: countless
serene: very quiet and peaceful

artifacts: characteristic items of the culture

3   On Saturdays, I visit the local plaza and drink in the sights and sounds of Indians wearing and selling their traditional costumes and **artifacts** made with clay by hand, a phenomenon almost unique to the town. On Sunday mornings the plaza looks quiet and almost deserted because virtually the entire population is in church. But by noon of the same day the village square is alive with flocks of brightly costumed children at play under the tolerant eyes of their parents and elder siblings, while on the main stage of the *zocalo* (the town square), the *marimbas* (the national instrument of Guatemala) are casting their magical spell as people of all ages dance and sing around them, and I enjoy such savory appetizers as Guatemalan tamales and *atole de elote* (the delicious corn soup for which the Mayans are renowned through the world).

inestimable: countless

4   As the magnificent evening sunset filters slowly down through the magically changing blues and greens of the mountain rivers, I reflect once more on the **inestimable** treasures of spiritual beauty with which our humble people have been blessed.

Questions for Analysis

1. What is the main point that Max Rodriguez makes?
2. Max includes several Spanish words, which he then defines or describes in parentheses. Would the description be less effective with the Spanish words removed? Why or why not?
3. Max mixes action along with description. Identify several places in which he does this.
4. Examine the organization of each paragraph. What transitions help you follow the organization? Underline them. How is the whole essay organized?

Writing Assignments

1. Imagine you are composing a letter to a friend who lives far away from you. Describe a place your friend would find beautiful or exciting.
2. For the same audience, describe the activities of a busy place at different times of the day, week, or season.

3. Max Rodriguez's description of the town square reveals some of the customs and traditions of his Mayan culture. Describe one activity that reveals something about your culture or society.

4. Both Giuliano Correia, in the previous essay, and Max Rodriguez describe places of natural beauty, but in quite different environments—urban and rural. Compare or contrast the descriptions. Would you enjoy visiting both places, or would you prefer one to the other? Explain.

The Natchez Indians
Adapted from *The People's Almanac #3*

* * * *

We tend to think that the customs of our culture and community are "natural." Men, women, and children have certain roles, and so do the leaders of the community. Think about who takes or took the main responsibility for raising the children in your family. Think about the class structure in your society or culture. Who are your leaders? Whom do you look up to? What determines membership in the higher or lower classes? The following essay describes a culture that has disappeared, but that, while it existed, was unique. As you read it, notice its descriptions and classifications of the four levels within the society. Notice its discussion of the importance of women. And notice its discussion of how and why the society disappeared.

1   The Natchez were a Native American tribe that lived on the bank of the Mississippi River near what is now Natchez, Mississippi. They may have come to that area from Mexico. Although they were farmers, they also hunted, made pottery, and wove clothes. They created a society in which everyone knew his and—more important—*her* role. Unfortunately, their way of life, and the people themselves, died out in a period of less than 200 years.

2   The society of the Natchez was based on their religion. The high priest ruled the Natchez, who worshiped him as the "Great Sun," a descendant of the sun god. There were four classes in the Natchez society. The highest class was the Suns, who were rulers and priests and relatives of the Great Sun. The second highest class were the Nobles, and the third highest were the Honored Men. The lowest class, known as Stinkards, served the upper classes. But people rose from one class to another because all people of the upper classes had to marry below them.

3   Although the high priest was the main ruler, the true powers behind Natchez society were women. When a Great Sun died, for example, his mother or sister chose the next Great Sun from among his brothers or sons. Female Suns also led privileged lives. Their husbands were commoners and had to wait on them and obey their commands. If the husband was unfaithful to a Sun woman, she could have him beheaded. But she could be unfaithful to her husband.

4   In 1700, about 4,000 Natchez people lived peacefully in farming communities and grew squash, corn, pumpkins, and beans. But they soon engaged in bloody battles with the French who had settled on their land. In 1729, the French commander of a fort on Natchez territory ordered them to give him their main village for his personal **plantation.** The Natchez were **outraged.** They killed 200 Frenchmen, captured 400 women and children, and burned the fort. The French fought back and slaughtered the Natchez.

plantation: a large farm
outraged: very angry

5   This was the beginning of the end of the tribe. About 400 surrendered and were sold into slavery in the Caribbean Islands. The rest of the survivors—no more than 450—joined other Native American tribes for protection. The slaves soon died, and the rest of the Natchez lost their tribal identity and language. During the 1800s, the United States government forced them to settle in a territory that is now part of Oklahoma. By 1900, there were only 20 Natchez left, and in a short time they disappeared. A **unique** culture and people were erased forever.

unique: very unusual, different from anything like it

Questions for Analysis

1. Find and underline topic sentences in paragraphs 2, 3, and 5. Does the topic sentence always begin the paragraph?
2. Much of the essay is presented in chronological order. Circle the transitional words and phrases that indicate the chronology.
3. Why is an entire essay necessary to define the Natchez? What is the purpose of each paragraph in the composition?
4. Which sentence in paragraph 1 provides a formal definition of the Natchez? What is the function of the body sentences of the paragraph? What is the function of the last sentence of the paragraph?
5. The last two sentences of the opening paragraph introduce key ideas discussed later in the essay. Underline those ideas. Which paragraphs specifically discuss each of the ideas? Identify the idea with a one- or two-word label.

Writing Assignments

1. Write a description of the differing roles of the people in your own family or immediate community. Who is primarily responsible for each important task (making money, caring for children, preparing meals, and so on)? Who shares these responsibilities? Give examples.
2. Describe a typical gathering of your family or community in which different generations perform different roles. It might be an important holiday, a reunion, a traditional dinner, or a monthly or yearly event. What things happen, and who does each one?
3. Describe how some tradition or behavior in your family or community has changed over time. Contrast what used to happen before the change and what happened or happens afterward. Give examples.
4. In your own words, write a short summary of the powers of women described in paragraph 3. Comment.
5. Summarize the essay and then respond. Do you admire the Natchez culture? Why or why not?

The Legacy of Generation Ñ
Christy Haubegger

* * * *

Like all minority groups, Latinos tend to be stereotyped in a number of ways. In the following essay, Christy Haubegger has a bit of fun with the negative stereotypes, and she also presents some surprising facts about Latinos. As you read, notice that Haubegger's main method of development is cause-effect. Also notice the topic sentences in each body paragraph, which also serve as transitions. Finally, notice how Haubegger uses statistics to support her main ideas.

Christy Haubegger was born in Houston, Texas, in 1968 and received a law degree from Stanford University. She is the founder, president, and publisher of Latina *magazine, the first magazine for Hispanic women.*

1   About 20 years ago, some mainstream observers declared the 1980s the "decade of the Hispanic." The Latino population was nearing 15 million! (It's since doubled.) However, our decade was postponed—a managerial oversight, no doubt—and eventually rescheduled for the '90s. What happens to a decade **deferred?** It earns compounded interest and becomes the next 100 years. The United States of the twenty-first century will be undeniably ours. Again.

defer: postpone, delay

a joke based on **manifest destiny:** a belief from the nineteenth century in the United States that "white" people will inevitably rule the native populations, from the Atlantic to the Pacific oceans

assimilate: adopt the customs of another group or country

coup: revolution

condiment: spice

Ricky Martin: a popular Hispanic singer

demographic: a statistical counting of a group with similar characteristics

pivotal: central

anorexia: a disorder in which someone intentionally eats too little

senescence: the beginning of the aging process

The Simpsons: a popular television comedy show

2   It's **Manifest *Destino*.** After all, Latinos are true Americans, some of the original residents of the Américas. Spanish was the first European language spoken on this continent. Which is why we live in places like Los Angeles, Colorado, and Florida rather than The Angels, Colored, and Flowered. Now my generation is about to put a Latin stamp on the rest of the culture—and that will ultimately be the Ñ legacy.

3   We are not only numerous, we are also growing at a rate seven times that of the general population. Conservative political ads notwithstanding, this growth is driven by natural increase (births over deaths) rather than immigration. At 30, I may be the oldest childless *Latina* in the United States. More important, however, while our preceding generation felt pressure to **assimilate,** America has now generously agreed to meet us in the middle. Just as we become more American, America is simultaneously becoming more Latino.

4   This quiet *revolución* can perhaps be traced back to the bloodless **coup** of 1992, when salsa outsold ketchup for the first time. Having toppled the leadership in the **condiment** category, we set our sights even higher. Fairly soon, there was a congresswoman named Sanchez representing Orange County, a taco-shilling Chihuahua became a national icon, and now everyone is *loca* for **Ricky Martin.**

5   We are just getting started. Our geographic concentration and reputation for family values are making us every politician's dream constituency. How long can New Hampshire, with just four Electoral College votes—and probably an equal number of Hispanic residents—continue to get so much attention from presidential candidates? Advertisers will also soon be begging for our attention. With a median age of 26 (eight years younger than the general market), Latinos hardly exist outside their coveted 18–34 **demographic.** Remember, we may only be 11 percent of the country, but we buy 16 percent of the lipliner.

6   The media will change as well, especially television, where we now appear to be rapidly approaching extinction. Of the 26 new comedies and dramas appearing this fall [2003] on the four major networks, not one has a Latino in a leading role. The Screen Actors Guild released employment statistics for 1998 showing that the percentage of roles going to Hispanic actors actually declined from the previous year. But, pretty soon, the cast of *Friends* will need to find some *amigos*. Seeing as they live in New York City, and there's almost 2 million of us in the metropolitan area, this shouldn't prove too difficult. [Editor's Note: The *Friends* season ended in 2004—with no Latinos cast.]

7   Face it: This is going to be a bilingual country. Back in 1849, the California Constitution was written in both Spanish and English, and we're headed that way again. If our children speak two languages instead of just one, how can that not be a benefit to us all? The re-Latinization of this country will pay off in other ways as well. I, for one, look forward to that **pivotal** moment in our history when all American men finally know how to dance. Latin music will no longer be found in record stores under FOREIGN and romance will bloom again. Our children will ask us what it was like to dance without a partner.

8   "American food" will mean low-fat enchiladas and hamburgers served with rice and beans. As a result, the American standard of beauty will necessarily expand to include a female size 12, and **anorexia** will be found only in medical-history books. Finally, just in time for the baby boomers' **senescence,** living with extended family will become hip again. *Simpsons* fans of the next decade will see Grandpa moving back home. We'll all go back to church together.

9   At the dawn of a new millennium, America knows Latinos as entertainers and athletes. But, someday very soon, all American children can dream of growing up to be writers like Sandra Cisneros, astronauts like Ellen Ochoa, or judges like José Cabranes of the Second Circuit Court of Appeals. To put a Latin spin on a famous Anglo phrase: It is truly *mañana* in America. For those of you who don't know it (yet), that word doesn't just mean tomorrow; *mañana* also means morning.

Questions for Analysis

1. What is Haubegger's thesis? Where does she state it?

2. According to Haubegger, what are some of the causes of the "decade of the Hispanic"? What will be some of the effects? Which topic sentences serve to introduce these causes and effects?

3. Who will benefit from these effects?

4. In paragraph 2, Haubegger writes an intentional fragment. Underline it. Why do you think she writes the fragment?

5. Haubegger mixes humorous or trivial statistics and details about Latinos with more significant information. Why? Underline the most significant information.

6. Haubegger also suggests that some common terms will need to be redefined. Which ones? How?

Writing Assignments

1. Write a causal analysis paper on how the influence of a group (for example, teenagers, a specific group of immigrants, or African Americans) has changed some aspect of American culture (food, music, dance, dress, speech, and so on) in the past decade or two.

2. Write a causal analysis paper explaining what has influenced you the most in any one of the following ways: your choice of dress, your decision to study in college, your choice of a profession, or your favorite leisure activities?

3. Write an essay in which you explain the most important benefits to American society that Haubegger thinks Latino culture is creating.

4. Summarize the article and then respond. Do you agree with Haubegger's argument? Do you see the culture of the United States being influenced by another group besides Spanish speakers?

Out of the Sweatshop and into the World
David Masello

* * * *

The experience of many immigrants in the United States is quite different from the myth of "the streets are paved with gold." In the essay that follows, David Masello, an editor of Arts & Antiques *magazine, describes some rather unromantic experiences of people who came from China many years ago. The essay first appeared in* Newsweek *on June 24, 2002.*

As you read the essay, note how Masello backs up his general claims by telling the story of two people. Note, too, how he uses authentic dialogue to make the story realistic. "Devil's Island" refers to a French prison colony in the nineteenth century.

anesthesiologist: a doctor in charge of preventing pain during operations

1   I was surprised last fall when my Chinese students didn't know the term "sweatshop." Lo, a woman in her mid-50s, told me during a class that she had spent 35 years working in a garment factory—not once getting a day off with pay. Sam, who is a few years younger, had stitched collars in Australia for 10 years before coming to New York and doing the same task for five more. He was an **anesthesiologist** in China but is content now to be working as an aide in an East Harlem nursing home where some of his medical training is put to use. Both he and Lo, co-workers at the Florence Nightingale Home, marveled at having two days off every week.

2   "Real luxury," Lo said, "no work two whole days."

3   Still not used to such luxury, Lo said she doesn't know how to use the time, so she often just sits in her favorite chair at home or goes to a second mass at church. And because Sam's workweek is now 40 hours, instead of the 70 he used to put in, he explained that he has time to attend to his Brooklyn garden growing Chinese eggplant, "much better than American eggplant," he insisted.

4   For several years, I have taught English, as a volunteer, to immigrants at Chinatown Manpower Project, a nonprofit organization that provides vocational training and tutoring for people of all ages. Sometimes, when I meet my students, I feel as if I've been handed the wrongly accused, people just released from a Devil's Island compound who never had the chance to learn the language of their adopted country or see neighborhoods beyond their own.

5   One evening a week, I stand before a blackboard in an old public-school classroom, the occasional blur of a mouse disappearing behind radiators, writing down phrases and idioms. Typical conversation topics include happy memories (weddings, births of children), superstitions (it's proper to sprinkle food at grave sites for relatives to enjoy), goals (living in a house with two bedrooms!), and first impressions of America (disappointment at **bleak** neighborhoods, awe at the variety of races).

bleak: without warmth, life, or kindness

6   When I used the word "sweatshop" and my students didn't understand, I sat at a desk pretending to stitch at a sewing machine, pumping an imaginary pedal, mopping my brow with the drama of a silent film star. "Sweating in a shop—or factory—as you work, getting very tired," I explained.

7   "Sweatshop," Lo said, "make sense. Meaning is correct."

wisp: small amounts

8   I've often seen **wisps** of steam funneling from clouded windows in old buildings in Chinatown. Now I know that within those places some of my students are hunched over sewing machines, feeding garments under bobbing needles. The faster they work the more money they make, for payment is by the piece and not the hour.

incurious: without curiosity

9   One of the first topics I cover each semester is which sites my students have visited. Lo, who has lived in New York 25 years, had been to Central Park once and never to the Metropolitan Museum of Art. I used to think some students were **incurious.** I've come to realize that after 70 hours a week at a sewing machine, with pay often below minimum wage, there is no time or energy to admire a Vermeer or see the whitecaps on the Central Park Reservoir some windy Sunday afternoon.

rep: representative
spritz: a spray

10   I take my students on occasional field trips and, during a tour of midtown last September, as we were about to enter Saks Fifth Avenue, Lo bragged that she had made sample fabrics for a fashion show there. When we went inside, an aggressive perfume-company **rep** approached her and asked if she wanted a **spritz** of fragrance and the chance to purchase it and an accompanying silk scarf at a special price. But Lo didn't understand her and laughed out of self-consciousness, whereupon the perfume rep turned to a co-worker and said, "This one hasn't got a clue about fashion."

placket: a hole that a button goes into

11   After class weeks later, Lo and I stopped at a bulletin board in a hallway that displays adult-student projects. Among the items pinned to the board were shirt collars, **plackets,** and zippers. I never knew there were four kinds of zippers—the kissing zipper, overlap, right fly, and invisible. Lo ran the zipper up and down the gleaming track of one of the samples, an invisible.

12   "This what I used to do. I was expert," she said with wistfulness, certainly remembering how hard the job was, but also how it allowed her to remain in the background of American life.

13   "Still scared at my job at nursing home," she admitted to me in class one day. "Too many responsibilities and nobody understand my accent."

14   Over the semester, Lo remained uneasy in her nursing-home job, but never said she missed the old work of zippers and plackets and collars.

Questions for Analysis

1. The first three paragraphs of David Masello's essay describe the history of Lo and Sam. Why does he begin by narrating their stories?
2. In paragraph 4, Masello says that he sometimes feels he has "been handed the wrongly accused." What's his point?
3. How does Masello feel about Lo and Sam? Cite evidence to support your viewpoint.
4. How does Lo feel about the work she used to do? Cite evidence to support your viewpoint.
5. How does Masello handle dialogue (quoted speech) in the essay? How is it punctuated? How are the speakers identified? How does dialogue affect paragraphing? Why has Masello chosen to quote "broken English" in his essay?
6. In paragraph 12, Masello says that Lo's former job allowed her "to remain in the background of American life." Why would Lo wish to be in the background?
7. Masello never directly states a thesis in his essay. What is his central point?

Writing Assignments

1. Did you feel uncomfortable when you first spoke English or another new language? Tell a story about one event—funny, embarrassing, or even frightening—that reveals how you felt.
2. Describe a past or current job that gave or gives you pride. Explain why.
3. Describe a past or current job that you hated or hate. Explain why.
4. Write a narrative about how you had to adjust to some cultural change—perhaps a change from the way things are done in your native country or your family to how they are done in your current environment.
5. Write an essay on any of the topics Masello mentions in paragraph 5.
6. Summarize the essay and then respond. How do you feel about the people Masello describes?

The Struggle to Be an All-American Girl
Elizabeth Wong

* * * *

Many people in the United States are bilingual, speaking one language at home or in their community and another language at school or work. And many people face conflicts between the traditions and desires of their parents and their own desires to assimilate—fit in—within the "all-American" culture. Elizabeth Wong was one of those people. Her mother insisted that Elizabeth and her brother attend a Chinese language school, and the essay that follows explores the conflicts involved. As you read it, notice the physical description that reinforces Wong's feelings toward the school. Notice the contrasts between the lessons of the Chinese school and the American school, the life in Chinatown and outside of Chinatown, and the attitudes toward speaking Chinese and speaking English.

Elizabeth Wong, who grew up in Los Angeles's Chinatown, is an award-winning Chinese playwright whose works focus on Asian American subject matter. Among her plays are China Doll, Letters to a Student Revolutionary, *and* Kimchee & Chitlins. *She was the staff writer for the television sitcom* All-American Girl.

stoic: without feeling or emotion

dissuade: persuade not to do something

repressed: self-controlled
maniacal: crazy

mustiness: damp smell

flanked: placed on both sides

ideograph: writing that represents ideas in pictures
blotches: puddles of ink

raunchy: crude, vulgar

pedestrian (adjective): slow or common

chaotic: out of control, wild
frenzied: desperate and crazy
gibberish: meaningless words

fanatical: extremely determined
pidgin: simplified language between people who speak different languages
smattering: tiny amounts
exasperation: frustration

infuriate: make very angry

1 It's still there, the Chinese school on Yale Street where my brother and I used to go. Despite the new coat of paint and the high wire fence, the school I knew 10 years ago remains remarkably, **stoically** the same.

2 Every day at 5 P.M., instead of playing with our fourth- and fifth-grade friends or sneaking out to the empty lot to hunt ghosts and animal bones, my brother and I had to go to Chinese school. No amount of kicking, screaming, or pleading could **dissuade** my mother, who was solidly determined to have us learn the language of our heritage.

3 Forcibly, she walked us the seven long, hilly blocks from our home to school, depositing our defiant tearful faces before the stern principal. My only memory of him is that he swayed on his heels like a palm tree, and he always clasped his impatient twitching hands behind his back. I recognized him as a **repressed maniacal** child killer, and knew that if we ever saw his hands we'd be in big trouble.

4 We all sat in little chairs in an empty auditorium. The room smelled like Chinese medicine, an imported faraway **mustiness.** Like ancient mothballs or dirty closets. I hated that smell. I favored crisp new scents. Like the soft French perfume that my American teacher wore in public school.

5 There was a stage far to the right, **flanked** by an American flag and the flag of the Nationalist Republic of China, which was also red, white, and blue but not as pretty.

6 Although the emphasis at the school was mainly language—speaking, reading, writing—the lessons always began with an exercise in politeness. With the entrance of the teacher, the best student would tap a bell and everyone would get up, kowtow, and chant, "Sing san ho," the phonetic for "How are you, teacher?"

7 Being ten years old, I had better things to learn than **ideographs** copied painstakingly in lines that ran right to left from the tip of a *moc but,* a real ink pen that had to be held in an awkward way if **blotches** were to be avoided. After all, I could do the multiplication tables, name the satellites of Mars, and write reports on *Little Women* and *Black Beauty.* Nancy Drew, my favorite book heroine, never spoke Chinese.

8 The language was a source of embarrassment. More times than not, I had tried to disassociate myself from the nagging loud voice that followed me wherever I wandered in the nearby American supermarket outside Chinatown. The voice belonged to my grandmother, a fragile woman in her seventies who could outshout the best of the street vendors. Her humor was **raunchy,** her Chinese rhythmless, patternless. It was quick, it was loud, it was unbeautiful. It was not like the quiet, lilting romance of French or the gentle refinement of the American South. Chinese sounded **pedestrian.** Public.

9 In Chinatown, the comings and goings of hundreds of Chinese on their daily tasks sounded **chaotic** and **frenzied.** I did not want to be thought of as mad, as talking **gibberish.** When I spoke English, people nodded at me, smiled sweetly, said encouraging words. Even the people in my culture would cluck and say that I'd do well in life. "My, doesn't she move her lips fast," they would say, meaning that I'd be able to keep up with the world outside Chinatown.

10 My brother was even more **fanatical** than I about speaking English. He was especially hard on my mother, criticizing her, often cruelly, for her **pidgin** speech— **smatterings** of Chinese scattered like chop suey in her conversation. "It's not 'What it is,' Mom," he'd say in **exasperation.** "It's 'What is it, what is it, what is it!'" Sometimes Mom might leave out an occasional "the" or "a," or perhaps a verb of being. He would stop her in mid sentence: "Say it again, Mom. Say it right." When he tripped over his own tongue, he'd blame it on her: "See, Mom, it's all your fault. You set a bad example."

11 What **infuriated** my mother most was when my brother cornered her on her consonants, especially "r." My father had played a cruel joke on Mom by assigning her an American name that her tongue wouldn't allow her to say. No matter how hard she tried, "Ruth" always ended up "Luth" or "Roof."

12 After two years of writing with a *moc but* and reciting words with multiples of meanings, I finally was granted a cultural divorce. I was permitted to stop Chinese school.

13 I thought of myself as multicultural. I preferred tacos to egg rolls; I enjoyed **Cinco de Mayo** more than Chinese New Year. At last, I was one of you; I wasn't one of them. Sadly, I still am.

Cinco de Mayo: Fifth of May, which is a Mexican national holiday celebrating its victory over France in a battle in 1862

Questions for Analysis

1. What is the thesis—the main point—of the essay? Wong develops her essay through a series of contrasts, often using very specific details. Underline each one. How do these contrasts support the thesis?

2. Wong's story combines description, narration, and comparison-contrast. What comparisons or contrasts does she make? Underline them.

3. What did Wong learn in Chinese school? Was it only the Chinese language?

4. Wong says in the eighth paragraph that Chinese "was a source of embarrassment." Why?

5. What do you think Wong means by her comments in paragraph 13, especially the concluding sentence?

Writing Assignments

1. Wong probably would never go back to the Chinese language school. Describe a place that you would never go back to again, and make clear to the reader why.

2. Describe a behavior of an adult (a parent, perhaps) that used to embarrass you, and explain why. Or, describe some aspect of your background that used to embarrass you, and explain why.

3. Visit a place, perhaps from your childhood, that you haven't been to in a long time. Describe it now, and compare it to how you remembered it.

4. Contrast at least one way in which your behavior at home is different from your behavior outside of home. Develop the contrast through specific examples.

5. Contrast one way in which a high school in another country differs from a high school in the United States—or the ways in which any two schools differ.

6. Explain why Elizabeth Wong was embarrassed by her grandmother's and mother's speech. Cite examples from Wong's essay to support your explanation.

7. Summarize the selection and then respond. Which of Wong's viewpoints toward being multicultural do you most agree with—the viewpoint she had as a child, or the one she seems to have as an adult? (Look again at the last paragraph of the essay.)

Melting Pot
Anna Quindlen

* * * *

As the title of this essay reminds us, America is supposed to be a great melting pot, in which people from many backgrounds melt together. But the melting is not easy. When new groups move in, the neighborhoods change, and not always in ways that the old groups like. Think about changes you've seen in the neighborhoods where you grew up or moved into. Think about the prejudices you've faced and perhaps felt. In the essay that follows, Anna Quindlen discusses the changes in her neighborhood in New York. As you read it, notice how it begins with a discussion of the melting pot, and then how it discusses both the hostility and friendliness between groups. Notice how the essay begins in the present tense and then switches to the past tense. Notice, also, how Quindlen is able to illustrate her main ideas with her own experiences, now and as a child.

Anna Quindlen, who was born in 1953, is a Pulitzer Prize–winning columnist who currently writes for Newsweek *magazine. She is the author of many best-selling books. Her nonfiction books include* Thinking Out Loud *and* A Short Guide to a Happy Life. *Her books of fiction include* One True Thing *and* Black and Blue.

1   My children are upstairs in the house next door, having dinner with the Ecuadorian family that lives on the top floor. The father speaks some English, the mother less than that. The two daughters are fluent in both their native and their adopted languages, but the youngest child, a son, a close friend of my two boys, speaks almost no Spanish. His parents thought it would be better that way. This doesn't surprise me; it was the way my mother was raised, American among Italians. I always suspected, hearing my grandfather talk about the "No Irish Need Apply" signs outside factories, hearing my mother talk about the neighborhood kids, who called her greaseball, that the American fable of the melting pot was a myth. Here in our neighborhood it exists, but like so many other things, it exists only person-to-person.

tabloid: a newspaper that includes sensational stories

2   The letters in the local weekly **tabloid** suggest that everybody hates everybody else here, and on a macro level they do. The old-timers are angry because they think the new moneyed professionals are taking over their town. The professionals are tired of being blamed for the neighborhood's rising rents, particularly since they are the ones paying them. The old immigrants are suspicious of the new ones. The new ones think the old ones are **bigots.** Nevertheless, on a micro level most of us get along. We are friendly with the Ecuadorian family, with the Yugoslavs across the street, and with the Italians next door, mainly by virtue of our children's sidewalk friendships. It took a while. Eight years ago we were the new people on the block, filling dumpsters with old plaster and lath, drinking beer on the stoop with our demolition masks banging around our necks like **goiters.** We thought we could feel people staring at us from behind the sheer curtains on their windows. We were right.

bigot: prejudiced against other people

goiter: growths on the neck

3   My first apartment in New York was in a gritty warehouse district, the kind of place that makes your parents wince. A lot of old Italians lived around me, which suited me just fine because I was the granddaughter of old Italians. Their own children and grandchildren had moved to Long Island and New Jersey. All they had was me. All I had was them.

glazier: a glass installer

4   I remember sitting on a corner with a group of half a dozen elderly men, men who had known one another since they were boys sitting together on this same corner, watching a **glazier** install a great spread of tiny glass panes to make one wall of a restaurant in the ground floor of an old building across the street. The men laid bets on how long the panes, and the restaurant, would last. Two years later two of the men were dead, one had moved in with his married daughter in the suburbs, and the three remaining sat and watched **dolefully** as people waited each night for a table in the restaurant. "Twenty-two dollars for a piece of veal!" one of them would say, **apropos** of nothing. But when I ate in the restaurant they never blamed me. "You're not one of them," one of the men explained. "You're one of me." It's an argument familiar to members of almost any **embattled** race or class: I like you, therefore you aren't like the rest of your kind, whom I hate.

dolefully: sadly
apropos: referring to

embattled: discriminated against

5   Change comes hard in America, but it comes constantly. The butcher whose old shop is now an antiques store sits day after day outside the pizzeria here like a lost child. The old people across the street cluster together and discuss what kind of money they might be offered if the person who bought their building wants to turn it into condominiums.

gourmands: food lovers

plantain: a type of fruit

bodega: a store specializing in Hispanic foods

6

calamari: squid served as a special food

sushi: Japanese food, typically fish, that is spiced and served raw

firebrand: politically radical or extreme

pressure cooker: a special pot for cooking foods under high pressure

8

The greengrocer stocks yellow peppers and fresh rosemary for the **gourmands,** plum tomatoes and broad-leaf parsley for the older Italians, mangoes for the Indians. He doesn't carry **plantains,** he says, because you can buy them in the **bodega.**

Sometimes the baby slips out with the bath water. I wanted to throw confetti the day that a family of rough types who propped their speakers on their station wagon and played heavy metal music at 3:00 A.M. moved out. I stood and smiled as the seedy bar at the corner was transformed into a slick Mexican restaurant. But I liked some of the people who moved out at the same time the rough types did. And I'm not sure I have that much in common with the singles who have made the restaurant their second home.

7

Yet somehow now we seem to have reached a nice mix. About a third of the people in the neighborhood think of squid as **calamari,** about a third think of it as **sushi,** and about a third think of it as bait. Lots of the single people who have moved in during the last year or two are easygoing and good-tempered about all the kids. The old Italians have become philosophical about the new Hispanics, although they still think more of them should know English. The **firebrand** community organizer with the storefront on the block, the one who is always talking about people like us as though we stole our houses out of the open purse of a 90-year-old blind widow, is pleasant to my boys.

Drawn in broad strokes, we live in a **pressure cooker:** oil and water, us and them. But if you come around at exactly the right time, you'll find members of all these groups gathered around complaining about the condition of the streets on which everyone can agree. We melt together, then draw apart. I am the granddaughter of immigrants, a young professional—either an interloper or a longtime resident depending on your concept of time. I am one of them, and one of us.

Questions for Analysis

1. Anna Quindlen is the child of parents of two different nationalities. Based on the information in paragraph 1, what are those nationalities?

2. Quindlen states her thesis in the first paragraph. Underline it. How does she support her thesis?

3. The term "moneyed professionals" appears in paragraph 2. From context, what do you think it means? Likewise, the terms "macro level" and "micro level" also appear. What, from context, do they mean?

4. Based on the information in paragraphs 3 and 4, what seems to be the main reason that Quindlen got along with her neighbors?

5. What is the topic sentence of paragraph 5? What point does the sentence about the greengrocer illustrate?

6. Paragraph 6 begins with an old expression about a baby and bath water. The paragraph then describes two groups who moved out of the neighborhood. Write, in your own words, a statement of what the baby-and-bath-water expression means in this context.

7. Paragraph 7 contains a sentence about how people in her neighborhood think of squid. But the point of the sentence really isn't about squid—it's about the people. Write, in your own words, a statement about what Quindlen is saying in that sentence. (Be sure you understand the words *calamari, sushi,* and *bait*.)

8. Quindlen says that the melting pot exists, but "only person to person." Explain what she means.

Writing Assignments

1. Have you ever encountered prejudice against your nationality, religion, or race? What happened? How did you react?

2. Have you ever moved from one community or country to another? Discuss one or more adjustments that you had to make.

3. Describe a change that you've seen in your neighborhood or community. What has resulted from that change? If the change was supposed to benefit the people there, has everyone benefited? Give examples.

4. Quindlen uses the terms *melting pot* and *pressure cooker* to describe the life in her neighborhood and society. Write an essay in which you define the terms and show how they apply to your life.

5. Summarize the article and then respond. Do you agree with Quindlen's viewpoint on different people's ability to get along with each other?

Common Irregular Verbs

Present tense	Past tense	Past participle
be (am, are, is)	was, were	been
beat	beat	beaten
become	became	become
begin	began	begun
bend	bent	bent
bet	bet	bet
bind	bound	bound
bite	bit	bitten
bleed	bled	bled
blow	blew	blown
break	broke	broken
breed	bred	bred
bring	brought	brought
build	built	built
burst	burst	burst
buy	bought	bought
cast	cast	cast
catch	caught	caught
choose	chose	chosen
come	came	come
cost	cost	cost
creep	crept	crept
cut	cut	cut
deal	dealt	dealt
dig	dug	dug
do	did	done
draw	drew	drawn
dream	dreamt (dreamed)	dreamt (dreamed)
drink	drank	drunk
drive	drove	driven
eat	ate	eaten
fall	fell	fallen
feed	fed	fed
feel	felt	felt
fight	fought	fought
find	found	found
fit	fit	fit
flee	fled	fled
fly	flew	flown
forget	forgot	forgotten
forgive	forgave	forgiven
freeze	froze	frozen

Present tense	Past tense	Past participle
get	got	gotten
give	gave	given
go	went	gone
grind	ground	ground
grow	grew	grown
hang	hung, hanged	hung, hanged
have	had	had
hear	heard	heard
hide	hid	hidden
hit	hit	hit
hold	held	held
hurt	hurt	hurt
keep	kept	kept
know	knew	known
lay	laid	laid
lead	led	led
leave	left	left
lend	lent	lent
let	let	let
lie	lay	lain
light	lit (or lighted)	lit (or lighted)
lose	lost	lost
make	made	made
mean	meant	meant
meet	met	met
pay	paid	paid
put	put	put
quit	quit	quit
read	read	read
ride	rode	ridden
ring	rang	rung
rise	rose	risen
run	ran	run
say	said	said
see	saw	seen
sell	sold	sold
send	sent	sent
set	set	set
shake	shook	shaken
shed	shed	shed
shine	shone, shined	shone, shined
shoot	shot	shot
show	showed	shown

Present tense	Past tense	Past participle	Present tense	Past tense	Past participle
shrink	shrank	shrunk	strive	strove	striven
shut	shut	shut	swear	swore	sworn
sing	sang	sung	sweep	swept	swept
sink	sank	sunk	swim	swam	swum
sit	sat	sat	swing	swung	swung
slay	slew	slain	take	took	taken
sleep	slept	slept	teach	taught	taught
slide	slid	slid	tear	tore	torn
slit	slit	slit	tell	told	told
speak	spoke	spoken	think	thought	thought
spend	spent	spent	throw	threw	thrown
spin	spun	spun	thrust	thrust	thrust
split	split	split	understand	understood	understood
spread	spread	spread	wake	woke	woken
stand	stood	stood	wear	wore	worn
steal	stole	stolen	weave	wove	woven
stick	stuck	stuck	win	won	won
sting	stung	stung	wind	wound	wound
stink	stank	stunk	withdraw	withdrew	withdrawn
strike	struck	struck	write	wrote	written

Commonly Misspelled Words

Add your own words to the list as you look up their correct spellings.

absenCe	diffERent/diffERence	mathematics	strenGTH
aCCept	diSAPPoint	miLLeNNium	SURpriSE
accomplish	DISease	misCHIEF	temPERature
accommodate	doESN'T	miSSpell	THROUGH
aCCurate	duRing	nIEce	thoROUGH
achIEvement	eiGHTH	ninETY	ThurSday
acquaintANCE	embaRRass	ninTH	toMoRRow
aCRoss	enTRANCE	oCCasion	unNECESsary
adverTISEment	enveLOPE	oCCuRRENCE	UNusually
adVICE/adVISE	enviRONment	opINion	WedNESday
A LOT	especIALLY	oPPortunity	
AnSWer	exaGGerate	oRIGinal	**Your own words:**
aPPropriate	EXcept	opTImist	
arGUment	existENCE	partiCULAR	
artiCLE	exPERIENCE	PAStime	
aTHLete	exPERIment	PERform	
attenDANCE	exPLANAtion	PERhaps	
availABLE	exTREMEly	phoNY	
bEAUtiful	familIAR	phySICAL	
begiNNing	faSCinate	poSSess	
behaVIOR	FeBRUary	preFER	
breaTH/breathE	forEIGN	prejudiced	
BUSiness	genIUS	PREscription	
calENDAR	goVERNment	preVALENT	
cEIling	gramMAR	priviLEGE	
certAINly	guarANtee	proBABly	
chIEf	hEIGHT	proNUNciation	
choiCe	iMMediate	PSYchology	
chOOse/chOse	imporTANT	PURsue	
coMMerCIAL	indepenDENCE	quIET/quITE	
coMMiTTee	inTEGration	REALize	
compETItion	inTELLectual	reCEIve	
conCentrate	inTERest/inTEResting	recoMMend	
congRATulate	inTERfere	RHyTHM	
conSCIENCE	inteRRupt	ridicULOUS	
conscious	iRRELevant	scenERy	
conSENSus	jUDGment	SCHEDule	
consEquently	jEWELry	SECRETary	
convenIEnce	knowLEDGE	SePARate	
counSelor	laBORATory	sIEge	
criticiSM/criticIZE	leiSURE	simILAR	
deFINITEly	liCenSe	sinCE	
desPErate	lONELiness	sinCEREly	
dESCribe	lOOse/lOse	spEEch	
develOP	mainTENance	straiGHT	

Infinitive and Gerund Objects after Verbs

Infinitives (for example, *to go, to do*) and gerunds (words ending in *-ing* such as *going, doing,* and so on) are formed from verbs but often function as nouns. Notice that the same sentence pattern of subject-transitive verb-object, shown below, can contain a noun object, an infinitive object, or a gerund object.

subject	verb	direct object
I	love	steak. (noun)
I	love	*to eat.* (infinitive)
I	love	*eating.* (gerund)

However, some verbs can take only an infinitive, other verbs can take only a gerund, and a few other verbs can take either. You may wish to memorize the following lists of the three types of verbs, or to use the lists for reference.

I. Transitive verbs that take infinitive objects

I decided to do it.

afford	decide	intend	propose
agree	demand	learn	remember
appear	deserve	manage	refuse
arrange	expect	mean	seem
ask	fail	need	start
attempt	get	offer	tend
begin	happen	prepare	try
choose	hate	pretend	want
come	hesitate	proceed	wait
continue	hope	promise	wish
dare			

II. Transitive verbs that take both an indirect object and an infinitive direct object

  i.o. d.o.
John asked *him to finish.*

  i.o. d.o.
I want *Julio to succeed.*

allow	expect	love	request
appoint	forbid	need	require
ask	force	order	select
cause	get	permit	send
choose	hire	persuade	teach
dare	instruct	prefer	tell
enable	invite	remind	want
encourage	like		

III. Transitive verbs that take an indirect object and the infinitive without *to*

> He *had* me finish.

have	help	make	see
hear	let	perceive	watch

IV. Verbs that take gerunds as objects

> I quit *doing* it.
>
> He dislikes *driving*.

admit	defer	hate	prefer
appreciate	delay	imagine	quit
avoid	deny	like	regret
begin	dislike	love	remember
complete	enjoy	mind	stop
consider	fear	miss	suggest
continue	finish	postpone	try

V. Verbs can take either an infinitive or a gerund object, although sometimes with different meanings

> Wanda remembered to do it. (She did it after she remembered.)
>
> Wanda remembered doing it. (She did it before remembering.)

begin	hate	love	remember
continue	like	prefer	try

Common Phrasal Verbs

Separable phrasal verbs

ask for, out
back up
blow up
break down, off, up
bring about, out
build up
burn up
call back
call off
check out, over
cheer up
clean out, up
cool off, down
cross off, out
cut off, up
do over
dress up
drink up
drive back

drop off
dry off, up
dust off, up
eat up
figure out
fill in, out, up
find out
fix up
follow up
get back, down, out
give away, up
hand in, out
hang up
have on
help out
hold up
keep down, on, up
knock out
leave on, out

let in, on, off, out, up
look over, up
make up
mix up
open up
pass out, up
pay off, out
pick out, up
plug in, up
point out
put aside, away, down,
    in, off, on, up
rub off
set up
shut down, off, out
slow down, up
speed up
stand up
straighten out, up

sweep out, up
take away, back, off, on, out,
    over, up
talk out, over, up
tear up
tell apart
think over
try on, out
turn around, down, in, into,
    off, on, out, over, up
use over, up
warm up
wash out, up
wear out
wipe off, up
work out
write down, off

Inseparable phrasal verbs

agree on
allow for
amount to
back out of
become of
bump into
care about
check up
come across
come along with
come back to, out of, over to, through
  with, up to
count on
deal in, with
do without
drop in, on, out of
feel like

get ahead of
get into, off, on, out of, over,
    through with
go into, on with
grow out of
hear about
hold on to
keep on with, up with
look at, for, out for
meet with
occur to
part with
plan on
put up with
read up on
run into, across, off, with, out of, over
see about

send for, away for
side with
speak about, for, of
stand by, up for
stick to
take up with
talk about, back to
think about, back on, of
try out for
turn into
wait for, on
walk out on
watch out for
work on

Common Expressions Using Prepositions

afraid *of* something

agree *with* someone *about* something

angry *at* someone

angry *with* something

approve *of* someone or something

argue *about* something

argue *with* someone *for* (or *about*) something

arrive *at* a place *in* a city or country

ashamed *of* something

ask someone *for* something

at the top of

aware *of* someone or something

because *of* something or someone

believe *in* something

blame someone *for* something

call *to* someone *from* a distance

call someone *on* the telephone

certain *of* something

close *to* something or someone

comment *on* someone or something

communicate something *to* someone

complain *to* someone *about* something

composed *of* something

concerned *about* someone or something

confidence *in* someone or something

confident *of* something

contribute *to* something

control *over* someone or something

copy *from* someone

correspond *with* someone

deal *with* someone or something

decide *on* something

demand something *of* someone

depend *on* someone *for* something

different *from* someone or something

disagree *with* someone *about* something

disappointed *in* or *by* something

disappointed *with* someone

do something *about* something

due *to* someone or something

engaged *to* someone

escape *from* something

excuse *for* something

explain something *to* someone

fall *in* love *with* someone

for the purpose *of*

full *of* something

grateful *to* someone *for* something

hear *about* something

hear *of* something

in case *of*

in favor *of*

in spite *of*

introduce someone *to* someone

invite someone *to* something

knock *at* or *on* a door

laugh *at* something or someone

listen *to* someone or something

look *at* someone or something

look *for* something or someone

look *up* something *in* a reference book

made *of* something

make something *for* someone

need *for* something

on account *of*

pay someone *for* something

pay something *to* someone

prejudiced *against* someone or something

punish someone *for* something

qualification *for* a job

quote something *from* someone

reason *for* something

related *to* someone

remind someone *of* something

reply *to* someone *about* something

result *from* a cause

result *in* a consequence

search *for* something

send *for* something

similar *to* someone or something

smile *at* someone

stare *at* someone

start *with* something

supply someone *with* something

sure *of* something

take advantage *of* someone or something

take care *of* someone or something

talk *to* someone *about* something

tell someone *of* or *about* something

think *of* or *about* or *over* something

wait *for* someone or something

worry *about* something

Glossary

A

Acronym: a word made up of the first letter of each word it represents, such as *Scuba* (self-contained underwater breathing apparatus)

Action verb: a verb that states what a subject does, did, or will do.

Active voice: a sentence structure in which the subject performs the action of the verb.

Adjective: a word or group of words that describe a noun or pronoun.

Adverb: a word or group of words that describe a verb (or a word formed from a verb, such as an *-ing word* or an *infinitive*), telling *when, where, why, how,* or *how often* the action happens or happened. Adverbs (especially adverbs such as *very, really, too,* and *somewhat*) can also describe adjectives or other adverbs.

Adverb clause: a clause beginning with a subordinating conjunction such as *if, because, when,* or *before* that functions as an adverb.

Agreement: the use of matching or correct forms between subject and verb or pronoun and antecedent. Singular or plural nouns or pronouns must agree in form with their verbs or with the pronouns that refer to them.

Antecedent: the word or words that come before a pronoun and which the pronoun refers to.

Apostrophe: a punctuation mark ['] that shows possession before or after *-s* on nouns, replaces omitted letters in contractions, or forms the plurals of letters before adding *-s*.

Appositive: a noun that adds identifying information about a noun that precedes it.

Articles: the words *a, an,* and *the,* which determine whether a noun is specific or not specific.

B

Block Organization: see *whole-to-whole organization.*

Body: the central part of a paragraph or essay that develops and explains the topic sentence of the paragraph or the thesis statement of the essay.

Brainstorming: a part of prewriting in which you list thoughts as they come to you.

C

Call for action: a persuasive appeal to an audience that they do something.

Causal analysis: an organization that examines the causes of an event or the results of an event. It is also called *cause-effect organization.*

Cause-effect organization: see *causal analysis.*

Chronological order: an organization of events according to how they occur in a time sequence. This organization is found most often in narratives, process analysis, and cause-effect papers.

Claim: a statement that needs proof, explanation, or both. Topic sentences and thesis statements usually make a claim.

Classification: an organization that divides the subject matter into categories determined by one criterion, or standard.

Clause: a group of words containing both a subject and a verb. Every sentence must contain at least one clause, although many sentences contain more than one.

Cliché: a tired and overused expression.

Climax order: an organizational arrangement going from the least important to the most important information and often ending dramatically.

Clustering: a part of prewriting in which you explore and organize your thoughts in a chart. Begin by writing and circling the topic in the middle of the page, then draw lines (or branches) to circles in which you write related ideas. You can also draw branches and attach circles to each of the related ideas until you fill up the whole page.

Coherence: the quality in which the relationship between ideas is clear throughout a paragraph or essay.

Collective noun: a noun such as *class, orchestra,* or *team* that represents a group of people or things. Most—but not all—collective nouns are grammatically singular in American English.

Colon: a punctuation mark [:] that functions like an equal sign. It is most often used to show that the last words of a grammatically complete statement are equal to what follows—usually a list or long quotation.

Comma: a punctuation mark [,] used for separating ideas or, with two commas, enclosing ideas.

Comma-spliced sentence: a sentence containing two independent clauses incorrectly joined by a comma. This is a serious, but common, grammatical error.

Command: a sentence that tells the reader what to do or what not to do. The command begins with a verb and omits the implied subject *you.*

Common noun: a noun that represents, but does not name, something and is therefore not capitalized.

Comparative form: the form of an adjective or adverb ending in *-er* or preceded by *more,* showing that the two things being compared are not equal.

Comparison-contrast: an organization that shows similarities and differences between two or more subjects. The organization can be whole-to-whole or part-to-part.

Complex sentence: a sentence containing an independent clause and a dependent clause that begins with a word such as *after, because, if, who, that,* or *which.*

Compound predicate: a predicate containing two or more verbs.

Compound sentence: a sentence containing two independent clauses, each of which could be a sentence by itself.

Compound subject: a subject consisting of two or more nouns and/or pronouns joined by *and.*

Compound word: a word formed by joining two complete words—sometimes with a hyphen and sometimes without.

Conclusion: the last sentence of a paragraph or last paragraph of an essay, which ties together the preceding ideas and strongly ends the work.

Conditional sentence: a sentence including a condition that is necessary for an event to occur. The condition is usually introduced by *if* or *unless*.

Conjunction: a joining word or phrase (see *coordinating conjunctions* and *subordinating conjunctions*).

Conjunctive adverb: a word that often follows a semicolon to explain how or in what way the two clauses joined by the semicolon are logically related. A conjunctive adverb is also called a *transitional word*.

Consonant: a sound represented by any of the letters of the alphabet that do not represent the vowel sounds.

Contraction: a joining of two words that requires the omission of a letter or several letters from the second word. An apostrophe occupies the spot of the missing letter(s).

Coordinating conjunction: a word that joins grammatically equal structures. There are only seven coordinating conjunctions: *for, and, nor, but, or, yet, so.*

Coordination: the joining of two or more grammatically equal structures, usually with a coordinating conjunction or a semicolon.

Count nouns: nouns that can be either singular or plural.

Criterion: the method used in classifying things—such as by size, frequency, or age.

D

Dangling modifier: a modifier that does not modify any word or phrase in a sentence.

Dash: a punctuation mark [—] used to separate and enclose items that dramatically interrupt a sentence. Internal items require two dashes, while end items require one.

Definite article: *the*, which makes a noun specific.

Definition: an organization that explains the meaning of a term, often by providing examples and contrasting it with similar terms.

Demonstrative adjectives: the pronouns *this, that, these,* and *those,* when used before nouns—as in "this man" or "these cars."

Demonstrative pronouns: the pronouns *this, that, these,* and *those,* when used without nouns (see *demonstrative adjectives).*

Dependent clause: a clause that cannot stand alone as a sentence but must be joined to an independent clause to complete its meaning. Most dependent clauses begin with words such as *because, although, if, that, which,* or *who.*

Detail: a smaller part of something larger. Details usually support generalizations.

Description: writing that creates a mental picture of something, often of a scene.

Direct object: the word or words (usually nouns or pronouns) following and receiving the action of a verb, following a word formed from a verb (such as an infinitive, a past participle, or an *-ing* word), or following a preposition.

Direct question: a question that forms a complete sentence ending in a question mark and places the verb (or first helping verb) before the subject.

Direct quotation: the exact words of a speaker or writer, placed in quotation marks.

Double negative: a type of grammatical error in which two negative words express one negative idea. Only one negative word should be used.

E

Edit: one of the last steps in the writing process in which you check over your second or third draft for misspelled words, words left out or repeated, grammatical errors, missing word endings, incomplete sentences, and incorrect punctuation.

Effect: the result of some action or event (see *causal analysis).*

Ellipsis marks: three dots (. . .) that indicate something has been omitted from a quote.

Essay: an organized discussion of a topic in a series of paragraphs—usually at least five paragraphs and often many more. Ideally, the introductory paragraph attracts the readers' attention, states the thesis of the essay, and outlines its structure. The body paragraphs present each main supporting point of the thesis. The concluding paragraph summarizes the ideas and brings the paper to a strong ending.

Example: a specific illustration of a concept.

Exclamation: a statement of strong emotion ending in an exclamation point [!].

Exclamation point: an end punctuation mark [!] that shows strong emotion.

F

Formal definition: the kind of explanation of a word's meaning found in a dictionary. A formal definition first places the word in a category and then explains its distinguishing characteristics.

Four Ws: *who, what, where, when*—usually included in a description of a scene or a narrative.

Fragment: an incomplete sentence because (1) it is missing either a subject, a verb, or both; (2) the verb is incomplete; or (3) it is only a dependent clause and must be attached to an independent clause.

Freewriting: exploring your ideas in paragraph form without concern for grammar, spelling, or organization.

Future perfect tense: a tense referring to an action or event completed before a later time in the future. This tense always contains three words: *will* + *have* + past participle.

Future progressive tense: a tense that expresses an action in progress at a later time. It is formed from *will* + *be* + the present participle.

Future true conditional: a statement that means "If this circumstance happens, the result will probably happen." It includes a clause beginning with *if* and a present tense verb and a clause in the future tense.

G

Gerund: a present participle used as a noun.

H

Have to: a verb phrase that expresses necessity in the present, past, or future. The phrase consists of *have/has/had/will have* + full infinitive. The negative form (*doesn't/don't/didn't have* + infinitive) expresses lack of necessity.

Helping verb: the parts of the verb before the main verb, conveying the most important information about verb tense or mood.

Hyphen: the punctuation mark [-] used for joining words and for separating words between syllables at the end of a line.

I

Imperative sentence: see *command*.

Indefinite article: the word *a* or *an*, which precedes singular, nonspecific count nouns.

Indefinite pronouns: pronouns such as *everyone, nowhere,* or *something* that do not refer to a specific person, place, or thing.

Independent clause: a clause that can stand alone as a sentence.

Indirect object: a noun or pronoun following a verb that receives a direct object.

Indirect question: a question contained within a larger statement that uses the word order of a statement. An indirect question does not end with a question mark.

Infinitive: a word formed from a verb but that does not have a tense and that functions as an adjective, adverb, or noun.

-ing word: a word formed from a verb that functions either as a noun, an adjective, or an adverb. An *-ing* word can also be part of a verb if some form of *to be* precedes it, such as *is going, was going,* or *will be going* (see *present participle*).

Interrogative pronoun: a pronoun, such as *who, which, what,* or *where,* that begins a question.

Intransitive verb: a verb that cannot take a direct object. Any object after an intransitive verb must be preceded by a preposition.

Introduction: the beginning of a paragraph or essay, which attracts the readers' interest and usually includes the point of the paragraph in a topic sentence or, for an essay, in a thesis statement.

Irregular nouns: nouns that do not form plurals by adding *-s*.

Irregular verbs: (1) verbs that do not simply add *-s* for present tense subject-verb agreement but make larger changes, or (2) verbs that do not form the past tense or past participle by adding *-ed*. These verbs change internally or do not change form at all.

L

Linking verb: a verb that does not express action but merely links the subject to the word or words that describe the subject. The most common linking verbs are *to be* (*is, am, was, were,* etc.) and the verbs representing the five senses: *look, feel, smell, sound,* and *taste*.

M

Main idea: the central idea, or claim, of a paragraph or essay.

Main verb: the last word in a verb phrase, conveying the most important information about the action the verb expresses.

Metaphor: a way to make writing livelier by discussing your actual topic (such as *thinking*) in terms of another (*brewing up* or *cooking up ideas*).

Modal verb: a helping verb that does not change form for tense or agreement and that expresses an attitude toward its subject. Modals include *can, could, may, might, must, ought to, should, will, would, had better* and *have to* (which does change form for tense and agreement).

Modifier: a word or group of words that function as an adjective or an adverb.

N

Narration: a story, usually told in a chronological order, or a sequence of consecutive events that build to a climax, which ends the story. A narration often includes dialogue.

Noncount nouns: nouns that represent an idea or subject that cannot be counted, such as *air, water,* or *furniture.*

Nonrestrictive relative clause: a clause that provides information not essential to the meaning of the noun it relates to, so the clause is enclosed by two commas.

Noun: a word that functions as a subject or an object and can be replaced by a pronoun. A noun usually represents a person, place, idea, or thing.

Noun clause: a clause that functions as a noun, usually beginning with *what, that, where, why,* or *when.*

Number: the singular or plural forms of nouns or pronouns.

O

Object: a word or words (usually nouns or pronouns) following action verbs; words formed from verbs (*-ing* words, past participles, and infinitives), prepositions, or other objects (see *direct object* and *indirect object*).

Object complement: in some sentence patterns, an adjective following an object that describes or renames it.

Object pronoun: a pronoun form (*me, us, you, him, her, it,* or *them*) that follows verbs, prepositions, or words formed from verbs.

Objective writing: reporting that focuses on the facts and does not include opinions or interpretations.

Outline: an organized list of the main ideas and supporting ideas, usually labeled with numbers and letters.

P

Paragraph: a group of sentences that discusses a topic. A paragraph can contain ten or more sentences—or as few as one sentence, especially when used for dialogue in a story. In most circumstances, paragraphs are smaller divisions of an essay.

Parallel construction (parallelism): the repetition of the same grammatical structure for coherence or emphasis.

Paraphrase: restating ideas in your own words and sentence structure—as opposed to quoting the idea.

Parentheses: punctuation marks [( )] that enclose incidental information in a sentence. They always come in pairs.

Partial infinitive: the infinitive with *to* omitted.

Part-to-part organization: a way of making comparisons and contrasts between subjects by examining one part of each subject, examining the second part of each, and so on.

Parts of speech: the eight grammatical categories of words—nouns, pronouns, verbs, adverbs, adjectives, prepositions, conjunctions, and interjections.

Passive voice: a clause in which the subject does not act but is acted upon. The passive voice is formed from *be* and the past participle of the verb in any tense, such as *has been done, is done, was done,* or *will be done.*

Past participle: a verb form that ends in *-ed* for regular verbs, although there are more than 100 irregular forms. The past participle functions as a main verb in perfect tenses (such as the present perfect *has locked,* or the past perfect *had locked*), in the passive voice (such as *is locked* or *was locked*). The past participle is also used as an adjective (a *well-locked* door).

Past perfect tense: a tense used to describe a past action or event occurring prior to a later time in the past. The past perfect tense is formed from *had* and the verb's past participle.

Past progressive tense: a tense showing an action in progress in the past, formed from the helping verbs *was* or *were* and an *-ing* word.

Past tense: a tense used to discuss completed actions in the past. All regular past tense verbs end in *-ed.* There are more than 100 irregular verbs (see *simple past tense*).

Past untrue conditional: a statement that is contrary to the facts in the past. It includes a clause in the past perfect tense and a clause with *would + have + past participle.*

Perfect modal: a verb phrase that begins with a modal verb and relates previous actions or circumstances to a later time. Perfect modals are formed from three words: modal + *have* + past participle.

Perfect progressive modal: a verb phrase that interprets past actions or circumstances in progress. Perfect progressive modals are formed from a modal + *have* + *been* + present participle.

Period: a punctuation mark [.] that ends a complete statement or is included in an abbreviation.

Person: a way of classifying personal pronouns: first person, *I* and *we;* second person, *you;* third person: *he, she, it,* and *they.*

Personal pronouns: the pronouns such as *I, we, you, he, she, it, they* or *me, us, you, him, her, it, them* that refer to people

Persuasion: the attempt to convince others that they should accept your views or do what you ask of them.

Phrasal verb: a two-word (and sometimes three-word) expression such as *get up,* which combines a verb with a second word to change the meaning of the verb.

Phrase: a group of two or more words. Unlike a clause, it does not contain a complete subject and verb.

Plural: more than one. Most plural nouns end in *-s,* but two or more nouns or pronouns can be joined to make a plural by *and.* Present tense plural verbs do not end in *-s.*

Possessive: a word that shows ownership or possession.

Possessive adjective: a possessive word—actually a pronoun, such as *my, our, your, his, her, its,* and/or *their,* that shows possession before a noun (see *possessive pronoun*).

Possessive noun: a possessive word formed by adding *'s* to singular nouns or *'* to plural nouns ending in *-s.*

Possessive pronoun: a possessive word, such as *mine, ours, yours, his, hers, its,* and *theirs,* which replaces a possessive noun or possessive adjective and the noun.

Predicate: the words that make a statement or ask a question about the subject. A predicate begins with a verb.

Predicting: a revising technique in which you read a topic sentence, think about what readers would expect to follow, and then examine and revise the paragraph so thatit meets some reasonable expectation.

Prefix: an addition to the beginning of a root word.

Preposition: a small word, such as *in, of, on, at,* or *around,* that precedes a noun or pronoun object (for example, *on the roof, by the road, under the rug, in a year*). The preposition and its object,

called a *prepositional phrase,* modify a noun or a verb.

Prepositional phrase: see *preposition.*

Present participle: an *-ing* word that functions as an adjective or adverb.

Present perfect progressive tense: a tense that describes a continuing action that began in the past and relates to the present. The tense is formed from *have/has + been +* the present participle.

Present perfect tense: a tense used to describe an action or condition in the past that continues up to the present. The tense is formed with *has/have* and the past participle.

Present progressive tense: a tense that discusses actions that are happening now or are planned for the future. All verbs in this tense include the helping verb *is, am,* or *are* and an *-ing* word.

Present tense: see *simple present tense.*

Present true conditional: a statement that means "If one circumstance happens, the result also happens." It includes a clause beginning with *if* and a present tense verb.

Present untrue conditional: a statement that is contrary to the facts at the present time. It includes a clause in the simple past tense (except that the verb *were* agrees with all subjects) and a clause with *would* as the modal.

Prewriting: the step in the writing process in which you think about your topic, purpose, and audience, and then explore your ideas through brainstorming, clustering, or freewriting.

Process analysis: an organizational structure that explains how to do something or how something works.

Proofreading: the last step in the writing process in which you examine the final copy for small errors and omissions.

Pronoun: a word that replaces a noun as a subject, object, or possessive word. Some pronouns have additional functions (see *relative pronouns, demonstrative pronouns,* and *reflexive pronouns*).

Proper noun: a noun that names someone or something and is therefore capitalized.

Purpose: the goal a paragraph or essay achieves for its audience. In general, the goal can be to inform, persuade, or entertain.

Q

Question mark: a punctuation mark [?] that ends direct questions.

Quotation marks: punctuation marks [" "] that enclose direct quotations, titles of short works, definitions, and words used in special ways.

R

Reflexive pronoun: a pronoun that both performs and receives the action of the verb (such as "I looked at *myself*"), or that is used for emphasis (such as "I *myself* wouldn't do that.") The pronoun's singular forms end in *-self*, and its plural forms end in *-selves*.

Regular verb: a verb that ends in *-ed* in the past tense or past participle, or that forms its third person singular form by adding *-s* or *-es*.

Relative clause: a clause that functions like an adjective, relating its information back to the noun that, in most cases, immediately precedes it.

Relative pronoun: the word that begins a relative clause, which relates its information back to a noun preceding the clause. The most common relative pronouns are *who, which, that,* and *whom.*

Report: a summary of decisions taken at a meeting, the details of some incident, the results of an experiment, or a set of observations.

Reported speech: a retelling in your own words of what the speaker or writer says or said. Reported speech never uses quotation marks.

Response: the interpretation of or reaction to materials discussed in a summary.

Restrictive relative clause: a clause that provides essential information about the noun it relates to, so the clause is not enclosed in commas.

Revision: the stage in the writing process in which you examine what you have written and then reorganize it, develop ideas further, eliminate ideas that don't support your point, and clarify your language.

Root word: a word to which a suffix or prefix is added.

Run-on sentence: a sentence containing two independent clauses with nothing that joins them together. This is a very serious grammatical error.

S

Semicolon: a mark of punctuation [;] that most commonly joins two independent clauses or, less commonly, separates items in a series that contains internal commas.

Sentence: a complete statement or question containing a subject (usually a noun or subject pronoun) and a verb, which begins the statement or question about the subject.

Sequential order: an organization in which ideas are presented in consecutive steps or a sequence.

Simile: a comparison using *like* or *as,* such as "He ran *like a deer.*"

Simple future tense: a tense that discusses future intentions, expectations, and promises. It is formed from *will* + base form of the verb.

Simple past tense: a tense that shows a completed action or idea in the past. Regular verbs in the simple past tense end in *-ed,* but more than 100 past tense verbs are irregular.

Simple present tense: a tense used to discuss habitual actions or states, facts, or conditions that are true of the present. All third-person-singular present-tense verbs end in *-es.*

Singular: only one. Singular nouns usually do not end in *-s,* but the present tense verbs that agree with them do end in *-s.*

Spatial order: an organization that presents details in space according to some arrangement such as top to bottom, left to right, or front to back. This organization occurs most often in description.

Speaker tag: a phrase such as *he said* or *she asked* that identifies the speaker or writer or material you quote.

Subject: the topic (who or what) a clause makes a statement or asks a question about. Most often the subject is a noun or subject pronoun. In statements, the subject usually precedes the verb; in questions, the verb precedes the subject.

Subject complement: a noun or adjective following a linking verb that describes or renames the subject

Subject of a paragraph or essay: The material the paragraph or essay discusses. See *claim, topic sentence,* and *thesis statement.*

Subject pronoun: a word that replaces a noun as the subject of a verb. The list of subject pronouns includes *I, we, you, he, she, it,* and *they.*

Subjective: writing that includes opinions and interpretations of material.

Subject-verb agreement: matching of singular subjects with singular verbs or plural subjects with plural verbs. With the exception of *to be* (*was/were*) in the past tense, only present tense verbs change form to agree with their subjects.

Subordination: joining two clauses by making one clause dependent on the other clause.

Subordinating conjunction: a word that joins two clauses by making one clause lower in importance and dependent on the second clause. The second clause is independent and completes the meaning of the dependent clause.

Suffix: an ending added to a root word.

Summary: a discussion of the main ideas, omitting most supporting details.

Superlative forms: the adjective or adverb form ending in *-est* or preceded by *most* that is used to show that one of three or more things compared is greater than the others.

Syllable: a grouping of one or more letters that contains a single vowel sound.

Synonym: a word with the same or nearly the same meaning as another word.

T

Tense: the form of the verb that shows when an action or idea occurs or occurred—in the *present, past, future,* and so on. In two-, three-, or four-word verbs, the first word always indicates the tense (*doesn't want*—simple present; *didn't want*—simple past; *is going*—present continuous; *was going*—past continuous, and so on).

Thesis statement: this sentence, included in the introductory paragraph of an essay, states the central point of the essay and often outlines the organization of the essay.

Topic sentence: a sentence that states the main idea, or point, of a paragraph, which the body of the paragraph develops. Most topic sentences come at the beginning of a paragraph.

Transition: a word, phrase, or sentence that explains how or in what way two ideas are logically related (see *conjunctive adverb*).

Transitive verb: a verb that takes a direct object.

U

Unity: a trait of an effective paragraph, in which each sentence develops the main idea, or topic, which is often expressed in the topic sentence.

Used to: a verb that expresses a habitual action or condition in the past that is no longer true of the present. The verb consists of *used* + full infinitive.

V

Verb: a word or phrase that usually follows the subject and expresses the action the subject performs. A few verbs also link descriptive words back to the subject. Verbs generally have a tense (present, past, future, etc.) and can contain as many as four words.

Verb phrase: a verb made up of two, three, or four words.

Vowel: a sound represented by the letters *a, e, i, o, u* (or a combination of these letters) that involves the passage of air through the vocal cords.

W

Whole-to-whole organization: a way of making comparisons and contrasts between subjects by examining everything about one subject and then everything about the other.

Index

Notes

Notes

Notes